THE INTERMEDIARY WORLD AND PATTERNS OF PERFECTION

IN PHILO AND HEBREWS

SOCIETY OF BIBLICAL LITERATURE

DISSERTATION SERIES

edited by

Howard C. Kee

and

Douglas A. Knight

Number 25

THE INTERMEDIARY WORLD AND PATTERNS OF PERFECTION

IN PHILO AND HEBREWS

by

Lala Kalyan Kumar Dey

SCHOLARS PRESS
Missoula, Montana

THE INTERMEDIARY WORLD AND PATTERNS OF PERFECTION

IN PHILO AND HEBREWS

by

Lala Kalyan Kumar Dey

Published by

SCHOLARS PRESS

for

The Society of Biblical Literature

Distributed by

SCHOLARS PRESS
University of Montana
Missoula, Montana 59801

THE INTERMEDIARY WORLD AND PATTERNS OF PERFECTION

IN PHILO AND HEBREWS

by

Lala Kalyan Kumar Dey
Drew University
Madison, New Jersey 07940

Th.D., 1974   Adviser:
Harvard University   Helmut Koester

Library of Congress Cataloging in Publication Data

Dey, Lala Kalyan Kumar.
    The intermediary world and patterns of perfection in
Philo and Hebrews.
    239 p.; 22 cm.
    (Dissertation series ; no. 25)
    Originally presented as the author's thesis, Harvard,
1974.
    Bibliography: p. 235-239
    1. Philo Judaeus. 2. Bible. N.T. Hebrews--Theol-
ogy. 3. Perfection--History of doctrines. 4. Jesus
Christ--History of doctrines--Early church. I. Title.
II. Series: Society of Biblical Literature. Disserta-
tion series ; no. 25.
B689.Z7D48 1975   227'.87'066   75-22457
ISBN 0-89130-022-8

Printed in the United States of America
Printing Department
University of Montana
Missoula, Montana 59801

TABLE OF CONTENTS

To my teacher and friend

JOHN STRUGNELL

ABBREVIATIONS

Philo's Works

Abr	=	De Abrahamo
Aet	=	De Aeternitate Mundi
Agr	=	De Agricultura
Cher	=	De Cherubim
Conf	=	De Confusione Linguarum
Congr	=	De Congressu Eruditionis gratia
Decal	=	De Decalogo
Det	=	Quod Deterius Potiori insidiari soleat
Ebr	=	De Ebrietate
Flacc	=	In Flaccum
Fug	=	De Fuga et Inventione
Gig	=	De Gigantibus
Hyp	=	Hypothetica
Jos	=	De Josepho
Leg	=	De Legatione ad Gaium
Leg All i, ii, iii	=	Legum Allegoriarum
Mig	=	De Migratione Abrahami
Mos i, ii	=	De Vita Mosis
Mut	=	De Mutatione Nominum
Op	=	De Opificio Mundi
Plant	=	De Plantatione
Post	=	De Posteritate Caini
Praem	=	De Praemiis et Poenis
Prov	=	De Providentia
Quis Her	=	Quis rerum divinarum Heres sit
Quod Deus	=	Quod Deus sit Immutabilis
Quod Omn Prob	=	Quod omnis Probus liber
Sac	=	De Sacrificiis Abelis et Caini
Sob	=	De Sobrietate
Som i, ii	=	De Somniis
Spec Leg i, ii, iii, iv	=	De Specialibus Legibus
Virt	=	De Virtute
Vit Cont	=	De Vita Contemplativa

(same as the Loeb edition)

INTRODUCTION

Scholarship on Hebrews has recognized the importance of understanding the history of religions context for its interpretation. There is, however, considerable difference of opinion concerning its precise character. On the one hand, there is the attempt of Ernst Kaesemann (Das wandernde Gottesvolk, 1938) to explain the religious traditions in Hebrews in terms of the gnostic myth of the redeemed redeemer. On the other hand, Michel (in his commentary) has tried to present a consistent picture in terms of apocalyptic traditions, although he acknowledges the use of Hellenistic language in Hebrews.[1] Generally, scholars recognize in Hebrews both the eschatological language of primitive Christianity as well as the language of Hellenistic Judaism (Philo/Alexandrinism, metaphysical dualism between heaven and earth, etc.). How these two aspects happened to come together in our writing find as varied explanations as there are writers. Such statements as: "Und mit der eschatologisch-kultischen Ausrichtung im alexandrinischen Schema von Entsprechung, Andersartigkeit und Überbietung ist jedenfalls der theologische Grundzug des Hb genau erfasst" (E. Grässer in his comprehensive review "Der Hebräerbrief 1938-1963," ThR 30(1964), p. 203), are inadequate since they state rather than solve the problem of understanding Hebrews.

On the whole, the history of religions picture of Hebrews that emerges from scholarship is a syncretism of apocalypticism and elements of hellenistic Judaism. The latter is considered by scholars like Michel and Spicq as mainly superficial and without any real effect on the author's religious thinking. As E. Grässer points out: "Das at'l Erbe gilt dieser Forschung a priori als legitimes Erbe, während das helln. Erbe ebenso a priori als 'Fremdeinfluss' abgewertet und auf ein Minimum reduziert wird" (ibid., p. 167 in the section on "Zum religionsgeschichtlichen Problem"). The historical context which motivated the writing of Hebrews has not really received an adequate explanation. It has

---

[1] On the difficulties in H. Kosmala's contention (Hebraer-Essener-Christen, 1959) that Hebrews is addressed to ex-Essenes and that its language is like that of Qumran, see J. Coppens, "Les affinites qumraniennes de l'Epitre aux Hebreaux," NRTh 94 (1962), 128-41, 257-82; F. F. Bruce, "'To the Hebrews' or 'To the Essenes'?" NTS 9(1962/63), 217-32.

1

received only the broadest and vaguest of explanations: the
failure of faith due to the delay of the parousia (M. Werner,
K. Immer, G. Vos); a general exhaustion of faith and adaptation
of the kerygma to a changed historical situation (Kaesemann); the
battle against the fatigue of the post-Apostolic period with the
ideas of early Christian tradition (Michel); against gnosis as
well as early Catholicism (Vielhauer); delay in Christian progress (W. Manson); scandal of the cross (O. Kuss); paradox of the
now and not yet (F. J. Schierse); manual for the conversion of
the Jews (Spicq), etc. (E. Grässer, ibid., p. 198ff.). None of
these really give a convincing motive which explains the particular content of the writing and its concerns. Related to this is
the abandonment by most scholars of the older view of the polemical character of Hebrews. This has resulted from the insistence
of both Kaesemann and Michel that the Christological kerygma in
Hebrews has been placed in the service of paraenesis. This is
quite unsatisfactory when one considers the result that under
such a point of view the intricate argument and scriptural interpretation, e.g., in Hb 7-10,18 would merely serve the purpose of
the exhortation in 10,19ff.

In our estimation, we do not have a satisfactory explanation
for the carefully reasoned attempts of the author to establish
the superiority of Jesus over the angels, Moses, Levitic and
Aaronide highpriesthood, an attempt which has no comparable parallels in the rest of the New Testament. A basic issue of interpretation is whether the author is addressing himself to dispa-
rate problems or whether these comparisons fit together in a
common frame of religious thought. If we assume the latter, how
do these comparisons relate to the exhortations which are inter-
posed? These exhortations are characterized by a strong insistence on the traditional concepts which describe Christian existence such as faith, hope and confidence, and yet they receive
rather unusual definitions (e.g., 3,6; 6,19-20; 11,1, etc.). The
author is at the same time anxious to move beyond the traditional
tenets as enumerated in 6,1-2 (repentance, faith on God, bap-
tisms, laying on of hands, resurrection and eternal judgement) on
the path to perfection. The question is what intrinsic connection do the peculiar features of these exhortations have to the
comparisons of Jesus with the angels, heavenly man, Moses, Levi,
Aaron and Melchizedek. How do they relate to the central concern
with perfection (2,10; 5,9; 7,11; 7,19. 28; 9,9; 10,1. 14; 11,40;
12,2. 23)? Furthermore, what is the rationale for what has been

considered major breaks in Hebrews, e.g., between 4,13 and 4,14
(Michel); between 5,10 and 5,11 (Spicq, Vanhoye), and between
chaps. 10 and 11 (most scholars)?

Since the discoveries of the literature from Qumran and Nag
Hammadi, our conception of the religious situation of the early
Christian period has undergone a fundamental change. The religious context of the New Testament can no longer be adequately
described in such general terms as "apocalyptic," "hellenistic,"
"gnostic," "wisdom," etc. We have become conscious of the religious pluralism and diversity within Judaism as well as in the
history of early Christianity (see essays by H. Koester in:
Robinson, J. M. and Koester, H., Trajectories through Early
Christianity). The implication of this changed conception of the
early Christian period has far reaching implications for the
study of the New Testament. It means that each New Testament
writing has its particular place within a diverse and pluralistic
situation and the explication of that particular context would
decisively advance our understanding of the literature. This
awareness of diversity calls for basic historical research which
would define and describe the particularities within such broad
categories as "hellenistic," "apocalyptic," etc.

For the interpretation of Hebrews it implies an attempt at
defining and describing the particular religious tradition or
traditions which have informed the writing and the nature of the
religious issues that are likely to emerge when different traditions meet and have to come to terms with each other. We will
attempt to set Hebrews in its particular history of religions
context, i.e., a particular kind of Judaism within which the features of its content become explicable. This can be done best,
not by examining a particular passage or theme in the writing,
but by attempting to describe the total framework of its religious thought. Religious ideas and concepts do not have an inde-
pendent life apart from the tradition in which they are incorpo-
rated, modified and reinterpreted. It is only when we are able
to place Hebrews in its particular religious context that the
significance of any concept or idea, the motivation behind it,
the purpose of the writing and its literary character can be
defined. For our endeavour we can examine two aspects of Hebrews.
First, since much of the argument is advanced by means of exege-
ses of the Old Testament, the location of such traditions in
earlier or contemporary literature would provide a firm basis for
understanding the character of its thought world. The fruitful-

ness of this approach has already been demonstrated by H. Koester ("Die Auslegung der Abraham-Verheissung in Hb 6," in G. von Rad Festschrift, 1961, pp. 95-109). Second, the author uses traditional concepts which are found in other parts of the New Testament, e.g., christological titles as "Son" and "Lord," the pattern of humiliation-exaltation christology (1,3ff., cf. Phil 2,6ff.; Col 2,10ff.), Old Testament proof texts (Ps 2; 110), fragments of early christological formulations (2,4; cf. Acts 2,22), the traditional concepts which describe Christian existence as faith, hope, endurance, love and good works. The way the author uses such traditions would provide a second perspective into the thought world of the writing.

The thesis does not intend to give a detailed interpretation of all of Hebrews, but to elaborate the religious context within which it should be interpreted. It will attempt to show the coherence in the progression of the themes of the superiority of Jesus over the angels, Moses, Levi and Aaron, and how the paraenetic sections fit within this progression. And what occasioned the need for such exegetical demonstrations that indeed Jesus has entered into the heavenly temple, having himself been made perfect, and has thereby prepared the path for a direct access to God and in a way superior to that of the Levitic-Aaronide priesthood.

PART I

THE INTERMEDIARY WORLD AND PATTERNS OF PERFECTION
IN PHILO - WITH BRIEF COMPARISONS WITH OTHER
LITERATURE OF JUDAISM

CHAPTER ONE

SYNONYMITY OF TITLES AND INTERCHANGEABILITY
OF FUNCTIONS IN THE INTERMEDIARY WORLD

Introduction: A basic argument of the thesis is that the
sequence of comparisons of Jesus as "Son" with the angels, heavenly man, Moses, Aaron, Levi and Melchizedek in Hebrews belong to
a single religious thought world. Here angels, logos, heavenly
man, wisdom, etc. have to a large degree synonymous titles and
interchangeable functions and they constitute the intermediary
world between God and man. As intermediaries they are the agencies of creation and revelation. To this correspond two levels
of religious existence. The intermediary world (logos-wisdom-
archangel-heavenly man-son) mediates an inferior revelation and
religious status of a secondary order. The higher level or
perfection is characterized by unmediated and direct access to
God and participation in the primary gifts. The supreme exemplars of this perfection were Moses who communicated with God
face to face, Aaron who as high priest divests himself of the
robe (= universe) and enters the Holy of Holies, the upper limits
of heaven where God dwells (i.e., allegorically understood),
Isaac who typified self-learnt and self-taught wisdom (automathēs
and autodidaktos), as did the priesthood of Melchizedek. It is
our contention that the readers addressed in Hebrews had analogous frame of religious thought and that this explains the
sequence of comparisons in Hebrews and the underlying issues.
The evidence for this is to be found in the religious thought of
Hellenistic Judaism, especially in Philo Judaeus.

The following chapters of Par I will describe the character
of the intermediary world in Philo and the patterns of religious
perfection as the general background for the understanding of
Hebrews, and with brief comparisons with other literature of
Judaism (Chapters 1-3). Part II and following will interpret
some major themes in Hebrews in terms of this general background
and in terms of the specific exegetical traditions used by the
author in his arguments.

Our presentation will first set forth the relevant texts
which will then be followed by analyses and summaries. The
detailed table of contents should be used as a guide.

7

8

A. Titles

<u>Texts</u>

Logos and Sophia

Leg All i,65: ποταμὸς ἢ γενικὴ ἐστιν ἀρετή, ἡ ἀγθότης, αὕτη
ἐκπορεύεται ἐκ τῆς Ἐδέμ, <u>τῆς τοῦ θεοῦ σοφίας, ἡ δέ</u>
<u>ἐστιν ὁ θεοῦ λόγος</u>. (Philo's interpretation of Gn 2,10).

Fug 97: προτρέπει δὴ τὸν μὲν ὡδυδρομεῖν ἱκανὸν συντείνειν
ἀπνευστὶ πρὸς τὸν ἀνωτάτω <u>λόγον θεῖον, ὃς σοφίας ἐστι</u>
<u>πηγή</u>, ἵνα ἀρυσάμενος τοῦ νάματος ἀντὶ θανάτου ζωὴν ἀίδιον
<u>ἆθλον</u> εὕρηται. (Interpretation of the six cities of
refuge in Nu 35; "the eldest, most secure and best
mother-city" is the divine logos, cf. 94.)

Som ii,242: κάτεισι δὲ ὥσπερ ἀπὸ <u>πηγῆς τῆς σοφίας</u> ποταμοῦ
τρόπον ὁ θεῖος λόγος . . . (refers to Gn 2,10; cf. 241-42
and Leg All i,65 above.)

Wis Sol 9,1b-2a: ὁ ποιήσας τὰ πάντα <u>ἐν λόγῳ σου καὶ τῇ σοφίᾳ σου</u>
κατασκευάσας ἄνθρωπον.

Aristobulus (Eus PE XIII,12,667a): . . . ὁ θεὸς τὸν ὅλον κόσμον
κατεσκεύακε, καὶ δέδωκεν ἀνάπαυσιν . . . <u>ἐβδόμην</u> ἡμέραν,
ἢ δὴ καὶ πρώτη φυσικῶς ἂν λέγοιτο φωτὸς γένεσιν . . .
μεταφέροιτο δ᾿ ἂν τὸ αὐτὸ καὶ ἐπὶ τῆς <u>σοφίας</u>, τὸ γὰρ πᾶν
φῶς ἐστιν ἐξ αὐτῆς.

667c: διασεσάφηκε δ᾿ ἡμῖν αὐτὴν ἔννομον, ἕνεκεν σημείου τοῦ
περὶ ἡμᾶς ἑβδόμου <u>λόγου</u> καθεστῶτος, ἐν ᾧ γνῶσιν ἔχομεν
ἀνθρωπίνων καὶ θείων πραγμάτων.[1]

Logos and Angel

Leg All iii,177: ὡραῖος οὗτος ὁ τρόπος, τροφέα τὸν θεόν, οὐχὶ
λόγον, ἡγεῖται, τὸν δὲ <u>ἄγγελον</u>, ὃς ἐστι <u>λόγος</u>, ὥσπερ
ἰατρὸν κακῶν. (Philo's interpretation of the angel in
Gn 48,15f.)

Conf 28: "ὁ λαὸς περιεκύκλωσαν ἅμα τὴν οἰκίαν, νέοι τε καὶ
πρεσβῦται" κατὰ <u>τῶν θείων καὶ ἱερῶν λόγων</u> συνομοσάμενοι,
οὓς καλεῖν ἔθος <u>ἀγγέλους</u>. (Passage refers to Gn 19,4,
the Sodomites surrounding Lot's house = "house of the
soul," cf. 27. Same interpretation of the incident in
Fug 144.)

---

[1]We have in the last phrase ("by which we have knowledge of
things human and divine") a commonplace definition of philosophy,
usually attributed to the Stoics, which is also found in Philo,
Cicero and Albinus. Cong 79: ἔστι γὰρ φιλοσοφία ἐπιτήδευσις
σοφίας, σοφία δὲ ἐπιστήμη θείων καὶ ἀνθρωπίνων καὶ τῶν τούτων
αἰτίων. Exactly the same definition is given by Philo in QG III,
43 and in much more elaborate form in Spec Leg III,185-91.
S.V.F. . . . τὴν φιλοσοφίαν φασὶν ἐπιτήδευσιν εἶναι σοφίας, τὴν
δὲ σοφίαν ἐπιστήμην θείων τε καὶ ἀνθρωπίνων πραγμάτων. For Cicero, see De Off. ii,5. Albinus, I: σοφία δ᾿ ἐστιν ἐπιστήμη
θείων καὶ ἀνθρωπίνων πραγμάτων. That reason/Logos is the basis
of philosophy is also a common topic, e.g., Albinus III: ἡ δὲ
τοῦ φιλοσόφου σπουδὴ κατὰ τὸν Πλάτωνα ἐν τρισὶν ἔοικεν εἶναι, ἔν
τε τῇ θέᾳ τῇ τῶν ὄντων, καὶ ἐν τῇ πράξει τῶν καλῶν, καὶ <u>ἐν αὐτῇ τῇ</u>
<u>τοῦ λόγου θεωρίᾳ</u> (i.e., dialectics.)

Quis Her 205: τῷ δὲ <u>ἀρχαγγέλῳ</u> καὶ <u>πρεσβυτάτῳ λόγῳ</u> δωρεὰν ἔδωκεν ἐξαίρετον ὁ τὰ ὅλα γεννήσας πατήρ, ἵνα μεθόριος στὰς τὸ γενόμενον διακρίνῃ τοῦ πεποιηκότος. (The reference is to Dt 5,5, i.e., Moses.)

Som i,239: . . . οὕτως καὶ τὴν τοῦ εἰκόνα, <u>τὸν ἄγγελον αὐτοῦ</u> <u>λόγον</u>, ὡς αὐτὸν κατανοοῦσιν. (The problem addressed is that of the appearance of God in the likeness of angels or men.)

Cher 3: . . . κατάγεται ὑπαντήσαντος <u>ἀγγέλου</u>, ὃς ἐστι <u>θεῖος</u> <u>λόγος</u>, εἰς τὸν δεσποτικὸν οἶκον . . . (The reference is to the angel who meets Hagar in Gn 16,6ff. The same identification of the angel with the divine word is also made in <u>Fug</u> 5.)

Cher 35: ἴδε τὸν ἀνθεστῶτα ἐξεναντίας <u>θεοῦ λόγον</u> ἐνωπλισμένον <u>ἄγγελον</u> . . . (The reference is to the armed angel in Nu 22,31. The same identification of the angel with the logos of God is made in Quod Deus 182.)

Mut 87: τὸν δὲ 'Ιακὼβ <u>ἄγγελος</u> ὑπερέτης τοῦ θεοῦ, <u>λόγος</u> (μετωνόμασεν). (Whereas God changed Abraham's name, the angel changed Jacob's name.)

Mig 173: ὁ δὲ ἐπόμενος θεῷ κατὰ τἀναγκαῖον συνοδοιπόροις χρῆται τοῖς ἀκολούθοις αὐτοῦ <u>λόγοις</u>, οὓς ὀνομάζειν ἔθος <u>ἀγγέλους</u>. (This is corroborated by reference to Gn 18,16.)

Post 91: τότε τῶν ἀρετῆς ἐκγόνων τοὺς ὅρους ἔστησεν ἰσαρίθμους <u>ἀγγέλοις</u>, ὅσοι γὰρ θεοῦ <u>λόγοι</u>, τοσαῦτα ἀρετῆς ἔθνη τε καὶ εἴδη. (This is part of the explanation of Dt 32,7-9, which is quoted in 89.)

Som i,115: The practiser's mind (hē askētikē dianoia) "in the time of fruitfulness and uplifting, there shine upon it the archetypal and incorporeal rays of the fountain of reason, God the consummator," ὅταν δὲ καταβαίνῃ καὶ ἀφορῇ, ταῖς ἐκείνων εἰκόσιν, ἀθανάτοις <u>λόγοις</u>, οὓς καλεῖν ἔθος <u>ἀγγέλους</u>. (This part of an extended explanation of the meaning of Gn 28,11--"he met a place . . . for the sun was set," cf. 72ff.)

Wis Sol 18,15: ὁ <u>παντοδύναμός</u> σου <u>λόγος</u> ἀπ' οὐρανῶν ἐκ θρόνων βασιλείων ἀπότομος <u>πολεμιστὴς</u> εἰς μέσον τῆς ὀλεθρίας ἥλατο γῆς ξίφος ὀξὺ τὴν ἀνυπόκριτον ἐπιταγήν σου φέρων . . . (A description of the agent of the destruction of the first born (Ex 12,29); the description which follows--"he touched heaven and walked on earth"--bears close resemblance to the warrior angel described in I Chron 21,16; the epithet "all-powerful" is applied to <u>sophia</u> in 7,23.)

Similar correlations between the logos and angel can be illustrated from numerous other passages, e.g., Sob 65; QG III,11; 27; 28; IV,44; 90; 91; QE II,13; Som i,148.[2]

---

[2]The identification of angel with Logos is to be found in Hellenistic philosophy and seems to be based on the interpretation of the heavenly messenger Hermes in Plato, Crat 407e: ἔοικε περὶ λόγον τι εἶναι ὁ "Ἑρμῆς," καὶ τὸ ἑρμηνέα εἶναι καὶ τὸ ἄγγελον . . . Speculation concerning Hermes in later literature is documented by Kleinknecht, <u>TDNT</u> IV, 86-88.

Logos and Anthropos

Fug 72:   λέγεται γὰρ "ἐποίησεν ὁ θεὸς τὸν ἄνθρωπον," τὸν ἀειδῆ
          καὶ ἄκρατον λογισμόν. (The distinction being drawn by
          Philo is between the creation of "mixed" man of logos and
          alogos by a plurality of creators (Gn 1,26) and the
          "true" man--pure mind, unmixed reason--whom God alone
          creates, Gn 1,27.)[3]

Det 83:   ὅτι ἀρχέτυπον μὲν φύσεως λογικῆς ὁ θεός ἐστι, μίμημα δὲ
          καὶ ἀπεικόνισμα ἄνθρωπος, οὐ τὸ δυφυὲς ζῷον ἀλλὰ τὸ τῆς
          ψυχῆς ἄριστον εἶδος, ὃ νοῦς καὶ λόγος κέκληται. (The
          context of the discussion is Gn 4,10; Philo distinguishes
          between blood as the ousia of the soul--Lv 17,11, and
          pneuma as the ousia of the soul--Gn 2,7. The former
          refers to the vital power--zotike dynamis--which we share
          with irrational creatures and the latter to the rational
          power, which is the true man.)

QG I,4:   "The moulded man is the sense-perceptible man and a
          likeness of the intelligible type. But the man made in
          accordance with (God's) form is intelligible and incor-
          poreal and a likeness of the archetype. . . . And he
          is a copy of the original seal. And this is the Logos of
          God, the first principle, the archetypal idea, the pre-
          measurer of all things." (Marcus: Loeb) (Interpre-
          tation of Gn 2,7.)

Conf 41: ἕνα καὶ τὸν αὐτὸν ἐπιγεγραμμένοι πατέρα οὐ θνητὸν ἀλλ'
          ἀθάνατον, ἄνθρωπον θεοῦ, ὃς τοῦ αἰδίου λόγος ὢν ἐξ
          ἀνάγκης καὶ αὐτός ἐστιν ἄφθαρτος. (This is an interpre-
          tation of Gn 42,11: "We are all sons of one man, we are
          peaceful," cf. Conf 62; 147.)

Quis Her 230-31: Philo distinguishes between two logoi, one of
          which stands above us and one we possess on the basis of
          Gn 1,27. (See below p. 22; cf. 118.)

Logos and Son

Agr 51:   ὁ ποιμὴν καὶ βασιλεὺς θεὸς ἄγει κατὰ δίκην καὶ νόμον,
          προστησάμενος τὸν ὀρθὸν αὐτοῦ λόγον καὶ πρωτόγονον υἱόν,
          ὃς τὴν ἐπιμέλιαν τῆς ἱερᾶς ταύτης ἀγέλης οἷά τις μεγάλου
          βασιλέως ὑπαρχος διαδέξεται. (The context of the dis-
          cussion is the dignity of the calling of a shepherd and
          the attribution of such a role to God, Ps 23,1.)

Quis Her 119: ὁ γὰρ διοιγνὺς τὴν μητρὰν (i.e., πρωτότοκος καὶ
          μονογενής of Ex 13,1-2) . . . ἀόρατος καὶ σπερματικὸς καὶ
          τεχνικὸς θεῖός ἐστι λόγος . . . (The interpretation of
          "arche" is the context of the passage.)

---

[3]Apart from the numerous instances in which "logismos" means
human rationality or reasoning, Philo does assert that the nature
of the Logos and "logismos" in us are inseparable (Quod Her 234:
ἄτμητοι μὲν οὖν αἱ δύο φύσεις, ἥ τε ἐν ἡμῖν τοῦ λογισμοῦ καὶ ἡ
ὑπὲρ ἡμᾶς τοῦ θείου λόγου, ἄτμητοι δὲ οὖσαι μυρία ἄλλα τέμνουσιν.)
In Spec Leg i,66 the angels are priests in the temple (=universe)
and are described as "pure intelligences" (λογισμοὶ ἀκραιφνεῖς).
It is a tenet in Philo that man ascends beyond the visible and
material world by means of "logismos" (see Leisegang, Index,
II,5, p. 489f.). Cf. the following passage--Det 83.

Som i,215: δύο γάρ, ὡς ἔοικεν, ἱερὰ θεοῦ, ἐν μὲν ὅδε ὁ κόσμος,
ἐν ᾧ καὶ ἀρχιερεὺς ὁ πρωτόγονος αὐτοῦ θεῖος λόγος . . .
(The context is the description of the highpriest's
robe.)

Conf 146: Logos is called prōtogonos (see below p. 32).[4]

Sophia - Angel - Anthropos - Son

QG I,92:   . . . "But sometimes he calls the angels 'sons of God'
because they are made incorporeal through no mortal man
but are spirits without body. But rather does the exhorter, Moses, give to good and excellent men the name 'sons
of God,' while wicked and evil men (he calls) 'bodies.'"
(Marcus: Loeb) (Refers to Gn 6.4.)

Conf 62: "ἰδοὺ ἄνθρωπος ᾧ ὄνομα ἀνατολή" (Zech 6,12) . . .

  63: τοῦτον μὲν γὰρ πρεσβύτατον υἱὸν ὁ τῶν ὅλων ἀνέτειλε
πατήρ, ὃν ἑτέρωθι πρωτόγονον ὠνόμασε . . . (The context
is the interpretation of "anatole" in Gn 11,2.)

Agr 51: See above p. 10. What follows immediately after the
statement concerning the "orthos logos and protogonos
huios" is: καὶ γὰρ εἴρηταί που, "'Ιδοὺ ἐγώ εἰμι,
ἀποστέλλω ἄγγελόν μου εἰς πρόσωπόν σου τοῦ φυλάξαι σε
ἐν τῇ ὁδῷ." (Ex 23,20)

Wis Sol 7,22: ἔστιν γὰρ ἐν αὐτῇ πνεῦμα νοερόν, ἅγιον, μονογενές,
πολυμερές, λεπτόν, . . . (i.e., Sophia.)

Analysis and Summary

What is characteristic of the correlations and identifications of the figures in the intermediary world in Philo is the
primacy of the Logos. Whether it is sophia or angel or anthropos, their significance lies in their identity with or relationship to the logos. Although the passages quoted above are not
exhaustive, most of them are from the allegorical writings of
Philo. The systematic way in which Philo identifies and corre-
lates the logos with sophia, angel, and anthropos is evidence
that this constitutes a basic principle in his allegorical interpretation. In this respect, Philo shares the common high estimation of rationality in the Hellenistic culture of the period.
This mode of interpretation in his allegorical writings is not
restricted to OT passages in which any of these terms occur
(e.g., in Fug 97, the eldest and most secure city of refuge--
Nu 35--is the "divine logos, which is the fount of sophia"; in

---

[4]Quod Deus 31 is incorrectly cited by Kleinknecht (TDNT IV,
p. 89, footnote 89) as calling the sense perceptible world (kosmos aisthētos) the Logos. Such a statement would be impossible
for Philo. In the middle of page 89 he incorrectly quotes Agr 51
as a reference to the creation of the intelligible world. The
passage refers to the created world over which God has set his
Logos and First Born Son as viceroy (of the great king).

reference to Dt 5,5, Moses is called the "archangel and eldest logos," Quis Her 205; cf. Agr 51; Som i,215).

The precedent to such correlations is to be found in Wis Sol (9,1b-2a: the instrumental role of logos and sophia in creation), Aristobulus (Eus PE XIII,12,667a,c: the metaphorical and symbolic understanding of the seventh day--hebdomē--as sophia and logos; cf. Philo, Mut 144; Mos ii,210; Decal 102; Spec Leg i,170; ii,56; Praem 154, etc.), Wis Sol (18,15: description of an angelic figure--a divine warrior--as "thy all-powerful logos"; 7,22: sophia = monogenes). The terms "son," "first-born" and "eldest" as descriptive of religious status and dignity are used in a similar way to describe the "just," "pious," "holy," "Israel" and idealized individuals in the Wis Sol, 3 Macc, Joseph and Asenath and Sib Or (to be discussed below).

The function of the interchangeability of the titles of figures in the intermediary world was to render the mythical stories, customs and anthropomorphic manifestations of God in the OT into religious-philosophical concepts which would be comprehensible and would appeal to the cultured milieu of the Hellenistic world (wisdom--understanding--knowledge, reason, virtue, paideia --the forming of the cultured man, perfection, etc. This will become clearer in chapter 2, below). This pattern of identifications and correlations is a part of the hermeneutics of Philo, through which stories in the OT acquire eternal and therefore contemporary significance (see below pp. 46-48). Thus the rivers in Genesis become "aretai," their source being sophia = logos (Leg All i,65; Som ii,242). The cities of refuge (Nu 35) form a hierarchy of religious attainments, the first city being the logos (Fug 97). The seventh day/rest is a metaphor and symbol of sophia and logos (Aristobulus, loc. cit.). The anthropomorphic manifestations of God are attributed to the fallibility of human apprehension (Som i,239; Post 1-6; Aristobulus, Eus PE VIII,10). The essential quality of being an "anthrōpos" is rationality-- logikē psychē (see above section on Logos and Anthropos). Furthermore, as we will show below, there is an essential correlation between the intermediary world and the attainment of religious status or perfection.

In summary, the titular characterizations of the intermediary world show considerable fluidity between logos, sophia, angel, anthropos and son, as well as consciously wrought identifications between them in the literature of Hellenistic Judaism. By this means the OT could be interpreted and given religious valuation in terms of the cultured religion of the Hellenistic world.

B. Functions

Texts

Agents and Sustainers of Creation

Leg All iii,96: ἑρμηνεύεται οὖν Βεσελεὴλ ἐν σκιᾷ θεοῦ, σκιὰ θεοῦ δὲ ὁ λόγος αὐτοῦ ἐστιν, ᾧ καθάπερ ὀργάνῳ προσχρησάμενος ἐκοσμοποίει. (The context of the discussion is Ex 31, 2ff.; cf. Mig 6.)

Spec Leg i,81: λόγος δ᾿ ἐστιν εἰκὼν θεοῦ, δι'οὗ σύμπας ὁ κόσμος ἐδημιουργεῖτο. (The context is the bodily perfection of the priest as symbolic of the perfection of the soul, ἣν φασι τυπωθῆναι κατὰ τὴν εἰκόνα τοῦ ὄντος.)

Cher 125: ὅτι ὁ θεὸς αἴτιον, οὐκ ὄργανον, τὸ δὲ γινόμενον δι᾿ ὀργάνου μὲν ὑπὸ δὲ αἰτίου πάντως γίνεται. πρὸς γὰρ τὴν τινος γένεσιν πολλὰ δεῖ συνελθεῖν, τὸ ὑφ' οὗ, τὸ ἐξ οὗ, τὸ δι᾿ οὗ, τὸ δι᾿ ὅ, καὶ ἔστι τὸ μὲν ὑφ' οὗ τὸ αἴτιον, ἐξ οὗ δὲ ἡ ὕλη, δι᾿ οὗ δὲ τὸ ἐργαλεῖον, δι᾿ ὃ δὲ ἡ αἰτία. (The reference is to the false view of Eve in her statement·: "ἐκτησάμην ἄνθρωπον διὰ τοῦ θεοῦ"--Gn 4,1. The organon is obviously either the logos or sophia.)[5]

Agr 51: See p. 10. God appoints the orthos logos, the first born son over the universe like a viceroy of the great king.

Leg All ii,86: . . . τὸ δὲ γενικώτατον ἐστιν ὁ θεός, καὶ δεύτερος ὁ θεοῦ λόγος, τὰ δ᾿ ἄλλα λόγῳ μόνον ὑπάρχει, . . . (The context is the interpretation of "manna"--the genus of all things, Dt 8,15f.)

Plant 8-10: . . . ὅτι οὐδὲν τῶν ἐν ὕλαις κραταιὸν οὕτως, ὡς τὸν κόσμον ἀχθοφορεῖν ἰσχῦσαι, λόγος δὲ ὁ ἀίδιος θεοῦ τοῦ αἰωνίου τὸ ὀχυρώτατον καὶ βεβαιότατον ἔρεισμα τῶν ὅλων ἐστίν. . . . δεσμὸν γὰρ αὐτὸν ἄρρηκτον τοῦ παντὸς ὁ γεννήσας ἐποίει πατήρ. . . . τὰς τῶν ἐναντίων ἀπειλὰς πειθοῖ τῇ συνόδῳ μεσιτεύοντος τε καὶ διαιτῶντος. (I.e., στοιχεῖα; The context is the criticism of the Stoic view of emptiness/kenon; cf. Quis Her 188; QE II,90.)[6]

---

[5]For a discussion of the origin of the four causes in Aristotle and its modification by Philo, see Wolfson I, 261-94. Wolfson's denial of intermediaries in Philo's thought and the reduction of their role to a mere pattern that God uses in creation is far fetched and this entire chapter may be deemed as proving otherwise.

[6]For the Stoic background of this concept of the Logos as the bond and pillar/support of the universe and the mediator and harmoniser of the elements, see Wolfson I, 338-39. A close parallel is Plutarch, Is. et Os., 373d: τὸ πᾶν ὁ λόγος διαρμοσάμενος σύμφωνον ἐξ ἀσυμφώνων μερῶν ἐποίησε. This is Plutarch's interpretation of the statue of Horus grasping the privy members of Typhon and the legend that Hermes cut the sinews of Typhon as strings for his lyre. Plutarch's treatment of Egyptian mythology is an exact parallel to the way Philo interprets the Hebrew scriptures.

14

Fug 12: γέγονέ τε γὰρ ὁ κόσμος καὶ πάντως ὑπ' αἰτίου τινὸς
γέγονεν, ὁ δὲ τοῦ ποιοῦντος λόγος αὐτός ἐστιν ἡ σφραγίς,
ᾗ τῶν ὄντων ἕκαστον μεμόρφωται. (This is the understanding of the company of Jacob in contrast to Laban
who does not know the "moving cause.") Cf. Som ii,45.

QG IV,110: . . . "the divine logos is the governor and administrator of all things." (Marcus: Loeb) (The context is
the discussion of Gn 24,22. Cf. M. Ant. VI,1: ὁ τὴν
οὐσίαν τῶν ὅλων διοικῶν λόγος.)

QE II,68: ὁ τοῦ θεοῦ λόγος μέσος ὢν οὐδὲν ἐν τῇ φύσει καταλείπει
κενόν, τὰ ὅλα πληρῶν καὶ μεσιτεύει καὶ διαιτᾷ τοῖς παρ'
ἑκατέρα διεστάναι δοκοῦσι, φιλίαν καὶ ὁμόνοιαν ἐργαζόμε-
νος. (Gk frg, Harris, p. 66; discussion of Ex 25,22b.)

Fug 109: . . . , διότι, οἶμαι, γονέων ἀφθάρτων καὶ καθαρωτάτων
ἔλαχεν, πατρὸς μὲν θεοῦ, ὃς καὶ τῶν συμπάντων ἐστι πατήρ,
μητρὸς δὲ σοφίας, δι'ἧς τὰ ὅλα ἦλθεν εἰς γένεσιν. (This
constitutes an interpretation of Lv 21,11.)

Det 54: . . . πατέρα μὲν τὸν γεννήσαντα (τὸν) κόσμον, μητέρα δὲ
τὴν σοφίαν, δι' ἧς ἀπετελέσθη τὸ πᾶν . . . (The reference is to Ex 20,12.)

Quis Her 199: ἔργῳ δὲ ὁ θείᾳ σοφίᾳ δημιουργηθεὶς κόσμος ἅπας
. . . (Refers to the whole world being a sacrifice and
offering--an interpretation of Ex 30,34-35.)

Ebr 30: τὸν γοῦν τόδε τὸ πᾶν ἐργασάμενον δημιουργὸν ὁμοῦ καὶ
πατέρα εἶναι τοῦ γεγονότος εὐθὺς ἐν δίκῃ φήσομεν, μητέρα
δὲ τὴν τοῦ πεποιηκότος ἐπιστήμην, ᾗ συνὼν ὁ θεὸς οὐχ ὡς
ἄνθρωπος ἔσπειρε γένεσιν. (ἐπιστήμη = σοφία; cf. 31;
context is an extended discussion on Dt 21,18-21.)

Conf 63: τοῦτον μὲν γὰρ πρεσβύτατον υἱὸν ὁ τῶν ὅλων ἀνέτειλε
πατήρ, ὃν ἑτέρωθι πρωτόγονον ὠνόμασε, καὶ ὁ γεννηθεὶς
μέντοι, μιμούμενος τὰς τοῦ πατρὸς ὁδούς, πρὸς παραδείγ-
ματα ἀρχέτυπα ἐκείνου βλέπων ἐμόρφου τὰ εἴδη. (The
reference is to the anthropos in Zech 6,12; see p. 11
above.)

Wis Sol 9,1b-2a: See above p. 8. Logos and Sophia--agents of
creation.

Sib Or III,20: ὃς λόγῳ ἔκτισε πάντα, καὶ οὐρανόν, ἠδὲ
θάλασσαν . . .

Wis Sol 7,21: ἡ γὰρ πάντων τεχνῖτις ἐδίδαξέν με σοφία. (I.e.,
things secret and manifest; God is called technites in
13,1.)

Sources of Knowledge and Virtue

Post 102: τὴν βασιλικὴν γοῦν ταύτην ὁδόν, ἣν ἀληθῆ καὶ γνήσιον
ἔφαμεν εἶναι φιλοσοφίαν, ὁ νόμος καλεῖ θεοῦ ῥῆμα καὶ
λόγον. (Reference to Nu 21,17.)

Quod Deus 143: ταύτην ἴσθι σοφίαν, διὰ γὰρ ταύτης ὁ νοῦς
ποδηγετούμενος εὐθείας καὶ λεωφόρου ὑπαρχούσης ἄχρι
τερμάτων ἀφικνεῖται, τὸ δὲ τέρμα τῆς ὁδοῦ γνῶσίς ἐστι
καὶ ἐπιστήμη θεοῦ. (Followed by reference to Nu 20,17-20;
the context of the passage being Gn 6,12--"his way"; cf.
159.)

Fug 76: τῷ μὲν γὰρ ἑαυτοῦ λόγῳ ὁ θεὸς πατρίδα οἰκεῖν τὴν
ἐπιστήμην ἑαυτοῦ, ὡς ἂν αὐτόχθονι δεδώρηται . . .
(The discussion is on Ex 21,13.)

Post 129: αὗται (ἀρεταὶ) δὲ καθάπερ ἐκ μιᾶς ῥίζης ἐκπεφύκασι
τοῦ θείου λόγου, ὃν εἰκάζει ποταμῷ . . . (Reference to
Gn 2,10.)

Conf 81: ὅτι παροικεῖ μὲν ὁ σοφὸς ὡς ἐν ξένῃ σώματι αἰσθητῷ,
κατοικεῖ δ᾽ ὡς ἐν πατρίδι νοηταῖς ἀρεταῖς, ἃς λαλεῖ ὁ
θεὸς ἀδιαφορούσας λόγων θείων. (The context is Gn 11,2
and the contrast between "dwelling" and "sojourning.")

Virt 8: τοῦτον τὸν πλοῦτον σοφία χορηγεῖ διὰ λογικῶν καὶ ἠθικῶν
καὶ φυσικῶν δογμάτων καὶ θεωρημάτων, ἐξ ὧν φύεσθαι τὰς
ἀρετὰς συμβέβηκεν, . . . (The context is the discussion
on courage against poverty.)

Wis Sol 9,11: οἶδε γὰρ ἐκείνη πάντα καὶ συνίει καὶ ὁδηγήσει με
ἐν ταῖς πράξεσί μου σωφρόνως . . . (i.e., sophia).

4Macc 1,30: ὁ γὰρ λογισμὸς τῶν μὲν ἀρετῶν ἐστιν ἡγεμών, τῶν δὲ
παθῶν αὐτοκράτωρ. (It is the thematic refrain of the
treatise; cf. 1,19.)

Mediators between God and Man

Quis Her 205: τῷ δὲ ἀρχαγγέλῳ καὶ πρεσβυτάτῳ λόγῳ δωρεὰν ἔδωκεν
ἐξαίρετον ὁ τὰ ὅλα γεννήσας πατήρ, ἵνα μεθόριος στὰς τὸ
γενόμενον διακρίνῃ τοῦ πεποιηκότος. ὁ δ᾽ αὐτὸς ἱκέτης
μὲν ἐστι τοῦ θνητοῦ κηραίνοντος αἰεὶ πρὸς τὸ ἄφθαρτον,
πρεσβευτὴς δὲ τοῦ ἡγεμόνος πρὸς ὑπήκοον. (Followed by
reference to Dt 5,5; i.e., Moses.)

Som i,141-42: ταύτας δαίμονας μὲν οἱ ἄλλοι φιλόσοφοι, ὁ δὲ ἱερὸς
λόγος ἀγγέλους εἴωθε καλεῖν προσφυεστέρῳ χρώμενος ὀνόματι,
καὶ γὰρ τὰς τοῦ πατρὸς ἐπικελεύσεις τοῖς ἐγγόνοις καὶ τὰς
τῶν ἐγγόνων χρείας τῷ πατρὶ διαγγέλουσι. παρὸ καὶ ἀνερ-
χομένους αὐτοὺς καὶ κατιόντας εἰσήγαγεν, οὐκ ἐπειδὴ τῶν
μηνυσόντων ὁ πάντη ἐφθακὼς θεὸς δεῖται, ἀλλ᾽ ὅτι τοῖς
ἐπικήροις ἡμῖν συνέφερε μεσίταις καὶ διαιτηταῖς λόγοις
χρῆσθαι διὰ τὸ τεθηπέναι καὶ δεδιέναι τὸν παμπρύτανιν
καὶ τὸ μέγιστον ἀρχῆς αὐτοῦ κράτος. (This is a portion
of the interpretation of Gn 28,12-13.)

QE II,13: "(Therefore) of necessity was the Logos appointed as
judge and mediator, who is called 'angel.'" (Marcus:
Loeb) (Reference is to Ex 23,20-21.)

QE II,94: "The incorporeal world is set off and separated from
the visible one by the mediating Logos as by a veil."
(Refers to Ex 26,33b--the veil separating the Holy of
Holies; Marcus: Loeb.)

Quod Deus 138: οἷς δ᾽ ὑφηγεῖται ὁ ἑρμενεὺς τοῦ θεοῦ λόγος καὶ
προφήτης ἔπηται. (The reference is to the soul which has
been visited by the "man of God"--1Kg 17,18.)

QE II,16: φωνὴν θεοῦ τὸν πρὸ μικροῦ λεχθέντα ἄγγελον ὑπονοητέον
μηνύεσθαι. τοῦ γὰρ λέγοντος ὁ προφήτης ἄγγελος κυρίου
ἐστιν. (Gk Frg: Harris, p. 54; refers to Ex 23,22.)[7]

---

[7]A striking example of the role of the angel/logos as mediator and revealer and which provides a close parallel to Philo is
Cornutus, Theol. Graec.,16: τυγχάνει δὲ ὁ Ἑρμῆς ὁ λόγος ὤν, ὃν
ἀπέστειλαν πρὸς ἡμᾶς ἐξ οὐρανοῦ οἱ θεοί, μόνον τὸν ἄνθρωπον τῶν
ἐπὶ γῆς ζῴων λογικὸν ποιήσαντες . . . ἀλλὰ πρὸς τὸ σῴζειν μᾶλλον
γέγονεν ὁ λόγος, ὅθεν καὶ τὴν Ὑγίειαν αὐτῷ συνῴκισαν . . . παρα-
δέδοται δὲ καὶ κῆρυξ θεῶν καὶ διαγγέλειν αὐτὸν ἔφασαν τὰ παρ᾽
ἐκείνων τοῖς ἀνθρώποις, . . . (quoted by Kleinknecht in TDNT IV,
87).

Analysis and Summary

The precedents concerning the instrumental role of logos and sophia in creation is indicated in Wis Sol (9,1a-2b; 7,21) and Sib Or (III,20). That God created the world through the instrumentality (organon) of the logos (Leg All iii,96; Cher 125; Mig 6; Spec Leg i,81), by means of sophia (Det 54; Quis Her 199; Ebr 30) and that the eldest and first-born son (= anthrōpos)--Conf 63 --gave shape to the forms by looking to the archetypal patterns of the Father, is simply assumed by Philo and occurs in contexts unrelated to the question of how God created the world. In the Opificio, the Logos is the place (topos) of the ideas, not place in the geographical sense (17-20), and constitutes the intelligible world which God created as a pattern of which the sensible world is an imitation (24-25; 29). The use of the divine logos as the paradeigmatic means of creation is clearly indicated in this treatise (cf. Fug 12). It is a commonly held view among middle-Platonic writers concerning creation and its "aitiai" (see note on: "Cosmological Language in Philo," pp. 23-27). The logos/first-born son sustains and preserves the world as viceroy of the Great King (Agr 51), governor and administrator (QG IV, 110), as support and bond (Stoic--see Wolfson I, pp. 338-39), and mediator and reconciler between antagonistic elements (stoicheia) --Plant 8-10; QE II,68.

Thus the logos, eldest, first-born son, and sophia function as agents of creation and sustainers and preservers of the order and harmony in it.

Furthermore, the logos/rhēma and sophia are the royal highway (Nu 20), which is identified with philosophy or the knowledge of God (Post 102; Quod Deus 143; cf. Congr 79; QG III,43). Sophia is omniscient (Wis Sol 9,11) and the logos dwells in God's knowledge as in a fatherland (Fug 76). Both logos and sophia are the sources of virtues (Post 129; Conf 81; Virt 8) and logismos is the chief of virtues (1Macc 1,30). Therefore, logos and sophia are the sources of knowledge and virtue.

The eldest logos and archangel stand as the frontier separating the creator from creation. He is the suppliant to God on behalf of afflicted mortality and God's ambassador to his subjects (Quis Her 205; Som i,141-42). The logos-angel is a mediator (QE II,94). The prophet like the logos is an interpreter (hermeneus) of God (Quod Deus 138) and God's voice is indeed both a prophet and angel (QE II,16). The correlation of the role of the angels and prophets as intermediaries and their titular iden-

tifications with the logos and each other can also be documented
from Abr 113, Congr 170 and Det 40. The mediating function of
the logos in creation is also indicated in Plant 8-10 and QE II,
68 (see above pp. 13-14). <u>Thus in various ways, logos, archangel,
prophet and angels serve as mediators between God and man, the
creator and creation</u>.

The manner in which Philo introduces these features of the
intermediary world in that they are interjected into contexts
which as such are not concerned with the question of creation
reveals a <u>pattern of thought</u> in Philo. This pattern in respect
to creation and mediation is triggered by an "associative" mode
of exposition (i.e., word-associations). <u>For example</u>, the main
context of Leg All iii,96 (quoted above, p. 13) goes back to the
interpretation of Gn 3,15-16 (65). The issue is the condemnation
of the serpent = pleasure without giving it an opportunity for
self defence, as in the case of Eve. The reason, according to
Philo, is that pleasure is bad in itself (68). Similarly, Er in
Gn 38,7 is slain without a charge since he represents our corpse-
like body (69-76). Then follow counter examples of good natures,
so pronounced without any manifest reason (Noah in Gn 6,8; Melchizedek in Gn 14,18; Abram in Gn 12,1; Isaac in Gn 17,17; Jacob
in Gn 25,23; Ephraim in Gn 48,19) and then Bezalel in Ex 31,12ff.
who receives a commendation without reference to any prior
praiseworthy deed (95). This is explained by the etymology of
Bezalel = shadow of God, which in Philo's mind is associated with
the logos, the instrument used by God to create the world and is
the paradigm for further creations. And this triggers the
thought of <u>Gn 1,27</u>, which is then quoted (95-96). One of the
keys to the understanding and interpretation of Philo would be to
locate <u>patterns of thought</u> which are triggered by means of <u>asso-
ciative</u> terms in the process of his exposition of the passages of
the OT. These <u>patterns of thought which emerge in various con-
texts</u> are, in my judgement, the principal avenues for understanding the religious thought of Philo in contrast to the synthetic
and genetic study of words and passages, which interpreters of
Philo usually use. In the course of this thesis we will outline
some of these patterns. It is thus in a variety of contexts,
diverse as well as unrelated, that this pattern of thought,
namely, the interchangeability of titles and synonymity of functions in the intermediary world, is to be seen.

A Note on the Cosmological Language in Philo

The cosmological language of Philo bears close resemblance to middle-Platonic writers and is structurally identical with them. God created the world by means of the Logos (= intelligible world, archetypal idea, cf. Op 24-25) which served as an "instrument," "seal," and "paradigm" for creation.

Albinus speaking of the three "archai": Ἀρχικὸν δε λόγον ἐπεχούσης τῆς ὕλης ἔτι καὶ ἄλλας ἀρχὰς παραλαμβάνει, τήν τε παραδιεγματικήν, τουτέστι τὴν τῶν ἰδεῶν, καὶ τὴν τοῦ πατρὸς καὶ αἰτίου πάντων θεοῦ. ἔστι δὲ (καὶ) ἡ ἰδέα ὡς μὲν πρὸς θεὸν νόησις αὐτοῦ, ὡς δὲ πρὸς ἡμᾶς νοητὸν πρῶτον, ὡς δὲ πρὸς τὴν ὕλην μέτρον, ὡς δὲ πρὸς τὸν αἰσθητὸν κόσμον παράδειγμα, ὡς δὲ πρὸς αὐτὴν ἐξεταζομένη οὐσία. καθόλου γὰρ πᾶν τὸ γινόμενον κατ' ἐπίνοιαν πρός τι ὀφείλει γίνεσθαι, οὗ ὥσπερ εἰ ἀπό τινός τι γένοιτο, ὡς ἀπ' ἐμοῦ ἡ ἐμὴ εἰκών, δεῖ τὸ παράδειγμα προυποκεῖσθαι. (Cf. Philo, Op 25: εἰ δ' ὁ σύμπας αἰσθητὸς οὑτοσὶ κόσμος, ὁ μεῖζον τῆς ἀνθρωπίνης ἐστίν, μίμημα θείας εἰκόνος, δῆλον ὅτι καὶ ἡ ἀρχέτυπος σφραγίς, ὃν φαμεν νοητὸν εἶναι κόσμον, αὐτὸς ἂν εἴη (τὸ παράδειγμα, ἀρχέτυπος ἰδέα τῶν ἰδεῶν) ὁ θεοῦ λόγος.) . . . ὁ κόσμος μὴ ἐκ ταὐτομάτου τοιοῦτός ἐστιν, οὐ μόνον ἐκ τινός ἐστι γεγονῶς, ἀλλὰ καὶ ὑπό τινος, καὶ οὐ μόνον τοῦτο, ἀλλὰ καὶ πρός τι. τὸ δὲ πρὸς ὃ γέγονε τί ἂν ἄλλο (γέγονεν) ἢ ἰδέα; (Chap. IX). To this compare Cher 125, quoted above; in Spec Leg 327-29, Philo argues against those who deny the existence of "ideas" that they reduce everything to the formless and quality-less nature of matter (ἡ δὲ πολλὴν ἀταξίαν εἰσηγεῖται καὶ σύγχυσις, ἀναιροῦσα γὰρ ταῦτα (i.e., ἰδέαι), δι' ὧν αἱ ποιότητες, συναιρεῖ ποιότητας . . . --329). Similar arguments are pursued by Albinus in Chap. VIII, where the formlessness of matter is asserted to be prior condition for receiving form and quality. In Chap. IX, Albinus attempts in various ways to prove the existence of "ideas"--a point which therefore seems to have been a matter of dispute among the schools. πατὴρ δέ ἐστι τῷ αἴτιος εἶναι πάντων καὶ κοσμεῖν τὸν οὐράνιον νοῦν καὶ τὴν ψυχὴν τοῦ κόσμου πρὸς ἑαυτὸν καὶ πρὸς τὰς ἑαυτοῦ νοήσεις. κατὰ γὰρ τὴν ἑαυτοῦ βούλησιν ἐμπέπληκε πάντα ἑαυτοῦ, τὴν ψυχὴν τοῦ κόσμου ἐπεγείρας καὶ εἰς ἑαυτὸν ἐπιτρέψας, τοῦ νοῦ αὐτῆς αἴτιος ὑπάρχων, ὃς κοσμηθεὶς ὑπὸ τοῦ πατρὸς διακοσμεῖ σύμπασαν φύσιν ἐν τῷδε τῷ κόσμῳ. (Chap. X)

The creative role of the "nous of the soul of the universe" may be compared to the similar role of the "first born son" in Philo, Conf 63, quoted on p. 14. That God fills all things with himself is often reiterated in Philo, cf. Leg All iii,4: πάντα γὰρ πεπλήρωκεν ὁ θεὸς καὶ διὰ πάντων διελήλυθεν καὶ κενὸν οὐδὲν οὐδὲ ἔρημον ἀπολέλοιπεν ἑαυτοῦ. In QE II,68 (quoted on p. 14) the Logos fills all things; QG IV,130--God fills all things with His powers. The same ambiguity between God as creating or some intermediary is also true in Albinus, as the following will illustrate in comparison to the passage quoted above from Chap. X (cf. Conf 63). ἀναγκαῖον καὶ τὸ κάλλιστον κατασκεύασμα τὸν κόσμον ὑπὸ τοῦ θεοῦ δεδημιουργῆσθαι πρός τινα ἰδέαν κόσμου ἀποβλέποντος, παράδειγμα ὑπάρχουσαν τοῦδε τοῦ κόσμου . . . ἐκ τῆς πάσης οὖν ὕλης αὐτὸν ἐδημιούργει. (Chap. XII)

The same cosmological language can also be documented from the Pseudo-Platonic Timaeus Locri and Apuleius.

Timaeus Locri: . . . "that of all the things in the Universe there are two causes, Mind, of things existing according to reason, Necessity, of things by force . . . and that the former of these is of the nature of the good, and is called god, and the principle of things that are best; but what comes after this and are co-causes, are referred to Necessity; but that, as regarding the things of the universe, there are Form and Matter . . . and that the former is unproduced, unmoved, stationary, of the nature of the same, perceptible by the mind and pattern of such things produced . . ." (Chap. I). The description of matter that follows is very similar to Albinus, Chap. VIII.

"Before, then, the heaven existed, there were, reasonably, Form, Matter and God, who is the demiurgos of the better. . . . He made, therefore, this world out of the whole of Matter, . . . one, only-begotten, perfect, endued with soul and reason" (Chap. 2). Cf. Philo, Quod Deus 31; 106; Ebr 30.

Apuleius, De Platone et eius Dogmate: "Initia rerum tria esse arbitratur Plato: deum et materiam rerumque formas, quas "ideas" idem vocat . . . " (I,V). The description of matter that follows is again analogous to Albinus, Chap. VIII and Timaeus Locri, Chap. I.

"'ideas' vero, id est formas omnium, simplices et aeternas esse nec corporales tamen; esse ex his, quae deus sumpserit, exempla rerum . . . " (I,VI). In Chap. VIII, the commonplace assertion is made that the world was made out of all the elements and nothing was left outside of the world.

In contrast, the Stoics recognized only two principles, the active and the passive, the active (Logos) being inherent in matter, which is passive: Δοκεῖ δ᾽ αὐτοῖς ἀρχὰς εἶναι τῶν ὅλων δύο, τὸ ποιοῦν καὶ τὸ πάσχον. τὸ μὲν οὖν πάσχον εἶναι τὴν ἄποιον οὐσίαν τὴν ὕλην, τὸ δὲ ποιοῦν τὸν ἐν αὐτῇ λόγον τὸν θεόν. . . .

20

διαφέρειν δέ φασιν ἀρχὰς καὶ στοιχεῖα, τὰς μὲν εἶναι ἀγενήτους (καὶ) ἀφθάρτους, τὰ δὲ στοιχεῖα κατὰ τὴν ἐκπύρωσιν φθείρεσθαι. (DL VII, 134) For this viewpoint Diogenes Laertius cites Zeno, Cleanthes, Chrysippus, Archedemus, and Posidonius. Marcus Aurelius refers consistently to these two principles as "matter" and "cause," e.g., IV,21: Τίς ἐπὶ τούτου ἡ ἱστορία τῆς ἀληθείας; διαίρεσις εἰς τὸ ὑλικὸν καὶ εἰς τὸ αἰτιῶδες. (Cf. V,13; VII,29; VIII,11; IX,25, 37; XII,10, 18, 29.) Kleinknecht (TDNT IV,84-85) adduces some interesting examples to show the identity of the Logos with God, cosmos, fate, law, nature, etc. The function of the Logos in the cosmology of Philo and its relationship to middle Platonism is left unelucidated in his article.

In light of the passages quoted from Albinus, Timaeus Locri and Apuleius, Wolfson incorrectly attributes to Philo the identification of the Aristotelian forms with the intelligible world, the world of ideas. It is a commonplace in middle-Platonism (see Wolfson I, 231 and 264). The language of "causes" is borrowed from Aristotle but the structure of thought is Platonic. For a diagrammatic presentation, see below p. 140.

C. Anthropos: Heavenly & Earthly

The Problem

That genetic and synthetic interpretations of Philo can be misleading can be illustrated from the way Jervell has treated the distinctions that are made in the understanding of anthropos, especially in terms of Philo's interpretation of Gn 1,26 and 27 and Gn 2,7, etc. It seems to be a commonplace that Philo distinguished between a "heavenly" or "image-like" or "ideal man" in Gn 1,27 and an "earthly" man in Gn 2,7, e.g.,

> "Finally, on the sixth day, He created land animals, the mind of man or the ideal man, which is referred to in the first account of the creation of man, and the corporeal or individual man, which is referred to in the second account of the creation of man." Wolfson I,310. "Philo finds his exegetical basis for the distinction in the twofold account of man's creation in Gn. 1:26f. and Gn. 2:7. This gives rise to the frequently described or assumed distinction, which characterises all Philo's theology and anthropology, between the heavenly man who in Gn. 1:26f. is created as the eikōn theou and has no part in mortality or earthliness and the earthly man who according to Gn. 2:7 is fashioned out of dust (Leg.All., I,31ff.; . . .)." Kittel in TDNT II, 394-95. "der Mensch in Gen 1,26f. wird als der Idee-Mensch verstanden, während von dem irdisch-empirischen Menschen erst in Gen 2,7 geredet wird." Jervell, Imago Dei, 70. "Philo unterscheidet an vielen Stellen zwischen dem ebenbildlichen Menschen in

Gen 1,27 und dem irdischen Menschen in Gen 2,7."
Eltester, Eikon, 54.

Furthermore, in an attempt to interpret Philo by means of synthetic word studies and by neglecting the context, Jervell has
made innumerable errors in his interpretation of Philo. For
example:

"Wir sehen weiter, dass das Abbild im Menschen der wahre
Anthropos genannt wird. Nun finden wir gerade unter dieser
Bezeichnung den Logos des Weltalls, De conf. ling. 41.62.
146," p. 57. If one reads the texts mentioned by Jervell,
not a single one mentions the "true man." Besides in Philo
this designation--"true man"--is exclusively used to describe the "nous," "logikē psychē," "Israel" and the
"elenchos in the soul" (Plant 42; Fug 71; Quis Her 231;
Som i,215; Spec Leg i,303; Fug 131). In his discussion
on the soul: Die menschliche Seele nach dem Logos
geschaffen, 58-60, Jervell fails to notice in Philo the
distinction between rational soul and irrational, and
that it is only the former, i.e., mind, which is created
according to the Logos Cf. Op 137-39. Hence he confuses
the "earthly" man with this section of his discussion.
(These distinctions will be described below.) At the end
of the section he reaches the conclusion that the Logos
and the nous in men are identical. However, the preser-
vation of this distinction is the crucial point in Philo's
exegesis of Gn 1,27 (see below).

The same synthetic procedure leads both Jervell and Eltester to
read the terms "eikōn" and "logos" as equivalent and by combining
two separate sets of passages they conclude that logos is the
decisive concept in Philo's interpretation of Gen 1,26f. and 2,7,
etc. (Jervell, p. 70; Eltester, p. 57).

On the basis of passages in which the Logos is called the
eikōn of God, both Jervell and Eltester deduce that the
logos is central to the distinctions Philo draws on the
basis of Gn 1,27. Hence the term eikōn is read in these
contexts as equivalent to Logos. "Bei Philo ist die Auslegung von Gen 1,26f. hauptsächlich von seiner Vorstellung
vom Logosbegriff bestimmt." Jervell, p. 70. The word is
given a substantive significance and Jervell seems igno-
rant of the wide and diverse use of this plastic imagery
in Greek literature as well as in Philo. "Das 'Bild' oder
die eikōn ist nunmehr eine selbständige Grösse, die weder
etwas an Gott noch am Menschen ist." Jervell, p. 54. "So
hat denn diese Unterscheidung zur Folge, dass der Begriff
eikōn tou theou eine Bezeichnung des Mittlers geworden ist,
eine Bezeichnung, die nicht ein Humanitätsprädikat, sondern
ein Charakteristikum der Gottheit ist," Jervell, p. 55.
That such conclusions are unwarranted can be easily seen
from common use of such plastic imagery in Philo in a
variety of contexts.

Quod Omn Prob 62: . . . καὶ ἐφ' ἡμῶν αὐτῶν ἔτ' εἰσιν ὥσπερ
εἰκόνες ἀπὸ ἀρχετύπου γραφῆς, σοφῶν ἀνδρῶν καλοκἀγαθίας,
τυπωθέντες. (The context is an introduction to examples
of wise men who are free.)

Praem 114: αἱ γὰρ συνεχεῖς τῶν καλῶν παραδειγμάτων φαντασίαι
παραπλησίας εἰκόνας ἐγχαράττουσι ταῖς μὴ πάνυ σκληραῖς

καὶ ἀποκρότοις ψυχαῖς. (The exemplary worth of the good
man--spoudaios--is hereby expressed.)

These two examples will suffice from the hundreds of such uses of
the plastic imagery in Philo to show that these terms, paradeigma,
archetypos, eikōn, ekmageion, etc., are terms which describe relations and are not substantive in their meaning. They describe
sets of relationships and are not restricted to the interpretation of Gn 1,27. The nature of these relationships will be
described below.

Texts

What follows are texts from Philo which interpret Gn 1,26f.
and 2,7, etc. and in a form which enables us to see the character
of the distinctions and their basis.

Op 69 (Gn 1,26 and 27)

μετὰ δὴ τἆλλα πάντα, καθάπερ ἐλέχθη, τὸν ἄνθρωπόν φησι γεγενῆσθαι,
"κατ' εἰκόνα θεοῦ" καὶ "καθ' ὁμοίωσιν" (Gn 1,26 and 27)

1. πρὸς γὰρ ἕνα, τὸν τῶν ὅλων ἐκεῖνον ὡς ἂν ἀρχέτυπον
   (= νοῦς)

2. (ἡ δὲ εἰκὼν λέλεκται κατὰ τὸν τῆς ψυχῆς ἡγεμόνα
   νοῦν . . .) ὁ ἐν ἑκάστῳ τῶν κατὰ μέρος ἀπεικονίσθη . .

Fug 71 (Gn 1,26 vs 1,27)

διὸ καὶ λεχθέντος πρότερον "ποιήσωμεν ἄνθρωπον" (Gn 1,26) ὡς ἂν
ἐπὶ πλήθους, ἐπιφέρεται τὸ ὡς ἂν ἐφ' ἑνός, "ἐποίησεν ὁ θεὸς τὸν
ἄνθρωπον" (Gn 1,27)

2. τοῦ μὲν γὰρ πρὸς ἀλήθειαν ἀνθρώπου, ὃς δὴ νοῦς ἐστι
   καθαρώτατος, εἷς ὁ μόνος θεὸς δημιουργός,

3. τοῦ δὲ λεγομένου καὶ κεκραμένου μετ' αἰσθήσεως τὸ
   πλῆθος.

Quis Her 230-31 (Gn 1,27)

. . . δύο λόγους, ἕνα μὲν ἀρχέτυπον (τὸν) ὑπὲρ ἡμᾶς, ἕτερον δὲ
μίμημα καθ' ἡμᾶς ὑπάρχοντα.

2α. καλεῖ δὲ Μωυσῆς τὸν μὲν ὑπὲρ ἡμᾶς εἰκόνα θεοῦ
2β. τὸν δὲ καθ' ἡμᾶς τῆς εἰκόνος ἐκμαγεῖον.

"ἐποίησε" γάρ φησιν "ὁ θεὸς τὸν ἄνθρωπον" οὐχὶ εἰκόνα θεοῦ, ἀλλὰ
"κατ' εἰκόνα" (Gn 1,27),

2β. ὥστε τὸν καθ' ἕκαστον ἡμῶν νοῦν, ὃς δὴ κυρίως καὶ πρὸς
    ἀλήθειαν ἄνθρωπός ἐστι, τρίτον εἶναι τύπον

1. ἀπὸ τοῦ πεποιηκότος

2α. τὸν δὲ μέσον <u>παράδειγμα τούτου</u> (2β), <u>ἀπεικόνισμα</u> δὲ
ἐκείνου (1).

Leg All iii,96 (Gn 1,27)

"καὶ ἐποίησεν ὁ θεὸς τὸν <u>ἄνθρωπον κατ᾽ εἰκόνα θεοῦ</u>" (Gn 1,27),
2α. ὡς τῆς μὲν <u>εἰκόνος κατὰ τὸν θεὸν</u> ἀπεικονισθείσης,
2β; τοῦ δὲ <u>ἀνθρώπου κατὰ τὴν εἰκόνα</u> λαβοῦσαν δύναμιν
παραδείγματος.

Op 134 (Gn 2,7)

μετὰ δὲ ταῦτά φησιν ὅτι "<u>ἔπλασεν</u> ὁ θεὸς τὸν ἄνθρωπον χοῦν λαβὼν
ἀπὸ τῆς γῆς, καὶ ἐνεφύσησεν εἰς τὸ πρόσωπον αὐτοῦ <u>πνοὴν ζωῆς</u>" (Gn
2,7). ἐναργέστατα καὶ διὰ τούτου παρίστησιν ὅτι διαφορὰ παμμε-
γέθης ἐστὶ τοῦ τε νῦν <u>πλασθέντος ἀνθρώπου</u> καὶ τοῦ <u>κατὰ τὴν εἰκόνα</u>
<u>θεοῦ</u> γεγονότος πρότερον (Gn 1,27),
2. ὁ δὲ <u>κατὰ τὴν εἰκόνα</u> ἰδέα τις ἢ γένος ἢ σφραγίς, νοητός,
ἀσώματος, οὔτε ἄρρεν οὔτε θῆλυ, ἄφθαρτος φύσει.
3. ὁ μὲν γὰρ <u>διαπλασθεὶς</u> αἰσθητὸς ἤδη μετέχων ποιότητος,
ἐκ σώματος καὶ ψυχῆς συνεστώς, ἀνὴρ ἢ γυνή, φύσει
θνητός, . . .

Leg All i,31 (Gn 2,7)

"καὶ <u>ἔπλασεν</u> ὁ θεὸς τὸν ἄνθρωπον <u>χοῦν</u> λαβὼν ἀπὸ τῆς <u>γῆς</u>, καὶ
ἐνεφύσησεν εἰς τὸ πρόσωπον αὐτοῦ πνοὴν ζωῆς, καὶ ἐγένετο ὁ ἄνθρωπος εἰς <u>ψυχὴν ζῶσαν</u>" (Gn 2,7). <u>διττὰ</u> ἀνθρώπων γένη, . . .
2. ὁ μὲν οὖν <u>οὐράνιος</u> ἅτε <u>κατ᾽ εἰκόνα θεοῦ</u> γεγονὼς φθαρτῆς
καὶ συνόλως γεώδους οὐσίας ἀμέτοχος,
3. ὁ δὲ <u>γήϊνος</u> ἐκ σπόραδος ὕλης, ἣν <u>χοῦν</u> κέκληκεν, . . .

Quis Her 56-57 (Gn 2,7 and 1,27)

"ἐνεφύσησεν" γάρ φησιν ὁ ποιητὴς τῶν ὅλων "εἰς τὸ πρόσωπον αὐτοῦ
<u>πνοὴν ζωῆς</u>, καὶ ἐγένετο ὁ <u>ἄνθρωπος</u> εἰς ψυχὴν ζῶσαν" (Gn 2,7), ᾗ
καὶ <u>κατὰ τὴν εἰκόνα</u> τοῦ ποιητοῦ λόγος ἔχει τυπωθῆναι (Gn 1,27).
ὥστε <u>διττὸν</u> εἶδος ἀνθρώπων,
2β. τὸ μὲν <u>θείῳ πνεύματι</u> λογισμῷ βιούντων,
3. τὸ δὲ <u>αἵματι καὶ σαρκὸς</u> ἡδονῇ ζώντων. τοῦτο τὸ εἶδός
ἐστι <u>πλάσμα γῆς</u>,
ἐκεῖνο δὲ <u>θείας εἰκόνος</u> (2α.) ἐμφερὲς <u>ἐκμαγεῖον</u>.

Plant 18-19 (Gn 2,7 and 1,27)

ὁ δὲ μέγας Μωυσῆς οὐδενὶ τῶν γεγονότων <u>τῆς λογικῆς ψυχῆς</u> <u>τὸ εἶδος</u>
ὡμοίωσεν, ἀλλ᾽ εἶπεν

2β. αὐτήν

1. τοῦ <u>θείου</u> καὶ· ἀοράτου <u>πνεύματος</u> ἐκείνου

2β. <u>δόκιμον</u> εἶναι <u>νόμισμα</u> σημειωθὲν καὶ τυπωθὲν

2α. <u>σφραγῖδι θεοῦ</u>, ἧς ὁ χαρακτήρ ἐστιν <u>ὁ ἀίδιος λόγος</u>

"<u>ἐνέπνευσε</u>" γάρ φησιν "ὁ θεὸς εἰς τὸ πρόσωπον αὐτοῦ <u>πνοὴν ζωῆς</u>"
(Gn 2,7), ὥστε ἀνάγκη πρὸς τὸν ἐκπέμποντα   τὸν δεχόμενον
ἀπεικονίσθαι, διὸ καὶ λέγεται <u>κατ' εἰκόνα θεοῦ</u> τὸν ἄνθρωπον
γεγενῆσθαι, . . . (Gn 1,27).

Leg All i,53 (Gn 2,8 vs 2,15)

<u>ὃν δὲ ἔπλασεν</u> <u>ἄνθρωπον</u> τιθέναι φησὶν <u>ἐν τῷ παραδείσῳ</u> νυνὶ μόνον
(Gn 2,8), τίς οὖν ἐστιν, εφ' οὗ ὕστερόν φησιν ὅτι "ἔλαβε κύριος
ὁ θεὸς τὸν ἄνθρωπον <u>ὃν ἐποίησε</u> καὶ ἔθετο αὐτὸν ἐν τῷ παραδείσῳ,
ἐργάζεσθαι αὐτὸν καὶ φυλάσσειν" (Gn 2,15); μήποτ' οὖν ἕτερός
ἐστιν ἄνθρωπος οὗτος, ὁ <u>κατὰ τὴν εἰκόνα</u> καὶ τὴν ἰδέαν γεγονώς,
ὥστε <u>δύο ἀνθρώπους</u> εἰς τὸν παράδεισον εἰσάγεσθαι,

2. τὸν δὲ <u>κατ' εἰκόνα</u>

3. τὸν μὲν <u>πεπλασμένον</u>

Det 83 (Gn 2,7 vs Lv 17,11; cf. 80)

ἡ μὲν οὖν κοινὴ πρὸς τὰ ἄλογα δύναμις οὐσίαν ἔλαχεν <u>αἷμα</u>, ἡ δὲ ἐκ
τῆς λογικῆς ἀπορρυεῖσα πηγῆς τὸ <u>πνεῦμα</u> . . . ἣν ὀνόματι κυρίῳ
Μωυσῆς <u>εἰκόνα</u> καλεῖ, δηλῶν ὅτι

1. <u>ἀρχέτυπον</u> μὲν <u>φύσεως λογικῆς</u> ὁ <u>θεὸς</u> ἐστι,

2. <u>μίμημα</u> δὲ καὶ <u>ἀπεικόνισμα</u> <u>ἄνθρωπος</u>,

3. οὗ τὸ <u>δυφυὲς ζῷον</u>,

ἀλλὰ τὸ τῆς ψυχῆς ἄριστον εἶδος, ὁ <u>νοῦς</u> καὶ <u>λόγος</u> κέκληται.

<u>Analysis</u>

It is clear from the passages above that the distinctions
which Philo draws between the two types of anthrōpos is not based
on a distinction between Gn 1 and Gn 2 but is made on the basis
of either one or several phrases from Gn 1,26f. 2,7, 2,8 and 2,15.
Thus in <u>Op 69</u>, the phrases "kata eikōn theou" of Gn 1,27 and
"kath' homoiōsis" of Gn 1,26, in terms of the plastic imagery,
are seen to be equivalent and to refer to the "nous" in each of
us which is "imaged" after the archetypal "nous of the universe,"
i.e., God.

> Jervell incorrectly reads "nous of the universe" to mean
> the Logos and dismisses Eltester's view that Philo can
> speak of the human mind as a direct eikōn of God as false
> (p. 55; esp. f.n. 114a). That Philo speaks of God as the
> "nous of the universe" is clear from the following passages,
> whereas I do not know of a single instance where Philo
> speaks of the logos as the nous of the universe:

Leg All iii,29: ὁ γὰρ ἀποδιδράσκων <u>θεὸν</u> καταφεύγει εἰς ἑαυτόν.
δυοῖν γὰρ ὄντων τοῦ τε <u>τῶν ὅλων νοῦ</u>, <u>ὅς ἐστι θεός</u>, καὶ
τοῦ ἰδίου, ὁ μὲν φεύγων ἀπὸ τοῦ καθ᾽ αὑτὸν καταφεύγει ἐπὶ
τὸν συμπάντων . . . (Interpretation of Gn 3,9; i.e.,
Adam's hiding from the presence of God.)

Post 41: τὸ μὲν οὖν "χάρις σου" λέγεται μὲν πρὸς <u>τὸν ἐν ἡμῖν</u>
<u>νοῦν</u> ὑπ᾽ ἐνίων, λέγεται δὲ καὶ πρὸς <u>τὸν τῶν ὅλων</u> ὑπὸ τῶν
ἀμεινόνων. (Enoch is interpreted to mean "charis sou";
there are two Enochs, descendant of Seth and that of Cain
(Gn 4,17 § 5,18); one acknowledges everything to be the
"gift of God," the other the gift of one's own mind. Cf.
Fug 46.)

Mig 4: μὴ θαυμάσῃς δέ, εἰ νοῦ τὸν λόγον ἐν ἀνθρώπῳ κέκληκεν
οἶκον, καὶ γὰρ <u>τὸν τῶν ὅλων νοῦν</u>, <u>τὸν θεόν</u>, οἶκον ἔχειν
φησὶ τὸν ἑαυτοῦ λόγον. (The context is the interpretation of "father's house" in Gn 12,1 as a reference to the
human logos [= house] as the house of the mind
[= father].)

On the other hand, "let us make" of Gn 1,26 and the singular of
Gn 1,27 become the basis in <u>Fug 71</u> for the distinction between
the pure nous--the true man--and the man mixed with the senses.

Similarly, on the basis of Gn 2,7a--"moulded"--in <u>Op 134</u> and
<u>Leg All i,31</u>, Philo distinguishes between the man made "according
to the image" (Gn 1,27) or "heavenly man" and "moulded" man
formed of body and soul or "earthly man." On the other hand,
Gn 2,7b is combined with Gn 1,27 as basis of distinguishing between those who live reasonably according to the divine spirit
and those who live by the pleasures of flesh and blood, the former being the "impression of the (seal) of the divine image" and
the latter "mould (plasma) of the earth"--<u>Quis Her 56-57</u>. In
<u>Plant 18-19</u> also Gn 2,7b and 1,27 is cited as proof that "the
form of the rational soul (logikē psychē)" is the "approved coinage" of the "divine, invisible spirit," i.e., God. In <u>Det 83</u> the
"spirit" (Gn 2,7b) is named by Moses "eikōn," on which basis the
distinction is made between God as the archetype of the rational
soul and "anthrōpos" who is its "image and imitation."

On the basis of reading in Gn 2,15 as "whom he made" (LXX
has "whom he moulded") and in 2,8 as "whom he formed," Philo
draws the distinction between man "according to the image" and
the "moulded" man--<u>Leg All i,53</u>.

This is enough to show that the basis of Philo's distinctions in the concept of "anthropos" is not that between the first
creation story and the second or Gn 1 and 2, as is commonly sup-
posed, but the distinctions can be drawn on the basis of anyone
of the phrases in both chapters. Furthermore the kinds of distinctions that are made on the basis of these passages cannot be
predicted and depend on the individual cases.

Although each individual case varies in its focus of concern, there is nevertheless a basic pattern which we have numbered in the texts. The basic pattern is a threefold one:

1. God; Universal Mind (Nous, never Logos); Divine, Eternal Spirit.

2. Mind = true man; Man according to the image; Heavenly Man.

3. Man mixed with senses; Moulded; Earthly; Mould of Earth; Dual-Natured Man.

What has often confused scholars is the fact that at times Philo introduces a further distinction on the second level between:

2a. Image of God; Image according to God; Seal of God = Eternal Logos; Divine Image.

2b. Man according to the image; Stamp of the Image; Human Mind = True Man; Rational Soul.

This distinction on the second level is explicitly made in Quis Her 230-31 to explain the distinction between the "Logos" and the logos in us and in Leg All iii,96 as an explanation of the fact that the Logos which is the eikōn of God is in its turn the archetypos or paradeigma of others (cf. QG I,4; Op 139). (For the whole context see p. 17 above.)   It is implicit in the formulations of Quis Her 56-57 and Plant 18-19. In the case of the former two passages, Gn 1,27 is used as the proof text. It is in this differentiation that the logos plays a role.

> Eltester has correctly recognized this threefold or fourfold pattern of steps (pp. 49-50). Jervell seems quite oblivious of these differentiations when he states: "Der irdische Mensch ist der ὁ κατ' εἰκόνα ἄνθρωπος," p. 64.

Once we recognize that Philo introduces the distinction between 2a and 2b in some cases and does not in others, the root of much confusion in understanding Philo at this point is eliminated.

His basic distinction is between the "ideal man" in the intelligible world and the "empirical" man of the sense perceptible world and it is this Platonic distinction which is decisive rather than his Logos theory--contrary to Eltester and Jervell. See especially Op 134; Fug 71; Leg All i,31.

> Since Jervell has missed these distinctions made by Philo and especially that Philo's argument is not based on a differentiation between Gn 1 and 2, he is led to postulate a Platonic interpretation of Gn 1,26f. in contrast to a logos interpretation, pp. 64-66. "Nun sehen wir aber, dass Philo in demselben Traktat (i.e., Op) schon in Gn 1,26f. die Schöpfung des irdischen Menschen gefunden hat, 25,69ff. Wir können also hier feststellen, dass er verschiedene Auslegungen derselben Stelle hat," p. 64.

The "true man," "pure mind" vs "mixed with senses" (Fug 71); the man "according to the image" is "idea," "genus," "intelligible," "incorporeal," "neither male nor female," "immortal by

nature" in contrast to the "moulded" man who is "sense perceptible," "partakes of quality," "composed of body and soul," "male
or female," "mortal by nature" (Op 134); the "heavenly" man is
"according to the image," "totally without corruptible and earthly substance" contrasted to the "earthly" man made from "matter,"
called "clay" (Leg All i,31). The language used in this contrast
is Platonic--the contrast between the intelligible world and
sense perceptible world. In making this distinction between a
heavenly man and an earthly man, Philo also speaks of it in terms
of "two genuses of men" (Leg All i,31, cf ii,4), "two forms of
men" (Quis Her 57) or just "two men" (Leg All i,53). The distinction between the eikōn and the anthrōpos kata eikona ought
not to be confused with the distinction between the heavenly and
earthly man. It belongs to second level in the basic pattern.
Thus Philo can simply call the human mind eikōn of God (Op 69);
anthrōpos, the best form of the soul = logos and nous, the imitation and image (apeikonisma) of God who is the archetypos of the
logikē psychē (Det 83; cf. 86-87: Mind = eikōn theou). Hence it
is not a contradiction for Philo to identify the Logos of God
along with the man according to God's image in Conf 146 (see
below p. 32). What is crucial is the level at which Philo wishes
to draw the distinction.

For clarity it should be reiterated (see above, pp. 21f.) that
the plastic or sculptural imagery of such terms as archetypos/
paradeigma--eikōn/apeikonisma/ekmageion, etc. is used widely by
Philo in a variety of contexts and it is the fallacy of word
studies which attributes to them technical significance and substantive meaning, as is done by both Eltester and Jervell. The
relational character of these terms may be illustrated by two
further passages (see above pp. 21f.):

Fug 12: ὁ δὲ τοῦ ποιοῦντος λόγος αὐτός ἐστιν ἡ σφραγίς, ᾗ τῶν
ὄντων ἕκαστον μεμόρφωται, παρὸ καὶ τέλειον τοῖς γινομέ-
νοις ἐξ ἀρχῆς παρακολουθεῖ τὸ εἶδος, ἅτε ἐκμαγεῖον καὶ
εἰκὼν τελείου λόγου.

There is the creator, his logos = seal, and the form which accom-
panies the things that have come into existence and this form is
perfect since it is the stamp and image (eikōn) of the perfect
logos. The term eikōn does not necessarily belong to the middle
level, it is a relational term and its occurrence does not tell
us anything concerning the level at which the distinction is
being made. Similarly the terms paradeigma and archetypos also
by themselves do not indicate at what level the differentiation
lies, e.g.,

Leg All iii,96: αὕτη δὲ ἡ σκιά (= λόγος θεοῦ) καὶ τὸ ὡσανεὶ
ἀπεικόνισμα, ἑτέρων ἐστὶν <u>ἀρχέτυπον</u>, ὥσπερ γὰρ ὁ θεὸς
<u>παράδειγμα</u> τῆς εἰκόνος, ἣν σκιὰν νυνὶ κέκληκεν, οὕτως
ἡ εἰκὼν ἄλλων γίνεται <u>παράδειγμα</u> . . .

An examination of the context of the passages quoted in pp.
22 - 24 confirms our observation that <u>patterns of thought</u> recur in
Philo in various contexts and one must observe these patterns to
be able to interpret him accurately. For example, the context of
<u>Det 83</u> is Gn 4,10--"voice of thy brother's blood"--which triggers
in Philo's mind passages like Lv 17,11, "<u>the soul of all flesh is
blood</u>," and by association this is contrasted with Gn 2,7--"<u>spir-
it</u> of life," "<u>living soul</u>," and this forms the basis for distinguishing the nous and logos of the soul, whose archetype is God,
and the two natured man. Philo then elaborates upon the qualities of the nous, which alone makes the conception of the invisible God possible since it is an eik$\overline{o}$n of God (86-87), followed by
a description of the noetic experience of transcending space and
time, analogous to <u>Op 69ff</u>, which is explained by the fact that
the mind is an <u>apospasma</u> of the universal soul (90; cf. Det 90;
Som i,34). In briefer form, the same pattern of thought is triggered by Gn 15,2 (LXX)--etymology of Damascus = "blood of sack-
cloth"--in Quis Her 54ff. The contrast between Lv 17,11 and Gn
2,7 along with 1,27 becomes the basis for distinguishing "two
forms of men," those who live by logismos, i.e., the divine
spirit, and are a clear stamp of the divine image and those who
live by the pleasures of flesh and blood, whose form corresponds
to the "mould of earth." The context of <u>Fug 71</u>, speaks of the
cities of refuge (Ex 21,12-14); Philo explains verse 13--"not
intentionally, but God delivers him into his hands," i.e., unintentional homicide--as God's act of punishment but not of sin and
this has to be modified further in that it is unbecoming for God
to punish and in fact he punishes only through his ministers and
this is proven by interpreting Gn 1,26. The context of <u>Quis Her</u>
230-31 is Gn 15,10, the birds are the two logoi. In <u>Plant 18-19</u>,
the context is the description of God as the perfect planter and
creation of man who is distinguished from other creatures by his
erect posture and rational soul. In <u>Leg All i,31 & 53</u>, the sequence follows Gn 2,1ff; 2,1-3 heaven = mind, earth = sense perception; 2,6 spring = mind, face of the earth = senses; 2,7
distinguishes the heavenly and earthly man; 2,8 garden = virtue
and distinction between 2,8 and 2,15, the man according to the
image and the moulded man. <u>Opificio</u> with numerous digressions
describes the creation of the intelligible world on the basis of
Gn 1,1-3; the sense perceptible world Gn 1,6ff; in 69 the crea-

tion of the mind is described followed by a discussion of the
plural in Gn 1,26 (cf. Fug 65ff.), a digression on why man comes
last in creation (77-88), on the number seven (89-128) alluding
to Gn 2,1-3, a brief discussion of 2,4-5 as referring to the incorporeal ideas and pattern, and then the discussion of Gn 2,7 in
134. The contexts vary widely, but a pattern of thought is impel-
led by terminological or conceptual associations.

> Op 135-50 gives an extended description of the composite
> man or sense perceptible man made of "earthly substance"
> and "divine spirit." He is called "first man," "earth
> born," "progenitor" (archegetēs) of our race. His soul
> is an image and imitation of the divine logos (139). He
> surpassed all succeeding men in his faculties since they
> are "imitations of the archetype" (141). He is a cosmo-
> plitēs and the constitution is the logos of nature or
> divine nomos or thesmos (143). He is a sophos, self-
> learnt and self-taught, indeed a king (148). Woman or
> sense perception was the cause of his down-fall (151-52;
> cf. Quis Her 53). Virt 205: the first man is an eikon
> of God in some sense on account of the mind in the soul
> and he did not keep the eikon undefiled, and followed
> vice rather than virtue and thus exchanged mortality for
> immortality.

Summary

The basis of Philo's distinctions concerning anthrōpos is
not that between Gn 1 and 2 or the first story of creation and
the second, but the distinctions are drawn on the basis of terminology in both chapters. On the one hand we have, "καθ᾽ ὁμοίωσιν"
(Gn 1,26), "κατ᾽ εἰκόνα θεοῦ" (Gn 1,27), "καὶ ἐνεφύσησεν εἰς τὸ
πρόσωπον αὐτοῦ πνοὴν ζωῆς" (Gn 2,7b), "ἔλαβε κύριος ὁ θεὸς τὸν
ἄνθρωπον ὃν ἐποίησε . . ." (Gn 2,15) as the basis for description
of the mind, true man, man according to the image, heavenly man,
etc. as distinct from "ποιήσωμεν ἄνθρωπον" (Gn 1,26), "ἔπλασεν ὁ
θεὸς τὸν ἄνθρωπον χοῦν λαβὼν ἀπὸ τῆς γῆς (Gn 2,7a), ὃν δὲ ἔπλασεν
ἄνθρωπον τιθέναι φησὶν ἐν τῷ παραδείσῳ (refers--Gn 2,8) as the
basis for the description of the man mixed with sense, moulded,
earthly, two-natured, etc. The basic pattern of differentiation
is a threefold one: 1. God, 2. Man according to the image or
heavenly man, 3. Moulded/Composite or earthly man. On occa-
sions, Philo makes a further distinction on the second level
between the eikon = logos of God and that which is according to
the eikon of God. It is in this latter distinction only that his
concept of logos plays a role, otherwise the basic distinctions
are drawn in terms of the Platonic differentiation between the
intelligible and sense perceptible world. The plastic imagery
that is used in this context describes a set of relationships and
does not in and of itself indicate the level at which the

distinction is being drawn. It is used in Philo in innumerable contexts. This pattern of thought occurs in numerous contexts, and as we have indicated above, is triggered by terminological and conceptual associations. We have argued that this is a methodologically more sound way of understanding Philo than synthetic study of words or concepts that is usual.

There is thus the distinction between a heavenly, ideal man who is genus, intelligible, incorporeal, immortal and without any part in corruptible and earthly essence and the earthly man composed of body and soul, mortal and sense perceptible (Op 134). Such a distinction can also be expressed in terms of two types of existence--those who live by reason, the divine spirit and those who live by the principle of animate existence = blood and the pleasures of the flesh (Quis Her 56-57).

CHAPTER TWO

PATTERNS OF PERFECTION

Introduction: The pattern of thought which shows fluidity
as well as consciously wrought identifications between the logos,
sophia, angel, anthrōpos and son and a degree of synonymity of
functions as the intermediary world between God and man is closely related to differentiations in the levels of religious status,
perfection or existence. The intermediary world mediates an
inferior revelation and religious status of a secondary order.
The higher level or perfection constitutes an unmediated and
direct access to God and participation in the primary gifts.[1]

---

[1] Older scholars on Philo had already noticed that the highest knowledge of God in Philo was a direct and "intuitive" vision
of God (Drummond, Philo Judaeus, II, 5-9); that the Logos is a
revelation inferior to a direct intuition of God (Bréhier, Les
Idées, p. 100 and 104). Hence, it is all the more surprising
that Goodenough in his By Light, Light nowhere elaborates this
aspect of Philo and even seems unaware of it: "To Philo, we have
seen, the revelation of God, and the way to God, fell into two
stages. . . . There was the Way of the unwritten Law and Logos,
or of Sophia, a Way that was characterized by its utter lack of
contact or association with material existence. And there was
the Way represented by those Powers that could be projected into,
and represented in, the material world, the Way, we have seen
thus far, of the written Law" (p. 95). Walther Völker's Fortschritt und Vollendung elaborates the central theme in Philo as
being progress in virtuous life and perfection. Drawing upon
Drummond and Brehier, he correctly recognized that: "Der Fort-
schreitende hält sich an die Mittelwesen, verehrt sie und hat
durch sie Zugang zu Gott, während der Vollkommene in einem
direkten Verhältnis zu ihm steht, von ihm allein unterwiesen
wird, mit dem Logos selbst Schritt hält, weshalb er der helfenden
Zwischenglieder nicht mehr bedarf" (p. 260-61; cf. 280-81). In
this respect he seems mainly dependent on Drummond and Brehier.
In spite of its one-sided stress on the basic Jewishness of Philo,
it remains a much neglected presentation of Philo (Wolfson's two
volumes have virtually nothing to say on this theme of progress
and perfection and Völker is completely bypassed) with which I am
inclined to concur (cf. Goodenough, "Problems of Method in Studying Philo Judaeus," JBL 58 (1939), 51-58 = review of Volker).
Our study will elaborate on these patterns of perfection, especially as it is related to a direct access to God, beyond its
notice in Völker and will show its many-sided character and its
background in the ideals of Greek paideia. Furthermore, its
relation to the understanding of the cult in Philo has not been
noticed. Festugière in spite of his acquaintance with Völker
seems oblivious of this direct knowledge of God in Philo: "La
dernière étape de la contemplation consiste à se replier sur
soi-même" (La Révélation D'Hermès Trismégiste, II, 584).

32

Conf 145: οἱ δὲ ἐπιστήμῃ κεχρημένοι τοῦ ἑνὸς υἱοὶ θεοῦ προσαγο-
ρεύονται δεόντως, καθὰ καὶ Μωυσῆς ὁμολογεῖ φάσκων, "υἱοὶ
ἐστε κυρίου τοῦ θεοῦ" (Dt 14,1) καὶ "θεὸν τὸν γεννήσαντά
σε" (Dt 32;18) καὶ "οὐκ αὐτὸς οὗτός σου πατήρ;" (Dt 32,6).

146: κἂν μηδέπω μέντοι τυγχάνῃ τις ἀξιόχρεως ὢν υἱὸς θεοῦ
προσαγορεύεσθαι, σπουδαζέτω κοσμεῖσθαι κατὰ τὸν πρωτόγονον αὐτοῦ λόγον, τὸν ἀγγέλων πρεσβύτατον, ὡς ἂν ἀρχάγγελον, πολυώνυμον ὑπάρχοντα, καὶ γὰρ ἀρχὴ καὶ ὄνομα θεοῦ
καὶ λόγος καὶ ὁ κατ' εἰκόνα ἄνθρωπος καὶ ὁ ὁρῶν, Ἰσραήλ,
προσαγορεύεται.

147: διὸ προήχθην ὀλίγῳ πρότερον ἐπαινέσαι τὰς ἀρετὰς τῶν
φασκόντων ὅτι "πάντες ἐσμὲν υἱοὶ ἑνὸς ἀνθρώπου" (Gn 42,
11), καὶ γὰρ εἰ μήπω ἱκανοὶ θεοῦ παῖδες νομίζεσθαι
γεγόναμεν, ἀλλά τοι τῆς ἀειδοῦς εἰκόνος αὐτοῦ, λόγου
τοῦ ἱερωτάτου, θεοῦ γὰρ εἰκὼν λόγος ὁ πρεσβύτατος.

148: καὶ πολλαχοῦ μέντοι τῆς νομοθεσίας υἱοὶ πάλιν Ἰσραὴλ
καλοῦνται, τοῦ ὁρῶντος οἱ ἀκούοντες, ἐπειδὴ μεθ' ὅρασιν
ἀκοὴ δευτερείοις τετίμηται καὶ τὸ διδασκόμενον τοῦ χωρὶς
ὑπηγήσεως ἐναργεῖς τύπους τῶν ὑποκειμένων λαμβάνοντες
αἰεὶ δεύτερον.

This passage summarizes well our basic contentions and points
to some basic features in regard to the two levels of religious
status/perfection/existence. There are those (1) who can be
called sons of God--who live by the knowledge of the one God--and
(2) others who are not worthy or adequate (axiochreōs, hikanos)
of such status can aim at becoming sons of the first-born Logos.
The Logos represents the whole intermediary world, he is the
eldest of the angels, an archangel, and has many names: archē,
name of God, logos, man according to the image, the seeing one,
Israel. The Logos is also the eikōn of God. This second level
is equivalent to the title sons of Israel, that is hearers are
sons of the seeing one. These are two orders of religious status,
hearing is secondary to seeing,[2] and being taught is always second to the one who receives clear impressions of basic realities
without instruction. This may be schematized as follows:

---

[2]The superiority of sight over hearing can be traced to as
early as Heraclitus (fr. 101a: "The eyes are more accurate wit-
nesses than ears"). Aristotle speaks of the sense of sight being
loved more than all others (Met 980a 24). But this preeminence
of sight is by no means unambiguous and Plato speaks of both
sight and hearing as the noblest of senses (Laws 961d) on the one
hand and as sense perceptions neither clear nor accurate (Phaedo
65a-b). Both sight and hearing (and speech and music) are the
source of philosophy (Timaeus 47a-e; often misquoted as if sight
is the only source, e.g., Michaelis in TDNT V, 321 and Festugière,
La Révélation D'Hermès Trismégiste, II, p. 555; (cf. Philo, Op 53-
54, Abr 156-64; Spec Leg iii, 185-91, QG II, 34). It is described by Plato as similar to the soul (Republic 508a-d), most
like the sun (ibid., 518), the clearest of senses (Phaedrus 250d),
etc. The metaphor of sight is the most common means of describing the ascent to the beautiful (Symposium 211). See further
Michaelis in TDNT V, 319-24.

1	2
Sons of God	- Sons of the Logos = Eldest of angels; archangel; archē; name of God; logos; man according to the image; seeing one; Israel
Sons of God	- Sons of the One Man = Logos; image of God
Israel/Seeing One/Sight -- primary (in honour)	- Sons of Israel/sons of the Seeing One/ Hearing -- secondary
Without Instruction -- primary	- Taught -- secondary

In this single passage of Philo we observe the distinction between two levels of religious status, being the direct son of God and son of the Logos = intermediary world, the distinction between a primary level of honour and secondary level, that between sight and hearing and the common Greek preference in the realm of Paideia of natural talent over taught talent. That this constitutes a pattern of thought in Philo will be adequately shown below and can be demonstrated from this treatise alone.

The treatise (Conf) interprets Gn 11, 1-9 by means of a series of examples and counter-examples based on individual words and phrases. After meeting the accusation that this story is like the Homeric myth of the Aloeidae, etc. (1-15) Philo proceeds to give his interpretation: the phrase "the earth was all one lip and one voice" shows the symphony of evils which is illustrated by the deluge of the senses, story of the flood, Gn 14,3; 19,4; Ex 7,15; 14,30; most of which have the word "voice" or "lip" in them (16-38). Then follows a series of counter-examples of which the first is Gn 42,11 (see p. 10 for the text) to which attention is drawn above in 147; Jer 15,10; Nu 25,12 (39-57); and the most wonderful symphony in Ex 19,8:

58: θαυμάσιος μὲν οὖν ἡ λεχθεῖσα συμφωνία, θαυμασιωτάτη δὲ . . . καθ᾽ ἣν ὁ λαὸς ἅπας ὁμοθυμαδὸν εἰσάγεται λέγων, "πάντα ὅσα εἶπεν ὁ θεός, ποιήσομεν καὶ ἀκούσομεθα."

59: (Ex 19,8), οὗτοι γὰρ οὐκέτι ἐξάρχοντι πείθονται λόγῳ, ἀλλὰ τῷ τοῦ παντὸς ἡγεμόνι θεῷ, δι᾽ ὃν πρὸς τὰ ἔργα φθάνουσι μᾶλλον ἢ τοὺς λόγους ἀπαντῶντες. τῶν γὰρ ἄλλων ἐπειδὰν ἀκούσωσι πραττόντων, οὗτοι, τὸ παραδοξότατον, ὑπὸ κατοκωχῆς ἐνθέου πράξειν φασὶ πρότερον, εἶτα ἀκούσεσθαι, ἵνα μὴ διδασκαλίᾳ καὶ ὑφηγήσει δοκῶσιν, ἀλλὰ ἐθελουργῷ καὶ αὐτοκελεύστῳ διανοίᾳ πρὸς τὰ καλὰ τῶν ἔργων ὑπαντᾶν.

Thus there is the wonderful symphony of being the "sons of the one man," i.e., the Logos (41) and the most wonderful symphony is to supercede the Logos and trust in God, the Sovereign of All. This corresponds to the paideutic distinction between a taught and instructed mind and a self-motivated and self-impelled mind.

34

This _pattern of thought_ in the subsequent sections of the
treatise is elaborated in terms of the patriarchs and Moses who
are _exemplars_ of the different levels of perfection (60-141).
This will be discussed below (see pp. 46ff.).

A. The Intermediary World and Patterns
of Perfection

Texts and Analysis

Logos and Sophia

Conf 58-59: See above.

Fug 102: ὁ μὲν οὖν ἄνευ τροπῆς, ἐκουσίου μὲν ἄπαγε, ἀλλὰ καὶ τῆς
ἀκουσίου γεγονώς, αὐτὸν τὸν θεὸν κλῆρον ἔχων, ἐν αὐτῷ
μόνῳ κατοικήσει, οἳ δ᾽ οὐκ ἐκ προνοίας ἀλλ᾽ ἀβουλήτοις
χρησάμενοι σφάλμασι καταφυγὰς ἕξουσι τὰς εἰρημένας
ἀφθόνους καὶ πλουσίας οὕτως.

The discussion is on the six cities of refuge in Nu 35 for unintentional homicide, and they represent levels of religious attainments or perfection. The chief city is the Divine Logos.

94: μήποτ᾽ οὖν ἡ μὲν πρεσβυτάτη καὶ ἐχυρωτάτη καὶ ἀρίστη
μητρόπολις, οὐκ αὐτὸ μόνον πόλις, ὁ θεῖός ἐστι λόγος,
ἐφ᾽ ὃν πρῶτον καταφεύγειν ὠφελιμώτατον.

The spiritually swift are bidden to strive to the highest divine
Logos and those less gifted to the other five cities = powers of
God, namely: ποιητική, βασιλική, ἵλεως, προστάττουσα καὶ ἀπαγο-
ρεύουσα (96-99). With each of these levels there pertains a certain good (agathon); the first two have been enumerated. Those
who strive to the divine Logos gain eternal life, the next being
the knowledge of the Maker. The highest sinless level supercedes
the Logos and has God for its portion and has Him alone for its
abode.

Som i,64: . . . "ἦλθεν εἰς τὸν τόπον ὃν εἶπεν αὐτῷ ὁ θεός, καὶ
ἀναβλέψας τοῖς ὀφθαλμοῖς εἶδε τὸν τόπον μακρόθεν."
(Gn 22,3-4)

65: ὁ ἐλθὼν εἰς τὸν τόπον, εἰπέ μοι, μακρόθεν αὐτὸν εἶδεν;
ἀλλὰ μήποτε δυεῖν πραγμάτων ἐστιν ὁμωνυμία διαφερόντων,
ὧν τὸ μὲν ἕτερον θεῖός ἐστι λόγος, τὸ δὲ ἕτερον ὁ πρὸ
τοῦ λόγου θεός.

66: ὁ δὴ ξεναγηθεὶς ὑπὸ σοφίας εἰς τὸν πρότερον ἀφικνεῖται
τόπον, εὑράμενος τῆς ἀρεσκείας κεφαλὴν καὶ τέλος τὸν
θεῖον λόγον, ἐν ᾧ γενόμενος οὐ φθάνει πρὸς τὸν κατὰ τὸ
εἶναι θεὸν ἐλθεῖν, ἀλλ᾽ αὐτὸν ὁρᾷ μακρόθεν, μᾶλλον δὲ
οὐδὲ πόρρωθεν αὐτὸν ἐκεῖνον θεωρεῖν ἱκανός ἐστιν, ἀλλὰ τὸ
μακρὰν τὸν θεὸν εἶναι πάσης γενέσεως αὐτὸ μόνον ὁρᾷ . . .

117: καὶ τὸ ὑπαντᾶν μέντοι τόπῳ ἢ λόγῳ τοῖς μὴ δυναμένοις
τὸν πρὸ τόπου καὶ λόγου θεὸν ἰδεῖν αὐταρκεστάτη δωρεά, .
. .

148: ταῖς μὲν δὲ τῶν ἄκρως κεκαθαρμένων διανοίαις ἀψοφητὶ
μόνος ἀοράτως ὁ τῶν ὅλων ἡγεμὼν ἐμπεριπατεῖ - καὶ γὰρ
ἐστι χρησθὲν τῷ σοφῷ θεοπρόπιον, ἐν ᾧ λέγεται "περιπατήσω

ἐν ὑμῖν, καὶ ἔσομαι ὑμῶν θεός," Lv 26,12), ταῖς δὲ τῶν
ἔτι ἀπολουομένων, μήπω δὲ κατὰ τὸ παντελὲς ἐκνιψαμένων
τὴν ῥυπῶσαν καὶ κεκηλιδωμένην (ἐν) σώμασι βαρέσι ζωὴν
ἄγγελοι, λόγοι θεῖοι, φαιδρύνοντες αὐτὰς τοῖς καλοκάγαθίας δόγμασιν.

Jacob's dream in Gn 28,10-15 is interpreted in Som i,1-188 and
words and phrases are the foci for the interpretation--"well of
oath" (4-40), "Haran" (41-60) and "he met a place" (61-67).
There are three meanings of "place" (topos), (i) that filled by
a material body, (ii) the Divine Logos, which God has filled with
incorporeal powers and (iii) God himself in the sense that "he is
his own place"--a place of refuge for all. The last sense is
proven by Gn 22,3-4 which speaks of Abraham: "he came to the
place of which God spoke to him . . . he saw the place from
afar." This statement is understood to imply two meanings of
"place," the Divine Logos and God who is before the Logos. The
one led by wisdom reaches the former place, the Divine Logos, in
which position he is unable to reach God in his essence, and only
sees from afar the fact that God is far from all creation. Implicit here is the distinction between being led by Sophia and
reaching the Logos and superceding Sophia and Logos and reaching
God Himself.

Thus Jacob who goes to Haran (= sense perception) meets the
Divine Logos and not God Himself (68-71) and this is indicated
further in that "sun was set" (Gn 28,11). The sun is the symbol
of God and also for other things, e.g., the mind, etc. (72-114),
the net result being that the practicer's mind (askētikē), i.e.,
Jacob's is continually ascending and descending, and when the
rays of God have set, there arises the feebler light of the logoi
(115-116). The passage in 117, therefore, states that to meet
the logos (place) is an adequate gift for those who are unable to
see God who is prior to the logos/topos.

The context for the next passage (148) is the dream of the
stairway in Gn 28,12-13. The stairway is the air in the kosmos,
whose base is the earth and head is the heaven. It is populated
by incorporeal souls, some of which descend into bodies and
others which are most pure and excellent are the angels which
serve as mediators (mesitai), which are also called logoi (133-
45). In the case of the individual the stairway refers to the
soul, in which the logoi move up and down (146-47). Thus in 148
the distinction is drawn between minds which are totally cleansed
and in which God himself walks silent and invisible, and in those
minds still undergoing cleansing--stained and defiled by the burdens of the body--the angels (= divine logoi) walk.

36

Leg 5: . . . αἱ (i.e., ψυχαί) τὸ γενητὸν πᾶν ὑπερκύψασαι τὸ
ἀγένητον καὶ θεῖον ὁρᾶν πεπαίδευνται, τὸ πρῶτον ἀγαθὸν
καὶ καλὸν καὶ εὔδαιμον καὶ μακάριον. . . .

6: οὐ γὰρ φθάνει προσαναβαίνειν ὁ λόγος ἐπὶ τὸν ἄψαυστον
καὶ ἀναφῆ πάντη θεόν, . . .

The context speaks of the race of Israel, "the one who sees God,"
and they represent souls that have stretched or stepped over the
world of creation and have been educated to see the uncreated and
divine, etc. Whereas the Logos is unable to ascend to God who
cannot be touched or handled.

QE II,39: (Ex 24,11b) What is the meaning of the words, "They
appeared to God in the place and they ate and drank"?
Having attained to the face of the Father, they do not
remain in any mortal place at all, for all such (places)
are profane and polluted, but they send and make a migration to a holy and divine place, which is called by
another name, Logos. . . .

QE II,40: (Ex 24,12a) What is the meaning of the words, "Come
up to Me to the mountain and be there"? This signifies
that a holy soul is divinized by ascending not to the
air or to the ether or to heaven (which is) higher than
all but to (a region) above the heavens. And after the
world there is no place but God. (Marcus: Loeb)

We observe the distinction between the place = Logos and God
who is above it, between those who "attained to the face of the
Father"--remain in the Logos--and that soul which ascends beyond
the Logos/topos to God himself.

Angel

Som i,148 See above pp. 34-35.

Leg All iii,176: τρέφεται δὲ τῶν μὲν τελειοτέρων ἡ ψυχὴ ὅλῳ
τῷ λόγῳ. ἀγαπήσαιμεν δ' ἄν ἡμεῖς, εἰ καὶ μέρει τραφεί-
ημεν αὐτοῦ.

177: ἀλλ' οὗτοι μὲν εὔχονται θεοῦ λόγῳ τραφῆναι. ὁ δὲ 'Ιακὼβ
καὶ τὸν λόγον ὑπερκύψας ὑπ' αὐτοῦ φησι τρέφεσθαι τοῦ
θεοῦ, λέγει δ' οὕτως (quot. - Gn 48,15f.) . . . ὡραῖος
οὗτος ὁ τρόπος, τροφέα τὸν θεόν, οὐχὶ λόγον, ἡγεῖται, τὸν
δὲ ἄγγελον, ὅς ἐστι λόγος, ὥσπερ ἰατρὸν κακῶν. φυσι-
κώτατα, ἀρέσκει γὰρ αὐτῷ τὰ μὲν προηγούμενα ἀγαθὰ αὐτο-
προσώπως αὐτὸν τὸν ὄντα διδόναι, τὰ δεύτερα δὲ τοὺς
ἀγγέλους καὶ λόγους αὐτοῦ.

The interpretation of Gn 3,14 is the context of the passage (161)
which gives occasion to a discussion concerning food of the body
and food of the soul. The latter being elaborated in terms of
the manna (Ex 16,4; Dt 8,3) which is identified with the Logos.
Thus in the passage above, the soul of the more perfect is fed by
the whole Logos. The wilderness generation prays to be fed by
it. But Jacob stretches beyond the Logos and says that he is fed
by God himself.(Gn 48,15-16). The angel in the Gn passage is
identified with the Logos. We observe also the distinction

between the <u>primary goods/benefits</u> which God gives in person and
the <u>secondary goods</u> which angels and logoi give.[3]

Mig 174: ἕως μὲν γὰρ <u>οὐ τετελείωται, ἡγεμόνι τῆς ὁδοῦ χρῆται</u>
λόγῳ θείῳ, χρησμὸς γάρ ἐστιν (quot. - Ex 23,20-21) . . .

175: ἐπειδὰν δὲ πρὸς <u>ἄκραν ἐπιστήμην</u> ἀφίκηται, συντόνως
ἐπιδραμὼν <u>ἰσοταχήσει</u> τῷ πρόσθεν <u>ἡγουμένῳ τῆς ὁδοῦ</u>.
ἀμφότεροι γὰρ οὕτως <u>ὁπαδοὶ</u> γενήσονται τοῦ <u>πανηγεμόνος</u>
θεοῦ . . . (Quis Her 19)

Lot's travel with Abraham (Gn 12,4) is a mark of Abraham's imperfection (148ff.) and it leads to a discussion with the help of
examples of bad fellow-travellers and good fellow-travellers.
This leads to the present distinction between being led by angels
or logoi (Gn 18,6)--as long as one falls <u>short of perfection</u> he
is <u>led by the divine Logos</u>--and reaching the state of <u>complete
knowledge</u> when one's pace is equal to that of the Logos and both
become attendants of <u>God</u> who is now the <u>leader of the way</u> (175).

QE II,13: (Ex 23,20-21) What is the meaning of the words,
"Behold, I am sending My <u>angel</u> before thy face, that he
may guard thee on the way . . . " An <u>angel</u> is an intel-
lectual soul or rather wholly mind, wholly incorporeal,
made (to be) a minister of God, and appointed over certain needs and the service of the <u>race of mortals</u>, since
<u>it was unable</u>, because of its corruptible nature, <u>to
receive the gifts and benefactions extended by God.</u> For
it was not capable of bearing the multitude of (His) good
(gifts). (Therefore) of necessity was the <u>Logos</u>
appointed as judge and mediator, who is called "angel."

The same Exodus passage is interpreted in Mig 174-75 (see
above) according to the same pattern of thought. Here the angel =
Logos is to serve man because of his imperfection--"corruptible
nature"--which makes him unable to receive <u>God's direct benefac-
tions</u>. Hence the angel-Logos serves as a "mediator."

Som i,232: ταῖς μὲν οὖν <u>ἀσωμάτοις</u> καὶ θεραπευτρίσιν αὐτοῦ
ψυχαῖς εἰκὸς αὐτὸν <u>οἷός ἐστιν</u> ἐπιφαίνεσθαι διαλεγόμενον
ὡς φίλον φίλαις, ταῖς δὲ ἔτι ἐν σώματι <u>ἀγγέλοις</u>
<u>εἰκαζόμενον</u>, . . .

238: ὥσθ' ὅταν φῇ, "ἐγώ εἰμι ὁ θεὸς ὁ ὀφθείς σοι ἐν τόπῳ
θεοῦ," τότε νόησον, ὅτι <u>τὸν ἀγγέλου τόπον</u> ἐπέσχεν ὅσα
τῷ δοκεῖν, οὐ μεταβάλλων, πρὸς τὴν τοῦ μήπω δυναμένου
τὸν <u>ἀληθῆ θεὸν</u> ἰδεῖν ὠφέλειαν. (Cf. Mut 32-34)

The context of both the passages is Gn 31,13 and the problem of
the reference to the two Gods. This is explained in terms of the

---

[3]Goodenough's misunderstanding of the passage results from
his stopping of the reading of the text at 176. His explanation
runs as follows: "The contrast between the ordinary man in the
wilderness getting food in portions and the perfect"--(the text
actually reads 'more perfect')--"getting the Logos as a whole is
expanded to represent two mystic stages. The one is purificatory,
supervised by the lower divine agencies and angels and logoi.
The higher stage is where God acts directly to give the Logos as
a whole" (p. 208).

"place of God" as referring to the Logos and that the "existent
one" really has no proper name. This is proven by reference to
Ex 3,14 (226-31). In both passages his revelation through the
angel(s) is an accommodation to human incapacity and inferior to
his <u>direct revelation</u> (cf. Som i,115-17).

Anthropos

Leg All i,92: ἐντέλλεται δὲ τούτῳ (i.e., Ἀδάμ) καὶ <u>οὐχὶ τῷ κατ'</u>
<u>εἰκόνα</u> καὶ κατὰ τὴν ἰδέαν γεγονότι. ἐκεῖνος μὲν γὰρ καὶ
<u>δίχα προτροπῆς</u> ἔχει τὴν <u>ἀρετην αὐτομαθῶς</u>, οὗτος δ' <u>ἄνευ</u>
<u>διδασκαλίας</u> οὐκ ἂν φρονήσεως ἐπιλάχοι.

93: διαφέρει δὲ τρία ταῦτα, πρόσταξις, ἀπαγόρευσις, ἐντολὴ
καὶ παραίνεσις. ἡ μὲν γὰρ ἀπαγόρευσις περὶ ἁμαρτημάτων
γίνεται καὶ πρὸς φαῦλον, ἡ δὲ παραίνεσις πρὸς τὸν μέσον,
τὸν μήτε φαῦλον μήτε σπουδαῖον. . . .

94: <u>τῷ μὲν οὖν τελείῳ τῷ κατ' εἰκόνα</u> προστάττειν ἢ
ἀπαγορεύειν ἢ παραινεῖν οὐχὶ δεῖ, οὐδενὸς γὰρ τούτων
<u>ὁ τέλειος</u> δεῖται, <u>τῷ</u> δὲ <u>φαύλῳ</u> προστάξεως καὶ ἀπαγορεύσεως
χρεία, τῷ δὲ <u>νηπίῳ</u> παραινέσεως καὶ διδασκαλίας, . . .

95: εἰκότως οὖν <u>τῷ γηΐνῳ νῷ</u> (i.e., Adam) μήτε φαύλῳ ὄντι μήτε
σπουδαίῳ ἀλλὰ <u>μέσῳ</u> τὰ νῦν ἐντέλλεται καὶ παραινεῖ.

Gn 2,16-17 mentions Adam by name for the first time and Philo
raises the question as to who this Adam was (90ff.). He is identified with the "moulded" man, the "earthly and perishable mind"
as distinguished from the heavenly mind "according to the image."
Adam is commanded whereas the "one according to the image" has
<u>arete</u> which is <u>self-taught</u> and without need for exhortation
(protrope). This is explained further in terms of a threefold
distinction:

1. The <u>perfect</u>, the one <u>according to the image</u> = heavenly
   mind (90), the <u>good man</u> (spoudaios) needs neither command, nor prohibition nor exhortation. He has <u>self-</u>
   <u>taught virtue</u>.

2. <u>Adam</u>, <u>earthly mind</u>, the <u>middle</u>--neither good nor bad--,
   the <u>child</u> needs command, teaching and exhortation.

3. The <u>bad man</u> (phaulos) needs specifically prohibitions.

Thus the <u>perfect</u> man has superceded the necessity of commands,
prohibitions, teaching and exhortation. He possesses virtue
which is <u>self-taught</u>. This is a characteristic of the perfection
of the <u>sons of God</u> in contrast to the <u>sons of the Logos</u>, the
former are <u>without instruction</u> and the latter are taught (Conf
148, see above pp. 32-33; cf. Conf 59 and Leg 5, pp. 33 and 36).
The distinctions belong to the tradition of Greek paideia.

QG I,8: (Gn 2,8) Why does he place the moulded man in paradise,
but not the man who is made in His image? . . . But I
would say that <u>paradise</u> should be thought as a symbol of
<u>wisdom</u>. For the <u>earth-formed man</u> is a mixture, and

consists of body and soul, and <u>is in need of teaching and instruction</u>, desiring, in accordance with the laws of philosophy, that he may be happy. But <u>he</u> who was <u>made in His image</u> <u>is in need of nothing</u>, but is <u>self-hearing</u> and <u>self-taught</u> and <u>self-instructed</u> by nature.

The man according to the image therefore does not need sophia, or teaching or instruction. He belongs to the class of the perfect (see above) who are self-taught and self-instructed by nature.

Mut 24: δικαιοῖ γὰρ τὸν μὲν <u>φαῦλον</u> ὡς <u>ὑπὸ κυρίου</u> δεσπόζεσθαι,
. . . τὸν δὲ <u>προκόπτοντα</u> ὡς <u>ὑπὸ θεοῦ</u> εὐεργετεῖσθαι, ὅπως ταῖς εὐποιίαις <u>τελειότητος</u> ἐφίκηται, τὸν δὲ <u>τέλειον</u> καὶ ἡγεμονεύεσθαι ὑπὸ κυρίου καὶ εὐεργετεῖσθαι ὡς ὑπὸ θεοῦ. (Cf. Abr 124-25)

30: <u>μεγίστη</u> δὲ <u>δωρεὰ</u> τὸ αὐτοῦ λαχεῖν ἀρχιτέκτονος, οὗ καὶ σύμπας ὁ κόσμος ἔλαχε. <u>φαύλου</u> μὲν γὰρ <u>ψυχὴν</u> οὐ διέπλασεν – ἐχθρὸν γὰρ θεῷ κακία – τὴν δὲ <u>μέσην</u> οὐ δι᾽ ἑαυτοῦ μόνου κατὰ τὸν ἱερώτατον Μωυσῆν, ἐπειδὴ κηροῦ τρόπον ἔμελλεν αὕτη δέξασθαι καλοῦ τε καὶ αἰσχροῦ διαφοράν.

31: διόπερ λέγεται, "ποιήσωμεν ἄνθρωπον κατ᾽ εἰκόνα ἡμετέραν," (Gn 1,26) . . . πάντως οὖν <u>σπουδαῖος</u> ἐκεῖνός ἐστιν, ᾧ φησιν, "ἐγώ εἰμι θεὸς σός," (Gn 17,1), <u>ποιητοῦ μόνου λαχὼν ἄνευ συμπράξεως ἑτέρων</u>.

The context for these passages is the interpretation of Gn 17,1-- "I am thy God"--and the titles God and Lord are understood as divine powers (15-16) and their functions are distinguished in terms of the <u>bad-man</u>, the <u>progressing one</u>, and the <u>perfect</u> (24), or the <u>bad-man</u>, <u>middle</u> and <u>good man</u> (30-31). In the latter case, the greatest gift is to have God as one's architect. God does not create the bad-man, the middle one is made with the aid of co-workers (Gn 1,26), but the <u>spoudaios</u> has Him alone as his creator (cf. Leg All i,92-95, see above p. 38).

Quis Her 45: ζωῆς δὲ τριττὸν γένος, τὸ μὲν <u>πρὸς θεόν</u>, τὸ δὲ <u>πρὸς γένεσιν</u>, τὸ δὲ <u>μεθόριον</u>, <u>μικτὸν</u> ἀμφοῖν, τὸ μὲν οὖν <u>πρὸς θεὸν</u> οὐ κατέβη πρὸς ἡμᾶς οὐδὲ ἦλθεν εἰς τὰς σώματος ἀνάγκας. τὸ δὲ <u>πρὸς γένεσιν</u> οὐδ᾽ ὅλως ἀνέβη οὐδ᾽ ἐζήτησεν ἀναβῆναι, φωλεῦον δὲ ἐν μυχοῖς Ἅιδου τῷ ἀβιώτῳ βίῳ χαίρει.

46: τὸ δὲ <u>μικτὸν</u> ἐστιν, ὁ πολλάκις μὲν ὑπὸ τῆς <u>ἀμείνονος</u> ἀγόμενον <u>τάξεως</u> θειάζει καὶ θεοφορεῖται, πολλάκις δ᾽ ὑπὸ τῆς <u>χείρονος</u> ἀντισπώμενον ἐπιστρέφει. . . .

47: Μωυσῆς δὲ <u>τὸ τῆς πρὸς θεὸν ζωῆς</u> γένος ἀκονιτὶ <u>στεφανώσας</u> εἰς ἐπίκρισιν τὰ λοιπὰ ἄγει . . .

This classification follows from the interpretation of Masek as "the life with senses" (40-41; cf. esp. 42 and 52). This triple distinction is parallel to other such which have been indicated above. The <u>Godward life</u> in its utter perfection has never de-scended to man nor entered the constraints of the body. It does not mean that this bodily state is beyond human achievement--cf. <u>Mut 32-34</u>. What is indicated is its ideal purity as a type. The <u>creation-oriented life</u> is like that of the bad-man (phaulos)

utterly sunk in Hades. The mixed type or middle kind fluctuates
between the two orders (taxis) and corresponds to that of the
progressing one (cf. Som i,151 - the askētikē) in the passages
above.

Gig 60: μῦθον μὲν οὖν οὐδένα περὶ γιγάντων εἰσηγεῖται τὸ παράπαν,
βούλεται δὲ ἐκεῖνό σοι παραστῆσαι, ὅτι οἱ μὲν γῆς, οἱ δὲ
οὐρανοῦ, οἱ δὲ θεοῦ γεγόνασιν ἄνθρωποι. γῆς μὲν οἱ
θηρευτικοὶ τῶν σώματος ἡδονῶν ἀπολαυσίν τε καὶ χρῆσιν
ἐπιτηδεύοντες . . . οὐρανοῦ δὲ ὅσοι τεχνῖται καὶ ἐπιστή-
μονες καὶ φιλομαθεῖς - τὸ γὰρ οὐράνιον τῶν ἐν ἡμῖν ὁ νοῦς
(νοῦς δὲ καὶ τῶν κατ' οὐρανὸν ἕκαστον) τὰ ἐγκύκλια καὶ
τὰς ἄλλας ἅπαξ ἁπάσας ἐπιτηδεύει τέχνας, . . .

61: θεοῦ δὲ ἄνθρωποι ἱερεῖς καὶ προφῆται, οἵτινες οὐκ
ἠξίωσαν πολιτείας τῆς παρὰ τῷ κόσμῳ τυχεῖν καὶ κοσμο-
πολῖται γενέσθαι, τὸ δὲ αἰσθητὸν πᾶν ὑπερκύψαντες εἰς
τὸν νοητὸν κόσμον μετανέστησαν κάκεῖθι ᾤκησαν ἐγγραφέντες
ἀφθάρτων (καὶ) ἀσωμάτων ἰδεῶν πολιτείᾳ.

This constitutes an interpretation of Gn 6,4 as referring to
three classes of men, of earth, heaven, and God. Those of earth
prey upon the pleasures of the body and live by its use and enjoy-
ment. Those of heaven are lovers of learning who pursue the encyclical education. Those of God have risen beyond the sense perceptible world and live as citizens of the intelligible world.

The terminology associated with this threefold pattern of
perfection as it pertains to man may be summarized as follows:

1. τέλειος, ὁ κατ' εἰκόνα, σπουδαῖος, τὸ τῆς πρὸς θεὸν ζωῆς
γένος, ἄνθρωποι θεοῦ.
οὐχὶ δεῖ προστάττειν ἢ ἀπαγορεύειν ἢ παραινεῖν, ἄνευ
διδασκαλίας, δίχα προτροπῆς, αὐτοδίδακτος, αὐτομαθής,
ἀρχιτέκτονος αὐτοῦ - θεός, οὐδὲ ἦλθεν εἰς τὰς σώματος
ἀνάγκας, τὸ αἰσθητὸν πᾶν ὑπέρκυψας εἰς τὸν νοητὸν
κόσμον μετανέστη.

2. μέσος, νήπιος, Ἀδάμ, γήϊνος νοῦς, μίκτος, πεπλασμένος,
πρόκοπτων, μεθόριος, ἄνθρωποι οὐρανοῦ.
δεῖται παραινέσεως καὶ διδασκαλίας, οὐ δι' ἑαυτοῦ μόνου
(θεοῦ), πολλάκις μὲν ὑπὸ τῆς ἀμείνονος ἀγόμενος τάξεως,
πολλάκις δὲ ὑπὸ τῆς χείρονος, τὰ ἐγκύκλια ἐπιτηδεύει.

3. φαῦλος, τὸ τῆς πρὸς γένεσιν ζωῆς γένος, ἄνθρωποι γῆς.
δεῖται προστάξεως καὶ ἀπαγορεύσεως, οὐ διέπλασεν ὁ θεὸς
ψυχὴν φαύλου, οὐδ' ὅλως ἀνέβη οὐδ' ἐξήτησεν ἀναβῆναι,
ἀπόλαυσις καὶ χρῆσις ἡδονῶν σώματος.

Son--Sonship

Conf 145-48: see above pp. 32-33.

Som i,173: ὃς (i.e.,θεός) καὶ τοὺς ἀρχετύπους τῆς παιδείας ἡμῶν
τύπους ἀδηλουμένους ἐμόρφωσας, ἵν' ἐμφανεῖς ὦσιν,
Ἀβραὰμ μὲν διδάξας, Ἰσαὰκ δὲ γεννήσας, τοῦ μὲν γὰρ

ὑφηγητής, τοῦ δὲ πατὴρ ὑπέμεινας ὀνομασθῆναι, τῷ μὲν
τὴν γνωρίμου τάξιν, τῷ δὲ τὴν υἱοῦ παρασχών
(cf. Det 123-24).

Gn 28,13 provides the context of the discussion of which this is
a part (159ff.). Attention is focused upon the difference
between "Lord God of Abraham" and "God of Isaac." Abraham and
Isaac are archetypes of Israel's paideia on the basis of which a
series of distinctions are made:

(i)	(ii)
Abraham	Isaac
God teaches	God begets
God is Instructor	God is Father
Order of pupil	Order of Son

Isaac, as we will show below, belongs to the class of the self-
taught and self-instructed.

QG I,92: (Gn 6,4) Why were the giants born from angels and
women? . . . But sometimes he calls angels "sons of God"
because they are made incorporeal through no mortal man
but are spirits without body. But rather does that
exhorter, Moses, give to good and excellent men the name
of "sons of God," while wicked and evil men (he calls)
"bodies." (Marcus: Loeb)

QG IV,153: (Gn 35,8) Why is it said that "he was added to his
people"? . . . And (Scripture) in another passage calls
him (i.e., Abraham) "forefather" but not "first born"
inheriting all from his divine Father and being without
share in a mother or female line. (Marcus: Loeb)

The latter reference is to Isaac who has a superior status than
Abraham and the appellation "first-born" is peculiarly his; his
origin is from God and without any female portion (cf. Som i,173
above). Israel--"the seeing one"--belongs to this first level of
perfection (cf. pp. 32-33) and this can be illustrated further
from:

Fug 208: ἑρμηνεύεται γὰρ 'Ισμαὴλ ἀκοῇ θεοῦ. ἀκοῇ δ' ὁράσεως τὰ
δευτερεῖα φέρεται, ὅρασιν δὲ ὁ γνήσιος υἱὸς καὶ πρωτόγονος 'Ισραηλ κεκλήρωται.

The exalted status of the claim to be a "son of God" can be
documented from other literature of Hellenistic Judaism. It reveals developments which are analogous to Philo.

Wis Sol 2,12c: καὶ ὀνειδίζει ἡμῖν ἁμαρτήματα νόμου καὶ
ἐπιφημίζει ἡμῖν ἁμαρτήματα παιδείας ἡμῶν

13: ἐπαγγέλλεται γνῶσιν ἔχειν θεοῦ καὶ παῖδα κυρίου ἑαυτὸν
ὀνομάζει. . . .

16d: καὶ ἀλαζονεύεται πατέρα θεόν

Striking is the understanding of the Law as "our culture/paideia."
It is a significant concept in the formation of Hellenistic Judaism. The charge of the "impious" against the "righteous" is his
boast and claim to have "knowledge of God" (cf. Quod Deus 143;

42

see above p. 14), to claim to be "child of the Lord" and that God
is his Father (cf. Jn 1,18; 5,18). On the day of judgment the
impious finally will acknowledge:

Wis Sol 5,5: πῶς κατελογίσθη ἐν υἱοῖς θεοῦ καὶ ἐν ἁγίοις ὁ
κλῆρος αὐτοῦ ἐστιν;

In the later chapters the title "son" or "child" of God is consistently applied to the "people" or "Israel" (cf. 12,7.19.21;
16,10.21.26; 18,4.9.13, etc.).

Joseph and Asenath VI(46),11: ἢ πῶς ὄψεταί με 'Ιωσὴφ ὁ υἱὸς τοῦ
θεοῦ, διότι λελάληκα ἐγὼ περὶ αὐτοῦ κακά; οἴμοι τῇ ἀθλίᾳ
ποῦ ἀπελεύσομαι καὶ κρυβήσομαι, ὅτι πᾶσαν ἀποκρυβὴν αὐτὸς
ὁρᾷ, καὶ πάντα γινώσκει, καὶ οὐδὲν κρυπτὸν λέληθεν αὐτὸν
διὰ τὸ φῶς μέγα τὸ ὂν ἐν αὐτῷ; . . . νῦν οὖν ὡς ἥλιος
ἐκ τοῦ οὐρανοῦ ἥκει πρὸς ἡμᾶς ἐν τῷ ἅρματι αὐτοῦ . . .
καὶ οὐκ ᾔδειν ὅτι 'Ιωσὴφ υἱὸς θεοῦ ἐστι. (Cf. 11,1)

In this dramatic passage Asenath states the impact of Joseph's
sight as he entered her parent's house. The divine and luminary
quality of being the "son of God" and his omniscience point to
its background in the traditions concerning the sophos and sophia
(cf. Wis Sol 9,11). In fact, Joseph is called a sophos.

Joseph and Asenath XIII(58),4-7: . . . καὶ λελάληκα περὶ αὐτοῦ
πονηρά, μὴ εἰδυῖα ὅτι υἱός σού ἐστι. τίς γὰρ ἀνθρώπων
ἔτεκεν ἢ τέξεται τοιοῦτον κάλλος ποτέ, ἢ τίς ἄλλος
ὑπάρχει (τοιοῦτος) σοφὸς καὶ δυνατὸς ὡς πάγκαλος 'Ιωσήφ;

The title "son of God" is used for Joseph in other passages as
well--XVIII(68),20; XXI(71),15; XXIII(75),4. In XIX, Asenath is
renamed "city of refuge" (katafugē) by the angel, and the proselytes are called "sons of the living God" who will dwell in the
city of her refuge and God will reign over the nations.

Thus in Philo, Wisdom of Solomon and Joseph and Asenath the
title "son of God" describes religious status of the first order
and being descriptive of status, the terms "son," first-born and
only-begotten can be used to characterize the logos (see above
pp. 10f.), sophia, angels, and anthropos (see above pp. 11f.).
Philo alone however distinguishes between the different levels or
orders of sonship. In the passages above, the title has been
used to describe Isaac as contrasted to Abraham, angels, good and
excellent men, and Israel--the seeing one (i.e., in Philo). And
to describe the "just" as contrasted to the "impious" in the
Wisdom of Solomon, and Joseph in Joseph and Asenath.

Summary

We could best summarize the patterns of perfection and its
relationship to the intermediary world in the form of a schema
which would highlight the vocabulary associated with the distinctions and would reveal the pattern of thought in its various

applications:

Conf 145-48: See above p. 33.

Logos

	(1)	(2)
Fug 102	Sinless have God as allotment and abode	Involuntary errors--cities of refuge; best and most secure = Logos
Som i, 64-66	God who is prior to the Logos; God in his Being	Led by Sophia one reaches the Topos = Divine Logos (Gn 22,3-4)
Som i, 117	God who is prior to Topos/Logos	To meet Topos/Logos is all sufficient gift for those unable to see God himself
Som i, 148	God walks silent and invisible in wholly cleansed minds	Angels/Divine Logoi in minds undergoing cleansing and burdened with bodies
Leg 5	Israel/souls rise above the created and educated to see the uncreated and divine	Logos unable to ascend to God who cannot be touched or handled
QE II, 39-40	Ex 24,11a: holy soul ascends beyond heaven, no Topos, to God	Ex 24,12a: migration to holy and divine Topos = Logos

Angel

	(1)	(2)
Leg All iii,176-177	Jacob rises above the Logos and is fed by God himself	Soul of more perfect is fed by the Logos of God = Angel
	God himself gives primary goods	His angels and logoi give the secondary
Mig 174-175	State of full knowledge--God is Leader, Logos is companion	Short of perfection--led by the Divine Logos/ led by angels/logoi
QE II, 13	God's gifts and benefactions	Mortals, corruptible by nature unable to receive such--Logos/ Angel is mediator
Som i, 232	God appears as he is to incorporeal and worshipping souls, as a friend to friends	To souls in the body in the likeness of angels
Som i, 238	To see the true God	Appears in the topos of angel to those unable to see the true God

Anthropos

Leg All i,92-95	Perfect, according to the image/heavenly mind, good man	Child, Adam/earthly mind, middle (neither good nor bad)
	needs no teaching, command, prohibition nor exhortation, = self-taught virtue	needs command, teaching and exhortation

44

<table>
<tr><th></th><th>(1)</th><th>(3)</th></tr>
<tr><td></td><td></td><td>Bad <u>man</u> needs prohibitions and <u>commands</u></td></tr>
<tr><td>QG I,8</td><td>Man according to image needs nothing, does not need Sophia. Self-taught, self-instructed by nature</td><td>Moulded man, earth-formed, body and soul needs teaching, instruction, laws of philosophy</td></tr>
<tr><td>Mut 24</td><td>Perfect led by Lord, benefited by God</td><td>Progresser benefited by God so as to reach perfection by good deeds</td></tr>
</table>

(2)

(3) Bad man is ruled by Lord

<table>
<tr><td>Mut 30</td><td>God alone maker of the soul of good man - greatest gift</td><td>With coworkers - the soul of middle man</td></tr>
</table>

(3)

Go did not form the soul of the bad man

<table>
<tr><td>Quis Her 45-47</td><td>Godward life did not come down or enter the constraints of the body</td><td>Middle/mixed life fluctuates between the better and worse orders (taxis)</td></tr>
</table>

(3)

Creation-oriented life does not ascend nor seeks to ascend - sunk in Hades

<table>
<tr><td>Gig 60-61</td><td>Men of God rise above sense-perceptible world, citizens of intelligible world</td><td>Men of heaven pursue encyclical education</td></tr>
</table>

(3)

Men of earth live by the pleasures of the body

Son-Sonship

<table>
<tr><td>Som i, 173</td><td>God begets Isaac, God is Father of Isaac

Order of Son</td><td>God teaches Abraham, God is instructor of Abraham

Order of pupil</td></tr>
<tr><td>QG I, 92</td><td>"Sons of God" - name of good and excellent men</td><td>(3)
Wicked and evil men are called "bodies"</td></tr>
<tr><td>QG IV, 153</td><td>"First-born" - Isaac</td><td>Abraham is "forefather" - nor first-born</td></tr>
<tr><td>Fug 208</td><td>To the genuine and first-born son Israel sight is allotted

Sight is primary</td><td>Ishmael = hearing of God

Hearing is secondary</td></tr>
</table>

Perfection is this pattern of thought thus means rising above the intermediary world of Logos, Sophia, Angel and Anthropos to the presence of God himself--unmediated access. This

appears in a variety of contexts and is expressed in numerous
ways, but there is remarkable consistency in its application of
the basic pattern of thought. We note the distinction between
the primary and secondary: sight is primary, hearing is secondary; that which is by nature is primary and what is taught is
secondary; God gives the primary benefits, the intermediary world
is the source of secondary. The revelation through the intermediary world is inferior to that given directly by God. Perfection is associated with Sight--Israel, sinless, wholly cleansed
minds, state of full knowledge, incorporeal and worshipping souls
(state which is possible for mankind; cf. Mut 32-34), man according to the image, good man (Stoic spoudaios), men of God, the
status of sonship to God, first-born, etc. In terms of the
paideutic ideals, the perfect belong to the class of the self-
taught and self-instructed and who have no need of the leading
of Sophia or the mediation of the Logos.

Imperfection, on the other hand, is defined in terms of
inability to rise beyond the intermediary world, need for instruction, teaching and exhortation, the guidance of Sophia and Logos.
Such are involved in involuntary errors, burdened with bodies,
minds still undergoing cleansing, mortals, corruptible by nature,
Adamic, composite of body and soul, progressing, fluctuating
between the better and worse. They receive an inferior revelation and gifts of a secondary order. The best they can do at
this stage is to become sons of the Logos and be guided by Sophia,
sons of Israel, and belong to the order of the pupil of God.

The exact terms "perfection, perfect, be perfected, etc."
occur in some of the passages but not in all. The structure of
thought, however, is remarkably clear and consistent.[4]

---

[4]Perfection is thus expressed in Philo in a variety of ways
and what is central is its unmediated relationship to God which
transcends the leading of Sophia and mediation of the Logos.
Völker, Fortschritt und Vollendung, rejects Reitzenstein's view
that "teleios" in Philo has its origin in oriental religion and
gnosis. His own view is that the main impulse comes from Judaism: "Vollkommenheit bedeutet für Philo nichts anderes als den
Lebensgipfel, wo mit der Höhe des Tugendlebens die Schau Gottes
verbunden ist, wo das ganze Dasein als ein Dienst Gottes und ein
Dienst den Brüdern aufgefasst, wo alles als ein Geschenk Gottes
empfunden und als μίμησις θεοῦ gestaltet wird" (p. 263). This
personal religious devotion to God is not peculiarly Jewish. For
Marcus Aurelius, life's motto is: "To worship and bless the
gods, and to do good to men" (V,33,6; cf. VI,30,4; III,6,2; VI,7;
referred to in Festugiere, Personal Religion Among the Greeks,
p. 115; cf. 110-21; the same personal piety is expressed in
Epictetus, I,16,16 and 20, and Cleanthes, Hymn to Zeus). This
tendency in Völker has received justified criticism. "His pro-

B. Exemplars of Perfection

Introduction: This pattern of perfection which distinguishes between a direct access to God and participation in his primary gifts over against the less perfect who need the mediation of the intermediary world and are beneficiaries of an inferior revelation and gifts of a secondary order, is also elaborated in Philo in terms of the patriarchs, Aaron, Levitic priesthood, Melchizedek and Moses. They serve as "exemplars" of the different levels of perfection and what is important is their exemplary character rather than their personal existence as mortal men. They represent different dispositions of the soul, characters, types and virtues. Philo's basic concern is not with the literal meaning of the Law, but with its significance for contemporary men, its existential meaning. Allegorical interpretation was the means by which past events acquired contemporary meaning and this meaning was understood in terms of its educative/paideutic role for contemporary man. It is in this sense that we have chosen the term "exemplars of perfection."

Som i,167: τὴν ἀρετὴν ἢ φύσει ἢ ἀσκήσει ἢ μαθήσει περιγίνεσθαί
φησι, διὸ καὶ τρεῖς τοὺς γενάρχας τοῦ ἔθνους σοφοὺς
πάντας ἀνέγραφεν, ἀπὸ μὲν τῆς αὐτῆς οὐχ ὁρμηθέντας ἰδέας,
πρὸς δὲ τὸ αὐτὸ τέλος ἐπειχθέντας.

168: ὁ μὲν γὰρ πρεσβύτατος αὐτῶν 'Αβραὰμ ἡγεμόνι ὁδοῦ τῆς πρὸς
καλὸν ἀγούσης ἐχρήσατο διδασκαλίᾳ, . . . ὁ δὲ μέσος
'Ισαὰκ αὐτήκόῳ καὶ αὐτομαθεῖ τῇ φύσει, ὁ δὲ τρίτος 'Ιακὼβ
ἀσκητικαῖς μελέταις, καθ' ἃς οἱ ἔναθλοι καὶ ἐναγώνιοι
πόνοι. . . .

171: ἐὰν μέντοι ὁ ἀσκητὴς οὗτος εὐτόνως δράμῃ πρὸς τὸ τέλος
καὶ τηλαυγῶς ἴδῃ ἃ πρότερον ἀμυδρῶς ὠνειροπόλει, μετα-
τυπωθεὶς τῷ κρείττονι χαρακτῆρι καὶ προσαγορευθεὶς
'Ισραήλ, ὁ θεὸν ὁρῶν, ἀντὶ τοῦ πτερνίζοντος 'Ιακὼβ πατέρα
οὐκέτι τὸν μαθόντα 'Αβραάμ, ἀλλὰ τὸν φύσει γεννηθέντα
ἀστεῖον 'Ισαὰκ ἐπιγράφεται.

172: ταῦτα δὲ οὐκ ἐμός ἐστι μῦθος, ἀλλὰ χρησμὸς ἐν ταῖς ἱεραῖς
ἀναγεγραμμένος στήλαις, "ἀπάρας" γάρ φησιν "'Ισραὴλ αὐτὸς
καὶ πάντα τὰ αὐτοῦ ἦλθεν ἐπὶ τὸ φρέαρ τοῦ ὅρκου, καὶ
ἔθυσε θυσίαν τῷ θεῷ τοῦ πατρὸς αὐτοῦ 'Ισαάκ." (Gn 46.1)
ἆρ' ἤδη κατανοεῖς ὅτι οὐ περὶ φθαρτῶν ἀνθρώπων, ἀλλ', ὡς
ἐλέχθη, περὶ φύσεως πραγμάτων ἐστιν ὁ παρὼν λόγος; ἰδοὺ

---

cedure is basically the same. At each step he shows that Philo had two ways of expressing himself, a Greek and a Jewish. . . . Having reduced the Greek element thus to the formal, he then adduces passages which seem more Jewish in inspiration, and then, reasons, in substance: Philo's motivations were religious (which is true); the Greek elements (which Völker adduces) are not religious; therefore Philo must have been basically Jewish in his motivation, and the Greek elements are all "Nebenströmmungen," an essentially extraneous terminology which Philo has put on, but which never affected his basic meaning." (E. R. Goodenough's review of Völker, *JBL* 58 (1939), 55-56.)

γὰρ τὸ αὐτὸ ὑποκείμενον τοτὲ μὲν ᾿Ιακὼβ ὀνομάζεται πατρὸς
᾿Αβραάμ, τοτὲ δὲ ᾿Ισραὴλ πατρὸς ᾿Ισαὰκ καλεῖται διὰ τὴν
ἠκριβωμένην αἰτίαν.

This passage which is a digression (164-72) on the interpretation
of Gn 28,13 (159ff.) discusses the nature of allegorical interpretation and the Genesis passage is used as an example. The
question is why in Gn 28,13 Abraham who is actually the grandfa-
ther of Jacob is called his father and it mentions the "God of
Isaac" without referring to Isaac as his father. This is explained by the standard identification in Philo of the three
patriarchs with the three paideutic types or natures (cf. Mut 12)
--natural talent, practice and study (see Jaeger, Paideia III,
63). They are all sophoi but they do not begin from the same
nature though they aim at the same goal of perfection. Abraham
represents virtue which is taught, Isaac is self-taught and self-
hearing by nature and Jacob represents virtue which is acquired
by practice and exercise. Thus Jacob calls Abraham his father
while he is yet a practicer, since learning and practice are
closely related (169-70). But when Jacob reaches the goal of
clear sight and receives the form of a better character, he is
called Israel, the one who sees, at which point he calls as
father that which is naturally born good, namely, Isaac, and not
Abraham--the learner. This is proven by Gn 46,1. Thus the same
subject is called Jacob at one point, whose father is Abraham,
and Israel at another point, whose father is Isaac. From this
fact, Philo makes his point that in terms of the deeper allegorical meaning we are concerned here with "facts of nature" and not
with "mortal men."

QG IV,88: . . . And so, necessarily allegorizing, we might most
naturally say that Isaac has no need of exhortation, for
he has never taken a wife from among the Canaanites. And
I say this, not concerning man and woman, but concerning
the traits of the soul, to which the symbols of the names
here used refer. For Isaac is the mind, the self-teacher
and the self-taught, the distinct among the indifferent,
rejoicing always and daily in his Father and God and in
His works. (Passage under discussion is Gn 24,3; Marcus:
Loeb)

QG IV,103: (Gn 24,18) Why does she say in addition, "Master,"
(although she was) almost the mistress of the servant?
This is an indication and proof of theoretical matters
from which one ought to see that the passage is not about
mortal men but about characters (footnote j, "types") of
good men, who are zealous for immortality. (Rebecca is
identified with sophia; Marcus: Loeb)

QG IV,137: . . . For the inquiry of the theologian is about
characters and types and virtues and not about persons
who were created and born. (Marcus: Loeb)

The same point is made in QG IV,144; 230 (cf. Abr 217). The contemporary significance of the OT is indicated in QG IV,157: "And
these things are said to us, for who does not know that heaven
has no share or mixture or part of evil, etc." This follows an
elaboration on the four possible meanings of Gn 25,23.

Thus Philo has a philosophy of history in which the OT
patriarchs function as "traits of the soul," "characters,"
"types" and "virtues"--i.e., paideutic examples of heroic virtue
to be followed and imitated and which has its roots in the classic understanding of paideia beginning with Homer (cf. Marrou,
History, 33-34; Jaeger, Paideia I, 32-34), and not merely mortal
men of the past whose influence has ceased with their death. For
Philo the Law is preeminently paideutic in nature and not legal-
istic or to be understood in terms of enforcement (Mos ii,51-52;
on the protreptic and its background in the Isocratean method of
education, see Jaeger, Aristotle, 54-101).

Texts and Analysis

Abraham

Leg All iii,244: ἑτέρα δὲ πειστέον γυναικί, οἵαν συμβέβηκε
Σάρραν εἶναι, τὴν ἄρχουσαν ἀρετήν. καὶ πείθεταί γε ὁ
σοφὸς 'Αβραὰμ αὐτῇ παραινούσῃ ἃ δεῖ. πρότερον μὲν γὰρ
ὅτ' οὔπω τέλειος ἐγεγένητο, ἀλλ' ἔτι πρὶν μετονομασθῆναι
τὰ μετέωρα ἐφιλοσόφει, ἐπισταμένη ὅτι οὐκ ἂν δύναιτο
γεννᾶν ἐξ ἀρετῆς τελείας, συμβουλεύει ἐκ τῆς παιδίσκης
τουτέστι παιδείας τῆς ἐγκυκλίου παιδοποιεῖσθαι τῆς "Αγαρ
(Gn 16,2ff.), ὃ λέγεται παροίκησις. ὁ γὰρ μελετῶν ἐν
ἀρετῇ τελείᾳ κατοικεῖν, πρὶν ἐγγραφῆναι τῇ πόλει αὐτῆς,
τοῖς ἐγκυκλίοις μαθήμασι παροικεῖ, ἵνα διὰ τούτων πρὸς
τελείαν ἀρετὴν ἀφέτως ὁρμήσῃ.

Adam's listening to his wife (Gn 3,17) is the context of the passage and this is interpreted as the listening of the mind to
sense perception. This results in confusion and conflagration
and this suggests to Philo the women who set fire in Moab
(= mind) in Nu 21,30 (LXX) and this is contrasted to those who
trust God rather than their own reasoning--Abraham and Moses (Gn
15,6 and Nu 12,7). Joseph's flight from Potiphar's wife is contrasted with Phinehas who pierced the Midianite woman. Then follow counter examples of women who should be listened to, namely
midwives in Ex 1,20 who saved the male offspring of the soul and
Sarah who is the principal virtue (222-44). The sophos Abraham
obeys her instruction to beget children from encyclical paideia,
Hagar, while he is not yet perfect to beget from perfect virtue
(= Sarah). Encyclical education was preparatory to philosophy
which was true virtue or excellence and knowledge (epistēmē),
whereas the former are the arts (technē), (cf. Congr 139-42).

49

Mut 34: φθείρεται οὖν εἰκότως τὸ γεῶδες καὶ καταλύεται, ὅταν
ὅλος δι᾽ ὅλων ὁ νοῦς εὐαρεστεῖν προέληται θεῷ. σπάνιον
δὲ καὶ τὸ γένος καὶ μόλις εὑρισκόμενον, πλὴν οὐκ
ἀδύνατον γενέσθαι. δηλοῖ δὲ τὸ χρηθὲν ἐπὶ τοῦ Ἐνὼχ
λόγιον τόδε, "εὐηρέστησε δὲ Ἐνὼχ τῷ θεῷ, καὶ οὐχ
εὑρίσκετο." (Gn 5,24)

39: οὗτοι μὲν δὴ τὴν ἔνθεον μανίαν μανέντες ἐξηγριώθησαν,
ἕτεροι δ᾽ εἰσὶν οἱ τῆς τιθασοῦ καὶ ἡμέρου σοφίας ἑταῖροι.
τούτοις καὶ εὐσέβεια διαφερόντως ἀσκεῖται καὶ τὰ ἀνθρώ-
πεια οὐχ ὑπεροράται. μάρτυρες δ᾽ οἱ χρησμοί, ἐν οἷς
λέγεται τῷ Ἀβραμμ ἐκ προσώπου τοῦ θεοῦ, "εὐαρέστει
ἐνώπιον ἐμοῦ," (Gn 17,1), τοῦτο δ᾽ ἐστὶ μὴ ἐμοὶ μόνῳ,
ἀλλὰ καὶ τοῖς ἐμοῖς ἔργοις παρ᾽ ἐμοὶ κριτῇ, ὡς ἐφόρῳ
καὶ ἐπισκόπῳ.

These passages follow the interpretation of Gn 17,1 ("I am thy
God," see above p. 39) as refering to the good man of whom God
alone is creator. There are men (thiasoi) who by paideia have
mastered their bodies and have become unbodied minds (32-33).
The earthly portion is destroyed and dissolved when the mind
devotes itself exclusively or entirely to pleasing God (directly)
and Enoch belongs to this class (34) and such are hidden and
separate from common men and have migrated from mortal life to
the immortal (38). There are followers of a more tame and gentler sophia who practice piety and do not overlook human concerns
like Abraham who are pleasing in the presence of God, i.e., not
to him alone but also to his works which are enumerated in 40 as
honouring parents, mercy to the poor, etc. The distinction is
between being pleasing to God alone or directly unencumbered by
the body and human concerns (Enoch) and that pleasing which is
indirect, "before him," by means of good deeds (Abraham).

Mig 139: See below pp. 53-54.

Mig 166: δηλοῖ δὲ τὸ λόγιον ἐν ᾧ σαφῶς εἴρηται, διότι
"πορευθέντες ἀμφότεροι ἅμ᾽ ἦλθον ἐπὶ τὸν τόπον ὃν εἶπεν
ὁ θεός" (Gn 22,8).

167: ὑπερβάλλουσά γε ἰσότης ἀρετῶν ἁμιλλησαμένων πόνου μὲν
πρὸς εὐεξίαν, τέχνης δὲ πρὸς τὴν αὐτοδίδακτον φύσιν, καὶ
δυνηθέντων ἴσα τὰ ἆθλα τῆς ἀρετῆς ἐνέγκασθαι . . .

When Abraham travels with Eshcol (= natural ability - eyphuia)
and Aunan (= lover of seeing - philotheamon) in Gn 14,24, he
finally reaches the perfection or virtue of Isaac in Gn 22,8, at
which point labour and natural gift, art and self-taught nature
reach equality of excellence/perfection/virtue. In Mig 173-75,
until perfection Abraham has the Divine Logos and angels as his
leader, and when he reaches the state of full knowledge his pace
becomes equal to the Logos and both become companions with God as
leader (see above p. 37; cf. also Som i,64-66, pp. 34-35).

Mut 270: τὸ δὲ "συνετέλεσε λαλῶν πρὸς αὐτόν" (Gn 17,22) ἴσον
ἐστὶ τῷ τὸν ἀκροατὴν αὐτὸν ἐτελείωσε κενὸν ὄντα σοφίας

πρότερον καὶ ἀθανάτων λόγων ἐπλήρωσεν. ἐπεὶ δὲ <u>τέλειος</u>
<u>ὁ μαθητὴς</u> ἐγένετο, "ἀνέβη" (φησὶ) "κύριος ἀπὸ 'Αβραάμ"
δηλῶν, οὐχ ὅτι διεζεύχθη - <u>φύσει γὰρ θεοῦ ὁπαδὸς ὁ σοφός</u>
- ἀλλὰ τὸ <u>ἑκούσιον</u> τοῦ μαθητοῦ βουλόμενος παραστῆσαι,
ἵν΄, ὅπερ ἔμαθε, μηκέτι ἐφεστῶτος τοῦ διδάσκοντος χωρὶς
ἀνάγκης αὐτὸς ἐπιδεικνύμενος, <u>ἐθελουργῷ</u> καὶ <u>αὐτοκελεύστῳ</u>
προθυμίᾳ χρώμενος, ἐνεργῇ δι᾿ ἑαυτοῦ.

This is from the concluding section of the treatise, and Abraham
who symbolizes virtue through learning is perfected by God. As a
learner Abraham needed sophia contrary to Isaac who needs no
instruction and his perfection attains the level of the latter in
its <u>voluntary</u>, <u>self-willed</u> and <u>self-impelled</u> character (cf. <u>Conf</u>
59, see above p. 33). On this level he as a sophos becomes an
attendant of God (cf. <u>Mig 173-75</u>, p. 37 above). It is clear from
the usage thus far that the term "sophos" does not by itself indi
indicate the level of perfection attained (cf. <u>Leg All iii,244</u>,
p. 48 above; this fact is explicitly stated in <u>Som i,167</u>: "wherefore he also recorded three ancestors of the race, all sophoi,
who did not start from the same form of character, but pressed
to the same goal," p. 46 above).

In comparison to Philo, Abraham's excellencies--nobility of
birth, wisdom, vision of God, pattern for imitation, etc.--in
other literature of Hellenistic Judaism is without reservations.
Eupolemus (Eus PE IX,17: 418d): . . . ἐν τρισκαιδεκάτῃ
γενέσθαι 'Αβραὰμ γενεᾷ, <u>εὐγενείᾳ καὶ σοφίᾳ πάντας ὑπερ-</u>
<u>βεβηκότα</u>, ὃν δὴ καὶ τὴν ἀστρολογίαν καὶ Χαλδαϊκὴν εὑρεῖν,
ἐπί τε τὴν εὐσέβειαν ὁρμήσαντα <u>εὐαρεστῆσαι τῷ θεῷ</u>.

The author is considered to be different from the one found in
other fragments quoted in Eusebius in that Abraham is received as
a guest in the temple of the city of Agrarizin (most probably
Gerizim)--a Samaritan trait not found in other fragments ascribed
to Eupolemus. Abraham is described as excelling all in <u>nobility</u>
and <u>wisdom</u> and <u>pleasing God</u> by his piety.
Aristobulus (Eus PE XIII,12: 665c):
οὐ γὰρ κέν τις ἴδοι θνητῶν μερόπων κραίνοντα εἰ μὴ
<u>μουνογενής</u> τις ἀπορρὼξ φύλου ἄνωθεν Χαλδαίων.

The reference is to Abraham (monogenḗs)--a stem from the Chaldean
race--who alone among mortals has seen God. This is the closest
parallel to <u>Jn 1,18</u> and does not seem to have been noticed by
most commentators. The invisibility of God, that he cannot be
seen by mortal eyes is a standard reiteration in Hellenistic Jewish literature (cf. Ezekiel Tragedian, Eus PE IX,29: 441a; Sib
Or III,17; IV,10-12).
4Macc 14,20: ἀλλ᾿ οὐχὶ <u>τὴν 'Αβραὰμ ὁμόψυχον</u> τῶν νεανίσκων
μητέρα μετεκίνησεν συμπάθεια τέκνων.
4Macc 15,28: ἀλλὰ <u>τῆς θεοσεβοῦς 'Αβραὰμ καρτερίας</u> ἡ θυγάτηρ
<u>ἐμνήσθη</u>.

4Macc 17,5-6: οὐχ οὕτως σελήνη κατ᾿ οὐρανὸν σὺν ἄστροις σεμνὴ
καθέστηκεν, ὡς σὺ τοὺς ἰσαστέρους ἑπτὰ παῖδας φωταγωγή-
σασα πρὸς τὴν εὐσέβειαν ἔντιμος καθέστηκας θεῷ καὶ
ἐστήρισαι σὺν αὐτοῖς ἐν οὐρανῷ. ἦν γὰρ ἡ παιδοποιία
σου ἀπὸ ᾿Αβραὰμ τοῦ πατρός.

The three passages from 4Macc all refer to the mother of the
seven sons whose martyrdom form the subject matter of the book.
The mother is of like-soul to Abraham in that sympathy for children did not move her, as a daughter of Abraham she remembered
Abraham's fortitude. At her death she stands honoured by God
with her seven starlike sons in heaven. Her child-bearing was
from Abraham, which obviously implies a spiritualized understanding of the passages in Genesis in which Abraham's descendants are
promised to be as numerous as the stars of heaven (Gn 22,17,
etc.). This is understood here in terms of the heavenly destiny
of his children. Thus Abraham and his sacrifice of Isaac is the
model for the mother's endurance, character and child-bearing
(cf. 13,12; 16,20). The ideology which informs this tradition
is paideutic.

The psychological elaboration of Abraham's filial feelings
for Isaac is a portion of a traditional exegetical theme. Wisdom
of Solomon 10,5c states that sophia: καὶ ἐπὶ τέκνου σπλάγχνοις
ἰσχρὸν ἐφύλαξεν. The reference being to Abraham.

Jacob/Israel

Ebr 82: ἡνίκα γοῦν ὁ ἀσκητὴς ᾿Ιακὼβ καὶ τοὺς ἀρετῆς ἄθλους
διαθλῶν ἔμελλεν ἀκοὰς ὀφθαλμῶν ἀντιδιδόναι καὶ λόγους
ἔργων καὶ προκοπὰς τελειότητος, τοῦ φιλοδώρου θεοῦ
βουληθέντος αὐτοῦ τὴν διάνοιαν ἐνομματῶσαι, ἵνα ταῦτ᾿
ἐναργῶς ἴδῃ ἃ πρότερον ἀκοῇ παρελάμβανε - πιστοτέρα γὰρ
ὄψις ὤτων -, ἐπήχησαν οἱ χρησμοί, "οὐ κληθήσεται τὸ ὀνομά
σου ᾿Ιακώβ, ἀλλ᾿ ᾿Ισραὴλ ἔσται σου τὸ ὄνομα, ὅτι ἴσχυσας
μετὰ θεοῦ καὶ μετὰ ἀνθρώπων δυνατός." (Gn 32,28) ᾿Ιακὼβ
μὲν οὖν μαθήσεως καὶ προκοπῆς ὄνομα, ἀκοῆς ἐξηρτημένων
δυνάμεων, ᾿Ισραὴλ δὲ τελειότητος, ὁρασιν γὰρ θεοῦ μηνύει
τοὔνομα. (Cf. Conf 72; Mig 200-201; Som i,167-72,
pp. 46-47.)

That wine is a symbol of foolish talking and raving is the context of this passage and its cause is apaideusia. This is illustrated by Dt 21,18-21. The father and mother in the Dt text can
mean God and Sophia, or their associates, the father being the
orthos Logos and the mother being the encyclical paideia (3-33).
There are four classes of children, those who obey both, those
who obey neither, and those who obey one or the other of the
parents. Jacob the practicer is cited as the example who obeys
both parents. When he reaches perfection, he exchanges hearing
for sight, words for deeds, and progress for perfection and this

is shown by the change of his name in Gn 32,28. Jacob is the
name for learning and progress, Israel is the name for perfec-
tion--vision of God. "And what among virtues/excellencies could
be more perfect than seeing the One who truly exists" (83). The
one who looks forward to this good is commended by both parents--
the earlier educators (83).

Mig 28: ἀλλὰ μετανάστην χρὴ γενέσθαι εἰς τὴν πατρῴαν γῆν τὴν
ἱεροῦ λόγου καὶ τρόπον τινα τῶν ἀσκητῶν πατρός. ἡ δ'
ἔστι σοφία, τῶν φιλαρέτων ψυχῶν ἄριστον ἐνδιαίτημα.

29: ἐν ταύτῃ τῇ χώρᾳ καὶ γένος ἐστί σοι τὸ αὐτομαθές, τὸ
αὐτοδίδακτον, τὸ νηπίας καὶ γαλακτώδους τροφῆς ἀμέτοχον,
. . . ἐπίκλησιν Ἰσαάκ.

30: οὗ τὸ κλῆρον παραλαβὼν ἐξ ἀνάγκης ἀποθήσῃ τὸν πόνον. αἱ
γὰρ ἀφθονίαι τῶν ἑτοίμων καὶ κατὰ χειρὸς ἀγαθῶν ἀπονίας
αἴτιαι. πηγὴ δέ, ἀφ' ἧς ὀμβρεῖ τὰ ἀγαθά, ἡ τοῦ φιλοδώρου
θεοῦ σύνοδός ἐστιν.

The basis of the discussion is Gn 12,1, "depart," and Gn 31,3 is
quoted as one example (27). The "perfect athlete" having won
prizes and virtues must cease from fondness of strife (philonei-
kos) and reap the fruits of his toil (27-28). Jacob (the athlete) therefore must return to the land of his father, which is
both Logos and Sophia. In this land there awaits Isaac, the
self-learnt and self-taught kind which does not partake of infant
diet of milk. The inheritance of Isaac is without toil and the
source of such goods is the companionship of the bountiful God.
Thus the perfection which Jacob attains at the end is what Isaac
has by nature.

Mig 38: ὁ δὲ ὁρῶν ἔστιν ὁ σοφός, τυφλοὶ γὰρ ἢ ἀμυδροὶ τὰς ὄψεις
οἵ γε ἄφρονες. διὰ τοῦτο καὶ τοὺς προφήτας ἐκάλουν
πρότερον τοὺς βλέποντας   (ISam 9,9). καὶ ὁ ἀσκητὴς
ἐσπούδασεν ὦτα ὀφθαλμῶν ἀντιδοὺς ἰδεῖν ἃ πρότερον ἤκουε,
καὶ τυγχάνει τοῦ καθ' ὅρασιν κλήρου τὸν ἐξ ἀκοῆς ὑπερβάς.

39: εἰς γὰρ τὸν ὁρῶντα Ἰσραὴλ μεταχαράττεται τὸ μαθήσεως
καὶ διδασκαλίας νόμισμα, οὗπερ ἐπώνυμος ἦν Ἰακώβ, δι'
οὗ καὶ τὸ ὁρᾶν γίνεται φῶς τὸ θεῖον, ἀδιαφοροῦν
ἐπιστήμης . . . (Cf. Quis Her 78)

The thing shown in Gn 12,1, according to Philo, is the "perfect
good" or virtue and this is attested by Ex 15,25 and Gn 2,9. The
one who sees it is the sophos, namely, the practicer Jacob who is
eager to exchange ears for eyes and to obtain the lot of sight by
rising above that which comes by hearing. From Jacob which is
the name for learning and teaching he is reminted into Israel--
who sees (cf. Ebr 82 above).

Fug 43: ὁ γοῦν Ἰακὼβ καὶ τὸν Ἡσαῦ ἀποδιδράσκει καὶ τῶν γονέων
διοικίζεται. ἀσκητικὸς γὰρ ὢν καὶ ἔτι διαθλῶν φεύγει μὲν
κακίαν, ἀρετῇ δὲ τελείᾳ καὶ αὐτομαθεῖ συζῆν ἀδυνατεῖ.

The subject is Jacob's flight from Esau (Gn 27,42-45) and his
inability, while yet a practicer, to aim for the best prize. The

best prize is described in 40 as the ministry to the only God, in 42 as the great highpriesthood to Him alone and in the passage above as self-learnt and perfect virtue. While Jacob is yet engaged in practice he flees evil and is incapable of sharing this perfection, namely, that associated with Isaac.

Isaac

That Isaac represents self-taught and self-learnt virtue, the highest level of perfection which the practicer Jacob attains when he becomes Israel--the one who sees God--, and Abraham (taught virtue) attains when God perfects him which is symbolized by his accompaniment with Isaac in Gn 22 and begetting through perfect virtue Sarah, has already been indicated in the passages quoted above: Som i,167-72; QG IV,88; Mig 166-67; 28-30; and Fug 43.

Conf 74: θέασαι γοῦν τὸν ἀσκητὴν οἷά φησιν, "ἄρατε τοὺς θεοὺς ἀλλοτρίους τοὺς μεθ᾽ ὑμῶν ἐκ μέσου ὑμῶν, καὶ καθαρίσασθε καὶ ἀλλάξατε τὰς στολὰς ὑμῶν, καὶ ἀναστάντες ἀναβῶμεν εἰς Βαιθήλ" (Gn 35,2-3), ἵνα κἂν λάβαν ἔρευναν αἰτῆται, ἐν ὅλῳ τῷ οἴκῳ μὴ εὑρεθῇ τὰ εἴδωλα, (ἀλλὰ) πράγματα ὑφεστηκότα καὶ ὄντως ὑπαρκτά, ἐστηλιτευμένα ἐν τῇ τοῦ σοφοῦ διανοίᾳ, ὧν καὶ τὸ αὐτομαθὲς γένος Ἰσαὰκ κληρονομεῖ. τὰ γὰρ ὑπαρκτὰ μόνος οὗτος παρὰ τοῦ πατρὸς λαμβάνει.

Shinar in Gn 11,2 is taken to mean "shaking out" (ektinagmos) and this is characteristic of evil men who shake out all semblance of good. The primary examples are the Egyptians (Ex 14,27) and the king of Moab (Nu 23,7) who desires to destroy not only perfection (Israel) but progress as well (Jacob)--68-72. Such minds shake and cast forth the whole nature of good, but the minds of good men only cast out the worthless (73). Thus the practicer Jacob commands that idols be cast away when they go to Bethel, since in his house no idols are found but realities which are the heritage alone of the self-learnt kind, Isaac.

Mig 139: τούτων δὴ τοῦτον ἐχόντων τὸν τρόπον τελειωθεὶς ὁ νοῦς ἀποδώσει τὸ τέλος τῷ τελεσφόρῳ θεῷ κατὰ τὸ ἱερώτατον γράμμα. νόμος γάρ ἐστι τὸ τέλος εἶναι κυρίου. πότε οὖν ἀποδίδωσιν; ὅταν "ἐπὶ τὸν τοπὸν ὃν εἶπεν αὐτῷ ὁ θεὸς τῇ ἡμέρᾳ τῇ τρίτῃ" (Gn 22,3) παραγένηται, παρελθὼν τὰς πλείους μοίρας τῶν χρονικῶν διαστημάτων

140: καὶ ἤδη πρὸς τὴν ἄχρονον μεταβαίνων φύσιν. τότε γὰρ καὶ τὸν ἀγαπητὸν υἱὸν ἱερουργήσει, οὐχὶ ἄνθρωπον - οὐ γὰρ τεκνοκτόνος ὁ σοφός -, ἀλλὰ τὸ τῆς ἀρετώσης ψυχῆς γέννημα ἄρρεν, τὸν ἐπανθήσαντα καρπὸν αὐτῇ, ὃν πῶς ἤνεγκεν οὐκ ἔγνω, βλάστημα θεῖον, οὗ φανέντος ἡ δόξασα κυοφορῆσθαι τὴν ἄγνοιαν τοῦ συμβάντος ἀγαθοῦ διηγεῖται φάσκουσα, "τίς ἀναγγελεῖ Ἀβραὰμ" ὡς ἀπιστοῦντι δήπου περὶ τὴν τοῦ αὐτο-μαθοῦς γένους ἀνατολήν, ὅτι "θηλάζει παιδίον Σάρρα" (Gn 21,7), οὐχὶ πρὸς Σάρρας θηλάζεται; τὸ γὰρ αὐτοδίδακτον

τρέφεται μὲν ὑπ' οὐδενός, τροφὴ δ' ἐστιν ἄλλων, ἄτε
ἱκανὸν διδάσκειν καὶ μανθάνειν οὐ δεόμενον.

The second part of the treatise begins with the statement: "On
the one hand therefore the subject of gifts has been dealt with,
which God is accustomed to bestow to those who will become perfect and through them to others" (127). The next passage for
discussion is Gn 12,4 which is interpreted to mean "to live in
consonance (akolouthos) with nature," to enter the straight path
of virtue, to walk in the footsteps of the orthos Logos and to
follow God. It is elaborated further until the passage quoted
above. (Cf. Plutarch, De recta rat. aud., 1: ταὐτον ἐστι τὸ
ἔπεσθαι θεῷ καὶ τὸ πείθεσθαι λόγῳ. Conf 58-59, see above p. 33.)
When the Abrahamic mind has been perfected the telos is repaid to
God (allusion to Nu 31,28ff.) when Abraham sacrifices the beloved
son (Gn 22,3) on the third day which signifies that he is already
passing into eternal nature having passed through the divisions
of time (probably--past, present and future). This beloved son
is no human but a divine offshoot, male, self-taught, is fed by
no one, is food for others, capable of teaching and himself not
needing to learn. This section is brought to a conclusion with
the statement: "This is the end (telos) of the way (hodos) of
those who follow the logoi and legal injunctions and go in what-
ever direction God may lead" (143). The goal is thus perfection,
that which is like Isaac's. The next sections deal with counter
examples to Abraham's following God.

Congr 36: τὸ δὲ αὐτομαθὲς γένος, οὗ κεκοινώνηκεν 'Ισαάκ, ἡ
          εὐπαθειῶν ἀρίστη χαρά, φύσεως ἀπλῆς καὶ ἀμιγοῦς καὶ
          ἀκράτου μεμοίραται, μήτε ἀσκήσεως μήτε διδασκαλίας
          δεόμενον, ἐν οἷς παλλακίδων ἐπιστημῶν, οὐκ ἀστῶν μόνον,
          ἐστι χρεία. θεοῦ γὰρ τὸ αὐτομαθὲς καὶ αὐτοδίδακτον
          ἄνωθεν ἀπ' οὐρανοῦ καλὸν ὀμβρήσαντος ἀμήχανον ἦν ἔτι
          δούλαις καὶ παλλακαῖς συμβιῶναι τέχναις, νόθων δογμάτων
          οἷα παίδων ὀρεχθέντα. . . .

       38: ἔχει γὰρ ἐν ἐτοίμῳ τέλεια τὰ τοῦ θεοῦ δῶρα χάρισι ταῖς
          πρεσβυτέραις ἐπιπνευσθέντα, βούλεται δὲ καὶ εὔχεται ταῦτα
          ἐπιμεῖναι.

On the basis of Gn 16,1-2 it is argued that those incapable of
receiving the seeds/sperms of virtue need encyclical education as
a preliminary and this is symbolized by Hagar (9). She is by
birth an Egyptian (symbol of that which is earthy and bodily) and
this underlines the necessity of the senses for such education
(20-21). Her name means "sojourning" in contrast to knowledge,
wisdom and virtue which are always native-born and indigenous
citizens (22-23). The virtue acquired through teaching (Abraham)
and that by practice (Jacob) need wives as well as concubines,
and the latter represent wisdom (phronēsis) and encyclical

preliminaries respectively (34-35). But the <u>self-learnt kind</u>, in
which <u>Isaac shares</u>, <u>needs neither practice nor teaching</u>. He has
at hand the <u>perfect gifts</u> of God breathed in by the <u>primary
graces</u> of God.

Fug 166: ἐν τούτῳ τάττεται πᾶς <u>αὐτομαθὴς</u> καὶ <u>αὐτοδίδακτος σοφός</u>.
οὐ γὰρ σκέψεσι καὶ <u>μελέταις</u> καὶ <u>πόνοις</u> ἐβελτιώθη,
γενόμενος δ' εὐθὺς εὐτρεπισμένην εὗρε <u>σοφίαν ἄνωθεν</u>
<u>ὀμβρηθεῖσαν ἀπ' οὐρανοῦ</u> . . .

The second part of this treatise (119ff.) deals with the theme of
finding (Gn 16,7), which is discussed under four heads: those
who neither seek nor find, seeking and finding, seeking and not
finding, and finding without seeking. The primary example of
finding without seeking is the <u>self-learnt</u> and <u>self-taught type</u>
of the sophos, namely, <u>Isaac</u>. This type is not improved by
searchings or practice or labours, but finds ready at hand wisdom
which has been rained from heaven above (cf. Congr 36: God rains
the "good" in this case rather than sophia).

Fug 167: οὗτός ἐστιν ὃν 'Ισαὰκ ὠνόμασαν οἱ χρησμοί . . . <u>οὐ</u> γὰρ
<u>ἄνθρωπος</u> ἦν ὁ γεννώμενος, ἀλλὰ <u>νόημα καθαρώτατον</u>, <u>φύσει</u>
μᾶλλον ἢ ἐπιτηδεύσει <u>καλόν</u>.

This <u>Isaac</u> is <u>not man</u> but the purest thought, <u>good by nature</u>
rather than by study. The self-learnt kind is <u>new</u> and <u>better
than the logos</u> and <u>divine</u> (168). This type is like the Hebrew
mothers who need no midwives (i.e., arts, sciences, systems,
etc.)--Ex 1,19; it is defined as that which is found quickly and
that which God delivered (Gn 27,20); it is that which comes up by
itself (Lv 25,11)--168-72.

Fug 172: <u>προκοπὰς</u> μὲν γὰρ ἐμποιῆσαι καὶ ὁ <u>διδάσκων</u> ἱκανός, τὴν
δ' ἐπ' <u>ἄκρον τελειότητα</u> ὁ <u>θεὸς μόνος</u>, <u>ἡ ἀρίστη φύσις</u>.

173: ὁ τούτοις <u>ἐντρεφόμενος</u> τοῖς δόγμασι τὴν <u>ἀίδιον εἰρήνην</u>
ἄγει, πόνων ἀφειμένος ἀτρύτων. <u>ἀδιαφορεῖ δ' ἑβδομάδος</u>
<u>εἰρήνη</u> κατὰ τὸν νομοθέτην. ἐν γὰρ αὐτῇ τὸ δοκεῖν ἐνερ-
γεῖν ἀποτιθεμένη <u>γένεσις ἀναπαύεται</u>.

174: προσηκόντως οὖν λέγεται, "καὶ ἔσται τὰ σάββατα τῆς γῆς
ὑμῖν βρώματα" (Lv 25,6), δι' ὑπονοιῶν, <u>τρόφιμον</u> γὰρ καὶ
<u>ἀπολαυστὸν μόνον</u> ἡ ἐν θεῷ ἀνάπαυσις, τὸ <u>μέγιστον ἀγαθὸν</u>
περιποιοῦσα τὴν ἀπόλεμον εἰρήνην.

The <u>teacher can produce progress</u>, but <u>God alone can produce full
perfection</u>, being the best nature. The connecting thought being
that that which grows by itself or by nature needs no artificial
tending (technē). The <u>one who is nourished by these principles</u>
(of the self-taught type) <u>lives in peace</u>, a peace which is no
different from the <u>seventh day rest</u> of creation. <u>Rest in God</u> is
alone nourishing and enjoyable and it secures the <u>greatest good</u>,
peace without war (Lv 25,6). This untoiling perfection of the
self-taught is further elaborated by reference to the lavish

supply that was at hand when God led one into Canaan (Dt 6,11-11), in 175-76 (cf. Mut 255, see below).

Mut 130: εἴπετο δ' εὐθὺς ἡ γένεσις Ἰσαάκ, καλέσας γὰρ τὴν
μητέρα αὐτοῦ Σάρραν ἀντὶ Σάρας φησὶ τῷ Ἀβραάμ, "δώσω
σοι (ἐξ αὐτῆς) τέκνον" (Gn 17,16). ἐν μέρει δ' ἕκαστον
ἀκριβωτέον.

131: ὁ τοίνυν κυρίως διδοὺς ὁτιοῦν ἴδιόν τι πάντως ἑαυτοῦ
δίδωσιν, εἰ δὲ τοῦτ' ἀψευδές ἐστι, γένοιτ' ἂν Ἰσαὰκ οὐκ
ὁ ἄνθρωπος, ἀλλ' ὁ συνώνυμος τῆς ἀρίστης τῶν εὐπαθειῶν,
χαρᾶς, γέλως ὁ ἐνδιάθετος, υἱὸς θεοῦ τοῦ διδόντος αὐτὸν
μείλιγμα καὶ εὐθυμίαν εἰρηνικωτάταις ψυχαῖς. (Cf. Det
123-24)

This section begins the interpretation of Gn 17,16. Since it is God who gives Isaac, he gives something which is peculiarly his own. Therefore Isaac is not a man, but the best of good emotions, joy and laughter within, son of God, who gives him as comfort and cheer to the most peaceful souls. (Cf. DL VII,116--joy as eupatheia; Völker, pp. 324-25.)

Mut 255: μάθε οὖν, ὦ ψυχή, ὅτι καὶ "Σάρρα," ἡ ἀρετή, "τέξεταί
σοι υἱόν" (Gn 17,19), οὐ μόνον Ἄγαρ, ἡ μέση παιδεία.
ἐκείνης μὲν γὰρ τὸ ἔγγονον διδακτόν, ταύτης δὲ πάντως
αὐτομαθές ἐστι.

256: μὴ θαυμάσῃς (δ'), εἰ πάντα φέρων σπουδαῖα ὁ θεὸς
ἤνεγκε καὶ τοῦτο τὸ γένος, σπάνιον μὲν ἐπὶ γῆς, πάμπολυ
δ' ἐν οὐρανῷ.

258: τί οὖν ἔτι θαυμάζεις, εἰ καὶ ἀρετὴν ἄπονον καὶ
ἀταλαίπωρον ὁ θεὸς ὀμβρήσει μηδεμιᾶς δεομένην ἐπιστασίας,
ἀλλ' ἐξ ἀρχῆς ὁλόκληρον καὶ παντελῆ; εἰ (δὲ) καὶ
μαρτυρίαν βούλει λαβεῖν Μωυσέως ἀξιοπιστοτέραν εὑρήσεις;
ὃς φησι τοῖς μὲν ἄλλοις ἀνθρώποις ἀπὸ γῆς εἶναι τὰς
τροφάς, μόνῳ δὲ ἀπ' οὐρανοῦ τῷ ὁρατικῷ.

259: . . . "ἰδοὺ ὕω ὑμῖν ἄρτους ἀπ' οὐρανοῦ" (Ex 16,4).
τίνα οὖν ἀπ' (οὐρανοῦ) τροφὴν ἐνδίκως ὕεσθαι λέγει, ὅτι
μὴ τὴν οὐράνιον σοφίαν;

260: ἣν ἄνωθεν ἐπιπέμπει . . . ἐν ἱερᾷ ἑβδόμῃ, ἣν σάββατον
καλεῖ. τότε γὰρ τὴν τῶν αὐτομάτων ἀγαθῶν φορὰν ἔσεσθαί
φησιν, οὐκ ἐξ ὅλης τέχνης ἀνατελλόντων, ἀλλ' αὐτογενεῖ
καὶ αὐτοτελεῖ φύσει βλαστανόντων καὶ τοὺς οἰκείους
φερόντων καρπούς.

Sections 252-63 deal with Gn 17,19 which is a reply to Abraham's request: "Let this Ishmael live before thee" (Gn 17,18). God instead grants him two, namely, the child of the lower paideia Hagar and the child of virtue Sarah, i.e., Isaac. The former represents virtue that is taught and the latter that which is self-learnt (see also 263). There are few of the latter kind on earth and numerous in heaven. This virtue/excellence which is without toil and trouble and requires no nurture is whole and perfect from the very beginning. God sends this excellence or virtue down like rain. The proof being Ex 16,4--bread from heaven. Other men receive food from earth, but only the seeing

<u>kind</u> (= Israel) receives <u>food from heaven</u>. This is identified
with the heaven sent <u>sophia</u> and the <u>sabbath year</u> (Lv 25,4ff.; cf.
Fug 172 above) which is characterized here as the automatic pro-
duction of goods, <u>self-productive</u> and <u>self-sufficient</u> in nature.

Som i,160: μὴ νομίσῃς δὲ παρέργως, τοῦ μὲν 'Αβραὰμ νυνὶ λέγεσθαι
κύριον καὶ θεόν, τοῦ δὲ 'Ισαὰκ θεὸν αὐτὸ μόνον. ὁ μὲν
γὰρ <u>αὐτηκόου</u> καὶ <u>αὐτοδιδάκτου</u> καὶ <u>αὐτομαθοῦς</u> φύσει περι-
γινομένης <u>σύμβολον ἐπιστήμης</u> ἐστίν, ὁ δὲ <u>Αβραὰμ διδασκο-
μένης</u>. καὶ τῷ μὲν <u>αὐτόχθονι</u> καὶ <u>αὐθιγενεῖ</u> συμβέβηκεν
εἶναι, τῷ δὲ <u>μετανάστῃ</u> καὶ <u>ἐπιλύτῳ</u>.

162: <u>οὗτος</u> μὲν δὴ <u>ὁ τρόπος</u> δυεῖν δυνάμεων τῶν ἐπιμελη-
σομένων ἐστι <u>χρεῖος, ἡγεμονίας</u> καὶ <u>εὐεργεσίας</u> . . . ὁ δ'
<u>ἕτερος τῆς κατὰ τὸ χαρίζεσθαι μόνης</u>, <u>οὐ γὰρ ὑπὸ νουθετού-
σης ἀρχῆς ἐβελτιώθη</u>, φύσει περιπεποιημένος τὸ καλόν,
ἀλλὰ <u>διὰ τὰς ὀμβρηθείσας ἄνωθεν δωρεὰς ἀγαθὸς</u> καὶ <u>τέλειος</u>
ἐξ ἀρχῆς ἐγένετο.

The passage under consideration is Gn 28,13 (159) which speaks of
"Lord God of Abraham and the God of Isaac." <u>Isaac</u> is the <u>symbol
of knowledge</u> which is <u>self-hearing</u>, <u>self-taught</u> and <u>self-learnt</u>,
and <u>Abraham</u> is the symbol of <u>knowledge</u> which is <u>taught</u>. Isaac is
a <u>native</u> and Abraham is an <u>immigrant</u> and <u>stranger</u>. Abraham <u>needs
both God's guidance</u> and kindness, whereas Isaac needs only God's
charis/gracious gift and is <u>not improved by the rule of admoni-
tion</u> but acquires by nature goodness/beauty and is good and
<u>perfect from the beginning</u> through gifts rained upon him from
above.

Isaac elsewhere is called <u>self-taught sophia</u>. In <u>Sac 78-79</u>,
when one receives the enlightenment of self-learnt sophia then
hearing of heroic deeds handed down by historians and poets
becomes idle since hearing has been replaced by sight. He will
no longer need the guidance of men but will become the pupil of
God. In <u>Det 29-30</u>, Isaac who is called self-learnt sophia has
God for his guide and fellow-traveller and desires to be alone
with Him (cf. QG IV,140).[5]

---

[5] The image of being "alone" with God expresses the highest
state of religious perfection (cf. Festugiere, <u>Personal Religion
among the Greeks</u>, pp. 138-39). In <u>Plotinus</u> VI,9.11, the image is
used to describe the supreme union of the soul with the One.
Other metaphors used in this passage are: <u>rest, entering into
the sanctuary, another kind of seeing, being out of oneself</u> and
<u>the secrecy of the mysteries</u>. The union of the soul with the One
is explicated by the principle of "like by like" (cf. V,3.7: "to
touch that Light and see It by Itself"). This principle is referred to frequently by Philo and Praem 46 is a close parallel to
Plotinus V,3.17 and points to their common background (cf. also
Det 1; 141; Gig 9; Conf 183; Mig 5; Mut 4-6; Praem 40; Prov 13).
Philo denies that one can see the essence of God (Praem 39-40).
In Plotinus the One is totally transcendent (above the Nous, V,
3.17; beyond Being, VI,9.11) and similarly in Philo God is "better than the good," "older than the monad," and "purer than the

58

4Macc 7,13: καίτοι τὸ θαυμασιώτατον, γέρων ὢν λελυμένων μὲν ἤδη
τῶν τοῦ σώματος τόνων, περικεχαλασμένων δὲ τῶν σαρκῶν,
κεκμηκότων δὲ καὶ τῶν νεύρων ἀνενέασεν 14: τῷ πνεύματι
διὰ τοῦ λογισμοῦ καὶ τῷ Ἰσακίῳ λογισμῷ τὴν πολυκέφαλον
στέρβλαν ἡκύρωσεν. 15: ὧ μακαρίου γήρως καὶ σεμνῆς
πολιᾶς καὶ βίου νομίμου, ὃν πιστὴ θανάτου σφραγὶς
ἐτελείωσεν.

The reference is to the martyrdom of Eleazar and he received
strength for it through an Isaac like reasoning (referring to Gn
22) and was perfected by the faithful seal of death. Similarly,
Isaac is the pattern for the martyrdom of the seven brothers in
13,12.

Highpriest/Priest: Aaron, Levi and Melchizedek

Leg All iii,45: καὶ γάρ εἰσι "αἱ χεῖρες Μωυσεῖ βαρεῖαι" (Ex 17,
12). ἐπειδὴ γὰρ αἱ τοῦ φαύλου πράξεις ἀνεμιαῖοί τε καὶ
κοῦφαι, γένοιντ᾽ ἂν αἱ τοῦ σοφοῦ βαρεῖαι καὶ ἀκίνητοι
οὐδ᾽ εὐσάλευτοι. παρὸ καὶ στηρίζονται ὑπό τε Ἀαρών, τοῦ
λόγου, καὶ Ὤρ, ὃ ἐστι φῶς, οὐδὲν (δὲ) τῶν πραγμάτων φῶς
ἐναργεστερόν ἐστι ἀληθείας. βούλεται οὖν διὰ συμβόλων
σοι παραστῆσαι, ὅτι αἱ τοῦ σοφοῦ πράξεις στηρίζονται ὑπὸ
τῶν ἀναγκαιοτάτων λογοῦ τε καὶ ἀληθείας. διὸ καὶ Ἀαρὼν
ὅταν τελευτᾷ, τουτέστιν ὅταν τελειωθῇ, εἰς Ὤρ, ὃ ἐστι
φῶς, ἀνέρχεται (Nu 20,25), τὸ γὰρ τέλος τοῦ λόγου ἀλήθειά
ἐστιν ἡ φωτὸς τηλαυγεστέρα, εἰς ἣν σπουδάζει ὁ λόγος
ἐλθεῖν.

Aaron and Or who held up Moses' hands are symbolically the Logos
and Light and since there is no brighter light than truth, they
represent Logos and Truth. This leads to the thought that when
Aaron died, that is when he was perfected, he went up into Or =
Light (Nu 20,25). The end/goal of the Logos is Truth and into it
the Logos is eager to enter since it represents the perfection of
the Logos. The context of the passage is Gn 3,8--Adam's hiding
in the wood of the garden (28ff.). This hiding is interpreted by
examples and counter examples. The latter are those who flee
from self to God (39ff.) and this is illustrated from Gn 15,5,
which in turn by associative ideas ("to lead out") leads Philo to
Gn 24,7, Ex 9,29 and this latter passage leads into Ex 17,12,
since both refer to the stretching out of Moses' hands.

Som ii,231: τούτῳ παραπλήσιόν ἐστι καὶ τὸ χρησθὲν λόγιον ἐπὶ τοῦ
μεγάλου ἱερέως, "ὅταν" γάρ φησιν "εἰσίῃ εἰς τὰ ἅγια τῶν
ἁγίων, ἄνθρωπος οὐκ ἔσται, ἕως ἂν ἐξέλθῃ" (Lv 16,17). εἰ
δὲ μὴ γίνεται τότε ἄνθρωπος, δῆλον ὅτι οὐδὲ θεός, ἀλλὰ
λειτουργὸς θεοῦ, κατὰ μὲν τὸ θνητὸν γενέσει, κατὰ δὲ τὸ
ἀθάνατον οἰκειούμενος τῷ ἀγενήτῳ.

---

one" (Praem 40; cf. Vit Cont 2; QE II,37: the one is a form and
likeness of God). See further in Festugiere, ibid., p. 128 where
he shows that Albinus understood Plato's concept of God to be an
"epekeina tēs ousias" (Republic VI, 509b, 8-9). Cf. E. Peterson,
"Herkunft und Bedeutung der ΜΟΝΟΣ ΠΡΟΣ ΜΟΝΟΝ - Formel bei Plotin,"
Philologus 88 (1932), 30ff.

232: τὴν δὲ <u>μέσην τάξιν</u> εἴληχεν, ἕως ἂν ἐξέλθῃ πάλιν εἰς τὰ
τοῦ σώματος καὶ τῆς σαρκὸς οἰκεῖα. . . .

234: τὸν μὲν οὖν <u>τέλειον</u> <u>οὔτε θεὸν</u> <u>οὔτε ἄνθρωπον</u> ἀναγράφει
Μωυσῆς, ἀλλ᾽, ὡς ἔφην, μεθόριον τῆς <u>ἀγενήτου καὶ φθαρτῆς</u>
<u>φύσεως</u>, τὸν δὲ <u>προκόπτοντα</u> πάλιν <u>ἐν τῇ μεταξὺ χώρᾳ ζώντων</u>
<u>καὶ τεθνηκότων</u> τάττει . . .

235: λέγεται γὰρ ἐπὶ ᾽Ααρὼν ὅτι "ἔστη ἀνὰ μέσον τῶν τεθνηκότων
(καὶ τῶν ζώντων), καὶ ἐκόπασεν ἡ θραῦσις" (Nu 16,48).
<u>ὁ γὰρ προκόπτων οὔτε ἐν τοῖς τεθνηκόσι</u> τὸν ἀρετῆς βίον
ἐξετάζεται, πόθον καὶ ζῆλον ἔχων τοῦ καλοῦ, <u>οὔτε ἐν τοῖς</u>
<u>μετὰ τῆς ἄκρας καὶ τελείας</u> ζῶσιν εὐδαιμονίας - ἔτι γὰρ
πρὸς τὸ πέρας ἐνδεῖ -, ἀλλ᾽ <u>ἑκατέρων ἐφάπτεται</u>.

The statement "I thought I stood" from Gn 41,17-24 forms the context. This is the statement of the self-lover who has no stability since stability belongs to God alone and His friends (215ff.).
Such friends are cited: Noah (Gn 9,11), Abraham the sophos (Gn
18,22), Moses (Dt 5,31 and 5,5). Moses is the kind (genos) between the mortal and immortal (228-29). And <u>Aaron</u> as the <u>great</u>
<u>priest when he enters the holy of holies</u> (Lv 16,17) <u>is perfect</u>,
<u>being neither man nor God</u>, but holds the <u>middle order</u> until he
comes out of the inner sanctuary to the realm of body and flesh.
But <u>outside</u> he is a <u>progressing one</u> and stands between the living
and the dead (Nu 16,48), <u>not among those dead to the life of vir-</u>
<u>tue nor among those who live in supreme and perfect happiness</u>,
i.e., <u>perfection</u> (see 236).

Quis Her 84: καὶ ὁ ἱερεὺς μέντοι "<u>ἄνθρωπος οὐκ ἔσται</u>" κατ᾽ αὐτὸν
ὅταν εἰσίῃ εἰς τὰ ἄγια τῶν ἀγίων, "ἕως ἂν ἐξέλθῃ" (Lv 16,
17), οὐ σωματικῶς, ἀλλὰ ταῖς κατὰ ψυχὴν κινήσεσιν. <u>ὁ γὰρ</u>
<u>νοῦς, ὅτε μὲν καθαρῶς λειτουργεῖ θεῷ, οὐκ ἔστιν ἀνθρώ-</u>
<u>πινος, ἀλλὰ θεῖος</u>, ὅτε δὲ ἀνθρωπίνῳ τινί, τέτραπται <u>κατα-</u>
<u>βὰς ἀπ᾽ οὐρανοῦ</u>, μᾶλλον δὲ πεσὼν ἐπὶ γῆν ἐξέρχεται, κἂν
ἔτι μένῃ τὸ σῶμα ἔνδον αὐτῷ.

The context is the interpretation of Gn 15,5 of which two phrases
are commented on: "look up" and "he led him out outside" (76ff.).
The former is represented by the seers (1Sam 9,9) and Israel--the
one who sees God. Some look to the earth and pursue earthly
things and others look up for the manna, the divine word, the
heavenly and incorruptible food. To be led outside is represented by those who go outside the prison of the body and is compared to the <u>priest who is not a man when he enters the Holy of</u>
<u>Holies</u>, not in the sense that he ceases to be a body but in terms
of the movements of the soul. The <u>mind</u> which <u>ministers to God in</u>
<u>purity</u> is <u>not human</u> but <u>divine</u>. When the priest <u>comes out</u> or
<u>serves anything human</u> he <u>descends from heaven</u> or rather <u>falls to</u>
<u>earth</u> although he may be still inside the Holy of Holies as far
as the body is concerned. In comparison with Som ii,231-35 above,
we observe that the pattern of perfection in one case is explic-

itly elaborated and is assumed in this case in the contrast
between being in the Holy of Holies = mind ministering to God in
purity, and being in <u>heaven</u> in a spiritual sense, and coming outside in the sense of ministering to anything human = fall to
<u>earth</u>. That this state of perfection is available to all and not
restricted to the priest is clearly stated:

Quis Her 82: ἢ οὐκ ἂν εἴποιτε, <u>τὸν μὴ τέλειον ἀρχιερέα</u>, ὁπότε
ἐν τοῖς ἀδύτοις τὰς πατρῴους ἀγιστείας ἐπιτελεῖ, ἔνδον
εἶναί τε καὶ ἔξω, <u>ἔνδον</u> μὲν τῷ <u>φανερῷ σώματι</u>, <u>ἔξω δὲ</u>
<u>ψυχῇ τῇ περιφοίτῳ</u> καὶ πεπλανημένῃ, καὶ ἔμπαλιν <u>τινα μηδὲ</u>
<u>γένους ὄντα τοῦ ἱερωμένου</u> θεοφιλῆ καὶ φιλόθεον <u>ἔξω</u> τῶν
περιρραντηρίων <u>ἑστῶτα ἐσωτάτω διατρίβειν</u>, ἀποδημίαν
ἡγούμενον ὅλον τὸν <u>μετὰ σώματος βίον</u>, ὁπότε δὲ δύναιτο
<u>τῇ ψυχῇ μόνῃ</u> ζῆν, ἐν <u>πατρίδι καταμένειν</u> ὑπολαμβάνοντα;

Thus the <u>highpriest who is not perfect</u> is wandering and astray
outside in his soul although bodily inside the inner shrine, on
the other hand, <u>one who does not belong to the priestly line</u> and
is a lover of God and loved by God dwells inside although he is
physically standing outside the area cleansed by lustration.
Such a character considers <u>life with the body a sojourning</u> but
<u>capacity to dwell in the soul alone as remaining in the father-</u>
<u>land</u>. The exemplars of perfection represent types and characters
of the soul and are possibilities for all as we have indicated
in the introductory section.

Congr 105: οἱ μὲν οὖν <u>πολλοὶ</u> τὰς ἐννέα ταύτας μοίρας καὶ τὸν
παγέντα κόσμον ἐξ αὐτῶν ἐτίμησαν, ὁ δὲ <u>τέλειος</u> τὸν
ὑπεράνω τῶν ἐννέα, δημιουργὸν αὐτῶν, δέκατον θεόν. <u>ὅλον</u>
<u>γὰρ ὑπερκύψας τὸ ἔργον</u> ἐπόθει τὸν τεχνίτην, καὶ <u>ἱκέτης</u>
<u>καὶ θεραπευτὴς</u> ἐσπούδαζεν αὐτοῦ γενέσθαι. διὰ τοῦτο
δεκάτην ἐνδελεχῇ τῷ δεκάτῳ καὶ μόνῳ καὶ αἰωνίῳ <u>ὁ ἱερεὺς</u>
ἀνατίθησι.

The context is one of Philo's favourite digressions on the number
ten (89ff.) and the passage above is based on Lv 6,20. The world
is composed of 9 parts: 7 wandering stars and 1 fixed star make
up the 8 parts of heaven, and earth, water and air make up the
ninth part. The <u>many</u> honour these nine parts, but the <u>perfect</u>,
i.e., <u>the priest, rises above the work of the Creator and desires</u>
<u>him</u> and is eager to become his <u>suppliant</u> and <u>servant</u>.

Sac 119: ὁ <u>καταπεφευγὼς</u> ἐπὶ θεὸν καὶ <u>ἱκέτης</u> αὐτοῦ γεγονὼς <u>λόγος</u>
<u>ὀνομάζεται Λευίτης</u>. τοῦτον ἐκ τοῦ μεσαιτάτου καὶ ἡγεμο-
νικωτάτου τῆς ψυχῆς λαβών, τουτέστι προσλαβόμενος καὶ
προσκληρώσας ἑαυτῷ, <u>τῆς τῶν πρεσβείων ἠξίωσε μερίδος</u>,
ὥστε ἐνθένδε δῆλον εἶναι, ὅτι ὁ μὲν 'Ρουβὴν τοῦ 'Ιακώβ,
ὁ δὲ <u>Λευὶ τοῦ 'Ισραὴλ</u> πρωτότοκός ἐστιν, ὁ μὲν τὰ <u>χρόνου</u>,
ὁ δὲ τὰ <u>ἀξιώματος καὶ δυνάμεως</u> φερόμενος <u>πρεσβεῖα</u>.

120: . . . καθάπερ οὖν τῶν 'Ησαῦ πρωτοτοκίων κληρονόμος
'Ιακὼβ ἀνευρίσκεται . . . οὕτως καὶ τὰ 'Ρουβὴν πρεσβεῖα
τοῦ εὐφυοῦς <u>ὁ κεχρημένος ἀρετῇ τελείᾳ Λευὶ</u> οἴσεται. <u>τῆς</u>
<u>τελειότητος</u> δεῖγμα ἐναργέστατον <u>πρόσφυγα</u> γένεσθαι <u>θεοῦ</u>,
<u>καταλιπόντα τὴν τῶν ἐν γενέσει πραγματείαν</u>.

This is an interpretation of Nu 3,12-13 which is quoted immediately prior to the passage. The Levite is the Logos which has taken refuge in God and is his suppliant. He is deemed worthy of the primary portion or portion of the elder and is the first-born of Israel in comparison to Reuben who is the first-born of Jacob. The latter has the primary rank in age and Levi in honour and power. Levi lives a life of perfect virtue/excellence, the most clear proof of perfection is his refuge in God having left dealings with created things. To this may be compared the description of the Levites in Fug 90-92: they are resolved into souls, destitute of body, sense perception, utterance (logos prophorikos) and thus left alone they cleave pure and undisturbed to the One Who is Alone.

Leg All iii,79: καὶ Μελχισεδὲκ βασιλέα τε τῆς εἰρήνης – Σαλὴμ
τοῦτο γὰρ ἑρμηνεύεται – (καὶ) ἱερέα ἑαυτοῦ πεποίηκεν
ὁ θεός (Gn 14,18), οὐδὲν ἔργον αὐτοῦ προδιατυπώσας, ἀλλὰ
τοιοῦτον ἐργασάμενος βασιλέα καὶ εἰρηναῖον καὶ ἱερωσύνης
ἄξιον τῆς ἑαυτοῦ πρῶτον. καλεῖται γὰρ βασιλεὺς δίκαιος,
βασιλεὺς δὲ ἐχθρὸν τυράννῳ, ὅτι ὁ μὲν νόμων, ὁ δὲ ἀνομίας
ἐστιν εἰσηγητής.

81: καλείσθω οὖν ὁ μὲν τύρρανος ἄρχων πολέμου, ὁ δὲ βασιλεὺς
ἡγεμὼν εἰρήνης, Σαλήμ, καὶ προσφερέτω τῇ ψυχῇ τροφὰς
εὐφροσύνης καὶ χαρᾶς πλήρεις . . .

82: ἀλλ᾽ ὁ μὲν Μελχισεδεκ ἀντὶ ὕδατος οἶνον προσφερέτω καὶ
ποτιζέτω καὶ ἀκρατιζέτω ψυχάς, ἵνα κατάσχετοι γένωνται
θείᾳ μέθῃ νηφαλεωτέρᾳ νήψεως αὐτῆς. ἱερεὺς γάρ ἐστι
λόγος κλῆρον ἔχων τὸν ὄντα καὶ ὑψηλῶς περὶ αὐτοῦ καὶ
ὑπερόγκως καὶ μεγαλοπρεπῶς λογιζόμενος . . .

The cursing of the serpent in Gn 3,14-15 without giving it an opportunity for defence is explained by the fact that the serpent (= pleasure) is bad in itself, e.g., Er in Gn 38,7 (65-76). This is followed by counter examples of those who are good without any indication of reason. Thus God made Melchizedek king of peace and His own priest and without expressing before hand a type of his deed, but produced him as such from the start as king, peaceable and worthy of His own priesthood. Contrast is made between king and tyrant (80-81) and between Melchizedek who offers food of joy and gladness to the soul and the Moabites and Ammonites who refused Israel--the seeing one--bread and water (81). Melchizedek instead of water offers unmixed wine to the souls that they may be seized by divine intoxication, more sober than sobriety itself; he is priest and Logos and has God for his portion (cf. Fug 102, pp. 34f. above) and his thoughts of God are high, vast and magnificent.

Congr 99: ἐνθένδε ὁ μὲν ἀσκητικὸς ὁρμηθεὶς εὐχόμενος εἶπε,
"πάντων ὧν ἄν μοι δῷς, δεκάτην ἀποδεκατώσω σοι" (Gn 28,
22), ὁ δὲ χρησμὸς ὁ μετὰ τὰς ἐπινικίους εὐχὰς ἀναγραφείς,

62

ἀς ὁ τὴν αὐτομαθῆ καὶ αὐτοδίδακτον λαχὼν ἱερωσύνην
ποιεῖται Μελχιϲεδέκ, "Ἔδωκε γὰρ αὐτῷ" φησίν "δεκάτην
ἀπὸ πάντων." (Gn 14,20)

The context is a digression on the number ten (89ff.) and the
present discussion is on Lv 27,30 and 32 (94ff.) which is understood as giving thanks to God for the senses and the mind--the
"rod" in vs. 32 is paideia--and the practicer (Jacob) and Abraham
are then cited as examples of such tithing. Melchizedek who
blessed Abraham after the victory received tithes from Abraham
and is described as the one who has received the self-learnt and
self-taught priesthood. That is, the same perfection and status
as Isaac.

4Macc 7,11: ὥσπερ γὰρ ὁ πατὴρ 'Ααρὼν τῷ θυμιατηρίῳ καθωπλισμένος
           διὰ τοῦ ἐθνοπλήθους ἐπιτρέχων τὸν ἐμπυριστὴν ἐνίκησεν
           ἄγγελον, 12: οὕτως ὁ 'Ααρωνίδης 'Ελεαζὰρ διὰ τοῦ πυρὸς
           ὑπερτηκόμενος οὐ μετετράπη τὸν λογισμόν.

The martyrdom of Eleazar, who was burnt, is compared with the
incidents of Nu 17,1-15 (LXX) and the reference to the "angel of
fire" is probably based on Nu 16,35. Eleazar did not swerve his
reasoning although consumed by fire just as Aaron overcame the
angel of fire. Aaron is the example of victory over fire and
Eleazar's martyrdom is patterned after it. In 7,14, Eleazar's
reasoning is described as an Isaac-like reasoning (see above
p. 58; cf. Wis Sol 18,20-25).

Joseph and Asenath XXII(73), 14-20: ἐκράτησε δὲ 'Ασενὲθ τὴν
           χεῖρα Λευί, διότι ἠγάπα αὐτὸν σφόδρα ὑπὲρ πάντας τοὺς
           ἀδελφοὺς 'Ιωσὴφ καὶ ὡς ἄνδρα προφήτην καὶ θεοσεβῆ καὶ
           φοβούμενον τὸν κύριον. ἦν γὰρ ἀνὴρ συνιῶν καὶ προφήτης
           ὑψίστου, καὶ αὐτὸς ἑώρα γράμματα γεγραμμένα ἐν τῷ οὐρανῷ
           καὶ ἀνεγίνωσκεν αὐτά, καὶ ἀπεκάλυπτεν αὐτὰ τῇ 'Ασενὲθ
           κρυφῇ, διότι καὶ αὐτὸς Λευὶ ἠγάπα τὴν 'Ασενὲθ πάνυ καὶ
           ἑώρα τὸν τόπον τῆς καταπαύσεως αὐτῆς ἐν τοῖς ὑψίστοις.

After Asenath's visit to Jacob, she is accompanied by Levi and
Simeon on each side and she holds Levi's hand on account of her
great love for him. Levi is described as a prophet, worshipper
of God and fearer of the Lord. As a prophet of the most high God
he read the writings in heaven (probably astrological knowledge)
and revealed them in secret to Asenath and he saw the place of
her rest in the highest regions (of heaven). We note here that
the terms "priest" and "prophet" have lost their institutional
specificity and have become terms which describe the religious
man in general.[6]

---

[6]Levi acquires striking importance in later Judaism and is
given precedence over Judah (Jub 31,14-15; TestR 6; Test Jud 21,
1-25,1). In the Damascus Document 4,15, Levi seems to have exer-
cised prophetic gifts by speaking of the three nets of Belial in
advance (see further TDNT IV, 236-37).

A similar understanding of the role of the prophet is to be found in Philo. Spec Leg iv,191-92: the true priest is necessarily a prophet and to a prophet nothing is unknown since he has within him the intelligible sun; Quis Her 260-62: all the just (dikaioi) are described as prophets-- Noah, Abraham, Isaac, Jacob and Moses; Quod Deus 138-39: the prophet is the Logos and interpreter of God. It would therefore appear that the title "prophet" in such litera- ture simply describes religious men, who were expected to have divine knowledge. In Wis Sol 7,27: those who possess wisdom are prophets. See TDNT VI, 821-23 for a more comprehensive discussion.

The title "priest" similarly describes in Philo religious status. The ascription of such titles in this generalized sense is to be found in Hellenistic philosophy. For the Stoics only the wise men are priests:

θεοσεβεῖς τε τοὺς σπουδαίους, ἐμπείρους γὰρ εἶναι τῶν περὶ θεοὺς νομίμων, εἶναί τε τὴν εὐσέβειαν ἐπιστήμην θεῶν θεραπείας. . . . μόνους θ' ἱερέας τοὺς σοφούς. (DL VII,119)

Marcus Aurelius describes the man who puts to use the divine genius enthroned within him so as to keep unstained from pleasure, etc. as: ἱερεύς τίς ἐστι καὶ ὑπουργὸς θεῶν . . . (III,4,3). For further discussion see TDNT III, 258-59.

Moses

Sac 5: . . . καὶ γὰρ ᾿Αβραὰμ ἐκλιπὼν τὰ θνητὰ "προστίθεται τῷ θεοῦ λαῷ" (Gn 25,8), καρπούμενος ἀφθαρσίαν, ἴσος ἀγγέλοις γεγονώς. ἄγγελοι γὰρ στρατός εἰσι θεοῦ, ἀσώματοι καὶ εὐδαίμονες ψυχαί. ὁ τε ἀσκητὴς τὸν αὐτὸν τρόπον ᾿Ιακὼβ λέγεται προστίθεσθαι τῷ βελτίονι (Gn 49,33), ὅτε ἐξέλιπε τὸ χεῖρον.

6: ὁ δὲ αὐτομαθοῦς ἐπιστήμης ἀξιωθεὶς ᾿Ισαὰκ ἐκλείπει μὲν καὶ αὐτὸς ὅσον σωματοειδὲς αὐτοῦ τῇ ψυχῇ συνύφαντο, προστίθεται δὲ καὶ προσκληροῦται οὐκεθ' ὡς οἱ πρότεροι λαῷ, "γένει" δέ, καθάπερ φησὶ Μωυσῆς (Gn 35,29). γένος μὲν γὰρ ἓν τὸ ἀνωτάτω, λαὸς δὲ ὄνομα πλειόνων.

7: ὅσοι μὲν οὖν μαθήσει καὶ διδασκαλίᾳ προκόψαντες ἐτελειώ- θησαν, προσκληροῦνται πλείοσιν. . . . οἱ δὲ ἀνθρώπων μὲν ὑφηγήσεις ἀπολελοιπότες, μαθηταὶ δὲ εὐφυεῖς θεοῦ γεγονότες, τὴν ἄπονον ἐπιστήμην ἀνειληφότες, εἰς τὸ ἄφθαρτον καὶ τελεώτατον γένος μετανίστανται κλῆρον ἀμείνω τῶν προτέρων ἐνδεδεγμένοι, ὧν ὁ ᾿Ισαὰκ θιασώτης ἀνωμο- λόγηται.

8: . . . εἰσὶ δὲ οὓς ἀνωτέρω προαγαγὼν εἴδη μὲν καὶ γένη πάντα ὑπερπτῆναι παρεσκεύασεν, ἵδρυσε δὲ πλησίον ἑαυτοῦ, καθὰ καὶ Μωυσῆς ᾧ φησι, "σὺ δὲ αὐτοῦ στῆθι μετ᾿ ἐμοῦ" (Dt 5,31).

"And he added" (Gn 4,2) is the subject under discussion (1-10). When the good opinion (dogma) Abel, which ascribes all things to God, is added, then the foolish opinion Cain, which ascribes all things to the human mind, is removed. This idea associated with the phrase "to add" leads to the comparisons in the passage quoted. When Abraham leaves mortality "he is added to the people of God" (Gn 25,8) and this is understood to mean that he gains immortality on the level of being made equal to the angels--the incorporeal and blessed souls. The same is true of the practicer Jacob (Gn 49,33).

But Isaac who is deemed worthy of self-learnt knowledge is added not to the people but to the "genus," which is one and above all, in contrast to the "people" who are many. Those who have been made perfect by progress through learning and teaching are alloted among the many. But the disciples of God with natural talent and who have dispensed with the instruction of men obtain knowledge without labour, are translated into the immortal and most perfect genus and receive a better lot than the former (Abraham and Jacob). Of this fraternity Isaac is the leader (thiasotēs).

There are others whom God leads higher and prepares them to soar above all species and genus and sets them beside himself-- just as Moses (Dt 5,31). Moses is translated by the word (rhema) and drawn up to God himself from earthly things through the same Logos by which God created the world. He is Sophos and Teleios and like God unchangeable (Ex 7,1; Dt 34,6; see 8-10; cf. Post 28). Thus the perfection of Moses and destiny after death of Moses is higher than Abraham, Jacob and Isaac. This is to be understood in terms of a hierarchy of proximities to God and Moses in his perfection stands closest. (Cf. Ebr 94)[7]

Post 76: λέγει (γὰρ) ἐπὶ μὲν τοῦ ᾿Αβραὰμ οὕτως (Gn 11,29), ἐπὶ (δὲ) τοῦ ᾿Ιακώβ (Gn 28,2), ἐπὶ δὲ τοῦ ᾿Ααρών (Ex 6,23).

77: ᾿Ισαὰκ δὲ καὶ Μωυσῆς λαμβάνουσι μέν, οὐ δ᾿ ἑαυτῶν δὲ λαμβάνουσιν, ἀλλ᾿ ὁ μὲν ᾿Ισαὰκ ὅτε εἰσῆλθεν εἰς τὸν οἶκον τῆς μητρὸς λαβεῖν λέγεται (Gn 24,67), Μωυσῆ δὲ ὁ ἄνθρωπος παρ᾿ ᾧ κατῴκησε τὴν θυγατέρα Σεπφώραν ἐκδίδοται (Ex 2,21).

78: τούτων δ᾿ οὐ παρέργως αἱ διαφοραὶ παρὰ τῷ νομοθέτῃ μεμήνυται. τοῖς μὲν γὰρ ἀσκηταῖς προκόπτουσι καὶ βελτιουμένοις ἡ ἑκούσιος αἵρεσις τἀγαθοῦ μαρτυρεῖται, ἵνα μηδ᾿ ὁ πόνος ἀστεφάνωτος ἀφεθῇ. τοῖς δὲ αὐτοδιδάκτου καὶ αὐτομαθοῦς σοφίας ἀξιωθεῖσιν ἕπεται τὸ μὴ δι᾿ ἑαυτῶν παρὰ θεοῦ δ᾿ ἐγγύασθαι λόγον καὶ λαμβάνειν τὴν σοφῶν σύμβιον ἐπιστήμην.

"And Lamech took to himself two wives . . ." (Gn 4,19) is the passage under discussion. Good men and evil men choose things appropriate to themselves. In each of the cases of Abraham (Gn 11,29), Jacob (Gn 28,2) and Aaron (Ex 6,23) there is the phrase "take to himself a wife." On the contrary, Isaac and Moses do not take to themselves, Isaac takes when he enters his mother's

---

[7] In the LXX, Logos and Rhēma are full synonyms which translate dābār (for statistics see TDNT IV, 92). Philo also uses them synonymously, e.g., he calls the manna in Fug 137: ῥῆμα θεοῦ καὶ λόγον θεῖον.

house (Gn 24,67) and Moses is given Zipporah (Ex 6,23). The contrast is between those who progress and become better through practice and voluntarily choose the good and those deemed worthy of self-taught and self-learnt wisdom, and who receive from God, and not through themselves, the Logos as their betrothed and knowledge--the life companion of the wise. Here Moses is classed with the self-learnt and self-taught Isaac, though in terms of proximity to God he ranks higher and thus also in terms of perfection (see Sac 5-8 above).

Quod Deus 109: παρατηρητέον δ' ὅτι τὸν μὲν Νῶε φησιν εὐαρεστῆσαι ταῖς τοῦ ὄντος δυνάμεσι, κυρίῳ τε καὶ θεῷ, Μωυσῆν δὲ τῷ δορυφορουμένῳ πρὸς τῶν δυνάμεων καὶ δίχα αὐτῶν κατὰ τὸ εἶναι μόνον νοουμένῳ, λέγεται γὰρ ἐκ προσώπου θεοῦ ὅτι "εὕρηκας χάριν παρ' ἐμοί" (Ex 33,17), δεικνύντος ἑαυτὸν τὸν ἄνευ πάντος ἑτέρου.

110: οὕτως ἄρα τὴν μὲν κατὰ Μωυσῆν ἄκραν σοφίαν ἀξιοῖ χάριτος ὁ ὢν αὐτὸς δι' ἑαυτοῦ μόνου, τὴν δὲ ἀπεικονισθεῖσαν ἐκ ταύτης δευτέραν καὶ εἰδικωτέραν οὖσαν διὰ τῶν ὑπηκόων δυνάμεων . . .

This is an interpretation of Gn 6,8 (6,9 LXX): "Noah found grace with the Lord God" (104ff.). Thus Noah was pleasing to the powers of God--Lord and God--whereas Moses was pleasing to God himself with none of the other powers (Ex 33,17). The One who is deems worthy of grace the supreme wisdom represented by Moses through the agency of His own self, whereas the wisdom which is its image--secondary and species-like--is deemed worthy of God's grace through his subject powers. What is at issue here is the directness of relationship to God.[8]

Plant 26: τοιγαροῦν Μωυσῆς ὁ ταμίας καὶ φύλαξ τῶν τοῦ ὄντος ὀργίων ἀνακεκλήσεται, λέγεται γὰρ ἐν Λευιτικῇ βίβλῳ, "ἀνεκάλεσε Μωυσῆν" (Lv 1,1). ἀνακεκλήσεται δὲ καὶ ὁ τῶν δευτερείων ἀξιωθεὶς Βεσελεήλ. καὶ γὰρ τοῦτον ἀνακαλεῖ ὁ θεὸς πρὸς τὴν τῶν ἱερῶν κατασκευήν τε καὶ ἐπιμέλειαν ἔργων.

27: ἀλλ' ὁ μὲν τὰ δευτερεῖα τῆς ἀνακλήσεως, Μωυσῆς δὲ ὁ πάνσοφος οἴσεται τὰ πρωτεῖα.

Plant 1-26 is a description of the universe and its parts which is made by the perfect planter God. Man is distinguished from other creatures by his erect body and mind which is made after God's image (Gn 2,7; 1,27). The eyes of the soul pass beyond the bounds of the universe to the uncreated. Such yearning for wisdom and knowledge is described in the sacred oracles as "to be

---

[8]Goodenough is inaccurate in his comment on this passage when he fails to note the distinction in Philo between reaching the Logos and God: "In contrast with Moses, Noah went only as far as the Powers. And so the conclusion is clear for the Mystery. The true goal for all is to rise like Moses to the ὁ ὢν or to ὁ τοῦ ὄντος λόγος" (p. 132).

called upwards" (17-23). <u>Moses</u> is thus called up (Lv 1,1). He
is compared to Bezalel who is also called up (Ex 31,2). But
whereas <u>Bezalel</u> bears the <u>secondary</u> honours of the call, <u>Moses</u>
bears the <u>primary</u> honours. Further comparisons are made in 27:
Bezalel makes the shadows (= images), but Moses makes the archetypes. (Cf. Leg All iii,102)

QE II,29: (Ex 24,2) Why does he say, "Moses alone shall come
near to God, and they shall not come near, and the people
shall not go up with them"?
O most excellent and God-worthy ordinance, that the
<u>prophetic mind alone should approach God</u> and that <u>those</u>
<u>in second place</u> should go up, making (lit. "cutting"--
prokoptōn) a path to heaven, while <u>those in the third</u>
<u>place</u> and the turbulent characters of the people should
neither go up above nor go up with them but those worthy
of beholding should be <u>beholders of the blessed path</u>
<u>above</u>. But that "(Moses) alone shall go up" is said most
naturally. For when the <u>prophetic mind</u> becomes divinely
inspired and filled with God, it becomes like a monad,
not being at all mixed with any of those things associated with duality. But he who is <u>resolved into the</u>
<u>nature of unity</u>, is said <u>to come near God</u> in a kind of
<u>family relation</u>, for having given up and left behind all
<u>mortal kinds</u>, he is changed into the divine, so that <u>such</u>
men become <u>kin to God</u> and <u>truly divine</u>. (Marcus: Loeb)

We observe the pattern of perfection according to one's proximity
to God. The prophetic mind, represented by Moses, alone "approaches God," "comes near God," is "kin to God," etc. Those on
the second level are the progressors and those on the third level
are merely beholders of the blessed path. That Moses is a representative of a certain type can be seen in the generalization at
first to "prophetic mind" and finally to "such men become kin to
God and truly divine."

QE II,46: (Ex 24,16b) Why is the mountain covered with a cloud
for six days, and Moses called above on the seventh day?
. . . But the <u>calling above of the prophet is a second</u>
<u>birth</u> better than the first. For the latter is mixed
with a body and had corruptible parents, while the former
. . . which has <u>no mother</u> but only a father, who is (the
Father) of all. Wherefore the calling above or, as we
have said, the <u>divine birth</u> happened to come about for
him <u>in accordance with the ever-virginal nature of the</u>
<u>hebdomad</u>. For he is called on the seventh day, in this
(respect) differing from the earth-born first-moulded man,
for the latter came into being from the earth with a body,
while the former (came) from the ether and without a body.
Wherefore the most appropriate number, six was assigned
to the earth-born man, while to the one differently born
(was assigned) the higher nature of the hebdomad.
(Marcus: Loeb)

Greek fragment: . . . ἡ δὲ ἀνάκλησις τοῦ προφήτου δεύτερα
<u>γένεσίς ἐστι</u> τῆς προτέρας ἀμείνων. ἑβδόμη δὲ ἀνακαλεῖται
ἡμέρᾳ, <u>ταύτῃ διαφέρων τοῦ πρωτοπλάστου</u>, ὅτι ἐκεῖνος μὲν
ἐκ γῆς καὶ μετὰ σώματος συνίστατο, οὗτος δὲ ἄνευ σώματος.
διὸ τῷ μὲν γηγενεῖ ἀριθμὸς οἰκεῖος ἀπενεμήθη ἑξάς, τούτῳ

δὲ ἡ ἱερωτάτη φύσις τῆς ἑβδομάδος. (Harris, pp. 60-61; quoted in Loeb)

The calling above of the prophet/Moses is described as a second birth. It is of the nature of the seventh--without mother and ever-virgin (cf. Mos ii,210; Decal 102; Spec Leg ii,56). He is superior to the earth-born man in that he has no body. What is implied hereby is probably that Moses in his perfection represents the pure mind (cf. Agr 80; Mut 207; QE II,44). This bodiless state of perfection is not beyond present human possibility --Mut 32-34.

Leg All iii,129: ἀλλ' οὗτος μέν (i.e., Aaron), ὡς ἔφην, ἔχων τὸ πάθος ἰᾶσθαι αὐτὸ πειρᾶται τοῖς λεχθεῖσι σωτηρίοις φαρμάκοις, Μωυσῆς δὲ ὅλον τὸν θυμὸν ἐκτέμνειν καὶ ἀποκόπτειν οἴεται δεῖν τῆς ψυχῆς, οὐ μετριοπάθειαν ἀλλὰ συνόλως ἀπάθειαν ἀγαπῶν.

131: . . . μοῖραν γὰρ ὁ θεὸς ἔνειμεν ἀρίστην τῷ σοφῷ τὸ ἐκτέμνειν τὰ πάθη δύνασθαι. ὁρᾷς πῶς ὁ τέλειος τελείαν ἀπάθειαν αἰεὶ μελετᾷ.

132: ἀλλ' ὅ γε προκόπτων δεύτερος ὢν 'Ααρὼν μετριοπάθειαν, ὡς ἔφην, ἀσκεῖ, ἐκτεμεῖν γὰρ ἔτι τὸ στῆθος καὶ τὸν θυμὸν ἀδυνατεῖ. φέρει δ' ἐπ' αὐτὴν τὸν ἡνίοχον σὺν ταῖς προσφυέσιν ἀρεταῖς λόγον, τὸ λογίον, ἐφ' οὗ δήλωσίς ἐστι καὶ ἀλήθεια.

135: . . . ἄπονος δ' ἐστὶν ᾧ ὁ θεὸς χαρίζεται κατὰ πολλὴν περιουσίαν τὰ ἀγαθὰ τέλεια. βραχύτερος δ' εὑρίσκεται καὶ ἀτελέστερος ὁ πόνῳ κτώμενος τὴν ἀρετὴν τοῦ ἀπόνως καὶ εὐμαρῶς αὐτὴν παρὰ θεοῦ λαβόντος Μωυσῆ, ὡς γὰρ αὐτὸ τὸ πόνειν βραχύτερον καὶ ἐλαττόν ἐστι τοῦ ἀπόνου, οὕτω καὶ τὸ ἀτελὲς τοῦ τελείου καὶ τὸ μανθάνον τοῦ αὐτομαθοῦς.

The context is the interpretation of Gn 3,14 (114ff.)--"On the breast and on the belly you shall go." The breast is the seat of anger (thymos) and the belly of desire (epithymia). These are curbed by reason and Ex 28,30 is used to illustrate this (118-28). Whereas Aaron attempts to cure the passion (thymos) with saving medicines ("Showing and "Truth"--virtues), he is inferior to Moses who cuts out the passion (Lv 8,29; 8,28 LXX). Moses is the Sophos and Teleios who received from God the best share, namely, the ability to cut off the passions, and to pursue or practice perfect lack of passion--Stoic "apatheia." Aaron of Ex 28,30 (see above pp. 58-59), the one who makes progress (prokoptōn), holds second rank to Moses and practices moderation--Aristotelian "metriopatheia"--being yet unable to cut off the breast, namely, anger (thymos).[9] This point is further illustrated from Lv 7,24

---

[9] Philo gives a different understanding of "apatheia" in QG IV,15 where it is understood as ungratefulness and shamelessness. This has caused unnecessary problems for scholars (see Völker, p. 267; Goodenough, p. 143) since the dual meaning of "apatheia" is a commonplace in Hellenistic philosophy. DL VII,177: φασὶ

68

LXX (133-34). The man to whom God bestows the <u>perfect goods</u>
in superabundance is <u>free from labour</u>. <u>He who acquires virtue/</u>
<u>excellence/perfection through labour falls short and is less</u>
<u>perfect than Moses who receives it from God without labour and</u>
<u>easily</u>. Labour itself is inferior to that which is free from
labour, imperfect to that which is perfect and that which is
learnt to that which is self-learnt. The same comparison between
the <u>perfect</u>, represented by Moses, and the <u>progressing one</u> is
drawn in the subsequent sections (140-60) which deals with the
"belly"--the symbol of pleasure.

The perfection of Moses is indicated in other ways by Philo.
<u>Leg All ii,80</u>: Moses loves incorporeal virtues, while we, unable
to put off the body, long after corporeal virtue. <u>Leg All ii,91-</u>
<u>92</u>: It is fitting for those not yet perfect to flee passions,
but the perfect Moses does not desist from warfare against passions. He takes the serpent pleasure by the tail and it becomes
a rod = paideia. <u>Virt 70</u>: Moses is the archetypal pattern for
all future leaders. <u>Mig 168-71</u>: Moses on the way to the supreme
vision of God has God as his guide on the way (Ex 33,15), whereas
Abraham until perfection has the Logos for his guide (see above
p. 37). Cf. Fug 140-41. <u>Mut 208</u>: Moses is the purest Nous and
Aaron is his logos. <u>QE II,44</u>: Moses/mind obtained the better
part, God, whereas Aaron/logos obtained the lesser, man (EX
24,14).

<u>Mos ii,288</u>: When Moses migrated from earth to heaven he was
immortalized and his body and soul were resolved into one nature
--mind as pure as sunlight (cf. Virt 76-77). <u>QG I,86</u>: Moses,
Enoch and Elijah had the gift of translation from earth to heaven
(cf. QE II,44).

Summary

The basis of the distinction among the exemplars of perfection is paideutic--between those who are progressing to perfection through teaching and practice and those who are perfect by
nature from the beginning and need neither teaching nor practice.
It is closely related to the pattern of thought which associates
perfection with exclusive and direct relationship with God compared to that which is indirect and mediated. The terminology
associated with these distinctions can be schematized as follows:

δὲ καὶ ἀπαθῆ εἶναι τὸν σοφόν, διὰ τὸ ἀνέμπτωτον εἶναι. εἶναι δὲ
καὶ ἄλλον ἀπαθῆ τὸν φαῦλον, ἐν ἴσῳ λεγόμενον τῷ σκληρῷ καὶ ἀτέγκ-
τῳ. Cf. Plutarch's description of Osiris as the Logos: λόγος
αὐτὸς καθ' ἑαυτὸν ἀμιγὴς καὶ ἀπαθής (Is. et Os. 373b).

	Progress	-	Perfection

Abraham

Leg All iii,244	To beget from encyclical paideia (=Hagar).	-	To beget from perfect virtue (=Sarah).
Mut 34, 39	Follower of gentler and tamer sophia - pleasing through good deeds.	-	Enoch pleases God alone unencumbered by body and human concerns.
Mig 139-40	Walk in the foot-steps of the Logos (128).	-	Passing into eternal nature.
Mig 166-67	Labour, art.	-	Natural gift, self-taught nature.
Mig 173-75	Divine Logos is leader	-	God is leader; Logos is co-attendant.
Mut 270	Empty of sophia	-	Self-willed and self-impelled character; Sophos is attendant of God.

Jacob/Israel

Ebr 82	Exchanges hearing, words and progress Jacob - name for learning and progress.	-	for sight, deeds and perfection. Israel - name for perfection and vision of God.
Mig 28-30	Perfect Athlete - Jacob; Logos is father of practicers and Sophia is dwelling place of virtue-loving souls.	-	In the land (= Logos and Sophia) awaits Isaac, self-learnt and self-taught type; does not partake of milk; inheritance without toil; companionship of God.
Mig 38-39	Practicer eager to exchange ears; rise above lot of hearing; Jacob is name for learning and teaching.	-	for eyes; obtain lot of sight; Israel is the one who sees.
Fug 43	Practicer Jacob flees evil (Esau) and unable to live with	-	perfect and self-learnt virtue.

Isaac

QG IV, 88		-	Has no need of exhortation; self-teacher and self-taught mind.
Conf 74		-	Isaac, self-learnt type alone inherits realities.
Mig 139-40		-	Divine offshoot; self-taught is fed by no one, food for others, capable of teaching, not needing to learn.
Congr 36,38		-	Self-learnt kind needs neither practice nor teaching nor arts; has at hand perfect gifts of God.
Fug 166-67		-	Self-learnt and self-taught sophos not

Progress	-	Perfection
		improved by searchings, practice or labours; finds sophia ready at hand; not man but purest thought, good by nature than by study.
Fug 172-74	Teacher can produce progress.	-	God alone, the best Nature, can produce full perfection; one nourished by the principles of self-taught type lives in peace = 7th day rest of creation; rest in God is alone nourishing, enjoyable and secures the greatest good.
Mut 130-31		-	God gives somethings peculiarly his own - Isaac; not man, joy and laughter within; son of God - comfort and cheer to peaceful souls.
Mut 255-60	Offspring of lower paideia (Hagar) - taught virtue. Food from earth for other men.	-	Offspring of virtue (Sarah) - self-learnt virtue. Virtue without labour and trouble; requires no nurture, perfect from the beginning; food from heaven for the seeing kind = heavenly sophia and sabbath year; self-productive and self-sufficient in nature.
Som i, 160, 162	Abraham is symbol of knowledge which is taught. He is immigrant and stranger. Needs God's guidance and kindness.	-	Isaac is symbol of knowledge which is self-hearing, self-taught and self-learnt. He is indigenous and native. Needs only God's grace; not improved by admonition; good and perfect from the beginning.
Sac 78-79		-	Self-learnt sophia does not need to hear heroic deeds - historians and poets - since hearing has been replaced by sight; pupil of God.
Det 29-30		-	Self-learnt sophia has God as guide and fellow-traveler; desires to be alone with Him.

High Priest/Aaron, Levi and Melchizedek

| Leg All iii,45 | | - | Aaron/Logos when perfected enters Hor = Light = Truth. |

	Progress	-	Perfection
Som ii, 231-35	Aaron outside the Holy of Holies, in the realm of body and flesh, is the progressing one. Not among those dead to the life of virtue nor among those who live in supreme and perfect happiness.	-	When he enters the Holy of Holies, he is not man but a minister of God, perfect, neither man nor God - middle taxis.
Quis Her 84	Priest/Mind when it serves anything human descends from heaven, falls to earth and comes out of the Holy of Holies even if his body is still inside.	-	Priest when he enters the Holy of Holies is not man; mind ministering to God in purity is not human but divine.
Congr 105	Many honour the nine parts of the universe.	-	The perfect/priest honours the tenth - God; rising above the work of the creator he desires the creator and is eager to be His suppliant and servant.
Sac 119-20	Reuben is first born of Jacob, has primacy in age. Jacob is heir of the first born's rights of Esau.	-	Levi is first born of Israel, has primacy in honour and power. Levi is heir of the prerogatives of Reuben = natural talent. Levite is Logos and suppliant and takes refuge in God; worthy of primary portion; Levi lives life of perfect virtue; clearest proof of perfection is refuge in God having left dealings with creation.
Leg All iii, 79-82			Melchizedek is from the start king, peaceable and worthy of God's own priesthood. He is priest and Logos and has God for his portion.
Congr 99		-	Melchizedek obtained the self-learnt and self-taught priesthood.
		Moses	
Sac 5-8		-	Abraham leaves mortality, added to people of God = angels; same is true of practicer Jacob. Those made perfect by progress through learning and teaching have their lot among the many (=people of God). Isaac, self-learnt knowledge, disciples of God

	Progress	-	Perfection
			with natural talent who have dispensed with instruction of men, receive a better lot than former - added to genus (one, perfect and immortal).
			Moses and others like him soar above species and genus and God sets them beside Himself.
Post 76-78	Abraham, Jacob and Aaron - those who progress and become better through practice, choose the good voluntarily.	-	Moses and Isaac, deemed worthy of self-taught and self-learnt wisdom, receive from God Logos as betrothed and knowledge, life companion of the wise (sophoi).
Quod Deus 109-10	Noah - wisdom is the image (of Mosaic wisdom), secondary and species-like, receives grace through God's powers.		Wisdom - Moses like - receives grace through God's own agency, without His powers.
Plant 26-27	Bezalel bears secondary honours of the upward call.		Moses bears primary honours of the upward call.
QE II, 29	Those in second place cut (prokoptōn!) a path to heaven.	-	Moses/prophetic mind alone approaches God; becomes like a monad, resolved into unity, comes near God; kin to God and truly divine.
QE II, 46		-	Calling up of the prophet Moses is a second birth (=divine birth); it is like the ever-virginal, motherless character of the Hebdomad; without body.
	Earth born first moulded man with body.		
Leg All iii,129-35	Aaron the progresser holds second rank to Moses, practices metriopatheia. Virtue through labour falls short and less perfect. That which is learnt.	-	Moses, sophos and perfect, received best portion from God, practices apatheia. Moses received it easily and without labour from God. That which is self-learnt.

For Philo the contemporary significance of the "sacred books"--especially that which deals with "genealogy" (the study of the descent of heroes in search of examples of human perfection/arete, cf. Marrou, Education, pp. 229-34, esp. 233-34)--lay in the eternal character of the OT persons as types of arete/excellence/perfection rather than in their past history as mortal men (cf. Mos ii,45-52). The content of sacred scripture is concerning facts of nature and not mortal men (Som i,167-72); not concerning man and woman, but traits of the soul (QG IV,88); not about mortal men but types of good men (QG IV,103); the inquiry of the theologian is about characters and types and virtues and not about persons created and born (QG IV,137). The statements that Isaac is not a man but purest thought, good by nature and not by study (Fug 166-67), best of good emotions and joy and laughter within (Mut 130-31) are to be understood in the same way as referring to Isaac's significance for contemporary man as a type of perfection. So also the priestly state of perfection is not restricted to one who is a priest by birth (Quis Her 82).

Abraham represents the type of character of virtue/perfection which progresses and is perfected by teaching and education (besides passages quoted above see QG IV,175 and Praem 27). His progress is characterized by encyclical paideia, pleasing God through good deeds, leadership of the Logos and walking in its footsteps, labour and art (technē). Perfection consists in his begetting from perfect aretē (=Sarah), leadership of God and coattendance of the Logos, passing into eternal nature, equality to angels and reaching equality with the self-taught and naturally talented perfection of Isaac.

Jacob is the type of perfection/virtue acquired through practice and exercise. It is the name for learning and progress, hearing and teaching and the Logos is its father. In perfection, he exchanges hearing for sight, progress for perfection and his name is changed to Israel, the one who sees God. Like Abraham, his perfection is to reach the level of the self-taught type, Isaac--an inheritance without labour/toil.

Isaac represents the highest type of paideutic perfection, namely, self-learnt and self-taught virtue. Or in other words, he is perfection in the fullest sense and the goal of both teaching and practice, Abraham and Jacob. He needs neither exhortation nor admonition, neither practice nor teaching nor the arts, needs no nurture, but is perfect and good by nature from the very beginning. This perfection is characterized by seventh day rest of God after creation, the sabbatical year, heavenly food/sophia, has God for its guide and fellow-traveller and is something which God alone can effect and is peculiarly his own--joy and inward laughter.

Aaron outside the Holy of Holies represents like Abraham and Jacob the progressing one who becomes better through practice. Inside the Holy of Holies he is neither man nor God but a minister (leitourgos) of God and perfect. At death Aaron (=Logos) when perfected enters Hor = Light = Truth. Levi (and Levite) is

Logos and suppliant of God and lives a life of perfect virtue the clearest proof of which is his refuge in God having left dealings with created things. His perfection like Isaac's represents "natural talent." The priest honours God and rising above creation is eager to be God's suppliant and servant. Melchizedek obtained a perfect priesthood which is characterized as self-learnt and self-taught. He is priest and Logos and has God for his portion. He is from the start king, peaceable and worthy of God's own priesthood. The best prize which the practicer Jacob is unable to aim for is ministry to the Only God (therapeia) and great high priesthood to Him alone (cf. Fug 40,42-43).[10]

Moses' perfection like that of Isaac's is self-learnt and self-taught. His relationship to God is one of immediacy--God sets him beside himself, receives grace through God's exclusive agency, approaches God, comes near God, is kin to God, etc. At times Philo places the perfection of Moses above that of Isaac in terms of his destiny after death (Sac 5-8) and winning the crown of the holy contests of virtues, namely, special rewards of being king, legislator, prophet and highpriest (see, Praem 49-53). His prophetic call is described as a second birth (=divine birth) which has the qualities of the Hebdomad--ever-virginal and motherless.

Some Other Aspects of Perfection

Perfection and Paraenesis: While Abraham is not yet perfect he is obedient to the paraenesis of Sarah (=perfect virtue; Leg All iii,244). The perfect Isaac on the other hand has no need of exhortation (QG IV,88) and is not improved by admonition (nouthetein) (Som i,160-62). This point has been noted above in connection with the anthropos (see above pp. 38-39; Leg All i,92 and QG I,8).

---

[10]Because of Goodenough's misunderstanding of the theme of perfection in Philo (see note at the end of p. 109), he has failed to notice the two aspects of Aaronic priesthood--as the one who is progressing outside the Holy of Holies and Aaron as perfect when truly inside the Holy of Holies. Goodenough's discussion of the 'Mystery of Aaron' (Chap. IV, By Light, Light), therefore, has serious errors. He states: "The Mystery of Aaron got its symbolism from the great Jerusalem cultus, the temple and the priesthood, and was a worship of God from the point of view of the material world. . . . The objective symbolism of the Higher Mystery was the holy of holies with the ark, a level of spiritual experience which was no normal part of even the high-priesthood" (p. 96). That this is untenable is clear from the passages we have discussed above (pp. 58-62).

Perfection and Immediacy to God: This is expressed in a
variety of ways.[11] The excellence of the type of Enoch lies in
the dissolution of the earthly portion and his total devotion to
pleasing God (Mut 34-39); in perfection the Logos and Abraham
become attendants (opadoi) of God as leader (Mig 173-75 and Mut
270); the inheritance of Isaac is without toil/labour and the
source of such goods is companionship (sunodos) of God (Mig 28-
30); the practicer Jacob is unable to reach the best prize--
ministry (therapeia) to the only God and high-priesthood to Him
alone (Fug 40,42); Isaac, self-learnt sophia, desires to be alone
with God, fellow-traveller and guide of his soul (Det 29-30);
Melchizedek has God for his portion (Leg All iii,79-82); the excellence of Moses over Isaac lies in his greater proximity to God
(Det 5,31; Sac 5-8); Moses, the prophetic mind, alone approaches

---

[11]The vision of God of which Israel is the main representative is only one among the several ways by which the theme of perfection and immediacy to God is expressed (cf. Som i,117, pp. 34-
35 above; Som i,238, p. 37 above; see under Jacob/Israel, pp.69ff.
above). It is also the one most noticed by scholars. The more
general background of this concern with a direct relationship to
God is the contemplative piety which had its roots in Plato and
flowered in the Hellenistic era (cf. A-J. Festugiere, Personal
Religion among the Greeks, esp. Chaps. VII and VIII; in conclusion he writes: "I have tried to show you that there was,
throughout the history of Greek religion, from at least the time
of Heraclitus and the tragedians, a desire to enter into direct,
intimate, and personal contact with the divinity," p. 139; His
sources in Chap. VIII are mainly Albinus and the Hermetic trac-
tates and he does not recognize that Philo is an important example of such piety). Both Völker and Festugiere deny that this
"mystical" union with God has its roots in mystery religion and
they agree that the language of ecstacy in Philo is purely literary (Festugière, La Révélation D'Hermès Trismégiste, II, p. 584,
f.n. 1; Völker, Fortschritt und Vollendung, pp. 283-88). Goodenough (JBL 58 (1939), p. 58) incorrectly accuses Völker of not
dealing with the mystical side of Philo. In fact, he devotes pp.
288-317 to the question of ecstatic experience and vision of God.
See especially Festugière, ibid., pp. 545-51 where he shows the
use of the language of initiations in Plato's Symposium and
Philo's dependence on it (Leg All i,44; iii,51; Som i,62-64; 184;
Fug 75). What is needed is a study of the language of mystery
religions and ecstatic phenomenon in Hellenistic philosophical
writings and the manner of its use therein for proper evaluation
of such language in Philo. (Cf. Plotinus VI. 9.11: literary use
of the language of mystery to describe the union of the soul with
the One. Examples of such literary usage in Plato are numerous.
Cf. Phaedrus 250b-252a.)

Furthermore, the vision of God in Philo is never that of the
essence of God (Spec Leg i,43-44; Post 167-69; Fug 161-65) but
only the existence of God (Praem 39-40). Wolfson's attempt to
show that the unknowability of God is probably original with
Philo is doubtful (Wolfson, Philo, II, 110-26; cf. Festugiere,
Personal Religion among the Greeks, 126-29).

God, comes near God and having left behind all mortal kinds becomes kin to God (QE II,29).

Perfection and the Body/Flesh/Creation: Aaron outside the Holy of Holies as the progresser is in the realm of body and flesh (Som ii,231-35); The priest's entry into the Holy of Holies is the ministry of the mind to God in purity (Quis Her 84); Levi takes refuge in God, having left dealings with created things-- the most clear proof of perfection (Sac 119-20); the second birth of Moses is without the body (QE II,46). In the paragraph imme- diately above, cf. Mut 34-39 and QE II,29.

Perfection and God's Grace; Metaphor of Rain: The idea of perfection/arete by nature (natural talent), that which is self- learnt and self-taught and good by nature rather than by study (Som i,160-62; 167; Fug 166-67), is easily associated in Philo's mind with the divine and that which stands in the closest rela- tionship to God. In fact, God is called in this context the "best nature" who alone can produce full perfection (Fug 172- 74).[12] That which is by nature is by divine agency, a free act of God's will (see Wolfson, Philo II, 196-200, for its background in Greek philosophy). The toilless inheritance of Isaac is the result of the readily available goods/benefits the source of which is companionship of the bountiful (philodoros) God, and these goods/benefits come down as rain from this source (Mig 28- 30); Isaac has at hand the perfect gifts of God breathed in by the primary/elder graces of God and God rains from heaven above the self-learnt and self-taught good (Congr 36,38); the self- learnt and self-taught sophos finds wisdom ready at hand rained

---

[12]A different understanding of physis is implied in Abr 53 and Mos ii,66 where it means the native talents necessary for education (cf. Albinus, Didaskalikos, I,2). W. Völker concludes incorrectly that the former is Aristotelian (Pol VII,13) and the supremacy of Isaac's virtue by nature is based on Philo's Jewish piety: "Wie man sieht, übernimmt Philo einen Terminus aus der platonisch-aristotelischen Philosophie, deutet ihn aber um, indem er ihn von seiner jüdischen frommen Haltung aus als ein gött- liches Gnadengeschenk auffasst" (Fortschritt und Vollendung, p. 156). But already in Aristotle in a discussion of the three types of virtue we find a different meaning of physis, namely, in the sense of "divine cause" (Eth Nic X,9,1179b,20-23; cf. Wolfson, Philo, II, 196-97). The idea that virtue really comes by divine dispensation and not by nature or teaching is the con- clusion of Pl Meno 99e-100. The idea of the superiority of natural talent goes back to the old aristocratic scorn for the self-educated (cf. Marrou, History of Education, p. 68; Jaeger, Paideia, III,63-64 and further in the index under "nature"). For the Stoics nature and God are synonymous, e.g., the active prin- ciple is called both God and Nature (DL VII,88; cf. Armstrong, An Introduction to Ancient Philosophy, p. 123).

from heaven above (Fug 166-67); God rains virtue that is without
toil and trouble (Mut 255-60); Isaac, knowledge self-learnt and
self-taught by nature, needs only God's grace (to charizesthai)
and became good and perfect through the gifts (doreai) rained
from above (Som i,160-62); the man to whom God graciously bestows
(charizesthai) the perfect goods is free from labour (Leg All
iii,135).

Grace/Charis constitutes for Philo a basic theological
principle. The asteios (cultured man) finds this to be
the highest truth, that χάριν ὄντα θεοῦ τὰ πάντα. God
bestows no gift of grace on Himself, He needs nothing.
Creation is motivated by His goodness (Platonic), the
eldest of the graces (Quod Deus 107-8); the cultic offerings of men are not something given to God but a small
symbol of thankfulness to God who needs no gifts but continually and always showers his graces for "all things
are his possessions and gifts" (Spec Leg ii,179-80); "for
all things, O Master, are thy graces and gifts" (ibid.,
219); "for to mortal creature there is nothing properly
his own, but all things are the gift and grace of God"
(QG III,3); the covenant is a symbol of grace which stands
between God and man and "the excelling benefaction is this
that there be nothing between God and the soul except
virgin grace" (Mut 52-53); A similar thought is expressed
in Wis Sol 8,21: the acquisition of sophia comes through
God and "prudence is the knowledge as to whose grace it
was"--that led to the finding of sophia.

Perfection and Rest/Anapausis: The toil-free and touble-
free character of perfection which is self-learnt and self-taught
shares in the rest of creation on the seventh day--rest in God
(Fug 172-74); it is also characterized as the bread rained from
heaven (= heavenly sophia) which is sent in the holy seventh--
sabbath year (of rest)--self-productive and self-sufficient by
nature (Mut 255-60).

Perfection and the Metaphor of Food: Originally paideia and
trophē were synonymous--the upbringing of children (see Jaeger,
Paideia, II, pp. 228, 244 and 252). The distinction between
teleios--nepios and between milky and solid food is rooted in
this context. The self-learnt and self-taught kind does not partake of infant and milky food (Mig 28-30); the self-taught is fed
by no one and is instead food for others, i.e., it is capable of
teaching and does not itself need to learn (Mig 139-40); rest in
God is alone nourishing and enjoyable (Fug 172-74); whereas
others receive food from earth, the seeing type (Israel) receives
food from heaven (Mut 258).

Perfection and Logos/Sophia: A Clarification: In connection with the intermediary world we noted that perfection implied
rising above Logos, Sophia, Angel and Anthropos and achieving
unmediated access to God (see above the summary, pp. 42-45).

Here too we have noted that perfection has to do with immediacy of relationship to God and the level or status to which one reaches is equal to the Logos and Sophia. These two aspects are not contradictory since unmediated access and immediacy of relationship to God does not imply full equality with God himself. To reach God one has to rise above the intermediary world on the one hand and the status one attains on the other hand is equal to the Logos and one possesses the highest sophia. In other words, when one stands on the level of the intermediary world his relationship to God is unmediated (cf. Fug 100-101). Short of perfection, Abraham is led by the Logos and when he attains supreme knowledge he and the Logos become attendants of God the leader (Mig 173-75; cf. Mut 270--Sophos is an attendant (opados) of God) possession of sophia in itself does not mean perfection--there is a gentler and tamer sophia which Abraham follows before perfection (Mut 34; 39) and the sophia of Noah is an image of the Moses-like sophia (Quod Deus 109-10); Logos is the father of practicers but when the practicer reaches the land of the Logos and Sophia there awaits him the perfection of Isaac--companionship of God (Mig 28-30); self-learnt and self-taught sophos finds sophia ready at hand (Fug 166-67); Moses and Isaac receive from God the Logos as betrothed and knowldge--the life companion of the wise (Post 76-78); Aaron, Levi and Melchizedek are all called Logos (Leg All iii,45; Sac 119-20; Leg All iii, 79-82). Similarly, Moses is often called Logos (cf. Mig 83; 122; Quis Her 205-6, etc.).[13]

Perfection in Other Hellenistic-Jewish Literature

It is in 4Maccabees that we find the understanding of the OT persons as exemplars for contemporary acts of piety in the face of martyrdom and the background for this lies in the assimilation of the ideals of paideia in such literature. Thus the mother of the seven brothers is of "like-soul to Abraham," as a "daughter of Abraham" she remembers his fortitude and her "child bearing was from Abraham" (see above pp. 50-51). Eleazar was victorious over torture through an "Isaac-like reasoning" and was "perfected

---

[13]Lack of clarity of the different ways in which Philo uses the terms "sophos" and "sophia" has led U. Wilckens to the view that it is sophia which is seen at the end: "Die σοφια aber ist nun nicht nur der Bereich Gottes, sondern zugleich auch der Weg u der Wegführer dorthin, die τελεία ὁδὸς ἡ πρὸς θεόν." "Die Identität von Weg, Wegführer u Ziel zeigt den mystischen Charakter der Weisheit als Offenbarungsmittler . . . " (TDNT VII, 501).

by the faithful seal of death" (7,13-15; see above p. 58). His
martyrdom is patterned after Aaron's victory over the angel of
fire--Nu 17--(7,11; see above p. 62). In Wisdom of Solomon the
early death of the righteous man is explained in terms of his
early perfection and translation like that of Enoch:

Wis Sol 4,7: Δίκαιος δὲ ἐὰν φθάσῃ τελευτῆσαι, ἐν ἀναπαύσει
    ἔσται, . . .
 10: εὐάρεστος θεῷ γενόμενος ἠγαπήθη καὶ ζῶν μεταξὺ ἀμαρτωλῶν
   μετετέθη. . . .
 13: τελειωθεὶς ἐν ὀλίγῳ ἐπλήρωσεν χρόνους μακρούς,
 14: ἀρεστὴ γὰρ ἦν κυρίῳ ἡ ψυχὴ αὐτοῦ, διὰ τοῦτο ἔσπευσεν ἐκ
   μέσου πονηρίας (cf. 4,16).

The association of perfection with death (cf. 4Macc 7,13-15; Leg
All iii,45 - p. 58 above) and with Enoch being pleasing to God
(Mut 34; p. 49 above) and with his translation (cf. QG I,86; see
p. 68 above) and "rest" (see p. 77 above) is therefore a tradition which Philo has in common with the Wisdom of Solomon. In
Wis Sol 6,15, the concern with wisdom is "perfection of understanding" (teleiotēs phronēseōs).[14]

 In conclusion we quote:

Abr 52: ταῦτα μὲν οὖν ἐπ᾿ ἀνδρῶν ὁσίων εἰρῆσθαι δοκεῖ, μηνύματα
  δ᾿ ἐστι φύσεως ἀδηλοτέρας καὶ πολὺ βελτίονος τῆς ἐν
  αἰσθητοῖς. τρόπους γὰρ ψυχῆς ἔοικεν ὁ ἱερὸς διερευνᾶσθαι
  λόγος, ἀστείους ἅπαντας, τὸν μὲν ἐκ διδασκαλίας, τὸν δ᾿
  ἐκ φύσεως, τὸν δ᾿ ἐκ ἀσκήσεως ἐφιέμενον τοῦ καλοῦ. . . .

 54: προσηκόντως οὖν καὶ τὴν τῶν τριῶν λόγῳ μὲν ἀνδρῶν ἔργῳ
  δ᾿ ὡς εἶπον ἀρετῶν οἰκειότητα συνῆψε, φύσεως, μαθήσεως,
  ἀσκήσεως, ἃς ἑτέρῳ ὀνόματι Χάριτας ἰσαρίθμους ἄνθρωποι
  καλοῦσιν, ἢ τῷ κεχαρίσθαι τὸν θεὸν τῷ ἡμετέρῳ γένει τὰς
  τρεῖς δυνάμεις πρὸς τελειότητα τοῦ βίου ἢ παρόσον αὗται
  δεδώρηνται ψυχῇ λογικῇ ἑαυτάς, δώρημα τέλειον καὶ
  κάλλιστον, ἵνα καὶ τὸ αἰώνιον ὄνομα τὸ δηλούμενον ἐν τοῖς
  χρησμοῖς ἐπὶ τριῶν μὴ ἐπ᾿ ἀνθρώπων μᾶλλον ἢ τῶν εἰρημένων
  δυνάμεων λέγηται.

 55: ἀνθρώπων μὲν γὰρ φθαρτὴ φύσις, ἄφθαρτος δ᾿ ἡ τῶν ἀρετῶν.

The opening sections of this treatise are crucial since they set
forth Philo's understanding of his task (1-59). He indicates

---

[14]Both Goodenough and Wolfson have missed what we have shown
to be a central and important theme in Philo, namely, religious
perfection as unmediated access to God. Speaking of the 'supreme
mystery' in Sac 59-60, Goodenough states: "We are now ready, as
far as metaphysics is concerned, for a free shifting back and
forth between the Powers and God, and an assertion that to find
the highest Powers or the Logos is to find God . . . " (p. 36:
underlining is my own); "But the whole objective of Philo's life
was to get beyond all material images, beyond the material cosmos
itself, and come through to the spiritual originals, at last to
the Logos or God as the ultimate spiritual original, of all
things." (p. 92; underlining is my own.) In this respect, Goodenough's understanding of Philo is quite incorrect. Wolfson, on
the other hand, has simply over-looked the entire subject of
religious perfection in Philo.

that it was preceded by a treatise on the manner in which the
world was created and ordered (2), probably the De Opificio. He
intends then to examine first the more general laws which are
archetypes of the particular laws, namely, "those who have lived
good and blameless lives, whose virtues are inscribed in the most
holy scriptures" (4) for the instruction (προτρέψασθαι) of the
readers. These men are living and rational laws (ἔμψυχοι καὶ
λογικοὶ νόμοι ἄνδρες ἐκεῖνοι; 5), who followed the unwritten law
and lived according to nature. (Of the projected treatises we do
not have those on Jacob and Isaac.) There follows the description of the first triad: Enos--the lover of hope, Enoch representing 'repentence' and Noah 'rest' and 'just' (7-47). Noah
represents perfection, though not of the absolute kind (36),
Enoch stands half way having devoted the earlier part of his life
to vice and the latter to virtue, and Enos last--in that he hoped
but did not attain the good (47). The second triad (Abraham,
Isaac and Jacob) are superior in as much as the exercises of
athletes is superior to the studies of children (48). The subject
matter seems to speak to pious men but are also statements of
Nature, which are less clear but superior to that perceived by
the senses. They pertain to kinds of souls--one which pursues
the good through teaching, one through nature and one through
practice (52). They are Abraham, Isaac and Jacob, symbols of
virtue acquired by teaching, nature and practice (53). Moses
associated the three together, nominally men but in fact virtues,
nature, teaching and practice. Men call them by another name--
Graces, which are also three in number, either because the three
powers are given to the Jewish race by God's grace for the perfection of life or because these have given themselves to the
rational soul as best and perfect gift. Thus the revelation of
the eternal name pertains not to men but rather to the powers (of
virtue). The nature of men is mortal but that of the virtues is
immortal (54-55). 56-59 speaks of the high dignity of the race
of Israel (the one who sees God), a royal priesthood and a holy
nation (Ex 19,6): οὐδὲν γὰρ ἀνωτέρω θεοῦ, πρὸς ὃν εἴ τις τὸ τῆς
ψυχῆς ὄμμα τείνας ἔφθακε, μονὴν εὐχέσθω καὶ στάσιν (58). And the
things which draw us downwards are of no avail ὅταν ἐκ τῶν αὐτοῦ
δυνάμεων ἀνακρεμάσας τὴν ψυχὴν ὁ θεὸς ὁλκῇ δυνατωτέρᾳ πρὸς ἑαυτὸν
ἐπισπάσηται (59).

The passage above will suffice as a conclusion to show that
the pattern of religious perfection in Philo that we have elaborated upon is a central theme in his writings. It is the ideals

of Greek paideia which give coherence to Philo's thought rather
than, as Goodenough proposed, 'mystery.' A traditional title of
the treatise sums up well our assertion: Φίλωνος βίος σοφοῦ τοῦ
κατὰ διδασκαλίαν τελειωθέντος ἢ νόμων ἀγράφων, ὅ ἐστι περὶ
ἀβραάμ (Parisinus gr.435).

CHAPTER THREE

THE ANGELIC WORLD AND THE CONCEPT OF PERFECTION
IN OTHER TRADITIONS OF JUDAISM:
A COMPARATIVE PERSPECTIVE

Introduction: We have shown above that there is a single
comprehensive thought world in which the intermediary world characterized by synonymous titles and interchangeable functions
mediates an inferior revelation and religious status compared to
a direct and unmediated access to God. Moses, Aaron, Levi, Melchizedek and Isaac exemplify this state of perfection. We intend
to argue that the sequence of comparisons of Jesus with the angel
angels, Moses, Aaron, Levi and Melchizedek and the problems dealt
with in Hebrews find their most satisfactory explanation in such
a thought world. Our major source in the depiction of this
thought world has been Philo, though we have tried to show that
many aspects of it have important precedents in other literature
of hellenized Judaism. Since the angelic world and the concept
of perfection does play a significant role in other traditions of
Judaism and these are drawn upon for the interpretation of
Hebrews, a comparison between the structure of thought that we
have elaborated and these other traditions will serve to clarify
the issues and advance our arguments in respect to Hebrews. We
do not intend to present any new ideas or documentation in this
respect except to highlight those comparative elements pertinent
to the thesis.

A. Angels

Texts and Analysis

The prolific growth of angelology in the intertestamental
period is usually understood in terms of the need for intermediaries between God and the world. The religious reasons for this
need are held to be the increasing emphasis on the transcendence
of God and the necessity for an explanation of evil and suffering
in the world, especially as it affects the righteous.[1] There is
ample evidence to support both these contentions regarding the
emphasis on God's transcendence and the problem of evil, but what

---

[1]Cf. D. S. Russell, The Method and Message of Jewish Apocalyptic, pp. 237-40.

is not clear is whether these created such a gulf between God and
the world that only intermediary beings could bridge it.[2]   In
other words, was the presence of the angels related to the problem of access and immediacy to God?

The evidence from Qumran shows that the activity and the
presence of the angels is in no way related to the problem of immediacy or distance from God. The activity of the angels is not
based on the view that God stands so far from the world that
other beings need to act on his behalf.

God has appointed two spirits, that of truth and perversity
until the time of his visitation when the spirit of perversity
will be destroyed for ever. There are two angels who hold dominion respectively over the sons of righteousness and the sons of
perversity, namely, the Prince of Lights (śar 'ôrîm) and the
Angel of Darkness (malak ḥôšek).[3] It is because of the Angel of
Darkness that the sons of righteousness go astray, commit sins
and inequities (1QS 3,18-23).

> (24) And all the spirits of his lot (i.e. Angel of
>   Darkness) cause the sons of light to stumble;
> but the God of Israel and His Angel of truth succour
>   all (25) the sons of light.[4]

At the last judgement the spirit of perversity is destroyed for
ever and God purifies his chosen (1QS 4,18-22)

> in order that upright be instructed in knowledge of
>   the Most High
> and the perfect of the way have understanding of wisdom
>   of the Sons of Heaven.[5]

Thus in this section of 1QS, in which the eschatological dualism

---

[2] Such a view is represented by Bousset-Gressmann, Die Religion des Judentums, in which they attribute the emergence of intermediaries to an inner duality between the principle of monotheism and national particularity. Jewish piety was unable to
hold fast to the personal character of God and monotheism under-
went polytheistic influences which resided in the folk soul.
"Ein ganzes Heer von Mittelwesen drängt sich zwischen den welt-
fern gewordenen Gott und die Menschen," p. 319. Such an understanding of intermediaries was questioned by G. F. Moore, "intermediaries in Jewish Theology," HTR 15 (1922), 41-85, in which he
shows that "memra" and "shekinah" are circumlocutions for God.
In Rabbinic theology, astronomical speculations concerning the
plurality of heavens and distances are discussed under the subject
of the nearness of God based on Dt 4,7 (Moore, Judaism, I, 368-69).

[3] Transliteration of the Hebrew follows that suggested by the
Catholic Biblical Quarterly.

[4] Translation of the texts from Qumran are taken from A.
Dupont-Sommer, The Essene Writings from Qumran. Otherwise alternative translations are indicated.

[5] Translation follows that of E. Lohse, Die Texte aus Qumran,
which follows the text more literally than Dupont-Sommer.

of Qumran receives full expression, the writer can speak of the activity of God and the Angel of Truth (= Prince of Lights) in the same breath. The knowledge of the Most High (daᶜat ᶜelyôn) stands in synonymous parallelism to the wisdom of the Sons of Heaven (ḥakmat bᵉnê sāmayim). There is no consciousness that belonging to the dominion of the Prince of Light creates a distance between God and the sect or that there are different levels of religious knowledge.

On the contrary, the sect sees itself in present fellowship with the angelic world and this joint community is their ultimate and final destiny/lot.

> He has given them an inheritance in the lot of the
>   holy ones,
> and with the sons of heaven has He associated their
>   company
> to be a council of unity and a foundation for a holy
>   building,
> to be an eternal plantation for all coming time.
> (1QS 11,7-8)[6]

> The perverted spirit didst Thou cleanse from much
>   transgression,
> that he may take his place in the host of the holy
>   ones
> and enter into community with the congregation of
>   the sons of heaven,
> and Thou hast cast for man an eternal lot with the
>   spirits of knowledge.
> (1QH 3,21f.)[7]

To the above may be added 1QH 6,13; 11,11-12. Given the fact that the sect calls itself the "lot of God" (gôral ʾel), it is clear that belonging to the lot (gôral), host (ṣabā) or congregation (ᶜēdāh) of the angels variously described as "holy ones" (qᵉdôsîm), "sons of heaven" (bᵉnê sāmayim) and "spirits of knowledge" (rûhôt daᶜat) and belonging to the lot of God mean one and the same thing for the sect. In other words, the world of angelic beings does not imply a distance between God and man or serve to bridge a gulf between the two as "intermediaries."

> 1QS 2,1f.: And the priests shall bless all (2) the men
> of the lot of God who walk perfectly in all His ways . . .
> 2,4f.: And the Levites shall curse the men (5) of the
> lot of Belial . . .
> 3,24f. (see above p. 84)

> 1QM 1,5: This shall be the time of salvation for
>   the people of God,
> the hour dominion for all the men of his lot and
> of final destruction for all the lot of Belial.

---

[6]Translation of H. Ringgren, The Faith of Qumran, p. 85. It follows the text more closely than Dupont-Sommer.

[7]Ringgren, ibid., pp. 85-86.

13,2: . . . and they shall execrate [Beli]al there
and all the spirits of his lot.
13,4: And cursed be all the spirits of his lot
13,5f.: For they are the lot of darkness whereas
the lot of God is for (6) [eterna]l light.
13,9f.: . . . and Thou hast caused us to fall in the
lot of light (10) unto Thy truth. And Thou didst
appoint the Prince of Light in former times to bring
us help, and [all the angels of justi]ce are
in his lot and all the spirits of truth are in his
empire. (See further 13,12; 15,1; 17,6f.)

We have on the one hand the "lot of God," "people of God" "lot of
light" over which God has appointed the "Prince of Light" in
whose lot and empire are "angels of justice" and "spirits of
truth," and on the other hand the "lot of Belial," "Lot of darkness," "spirits of his lot" (i.e., Belial's). These two camps or
or empires are ranged in opposition until the final battle, the
day of judgement, God's visitation, when Belial and his lot of
spirits and men will be destroyed for ever. Thus for the sect
belonging to the lot of God, present and ultimate fellowship with
the angels, belonging to the dominion of the Prince of Light(s)
and receiving his help (cf. 1QM 17,6f. and the passages quoted
above--1QM 13,10 and 1QS 3,24) and the aid of his angels or
spirits are terms which describe the religious self understanding
of the community. There is no consciousness that God stands in
such a distance from the world that access and immediacy to God
become overriding religious concerns.[8]

In apocalyptic and sapiential literature of the intertestamental period the angels perform a variety of functions: they
intercede for men (1En 15,2; 39,5; 47,2; 104,1; Tob 12,12; etc.);
propitiate God for the unconscious sins of the righteous (Test L
3,5); they are guardians of the righteous individuals as well as
nations (1En 100,5; Dan 10,13.20.21; 12,1; Jub 15,31-32; 35,17;
Sir 17,17; 1En 89,59ff.); they appear to the apocalyptic vision-

---

[8]Ringgren repeats the standard view of hypostases and intermediaries "who stand between God and the world and, so to say,
mediate his actions to the world. First and foremost among these
intermediary beings are the hypostases (Wisdom, the Shekinah, the
Word [mêmrā, dibbūr, etc.]) and angels . . . " (The Faith of
Qumran, p. 81). And this inspite of G. F. Moore's article (see
above f.n. 2). In the case of Qumran, he correctly sees a lack
of concepts of hypostases or intermediary roles: "For here the
angels seem to be--as in the Old Testament--God's heavenly court
rather than actual intermediary beings. They have not been
created to bridge the gulf between the divine, or heavenly, and
the earthly, but they have simply been taken over from the Bible
and the thought world of contemporary Judaism and been understood
as God's messengers and servants" (ibid., p. 82).

ary and lead him through the heavenly spheres, communicate God's messages to him, lead him to the presence of God, explain the heavenly terrain and inhabitants and reveal the apocalyptic secrets concerning the end time (cf. 1En 103,2; 106,19; 2Bar 81,4; 4Es 14,5, etc.).[9] The question that concerns us is whether these various functions of the angels are to be understood as evidence for a concept of God's transcendence of such a kind that the angels are to be conceived as "intermediary" beings who bridge the gulf between the transcendent God and the world and who mediate His actions to it. Some key examples will show that this popular view is questionable.

TestD 6,1: Καὶ νῦν φοβήθητε τὸν κύριον τέκνα μου, καὶ προσέχετε ἑαυτοῖς ἀπὸ τοῦ Σατανᾶ καὶ τῶν πνευμάτων αὐτοῦ.
2: Ἐγγίσατε τῷ θεῷ καὶ τῷ ἀγγέλῳ τῷ παραιτουμένῳ ὑμᾶς (α - παρεπομένῳ ὑμῖν), ὅτι οὗτός ἐστι μεσίτης θεοῦ καὶ ἀνθρώπων καὶ ἐπὶ τῆς εἰρήνης τοῦ Ἰσραηλ κατέναντι τῆς βασιλείας τοῦ θεοῦ (S¹ - ἐχθροῦ) στήσεται.[10]

The similarity in the language and ideas between the Testaments of the 12 Patriarchs and Qumran has been noticed and especially as it pertains to the doctrine of the two spirits.[11] The Testament of Dan is a perfect example of the eschatological dualism which forms the context of ethical exhortation in both groups of writings. The main theses of the TestD are as follows:

TestD 1,3: . . . ὅτι πονηρὸν τὸ ψεῦδος καὶ ὁ θυμὸς πᾶσαν κακίαν ἐδιδάσκοντα τὸν ἄνθρωπον.

1,6: τὸ γὰρ πνεῦμα τοῦ ζήλου καὶ τῆς ἀλαζονείας ἔλεγέ μοι, Καίγε σὺ αὐτὸς υἱὸς αὐτοῦ εἶ.

1,7: καὶ ἐκ τῶν πνευμάτων τοῦ Βελίαρ συνήργει μοι . . .

1,8: τοῦτο δὲ ἦν τὸ πνεῦμα τοῦ θυμοῦ τὸ πεῖθόν με . . . ἐκμυζῆσαι τὸν Ἰωσήφ.

2,1: καὶ νῦν, τέκνα μου, ἰδοὺ ἐγὼ ἀποθνήσκω, καὶ ἐν ἀληθείᾳ λέγω ὑμῖν, ὅτι ἐὰν μὴ φυλάξητε ἑαυτοὺς ἀπὸ τοῦ πνεύματος τοῦ ψεύδους καὶ τοῦ θυμοῦ, καὶ ἀγαπήσητε τὴν ἀλήθειαν καὶ τὴν μακροθυμίαν, ἀπολεῖσθε.

2,4: περιβάλλεται γὰρ αὐτὸν τὸ πνεῦμα τοῦ θυμοῦ τὸ δίκτυον τῆς πλάνης καὶ τυφλοῖ τοὺς ὀφθαλμοὺς αὐτοῦ. . . .

3,6: τοῦτο τὸ πνεῦμα ἀεὶ μετὰ τοῦ ψεύδους ἐκ δεξιῶν τοῦ Σατανᾶ πορεύεται . . .

4,7: ἔστι δὲ διπρόσωπον κακὸν ὁ θυμὸς μετὰ ψεύδους, καὶ συναίρονται ἀλλήλοις ἵνα ταράξωσι τὴν καρδίαν, ταρασσομένης δὲ τῆς ψυχῆς συνεχῶς, ἀφίσταται ὁ Κύριος ἀπ' αὐτῆς καὶ κυριεύει αὐτῆς ὁ Βελίαρ.

---

[9]Cf. Russell, ibid., pp. 241-43.

[10]The texts on the Testaments are taken from the critical edition of R. H. Charles, The Greek Versions of the Testaments of the Twelve Patriarchs.

[11]Cf. Ringgren, ibid., pp. 76-78, 91.

5,1: φυλάξατε οὖν, τέκνα μου, τὴν ἐντολὴν τοῦ κυρίου
καὶ τὸν νόμον αὐτοῦ τηρήσατε
ἀπόστητε ἀπὸ τοῦ <u>θυμοῦ</u>
καὶ μισήσατε τὸ <u>ψεῦδος</u>,
<u>ἵνα Κύριος κατοικήσει ἐν ὑμῖν</u>
<u>καὶ φεύξεται ἀφ' ὑμῶν ὁ Βελίαρ</u>.

5,4: ἐγὼ οἶδα ὅτι ἐν ταῖς <u>ἐσχάταις ἡμέραις</u>
ἀποστήσεσθε τοῦ Κυρίου,
καὶ προσοχθιεῖτε τῷ Λευί,
καὶ πρὸς τῷ 'Ιουδὰ παρατάξεσθε,
ἀλλ' οὐ δυνήσεσθε πρὸς αὐτούς,
<u>ἄγγελος γὰρ Κυρίου ὁδηγεῖ ἑκατέρους</u>, . . .

5:9: καὶ οὕτως ἐπιτρέψαντες πρὸς Κύριον ἐλεηθήσεσθε
καὶ ἄξει ὑμᾶς εἰς τὸ ἁγίασμα αὐτοῦ
καὶ δώσει ὑμῖν εἰρήνην.

5:10: καὶ ἀνατελεῖ ὑμῖν ἐκ τῆς φυλῆς ['Ιούδα καὶ]
τοῦ Λευὶ τὸ σωτήριον Κυρίου,
<u>αὐτὸς γὰρ ποιήσει πρὸς τὸν Βελίαρ πόλεμον</u> . . .

Anger and lying are spirits of Beliar, they go forth from the
right hand of Satan, their disturbance causes God to depart from
the soul and Beliar to gain domination over it, whereas the ob-
servance of God's law, departure from anger and hatred of lying,
causes God to dwell among them and Beliar to flee from them.
There is the angel of the Lord who guides the tribes of Levi and
Judah and protects them from harm. After the apostacy of the
children of Dan in the times when they turn back to the Lord they
shall receive mercy, access to his sanctuary and peace. And God
will raise salvation from the tribe of Levi, i.e., a messianic
figure, who will wage war against Beliar and deliver those held
in his captivity. The concluding exhortation in 6:1ff. urges
them to beware of Satan and his spirits, to draw near God and the
angel which intercedes on their behalf.[12] He is the <u>mediator</u>
(mesitēs) between God and man and stands against the <u>kingdom of</u>
<u>the enemy</u> for the peace of Israel. The doctrine of spirits or
angelology is in essential respects identical to that of Qumran
(see above pp. 83-86). We have here the same dualism of heavenly
powers--on the one hand God and His angel and on the other hand
Beliar/Satan with his spirits--and this forms the context for
ethical exhortation as in 1QS 4,2-11. We find in Qumran the virtues of truth and long suffering (1QS 4,3: 'ôrek 'appayim which
in the LXX is usually translated as makrothumia, e.g., Prov. 25,
15; and the adjectival form by makrothumos, e.g., Ex 34,6, etc.).
More telling is the metaphor of the snares and nets of Belial.

---

[12]Usually identified with the archangel Michael who is the
guardian angel of Israel. Cf. 1En 40,2 & 9; Jub 1,29; TestJud
25,2.

<u>1QH 4,9-14</u>: the passage speaks of false prophets who have lead the people astray, they have devised schemes of Belial against the writer, they have withheld knowledge from the people "(12) their straying might be gazed on, that they might be foolish concerning their feasts, and they might be taken in their nets. For Thou, O God, despisest every thought (13) of Belial . . . " The nets (m^eṣodôt) of the false prophets and the schemes of Belial are snares which entrap them (cf. 13-14). The expression "straying" (tā'ah) is translated by the LXX with planaō, e.g., Gn 21,14; Is 16,8, etc. We find a similar constellation of ideas in <u>CD 4,12-16</u>: "And in all those years (13) Belial shall be unleashed against Israel; as God said by the hand of the prophet Isaiah son of (14) Amoz, 'Terror and pit and snare are upon thee, O inhabitants of the land.' The explanation of this (is that) (15) these are Belial's three nets, of which Levi son of Jacob spoke, (16) by which he (Belial) ensnared Israel."

Hence the expression "net of deceit" (δίκτυον τῆς πλάνης) in TestD 2,4 belongs in this context. Passages like 1QH 3,24-36 should be interpreted within the same frame of reference.

As in Qumran, we observe here the same easy transitions from speaking of the direct activity of God (TestD 5,9-10), the leadership of the angel (5,4) and that God will raise a "messianic" figure from Levi to wage war against Beliar (5,10). The concluding exhortations speak of drawing near God and his angel (6,2), which indicate that for the author the angelic world and God belong together and there is no consciousness of the problem of a distant and transcendent God. The structure of thought is the same as that of Qumran.

Hence when the angel is called a "mesitēs" in 6,2 we ought not to understand his role in terms of an "intermediary" who bridges a gulf between a transcendent God and the world. What then does "mesitēs" mean in this context? The passage itself suggests an intercessory role (παραιτούμενος ὑμᾶς), an advocate, a middle man, whose task it is to represent the cause of a negotiating party, e.g., 1Enoch 15,2:

> And go say to the Watchers of heaven, who have
> sent thee to intercede for them: "You should
> intercede for men, and not men for you: . . . "

There is no clear evidence outside Judaism for such a meaning of "mesitēs" or its verbal form. The technical meaning in the vocabulary of Hellenistic law (mainly papyri) is that of an "umpire" in legal disputes, an arbiter. Other usages include "guarantor" of an agreement, a neutral with whom a sum is temporarily left, a pawnbroker, etc. (see O. Oepke, TDNT 4, 599-601). The only occurrence in the LXX is Job 9,33 where it is a mistranslation for bênênû. The meaning of "mesitēs" as an arbiter or umpire implies that he stands above the two contending parties. This is the sense in which the <u>Roman Emperor</u> is invoked as the mediator in Jos Ant 16,118; and <u>God in</u> 4, 133. In Josephus we find the first clear examples in which the noun and the verb are

used in the sense of a go-between or negotiator:[13]
Ant 7,193: Absalom persuades Joab to intercede with David
on his behalf and πεισθεὶς δ᾽ ὁ Ἰώαβος καὶ τὴν ἀνάγκην
αὐτοῦ κατοικτείρας ἐμεσίτευσε πρὸς τὸν βασιλέα καὶ
διαλεχθεὶς περὶ τοῦ παιδὸς οὕτως αὐτὸν ἡδέως διατίθησιν,
ὡς εὐθέως καλέσαι πρὸς αὐτόν. 16,24: καὶ τῶν παρὰ Ἀγρίππα
τισὶν ἐπιζητουμένων μεσίτης ἦν καὶ διεπράττετο μηδενὸς
ἀτυχῆσαι τοὺς δεομένους. . . . 26: Ἰλιεῦσι μέν γε αὐτὸν
διήλλαξεν ὀργιζόμενον . . . τοῖς δὲ ἄλλοις καθὸ δεηθεῖεν
ἕκαστοι παρίστατο. The passage refers to Herod's role as
mediator and reconciler of different parties with Agrippa,
the legate of Augustus. This particular meaning of
"mesitēs/mesiteuein" probably comes from a Semitic context
and corresponds to sarsôr, Aramaic sarsôrāh, which carries
the sense of "negotiator" in business and marriage deals
and is applied to Moses in Rabbinic literature (see TDNT 4,
602 & 615f.). This is probably the sense in which Moses as
the "mediator" (Latin - "arbiter_ and Greek in Gelasius,
Commentarius actorum concilii Nicaeni, is "mesitēs") of the
covenant in Ass Mos 1,14 and 3,12 should be understood.[14]

Philo's usage of the terms "mesitēs" and "mesiteuein" will illustrate for us how the same term can have entirely different conno-
tations and religious implications in a different structure of
thought when we compare it with the TestD.

Som i,141-42: (quoted on p. 15)
The context of the passage is the interpretation of Gn 28,12-13
(133ff.)--the dream of the stairway. In reference to the universe, the stairway represents air and is populated by incorporeal souls, some of which descend into bodies and others which
are most pure and best serve as viceroys (hyparchoi) of the Great
King (i.e., God). These are called "demons" by the philosophers
and "angels" by the sacred record (140-41). Not that God needs
informers, but it is to the advantage of mortals to avail themselves of the Logoi (i.e., angels) as "mediators" (mesitai) and
"negotiators" (diaitetai) on account of the awe and dread of the
universal Monarch and the exceeding power of his sovereignty
(142). It was this which led to the entreaty of Ex 20,19 to "one
of the mediators"--i.e., Moses. For we are incapable of receiving God's boons without the employment of "servants" (hyperetai).
Som i,148: (quoted on p. 35)
In reference to humans, the stairway refers to the soul, up and
down through the whole of which move the Logoi of God, drawing
the soul up to a vision worthy of our gaze, and descending on account of philanthropy, mercy, aid and alliance (146-47). In the
minds which are totally cleansed, God alone walks, but in the

---

[13]Text of Josephus quoted from B. Niese, Editio major.

[14]Cf. R. H. Charles, Apocrypha and Pseudepigrapha of the Old
Testament, II, note on Ass Mos 1,14, p. 415.

minds still undergoing cleansing and defiled by the burdens of
the body, there walk "angels," the "divine Logoi."

We observe that the term "μεσίτης" is used by Philo along
with others--ὕπαρχος, διαιτητής, ὑπηρέτης--to describe the intermediary role of the angels/logoi in the sense of bridging a gap
between a transcendent God (142) and mortal men. This mediating
role takes place both in the cosmic and psychic realm (133 § 146).
But the minds which are totally cleansed require no such mediation for God alone (monos) walks in them. Those who have not
reached this highest religious state need the services of medi-
ators--angels/logoi. They extend to them--φιλανθρωπία, ἔλεος,
ἐπικουρία καὶ συμμαχία--(147) making them bright with the teach-
ings of καλοκάγαθίας (148).

Mig 158: Ἔνιοι μὲν οὖν τὸν μιγάδα καὶ δασὺν τοῦτον ἀπορρίπτουσι
          καὶ διατειχίζουσιν ἀφ᾽ ἑαυτῶν <u>τῷ θεοφιλεῖ μόνῳ</u> γένει
          χαίροντες, ἔνιοι δὲ καὶ πρὸς αὐτὸν ἑταιρίαν τίθενται
          <u>μεσιτεύειν</u> τὸν ἑαυτῶν βίον ἀξιοῦντες καὶ <u>μεθόριον</u>
          <u>ἀνθρωπίνων τε καὶ θείων ἀρετῶν</u> τιθέντες, ἵν᾽ ἑκατέρων
          ἐφάπτωνται, καὶ τῶν ἀληθείᾳ καὶ τῶν δοκήσει.

The point of departure is the interpretation of Gn 12,4; Lot,
whose interpretation is "turning aside," follows Abraham while
Abraham is yet a novice in the contemplation of things divine
(148-50). It is the Lot-like character which hinders the soul
from making swift progress to virtue and is like the mixed multitude which hindered Israel's progress (151-54). There are some
who cast away this mixed and motley type and wall themselves off
from them and rejoice only in the God-beloved kind, others form
a fellowship with it, deeming their lives worthy of middle position (mesiteuein), holding an intermediate (methorion) place
between human and divine virtues, the true and the seeming.

This passage illustrates that for Philo the term μεσιτεύειν
carries the connotation of a less than perfect religious status
as compared with those who delight in the God-beloved kind of
virtue only. Any type of "mediation" implies an inferior religious status.

The intermediaries themselves, however, stand in close relationship to God and the same terms in reference to them imply the
highest religious dignity. Thus Moses in <u>Quis Her 205</u> (quoted
above on p. 9) is called an "archangel," the "eldest Logos" who
stands in between (μεθόριος) separating the creature from the
creator. He is a suppliant (ἱκέτης) to the immortal of afflicted
mortality and the ambassador (πρεσβευτής) of the ruler to the
subject. The attitude of Moses after the incident of the golden
calf is described as that of a μεσίτης καὶ διαλλακτής . . .

ὁ κηδεμὼν καὶ παραιτητής (Mos i,166). Similar terminology is
applied to the function of the Logos in mediating and reconciling
(μεσιτεύων τε καὶ διαιτῶν) the enmity of the elements (Plant 10,
quoted above on p. 13; cf. Quis Her 188; QE II,118). The term
μεθόριος is also applied to it in the same context. In Spec Leg
i,116, the exclusion of the high priest from mourning (Lv 21,1-
12) is explained by the fact that he has a nature higher than man,
approaching closer to the divine, an intermediate (διὰ μέσου
τινός) through whom they may propitiate God and for God to extend
his boons.

We thus have a number of terms which Philo uses to describe
the mediating role of intermediaries in that they bridge the gap
between a transcendent God and mortal men (μεσίτης, μεσιτεύειν,
διαιτητής, διαιτᾶν, διαλλακτής, παραιτητής, ὕπαρχος, ὑπηρέτης,
ἱκέτης, πρεσβευτής, μεθόριος, μέσος). The necessity of such mediation implies the imperfection of men, whereas the mediators
themselves stand in closest proximity to God, which implies religious perfection (see above pp. 77-78). The perfect need no such
mediation as we have shown.

Two further examples (Test L and Tobit) will illustrate for
our purposes that the angelic world does not function in apocalyptic and sapiential literature as intermediary between a distant
God and the human world. In the TestL, the angel in the vision-
ary journey (2,6ff.) acts as guide and interpreter of the hierarchy of the heavens and of the angelic beings and spirits which
dwell in them (3). In Chap. 5, the angel opens the gates of
heaven and Levi is addressed directly by God and the blessings of
priesthood are given to him (5,1-2). On being led to earth by
the angel, Levi pleads that the angel teach him his name that he
may call on him on the day of tribulation. The angel replied:
Ἐγώ εἰμι ὁ ἄγγελος ὁ παραιτούμενος τὸ γένος Ἰσραήλ, τοῦ μὴ
πατάξαι αὐτούς. Καὶ μετὰ ταῦτα ἔξυπνος γενόμενος εὐλόγησα τὸν
ὕψιστον (καὶ τὸν ἄγγελον τὸν παραιτούμενον τὸ γένος Ἰσραήλ καὶ
πάντων τῶν δικαίων - β,Α^β,S^1).

We observe no trace of consciousness in this vision that a
large gulf separates man from God which can only be bridged by
mediation of angels. Angels are guides, interpreters and inter-
cessors on behalf of men. Their aid and presence is eagerly
sought for and it is a mark of divine favor. The problems of immediacy and access to God and the unmediated character of perfection could not have arisen in this thought world.

The same is true in the book of Tobit. Raphael, an angel of

the presence, aids Tobit and his son; he is sent by God and it is God's will that he carries out: ὅτι οὐ τῇ ἐμαυτοῦ χάριτι, ἀλλὰ τῇ θελήσει τοῦ θεοῦ ἡμῶν ἦλθον. ὅθεν εὐλογεῖτε αὐτὸν εἰς τὸν αἰῶνα (12,18). . . . καὶ ἐξωμολογοῦντο τὰ ἔργα τὰ μεγάλα καὶ θαυμαστὰ θεοῦ καὶ ὡς ὤφθη αὐτοῖς ὁ ἄγγελος κυρίου (12,22, text = B/A). Thus the appearance and aid of Raphael is seen as God's work and activity for which He is to be praised. There is no consciousness that Raphael takes the place of a distant God.

Comparative Structures of Thought

On the basis of the evidence we have, we can outline and compare the function of the intermediary world in the structures of thought of Philo, Qumran, some intertestamental literature and Hebrews. In the case of Hebrews, although more detailed analysis will be provided in the chapters to follow, it would be useful to set forth some of the main contentions in this comparative perspective.

(1) We have shown above that the role of angels in Qumran is not to overcome a gulf that separates God from the community. Their presence does not create a problem of access or immediacy to God. On the contrary, the sect sees itself in present fellowship with the angelic world and its ultimate destiny is to belong to such a fellowship of the angels (see above pp. 85-86). The angels fight on the side of the children of light in the eschatological battle (1QM 12,1-9). The thought world of the Testament of Dan is very close to that of Qumran. In both, an eschatological dualism (God and His angel(s)/messiah are ranged against Belia(l,r) and his angels/spirits) forms the context of ethical exhortation (see above pp. 87-89). Drawing near to God and the intercessory angel are seen in conjunction rather than in disjunction (TestD 6,2; see above pp. 89-90). In Philo, on the other hand, the highest religious status or perfection requires that one pass beyond the intermediary world to God himself--an unmediated access. As long as the presence of the intermediaries becomes necessary, one has yet to attain perfection. Being in touch with the angels--a sign of divine intervention in apocalyptic Judaism (cf. Tobit, chapt. 12)--is in Philo a lack of immediacy to God and hence an inferior status. In Hebrews, access or immediacy to God together with perfection are crucial points in the author's argument (2,10-11: the leading of many sons into glory and the perfection of their leader through suffering; they are all brothers and have one origin; 4,14-16: that Jesus the high priest has

gone through the heavens implies that the Christians can freely approach the throne of grace; 6,19-20: hope which the Christians have as an anchor of the soul enters inside the veil where Jesus has entered as their forerunner; 7,18-19: the law perfected no one, but the arrival of a better hope is the means through which the Christians can draw near to God; that means perfection and access to God are alternative forms of expression, exactly as in Philo (see above p. 75); 10,19-20; Jesus has prepared a new and living way through the veil by which the Christians have free access into the holy of holies; such a conception of the cult and perfection is already visible in Philo and will be discussed further below). In this respect the thought world of Hebrews finds its closest analogy in Philo and not in the traditions of apocalyptic Judaism as exemplified by Qumran and the Testament of Dan. The religious understanding of perfection as immediacy and access to God, as we have shown above, could not have arisen in such a thought world and this will be verified in the next section when we deal with the concept of perfection in such literature. The proximity of the Qumran community to God belongs to a different thought world. It is proximity in the context of eschatological dualism, whether one belongs to the lot of God and his angels, an eschatological fellowship awaiting the final battle with Belial and his angels/spirits. In Hebrews and Philo, it is a question of proximity to the divine--the way into the holy of holies, religious status as perfection--and who exemplifies such access-- Moses, Levi, Aaron or Jesus and the Christians.

(2) The implications of divine proximity are conceived quite differently in each of these writings. In Qumran the presence of the angels demands cultic purity (1QM 7,4-6); the physically and mentally impaired (fools, madmen, deaf, lame, etc.) are excluded from the community "for the angels are in the midst" (4QD[b]; cf. 1QSa 2,3-9); certain ethical qualities are concomitant with those who walk in the Spirit of Truth (1QS 4,2-8). In TestD, similar to Qumran, the soul of man is the battle ground between God and Beliar with his spirits. The dominion of the former implies certain virtues and the dominion of the latter implies certain vices (see above pp.87f.). In Philo, divine proximity implies rising above the intermediary world and such perfection is characterized by sinlessness, fully cleansed minds, full knowledge, worship of God by incorporeal souls (see above pp. 44-45), self-learnt and self-taught virtue, requiring neither admonition nor exhortation, seventh day rest of God, existence inside the

holy of holies, rising above creation and eagerness to be God's
suppliant and servant, approach--nearness and kinship to God, the
quality of the seventh--ever virgin and motherless, etc. (see
above pp. 73-78). In Hebrews, proximity to God is characterized
by entry into the sabbath rest of God (4,3 & 10); sanctification
(2,11); hope which enters inside the veil and is the anchor of
the soul (6,19); a better hope (7,19); a way into the holy of
holies which is characterized by perfection of the conscience
(9,8-9); with one offering Jesus has perfected for ever those who
are being sanctified (10,14); fullness of faith, confession of
hope, love and good works which ought to attend the entry into
the holy of holies prepared by Jesus (10,19-24); the perfection
of faith (11,40; 12,2). Thus for Hebrews it is Christian faith
and hope which are the characteristics of perfection and access
to God. We will show below the relationship between the cult and
perfection in Philo and its close analogy to Hebrews. In these
respects, Hebrews has reinterpreted with the aid of Christian
beliefs a tradition which finds its closest analogy in Philo.

(3) What is lacking in both Philo and Hebrews are some of
the characteristic features of eschatological dualism, especially
as it pertains to angelology. Lacking in both is the dualism of
the opposed forces of God and His angels versus Belial with his
host of spirits or angels in Qumran and the Testament of Dan.
Lacking also is the concept of an eschatological battle which will
end with the rout and destruction of the forces of Belial. Neither is there the understanding of angels as revealers of the
apocalyptic mysteries.[15]

There are numerous other features which one finds in apocalyptic literature that are missing: names of the angels; their
hierarchical organization and numbers; concept of guardian angels;
the myth of the fall of angels, their responsibility for all the
evils in the world, their hosts and princes (Mastema, Beliar,
Satan, etc.); belief in wicked demons as the cause of sickness;
role of angels as guides and interpreters to the apocalyptic
visionaries, etc.[16]

The eschatological elements in Hebrews (eschaton, judgement,
destruction of the devil and death, second coming, heavenly Jerusalem and the unshakable kingdom) are traditional Christian

---

[15]For a detailed study of the concept see R. E. Brown, The
Semitic Background of the Term "Mystery" in the New Testament.

[16]Cf. Bousset-Gressmann, ibid., Chap. 16.

pieces which the author uses in his argumentation. This argumentation is directed to a quite different thought world than that
of apocalyptic as we have outlined above. These traditional
eschatological pieces are rather simple in comparison to the much
more elaborate apocalyptic themes in earlier Christian tradition
(Mk 13 and par.; 1Thess 4:13ff.; 2Thess; Rev., etc.) and are used
by the author mainly for the purpose of exhortation. Their function in the author's arguments will be analysed in the chapters
ahead.

> Hypostases: Bousset-Gressmann have correctly drawn
> attention to the multitude of intermediary beings (Mittel-
> wesen), the result of a "seltsame Zwitterbildungen eines
> kindlichen, zur vollen Abstraction noch unfähigen Denkens"
> (343), in the literature of the period (Chap. 18). Yet to
> lump together wisdom, glory, word, name of Jahweh, the
> powers of God (Philo and Rabbis), Primal-Man, chariot mys-
> tery, etc. under the same rubric of theological speculation
> is not very helpful. In the case of "memra" in the Targums,
> G. F. Moore has shown that it is a circumlocution for God
> and the motivation for its use is not to be found in the
> avoidance of anthropomorphism. That "in the Targums memra
> is not the term employed where the 'word of the Lord' is
> the medium or instrumentality of revelation, and that it is
> not the creative word in the cosmogony of Genesis or remi-
> niscences of it" ("Intermediaries in Jewish Theology,"
> HTR 15 (1922), 54). A distinction which suggests itself is
> one between clearly mythical figures as the Primal Man
> (Ezek 28,12ff; 2En 30,8-14), wisdom in such poetic sections
> as (Prov 8,22-31; Sir 24,3-6; 1Bar 3,9-4,4; Wis Sol 7,22-
> 27), and personalized attributes of God as glory, name,
> powers, word and spirit. It is in the Wisdom of Solomon
> that we observe the first clear traces of identifications
> between these two sets: wisdom is identical with the "holy
> spirit of paideia" and the "spirit of the Lord" which fills
> the world (1,4. 5 & 7; 9,17). Wisdom and the word (logos)
> occur in synonymous parallelism as the agents of creation
> (9,1-2; cf. 7,22). Wisdom is the vapour of the power of
> God (7,25), etc. Philo represents a further elaboration
> of the same tendency (see above pp. 8-17).
>
> In none of these cases (with the exception of Philo) can
> it be shown that these mythical figures and personalized
> conceptions are used to bridge the gap between a transcendent
> God and the world. In the Wisdom of Solomon, God directly
> grants wisdom to mankind (9,4; 9,17-18, etc.) and the activ-
> ity of God and of wisdom can alternate with ease (cf. 7,17
> & 7,22).

B. Perfection[17]

Texts and Analysis

At Qumran, the sectarian is one who has chosen the way

---

[17] General studies of the concept which take into account
most of the current literature are those of Du Plessis, ΤΕΛΕΙΟΣ:
The Idea of Perfection in the New Testament; C. Edlund, Das Auge
der Einfalt; Delling in TWNT VIII, 68-80.

(derek - 1QS 9,17-18); it is a term which describes the religious self-understanding of the sect. One of their self-designations is the "perfect of way" (t^emîmê derek - 1QH 1,36; 1QM 14,7). The perfection of the sectarian is characterized by complete commitment of himself and his possessions to the sect and full compliance with its religious view-point. The opening lines of 1QS 1 stress the total character of this commitment:

> " . . . to love all (4) that He has chosen and hate all that He has despised; to depart from all evil (5) and cling to all good works . . . "

> " . . . to walk perfectly before him (according to) all (9) the revelations concerning their regular feasts; and that they may love all the sons of light, each (10) according to his lot in the Council of God; and that they may hate all the sons of darkness, each according to his fault (11) in the Vengeance of God."

> " . . . shall bring all their understanding and powers and (12) possessions into the community of God, to purify their understanding in the truth of the precepts of God, and to order their powers (13) according to the perfection of His ways, and all their possessions according to His righteous Counsel. And they shall make no single step (14) from all the words of God concerning their times, they shall not anticipate their times, nor delay them (15) for any of their feasts. And they shall not depart from His precepts of truth to walk either to the right or to left."

> "And he shall establish his steps to walk perfectly (10) in all the ways of God, according to His Command concerning His regular feasts; and he shall step aside neither to right nor to left, and (11) shall make no single step from all His words." (1QS 3)

> "(1) In the Council of the Community (there shall be) twelve men and three priests, perfect in all that is revealed of all (2) the Law, to practice truth, righteousness, justice . . . " (1QS 8; cf. CD 7,5).

> "And let him (i.e., the maskil) keep true knowledge and right Justice for them that have chosen (18) the way. He shall guide each man in knowledge according to his spirit (and) according to the appointed moment of time; and likewise, he shall instruct them in the marvellous and true mysteries in the midst (19) of the members of the Community, that they may walk with one another in perfection in all that has been revealed to them." (1QS 9)

Perfection, therefore, means that the member of the community makes a total commitment (of understanding, powers and possessions) to understand the religious beliefs of the sect and to strictly adhere to the prescribed conduct. The key themes in the passages above show the apocalyptic nature of their religious beliefs: it is knowledge revealed concerning the festal calendar, the apocalyptic mysteries/secrets, knowledge of the full will of God (note the repeated use of "all"), dualism of the sons of light and the sons of darkness, love of one and hate of the

98

other in light of the day of God's vengeance. It is a sectarian
view of perfection in that belonging to the sect and perfection
are equivalent. The sect knows itself as "the House of holiness
for Israel for those who walk in perfection" (iQS 9,6), "men of
the Lot of God who walk perfectly in all His ways" (1QS 2,2),
etc. Thus the sect claims that it alone has the full knowledge
of God's will and that they alone uphold it. Perfection is total
fidelity to the sect, both in terms of its religious self-
understanding and appropriate conduct. This was subject to testing and grading by the community:

> . . . they shall examine (21) his spirit in common, (dis-
> tinguishing) between one and the other according to his
> understanding and his works with regard to the Law. . . .
> (23) And they shall inscribe them in order, one before the
> other, according to their intelligence and their works,
> . . . And they (24) shall examine their spirits and works
> year by year, in order to promote each man according to
> his understanding and the perfection of his way, or to
> demote him according to the faults which he has committed.
> (1QS 5)

The passage reveals the parallelism of "works" and "perfection of
his way." Perfection here means full conformity to the rules of
life and conduct of the sect. The person who has committed an
accidental offence is tried for two years "for the perfection of
his way and counsel" (1QS 9,2). Restitution into the community
requires that "his deeds/works are purified of all perversity and
he walks in perfection of way" (1QS 8,18).

Such total fidelity (perfection) and complete knowledge of
the eschatological will of God is God's work and the enablement
of the Spirit:

> For to God belongs my justification, and the perfection of
> my way, and the uprightness of my heart are in His hand;
> (3) by His righteousness are my rebellions blotted out.
> For he has poured forth from the fount of His knowledge
> the light that enlightens me, and my eyes have beheld His
> marvels and the light of my heart pierces the mystery (4)
> to come. (1QS 11; cf. 11,11)[18]

> And I, I know that righteousness is not of man, nor of the
> sons of men perfection (31) of way; to the Most High God
> belong all works of righteousness, whereas the way of man
> is not firm unless it be by the Spirit which God has cre-
> ated for him (32) to make perfect a way for the sons of
> men. . . . (1QH 4)

In inter-testamental literature, apart from Qumran, the concept of "perfection" is to be found in the Testaments of the
Twelve Patriarchs, which share with Qumran a similar eschatolog-

---

[18]Parallelism between "perfection" and "uprightness" is
frequent in the Old Testament, e.g., Ps 25,21; Prov 2,7; 1Kg 9,4;
Prov 11,5-6; 2,21.

ical dualism (see above pp. 87-89). Whereas the LXX has no settled rendition of the Hebrew (tām, tōm, tāmim), the Testaments of
the Twelve Patriarchs, according to C. Edlund, translates tōm
consistently with ἁπλότης.[19]

> TestR: The theme of the testament is a warning against
> fornication (ὅπως μὴ πορευθῆτε ἐν ἀγνοίᾳ νεότητος καὶ
> πορνείᾳ) and the gravity of this sin (μεγάλη γὰρ ἦν, οἷα οὐ
> γέγονεν ἐν Ἰσραὴλ οὕτως) - 1,6 & 10. This is followed by
> an enumeration of the seven spirits of deceit which forms
> the dualistic context for such exhortation (see above pp.
> 87-89) - Chaps. 2-3. Reuben's incest with Bilhah is de-
> scribed as an "abomination" and "impiety" (βδέλυγμα &
> ἀσέβεια - 3,12 & 3,14). (The "unclean," "abominable" and
> "defiling" character of incest and its polarity "God,"
> "holy nation," God's "possession" are underlined in Jub 33,
> where we find the tradition underlying TestR 3,11-15 in a
> more elaborate form).

> 4,1: μὴ οὖν προσέχετε, τέκνα μου, κάλλος γυναικῶν,
> μηδὲ ἐννοεῖσθε τὰς πράξεις αὐτῶν, ἀλλὰ πορεύεσθε
> ἐν ἁπλότητι καρδίας, ἐν φόβῳ κυρίου . . . ἕως οὗ ὁ
> κύριος δώῃ ὑμῖν σύζυγον, ἣν αὐτὸς θέλει, ἵνα μὴ ‑
> πάθητε, ὡς κἀγώ.

Fornication separates from God and brings near to idols
(4,6) and leads into destruction; brings reproach with men
and derision with Beliar (4,7). Joseph is the counter-
example of one who guarded himself from a woman and
cleansed/purified (ἐκαθάρισεν) his thoughts from all fornication (4,8). A key statement is thus: 4,11 ἐὰν γὰρ
μὴ κατισχύσει ἡ πορνεία τὴν ἔννοιαν ὑμῶν, οὐδὲ ὁ Βελίαρ
δύναται κατισχῦσαι ὑμῶν. We observe here that the primitive conception of sexual taboo, clean and unclean, holy
and profane, have been absorbed into a dualistic framework of God versus Beliar, and their respective spirits.
Chapter 5 speaks of the special susceptibility of women
to the spirit of fornication and this is evidenced by
their enticement of the Watchers in Gn 6. 6,1-4 concludes
with the exhortation to beware fornication and for purity
of mind (καθαρεύειν διανοίαν). 6,5-12 exhorts submission
to Levi whom God has made high priest and king for ever.

TestS: The first part of the testament deals with the
spirit of jealousy (τὸ πνεῦμα τοῦ ζήλου) with which the
prince of deceit (i.e., Beliar) blinds the mind of Simeon
against Joseph (2,6-11). His right hand stricken by God,
Simeon repents and prays to the Lord God that: ἀποκατα-
σταθῇ ἡ χείρ μου καὶ ἀποσχῶ ἀπὸ παντὸς μολυσμοῦ καὶ φθόνου
καὶ ἀπὸ πάσης ἀφροσύνης (2,13). Simeon has learnt that
"deliverance from envy comes by the fear of God" (3,4)
and that "if one takes refuge in the Lord, the evil spirit
runs away from him" (3,5). The good example of Joseph is
stated as a contrasting point (ἀγαθὸς ἀνήρ, καὶ ἔχων πνεῦμα
θεοῦ ἐν αὐτῷ, εὔσπλαγνος καὶ ἐλεήμων ὑπάρχων . . . cf.
2,4) - 4,4.

> 4,5: φυλάξασθε οὖν ὑμεῖς τέκνα μου, ἀπὸ παντὸς ζήλου
> καὶ φθόνου καὶ πορεύεσθε ἐν ἁπλότητι καρδίας, ἵνα δῷ
> καὶ ὑμῖν ὁ θεὸς χάριν καὶ δόξαν καὶ εὐλογίαν . . .
> καθὼς ἴδετε ἐν Ἰωσήφ.

---

[19]Cf. C. Edlund, ibid., pp. 53-61.

They are to love their brother with a good heart and the
spirit of envy will withdraw from them (4,7). 5,2ff.
warns against fornication in terms similar to TestR (cf.
5,3 with TestR 4,6). The remaining sections warn against
resisting Levi and speaks of the eschatological battle
(5,6), the defeat of the nations (6,3-4) and then the
spirits of deceit will be trodden underfoot and men will
rule over them (6,6).

TestL: Levi's prayer for salvation (1,4; 4,2) is answered
by a vision of the heavens where he sees the preparations
of the angels for the day of judgement when Beliar/spirits
will be routed (3,2-3), and Levi receives the blessings
of priesthood (5,1-2; cf. 4,2). He is directed by the
angel to execute vengeance on Shechem (5,3); it was because
of the abomination (βδέλυγμα) they did to Dinah (6,3), the
folly they wrought in Israel by defiling her (μιάναντες
τὴν ἀδελφήν μου) - 7,3. (This incident is used in Jubilees
as the basis of the choice of Levi as priest and for the
prohibition of all intermarriage with gentiles as "abominable," "unclean," "profanation of the divine name,"
"defilement of the sanctuary," for "Israel is holy unto
the Lord" and no uncleanness is to be found in Israel -
30.) A second vision confirms Levi's priesthood (Chap. 8).
Isaac then undertakes to instruct Levi in the laws of
priesthood (9,7) and to warn him against the spirit of
fornication (πνεῦμα τῆς πορνείας) - 9,9. Isaac predicts
that Levi's seed will pollute the holy place through fornication (9,9; cf. 14,5 - 16,1). 9,10 λαβὲ οὖν σεαυτῷ
γυναῖκα, ἔτι νέος ὤν, μὴ ἔχουσαν μῶμον μήτε βεβηλωμένην,
μήτε ἀπὸ γένους ἀλλοφύλων ἐθνῶν. 9,11 καὶ πρὸ τοῦ
εἰσελθεῖν σε εἰς τὰ ἅγια, λούου; καὶ ἐν τῷ θύειν σε,
νίπτου, καὶ ἀπαρτίζων πάλιν τὴν θυσίαν, νίπτου. What follows is Levi's fulfilment of Isaac's instructions (Chap.
11-12) on marriage and his own instructions to his children
(10,1ff. & 13,1ff.).

13,1: καὶ νῦν, τέκνα μου, ἐντέλλομαι ὑμῖν, φοβεῖσθε
Κύριον τὸν θεὸν ὑμῶν ἐξ ὅλης τῆς καρδίας ὑμῶν, καὶ
πορεύεσθε ἐν ἁπλότητι κατὰ πάντα τὸν νόμον αὐτοῦ.

Chaps. 14-16 describe the transgression of the Levites in
the "end of the ages." This transgression is described
mainly in terms of sexual taboos and with language of
ritual purity--clean/unclean, abomination, profaning, etc.:
14,6 . . . τὰς μὲν ὑπάνδρους βεβηλώσετε καὶ τὰς πόρναις
καὶ μοιχαλίσιν συναφθήσεσθε, θυγατέρας δὲ ἐθνῶν λήψεσθε
εἰς γυναῖκας, καὶ γενήσεται ἡ μῖξις ὑμῶν ὡς Σόδομα καὶ
Γόμορρα. 15,1 διὰ τοῦτο ὁ ναός, ὃν ἐκλέξεται κύριος,
ἔρημος ἔσται ἐν τῇ ἀκαθαρσίᾳ ὑμῶν, . . . 15,2 καὶ ἔσεσθε
βδέλυγμα αὐτοῖς, καὶ λήψεσθε ὄνειδος καὶ αἰσχύνην παρὰ τῆς
δικαιοκρισίας τοῦ θεοῦ. 16:1 καὶ νῦν ἐγὼ ἔγνωκα ὅτι
ἑβδομήκοντα ἑβδομάδας πλανηθήσεσθε, καὶ τὴν ἱερωσύνην
βεβηλώσετε καὶ τὰ θυσιαστήρια μιανεῖτε. Chap. 18 speaks
of the new priesthood when the Beliar and his spirits will
be bound, the gates of paradise opened and the threatening
sword against Adam removed. 19,1 concludes with the
exhortation to choose between light and darkness, between
the law of the Lord or the works of Beliar.

TestIss: Mss. b f S[1] add to the title (Διαθήκη Ἰσαχὰρ
τοῦ πέμπτου υἱοῦ Ἰακὼβ καὶ Λείας) περὶ ἁπλότητος. This
is not incorrect since the term appears 11 times and is
the one comprehensive virtue which seems to include all
others. Having upheld the continency (ἐγκράτεια) of his

stepmother Rachel and the motive of child-bearing rather
than love of pleasure (φιληδονία) on the part of his mother
Leah in respect to the transaction of the mandrakes (2,1
& 3), Issachar tells about his virtuous life. As a dili-
gent husbandman he walked in "uprightness of heart"
(εὐθύτης καρδίας) - 3,1; 3,2 καὶ ηὐλόγει με ὁ πατήρ μου
βλέπων με ὅτι ἐν ἁπλότητι πορεύομαι ἔμπροσθεν αὐτοῦ. He
is neither a "busybody," nor "envious," "malicious,"
"slandered nobody," etc., πορευόμενος ἐν ἁπλότητι ὀφθαλμῶν
(β-g,S[1]) - 3,4. He married at the age of thirty five, when
labour had consumed his strength, καὶ οὐκ ἐνενόουν ἡδονὴν
γυναικός . . . (3,5).

3,6: καὶ ἔχαιρε πάντοτε ἐπὶ τῇ ἁπλότητί μου ὁ πατήρ
μου διότι καὶ πᾶν πρῶτον γέννημα διὰ τοῦ ἱερέως τῷ
κυρίῳ προσέφερον, ἔπειτα καὶ τῷ πατρί μου. 3,7 καὶ
ὁ κύριος ἐμυριοπλασίασε τὰ ἀγαθὰ αὐτοῦ ἐν ταῖς χερσί
μου, ᾔδει δὲ καὶ ᾽Ιακὼβ ὁ πατήρ μου, ὅτι ὁ θεὸς συνεργεῖ
τῇ ἁπλότητί μου. 3,8 πάντα γὰρ πένησι καὶ θλιβομένοις
παρεῖχον ἐκ τῶν ἀγαθῶν τῆς γῆς ἐν ἁπλότητι καρδίας μου.
4,1 καὶ νῦν ἀκούσατέ μου, τέκνα, καὶ πορεύεσθε ἐν
ἁπλότητι καρδίας ὑμῶν . . .

The "perfect" (ὁ ἁπλοῦς) waits only for the will of God and
does not desire gold, or manifold dainties, varied apparel
or a long life (4,2-3). The "spirits of deceit" have no
power over him since he does not look on the beauty of
women, so that he may not pollute his mind (4,4).

4,6: πορεύεται δὲ ἐν ἁπλότητι ψυχῆς, πάντα ὁρᾷ ἐν
εὐθύτητι καρδίας, μὴ ἐπιδεχόμενος ὀφθαλμοὺς πονηροὺς
ἀπὸ τῆς πλάνης τοῦ κόσμου, ἵνα μὴ ἴδῃ διεστραμμένας
τὰς ἐντολὰς τοῦ κυρίου. 5,1 φυλάξατε οὖν τέκνα μου
νόμον θεοῦ, καὶ τὴν ἁπλότητα κτήσασθε, καὶ ἐν ἀκακίᾳ
πορεύεσθε, . . .

They are exhorted to love the Lord and neighbour, have
compassion on the weak, to practice husbandry, obey Levi
and Judah and τῇ ἁπλότητι τοῦ πατρος ὑμῶν περιπατεῖτε
(5,2-8). Issachar warns that in the end times his
descendants will forsake "perfection" (ἁπλότης) and cleave
to Beliar (6,1). In conclusion, Issachar contends that
he has not consciously committed any sin (7,1), did not
commit fornication (7,2), drank no wine, did not covet
his neighbour's desirables, had no guile, did not lie,
was charitable to the poor and was pious (7,3-5), loved
the Lord and every man (7,6), i.e., led a perfect life.
His concluding exhortation was:

7,7: ταῦτα καὶ ὑμεῖς, τέκνα μου, ποιεῖτε, καὶ πᾶν
πνεῦμα τοῦ Βελίαρ φεύξεται ἀφ᾽ ὑμῶν . . . ἔχοντες μεθ᾽
ὑμῶν τὸν θεὸν τοῦ οὐρανοῦ καὶ τῆς γῆς συμπορευόμενον
τοῖς ἀνθρώποις ἐν ἁπλότητι καρδίας.

TestB: The testament extols Joseph and exhorts imitation
of him (3,1; 4,1). The characteristic most praised is the
"good" or "pure" mind (ἀγαθὴ διάνοια; καθαρὰ διάνοια; 3,2;
4,1; 5,1; 6,5; 8,2). This is characterized in the following
manner:

3,2: καὶ ἔστω ἡ διάνοια ὑμῶν εἰς τὸ ἀγαθόν, ὡς κάμε
οἴδατε, ὅτι ὁ ἔχων τὴν διάνοιαν ὀρθὴν πάντα βλέπει
ὀρθῶς. 3,3 φοβεῖσθε κύριον καὶ ἀγαπᾶτε τὸν
πλησίον. . . . 3,4β ὁ γὰρ φοβούμενος τὸν θεὸν καὶ
ἀγαπῶν τὸν πλησίον ὑπὸ τοῦ πνεύματος τοῦ βελίαρ οὐ
δύναται πληγῆναι, σκεπαζόμενος ὑπὸ τοῦ φόβου τοῦ θεοῦ.

4,1: ἴδετε οὖν, τέκνα μου, τοῦ <u>ἀγαθοῦ ἀνδρὸς</u> τὸ τέλος,
μιμήσασθε ἐν ἀγαθῷ διὰ (β - μιμήσασθε οὖν <u>ἐν ἀγαθῇ
διανοίᾳ</u>) τὴν εὐσπλαγχνίαν αὐτοῦ . . .

4,2 ὁ γὰρ <u>ἀγαθὸς ἄνθρωπος</u> οὐκ ἔχει <u>σκοτεινὸν ὀφθαλμόν</u>,
ἐλεεῖ γὰρ πάντας, κἂν ἁμαρτωλοὶ ὦσιν.

4,3 . . . οὗτος τὸ ἀγαθὸν ποιῶν νικᾷ τὸ κακόν,
σκεπόμενος ὑπὸ τοῦ θεοῦ.

5,1: ἐὰν οὖν καὶ ὑμεῖς ἔχετε <u>ἀγαθὴν διάνοιαν</u>, καὶ οἱ
πονηροὶ ἄνθρωποι εἰρηνεύσουσιν μεθ' ὑμῶν, . . .

5,2 ἐὰν ἦτε ἀγαθοποιοῦντες καὶ τὰ <u>ἀκάθαρτα πνεύματα</u>
φεύξονται ἀφ' ὑμῶν, . . .

6,1: τὸ <u>διαβούλιον τοῦ ἀγαθοῦ ἀνδρὸς</u> οὐκ ἔστιν ἐν χειρὶ
<u>πλάνης πνεύματος Βελίαρ</u>, ὁ γὰρ <u>ἄγγελος τῆς εἰρήνης</u> ὁδηγεῖ
τὴν ψυχὴν αὐτοῦ. . . .

6,4 τὸ <u>ἀγαθὸν διαβούλιον</u> οὐ δέχεται δόξης οὐκ ἀτιμίας
ἀνθρώπων, . . .

6,5 ἡ <u>ἀγαθὴ διάνοια</u> οὐκ ἔχει δύο γλώσσας εὐλογίας καὶ
κατάρας . . . , ἀλλὰ μίαν ἔχει περὶ πάντας <u>εἰλικρινῆ
καὶ καθαρὰν διάθεσιν</u>. . . .

6,7 καὶ <u>καθαίρει τὴν διάνοιαν</u> αὐτοῦ πρὸς τὸ μὴ
καταγνωσθῆναι ὑπὸ τῶν ἀνθρώπων, ὁμοίως καὶ ὑπὸ θεοῦ.
ὁμοίως δὲ καὶ τοῦ <u>Βελίαρ</u> τὰ ἔργα διπλᾶ ἐστιν, καὶ
<u>ἁπλότητα</u> ἐν αὐτοῖς οὐκ ἔχουσιν (β-α,S[1] ὑπὸ θεοῦ καὶ
ἀνθρώπων, καὶ τοῦ Βελίαρ δὲ πᾶν ἔργον διπλοῦν ἐστι,
καὶ οὐκ ἔχει ἁπλότητα).

8,2:	c	/	β, S[1]	/	A
	ὁ γὰρ καθαρὸς	ὁ ἔχων <u>διάνοιαν καθα-</u>		ὁ γὰρ ἔχων	
	<u>νοῦς</u> οὐκ ἔχει	<u>ρὰν</u> ἐν ἀγάπῃ οὐχ ὁρᾷ		<u>αὐτὴν</u> (ἀγαθότης)	
	<u>μιασμόν</u>	γυναῖκα εἰς <u>πορνείαν</u>,		οὐχ ὁρᾷ γυναῖκα	
		οὐ γὰρ ἔχει <u>μιασμὸν</u>		εἰς <u>πορνείαν</u>	
				οὐδὲ γιγνώκει	
				<u>μιασμὸν</u>	

ἐν καρδίᾳ, ὅτι ἀναπαύεται ἐπ' αὐτὸν τὸ <u>πνεῦμα τοῦ θεοῦ</u>.

8,3: ὥσπερ γὰρ ὁ ἥλιος οὐ <u>μιαίνεται</u> προσέχων ἐπὶ <u>κόπρον</u>
καὶ <u>βόρβορον</u>, ἀλλὰ μᾶλλον ἀμφότερα ψύγει καὶ ἀπελαύνει
τὴν <u>δυσωδίαν</u>, οὕτω καὶ ὁ <u>καθαρὸς νοῦς</u> ἐν τοῖς <u>μιασμοῖς
τῆς γῆς</u> συνεχόμενος μᾶλλον οἰκοδομεῖ (emend to καθαίρει,
cf. 6,7 above; Charles suggests καθαρίζει), αὐτὸς δὲ οὐ
<u>μιαίνεται</u>.

The eschatological sections that follow (Chap. 9ff.) begin
with the prediction of Enoch (a common place in the Testaments, cf. TestS 5,4; TestL 14,5ff.) that the contemporary
generation will commit <u>fornication</u> like that of Sodom,
wanton deeds with women, etc.

The structure of thought in these testaments is a fairly

consistent one. In general, (a) the patriarch is about to die,

he calls his children and reveals to them the deepest secrets of

his heart (TestR 1,4; TestS 2,1; TestD 1,1-4); (b) this is fol-

lowed by exhortations on virtues and vices, the occasion for

which is provided by some biographical incident in the patri-

arch's life and by reference to typical examples of vices from

the Old Testament (TestR Bilhah--fornication, example of Joseph,

Watchers of Gn 6; TestS sale of Joseph--jealousy and envy, exam-

ple of Joseph; TestL Dinah, instructions of Isaac, example of

Joseph, intermarriage like that of Sodom and Gomorrah; TestJud

Tamar--fornication, drunkenness; TestIss Leah and Rachel--man-
drakes, continency, not love of pleasure; TestZ sale of Joseph--
compassion and mercy; TestD sin against Joseph, lying and anger,
truth and long-suffering; TestN order versus disorder, Sodom and
Watchers changed order of nature; TestG spirit of hatred (against
Joseph), spirit of love, law of love of one's neighbour, true
repentance, Esau (rich by evil means)--be not jealous; TestA two
ways; double-faced vs. single-faced, example of Sodom (sin
against angels); TestJos Egyptian woman--fornication vs. chastity,
prayer and fasting, brotherly love and endurance; TestB example
of Joseph, good and pure mind; fornication (like Sodom)); (c) the
concluding sections speak of the eschaton (i.e., the contemporary
period), warn against the apostasy of the later generations,
often by reference to predictions made in the writings of Enoch
(TestS 5,4 - fornication and harm to Levi; TestL 14,1 - transgressions; TestJud 18,1 - commit evils in the last days; TestD
5,6ff. - commit sin; TestN 4,1 - apostasy from the Lord, walking
in lawlessness of Gentiles and wickedness of Sodom), exhort obedience to Levi and sometimes Judah, whose salvific role in the
end times is stressed, and finally the victory of God over Beliar
and his spirits (TestR 6,5-12; TestS 5,4-7,2; TestL 14-19; Test-
Jud 21-25; TestIss 6-7; TestZ 8-10; TestD 5,4-6,10; TestN 4,1-8,
10; TestG 8,1-2; TestA 7,1-7; TestJos 19,1-12; TestB 9,1-11,5).

In particular, there are two over-arching and interpene-
trating themes which define the ideology of the Testaments.
First, the dualism between God (light, law of the Lord) and
Beliar (darkness, works of Beliar) - cf. TestL 19,1; TestN 2,6.
Second, the primitive distinction between clean and unclean, pure
and impure, especially as it pertains to sexual taboos (incest,
intermarriage, etc.). This accounts for the choice of biographical incidents in the patriarchs' lives and the frequent reference to the Watchers in Gn 6 and to Sodom and Gomorrah (see (b)
in the paragraph above). Exhortations to virtue and warnings
against vice are structured along these two dualities. It is
within this context that we find the exhortations "to walk in
perfection of heart."

The following summary schema will help us to see the dual-
isms in the structure of thought and the context in which the
concept of "perfection" occurs.

Dualism of

God/Light/Law of the Lord   versus   Beliar/Darkness/Works of Beliar

Testament of Reuben

- 7 spirits of deceit; 1st is spirit of fornication (2,1; 3,3); incest with Bilhah = abomination and impiety (3,12; 3,14; cf. Jub 33)

walk in "perfection of heart" in fear of the Lord   - beware of beauty and affairs of women (4,1)

fornication separates from God and brings near idols (4,6)

Joseph guarded himself ---------- from women and cleansed his thoughts ------- from all fornication (4,8)

if fornication doesnot overpower your mind neither can Beliar overpower you (4,11)

- women overcome more than men by spirit of fornication (e.g., Gn 6) - 5,3

pure in mind   - fornication; constant association with women is irremediable disease to them, and destruction of Beliar and eternal reproach to us (6,3)

Testament of Simeon

- prince of deceit; spirit of jealousy (2,7)

prays for restoration of his hand and to keep away ------- from all pollution, envy and folly (2,13)

deliverance from envy comes by fear of God; if one takes refuge in the Lord, the evil spirit runs away from him (3,4-5)

Joseph = good man; spirit of God in him

walk in "perfection of heart"   - beware of jealousy and envy (4,5)

love the brother with a "good heart" and spirit of envy will withdraw (4,7)

make hearts good; ways straight; - beware of fornication (5,2-3)

fornication is mother of evils which separates from God brings near to Beliar (5,3)

Testament of Levi

- abomination, folly and defilement done to Dinah (6,3; 7,3; cf. Jub 30)

Instructions of Isaac: - beware spirit of fornication take a wife without ------------- blemish
                    not ------------- defiled/polluted
                    not ------------- from foreign races
frequent bathing and washing in exercise of cult (9,7-11)

Levi's commands: fear the Lord -
with a "whole heart," walk in
"perfection" according to all
his law (13,1)

                        - Sins of Levites in the end
                          times: to pollute/defile
                          wedded women; be joined with
                          harlots and adulteresses; to
                          marry daughters of Gentiles
                          (=union like that of Sodom and
                          Gomorrah); will be unclean, an
                          abomination; will receive re-
                          proach and shame; will defile
                          priesthood and pollute sacri-
                          fices (Chaps. 14-16)

choose   light   - or darkness
              law of the Lord   or works of Beliar (19,1)

Testament of Issachar

self-control/continence   - love of pleasure (2,1; 2,3)

walked in "uprightness of heart" -

walked in "perfection"   -

walked in "perfection of eyes" - (not a) busybody, envious,
                                  malicious, slanderous (3,1-4)

Married late, did not think ----- on pleasure of women (3,5)

"perfection" = gave first fruits -
to the Lord, then to father (3,6)

God aided his "perfection" by -
multiplying His goods so that he
provided the poor and afflicted
"in perfection heart" from the
goods of the earth (3,7-8)

children, walk in "perfection -
of your heart" (4,1)

"The perfect" awaits the will - does not desire: gold, dain-
                                  ties, apparel, long life
                                  (4,2-3)

                 The spirits of deceit have no power over
                 him since he does not look on the beauty
                 of women, so that he may not pollute his
                 mind with corruption (4,4)

He walks in "perfection of soul" -
sees all things in "uprightness
of heart"
he does not admit --------------- evil eyes from the deceit of
                              the world (4,6)

keep the law of God, acquire -
"perfection," walk in guilelessness (5,1), love God and
neighbour, have compassion on
poor and weak, practise husbandry,
walk in the "perfection of your
father" (5,2-8)

                        - (in last times) your sons will
                          forsake "perfection" . . . and
                        will cleave to Beliar (6,1)

106

Issachar's perfection: no sin, -
no fornication, no wine, no
covetousness, no guile, no
lie; sympathy for afflicted,
charity to poor, practised
piety and truth; loved the
Lord and every man (7,1-6)

      do these things and every spirit of Beliar will
      flee from you . . . having God with you and
      walking with men in "perfection of heart" (7,7)

Testament of Benjamin

good mind/right mind sees right -
or straight; fear the Lord and
love neighbour (3,2-3)

      he who fears God and loves the neighbour cannot
      be smitten by the spirit of Beliar, being
      shielded by the fear of God (3,4; cf. Prov 2,7)

Good man does not have ---------- a dark eye,
has mercy even on sinners (4,2)

      he overcomes evil by doing good, shielded by
      God (4,3)

if you have a good mind --------- wicked men
are at peace with you, etc. (5,1)

      if you do well, unclean spirits will flee
      from you (5,2)

inclination of a good man
            is not ------- in the hand of the deceit of
                        the spirit of Beliar (6,1)

angel of peace guides his soul
good inclination does not
             receive ------- glory or dishonour of men (6,4)
good mind does not have --------- two tongues of praise and curse,
                        etc.
but has one clean and pure
disposition to all (6,5)

He purifies his mind so as not - works of Beliar are twofold,
to be condemned by men or God   there is no "perfection" in
                            them (6,7)

Clean mind does not look at ----- women for fornication
for it does not have ----------- defilement in heart,
because spirit of God rests
on him (8,2)

      For just as the sun is not defiled/polluted by
      approaching on dung and mire, but rather dries
      both and drives out the bad smell, so also the
      clean mind embroiled in the pollutions of the
      earth rather purifies (emended) and is not
      itself defiled (8,3)

            - present generation will commit
              fornication like that of Sodom
              and renew wanton deeds with
              women (9,1)

The obvious and most noticed meaning of "perfection of
heart" is its root meaning of wholeness or totality. Thus the

exhortation to fear God with a "whole heart" and to walk in "perfection" according to <u>all</u> his law (TestL 13,1) are synonymous expressions for complete fidelity to God's will. Acquisition of "perfection," keeping the law, walking in guilelessness, love of God and neighbour, compassion on the poor and weak are parallel expressions for full compliance with religious obligations (TestIss 5,1-2). Hence rendering of the first fruits to God and parents and acts of charity to the poor and afflicted are depicted as "perfection" (ibid., 3,6-8). Briefly, fulfillment of the great commandments (Mk 12,30-31) which emphasize wholeness (with all your heart, mind, etc.) also characterizes the nature of "perfection/wholeness" in the Testaments:[20]

> TestR 4,1 - walk in <u>perfection of heart</u> in <u>fear of the Lord</u>
> TestS 4,7 - <u>love the brother</u> with a <u>good heart</u> and the spirit of envy will withdraw (cf. 3,4-5)
> TestIss 5,1-2 - acquire <u>perfection</u> . . . <u>love God and neighbour</u>
> " 7,6 - <u>I loved the Lord</u>; likewise also <u>every man</u> with <u>all my heart</u>
> " 7,7 - <u>do these things</u> . . . and every spirit of Beliar will flee from you
> TestB 3,4 - who <u>fears God</u> and <u>loves neighbour</u> cannot be smitten by the spirit of Beliar (cf. 4,3; 5,2); see below TestJud 23,5; TestD 5,3; TestG 7,7; TestA 6,1

These examples show the dualistic framework in which these characteristic expressions are cast and phrases synonymous to "perfection of heart"--i.e., "good heart," "all my heart." The range of such latter expressions is wide and the meaning equivalent:

> TestS 5,2 - make hearts good . . . and ways straight
> TestJud 23,5 - when with perfect heart (teleia kardia) you repent and walk in all His commandments
> TestIss 3,1-4 - walked in uprightness of heart
>   walked in perfection
>   walked in perfection of eyes
> " 4,6 - walks in perfection of soul
>   sees all things in uprightness of heart
>   does not admit evil eyes from the deceit of the world
> TestZ 7,2 - give to every man with a good heart (cf. <u>TestIss</u> 3,7-8)
> TestD 2,4-5 - spirit of anger casts around him a net of deceit blinds his eyes, darkens his mind . . . hatred of heart, so as to be envious

---

[20]This aspect of the meaning of perfection has been underlined by C. Edlund: "In den Test. Patr. vereinigen sich zum ersten Mal im Frömmigkeitsleben des Judentums die beiden Gebote, die die Liebe zu Gott und die Liebe zum Nächsten betreffen. . . . Es gilt, <u>ganzherzig</u> im Verhältnis zu Gott und <u>weitherzig</u> im Verhältnis zu seinen Mitmenschen zu sein" (ibid., p. 79; see also p. 50).

```
TestD 3,3 - soul (of an angry man) does not see right
  "  5,3 - love the Lord . . . and one another with a true
           heart
TestN 3,1 - keeping silence in purity/cleanliness of heart
TestG 7,7 - put away jealousy from your souls, and love one
           another with uprightness of heart
TestA 1,2 - all that is upright in the sight of the Lord
  "  6,1 - attend to the commandments of the Lord following
           truth with singleness of face (cf. 4,1; 5,4)
TestJos 4,6 - Lord is pleased with those who approach him
           with clean/pure heart and undefiled lips versus
           uncleanness and adultery
TestB 3,2 - right mind sees rightly/correctly
  "  4,2 - good man does not have a dark eye
           (etc., see above p. 106).
```

Thus "perfection of heart" is one among several ways for expressing integrity of religious conduct; others being, "uprightness of heart," "perfection of eyes," "seeing right," "perfection of soul," "good heart," "true heart," "purity of heart," "singleness of face," "right mind," "good mind," "pure mind." The contrasts are: "evil eyes," "dark eye," "blinding of eyes," "darkening of mind," "hatred of heart," "double-faced," "twofold," etc.[21]

An aspect of the meaning of "perfection" in the Testaments, which seems to have been overlooked, is its close connection to the thought world of ritual purity--of clean and unclean, pure and impure, pollution, abomination, etc.--a second over-arching theme with the eschatological dualism. The predominance of this theme in the content and over-all structure of the writings has been indicated above (pp. 98-103). Specifically, it deals with sexual transgressions of incest and intermarriage or, generally, fornication (porneia). Such were the grave sins of the patriarchs and such will be the sins of the generation in the last days.[22] These sins belong to the realm of Beliar and his spirits. Reuben's incest with Bilhah is an abomination and impiety (cf. especially Jub 33) and he exhorts his children to beware the beauty and affairs of women and to walk in "perfection of heart" in the fear of the Lord (TestR 4,1). See further the summary chart above, p. 104, under TestR. Simeon prays for the restoration of his hand and that he be kept from "pollution," envy and folly (TestS 2,13); exhorts to make hearts good and ways straight and to beware fornication (5,2-3). Isaac's instructions

---

[21] It was the special burden of Edlund's work to show that "perfection of heart" and "perfection of eyes" are synonymous and which provide the clue for understanding Mt 6:22-23 (esp. pp. 62-79).

[22] Cf. TestL 14-16; TestB 9,1; TestJud 23,1-5; TestZ 9,5; TestD 5,5.

to Levi are to beware fornication, to take a wife without blemish, undefiled and not from a foreign race, and to wash and bathe
frequently in the exercise of the sacrificial cult (TestL 9,7-
11). In the TestB, a good and clean mind does not have two
tongues, or double sight and double hearing, but a single disposition, clean and pure. The works of Beliar are twofold and
there is no perfection in them (6, 5-7). A clean/pure mind does
not look at women for fornication, for it has no defilement in
the heart (8,2); and this is followed by the simile of the sun
(8,3; see above p. 106). This association of "perfection" with
ritual purity, in this case sexual taboos, is knit into the
dualistic theme of the Testaments partly with the aid of formu-
laic statements:

TestR 4,6: βόθρος γάρ ἐστι ψυχῆς ἡ ἁμαρτία τῆς πορνείας,
            χωρίζουσα ἀπὸ θεοῦ καὶ προσεγγίζουσα τοῖς εἰδώλοις, . . .
TestS 5,3: . . . ὅτι ἡ πορνεία μήτηρ ἐστι τῶν κακῶν, χωρίζουσα
            ἀπὸ τοῦ θεοῦ καὶ προσεγγίζουσα τῷ Βελίαρ.
TestR 4,11: ἐὰν γὰρ μὴ κατισχύσει ἡ πορνεία τὴν ἔννοιαν
            ὑμῶν, οὐδὲ ὁ Βελίαρ δύναται κατισχύσαι ὑμῶν.
TestIss 4,4: καί γε τὰ πνεύματα τῆς πλάνης οὐδὲν ἰσχύσουσιν
            πρὸς αὐτὸν (i.e., ὁ ἁπλοῦς), οὐ γὰρ εἶδεν ἐπιδέξασθαι
            κάλλος θηλείας, ἵνα μὴ ἐν διαστροφῇ μιάνῃ τὸν νοῦν
            αὐτοῦ. (cf. TestJud Chap. 18)

The association of fornication with idolatry is a traditional one
(Wis Sol 14,12; Philo, Spec Leg i,331f.; Conf 144; Decal 7-8; Mig
69; Decal 7-8) and we note above the parallelism of idols with
Beliar (TestR 4,6 and TestS 5,3). In the TestR the first of the
seven spirits of deceit is the spirit of fornication (2,1; 3,1).
The same association of fornication with idolatry is also found
in the New Testament (1Cor 10,7-8; Eph 5,5; Col 3,5; Rev 2,14;
2,20). The rationale for this association lies partly in the
fact that both idols and fornication or sexual taboos are rele-
gated to the realm of the "unclean" (Lv 18; 20; Eze 16,22; Isa
57,5; Dt 29,17; 1Kg 21,26; 2Kg 23,24; Eze 6,9; 16,36; 20,7; 23,
37, etc.; 2Ch 15,8); and one finds the frequent expression of
"going whoring/fornicating (zānāh) after their gods/demons," etc.
(Ex 34,15; 34,16; Lev 17,7; 20,5; Dt 31,16; Jg 2,17, etc.). One
also finds in the New Testament the association of such terms as
uncleanness/abomination/impurity with idols as well as with fornication (Acts 15,20; Rom 2,22; 2Cor 12,21; Gal 5,19; Eph 5,3;
Col 3,5; Rev 17,4; Eph 5,5). On the OT, see the extended note
at the end of this chapter, "Perfection in the Old Testament."

The meaning of "perfection" in the sense of ritual purity is
thus one which the Testaments of the Twelve Patriarchs shares
with the Old Testament and its specific contribution lies in the

casting of the concept into a dualistic framework and in its particular emphasis on sexual and racial purity. The ritual dimension is not absent in Qumran as can be seen in such a passage as 1QM 7,4-6 (see above p. 94), although the emphasis there is a sectarian one in that the "perfect of the way" is one who belongs to the community/sect and lives in total commitment to the ideology of the sect--i.e., its eschatological self-understanding (see above pp. 96-98).

Comparative Structures of Thought: Preliminary Comparisons with Philo and Hebrews

In the Old Testament, Testaments of the Twelve Patriarchs and in the literature of Qumran, there is no correlation between the concept of perfection and immediacy to the divine in terms of going beyond the world of intermediaries. As we have seen above (pp. 93-96), the presence of the angels does not raise the problem of access or immediacy to God. But it is precisely this correlation between perfection and immediacy which is central to the thought world of Philo and Hebrews (see above pp. 93-94).

In the Old Testament and Testaments of the Twelve Patriarchs, perfection describes a state of religious purity and full/total adherence to the religious obligations (both cultic and moral--a distinction which is not clearly made in this thought world). In Qumran, the term perfection acquires in addition a sectarian quality in that it implies belonging to the sect and full commitment and adherence to the religious ideology of the sect--observance of the ritual calendar, knowledge of the eschatological mysteries, life of purity in preparation for the eschatological battle, etc. The Testaments of the Twelve Patriarchs shares with Qumran a dualistic frame of thought, but with particular emphasis on sexual and racial purity.

On the other hand, in both Philo and Hebrews (as outlined above pp. 93-96), perfection implies going beyond the intermediary world and immediate access to God. Furthermore, one does not find in Hebrews the characteristic vocabulary associated with perfection in the Old Testament, Testament of the Twelve Patriarchs and Qumran, i.e., "walking in perfection of heart," "perfect of the way," "upright," "fear of God," "perfection of eyes," "good mind," "right mind," "duplicity" versus "singleness," "whole hearted" obedience to the law, terms in parallelism as "righteous," "faithful," "upright," etc. The overriding theme is the Christian's access to the holy of holies and this understanding of the cult in relation to perfection has its closest analogy in Philo.

Extended Note

Perfection in the Old Testament

It is not our intention to deal at length with the Old Testament background (see C. Edlund, Das Auge der Einfalt, Chap. II) and the controversy whether "perfection" is a moral or cultic term (G. von Rad: "The word that one translates "devout" (tamīm), following Luther, actually means "whole" or "complete," not, to be sure, in the sense of moral perfection but rather in relationship to God. It signifies complete, unqualified surrender. The demand, shortened here, is more fully stated in Deut. 18.13. . ." Genesis, A Commentary, p. 193--on Gn 17,1; " . . . does not mean "perfect" in an absolute (i.e., moral) sense; it is a term of sacred usage, and means the condition of a man (or a sacrifice) which conforms to the cult and is thereby pleasing to God," ibid., p. 122--on Gn 6,9. C. Edlund in his summary of the Old Testament meaning states: "Diese Bundestreue zeigt sich in Ganzheit: in g a n z h e r z i g e m Gehorsam gegenüber Jahve, kultisch wie ethisch, und in w e i t h e r z i g e r Güte, wenn es das Verhältnis zum Nächsten, zum Bundesbruder, gilt. Einige der grossen Vordergrundgestalten des Alten Testaments, Noah und Abraham, Hiob und David werden in diesem Sinn geschildert und religiös-ethisch charakterisiert," ibid., p. 47).

It seems to me that the distinction between moral or ethical and cultic is an inappropriate one for the Old Testament and especially as it pertains to the term "perfection." Its root meaning of "complete"/"whole"/"total" or its application to fulfilment of covenant stipulations is not in dispute, as can be seen from parallel expressions as "doing all the commandments" (1Kg 9,4) or "walking in the law of the Lord" (Ps 119,1). Nor is its association with terms as "righteous" (Gn 6,9; Ps 7,9; Job 22,3; Prov 11,3-6), "loyal/faithful" (Ps 18,26; 101,6) or "uprightness" (Ps 37,37; Job 1,8; 2,3; Ps 25,21; Prov 2,7, etc.) in dispute. The question is whether the basic sense can be deduced from these to be a relational one, as is asserted by both von Rad (ibid., p. 193) and Edlund ("Es handelt sich hier um die absolute und ganzherzige Zugehörigkeit zu Jahve," ibid., p. 50; i.e., in reference to Dt 18,13). And whether the covenant is the basic context for the understanding of the term is also questionable (as argued by Edlund).

Alternatively, if one attends to the "cultic" meaning of the term "perfection," which has to do with purity, holiness, cleanness, pollution, abomination, unclean, etc., and these as they relate to "ethical/moral" conduct, then one can suggest a different line of interpretation of the passages in which "perfection" is attributed to Old Testament personalities as well as in other cases:

Dt 18,13: Vs. 1-8 deal with the law relating to priesthood and 9-22 with the law concerning the prophets (cf. G. von Rad, Deuteronomy, A Commentary, pp. 122-25). In the latter case, the cultic and divination practices of the Canaanites are "abominations" (tôᶜebôt) which Israel is forbidden to practice and is the reason for the dispossession of the nations (9-12). "You shall be perfect (tamīm) before the Lord your God" (13). I would suggest that what this passage is saying is simply that Israel shall be "clean/pure/whole" by not committing these "abominations." That is its minimal contextual meaning. von Rad's comment, it seems to me, is both vague and misleading: "The expression is very typical of the religious thought of Israel which received its standards far less from ideas than from certain conditions of fellowship. It is not moral and religious 'perfection' which is demanded of Israel, but rather an undivided commitment, without any reinsurance by consulting strange gods, spirits of the dead, etc., to the conditions of fellowship with Yahweh" (ibid., p. 123). How one can speak of "certain conditions of fellowship" which are not "ideas" eludes me, as do terms such as "moral and religious perfection." If by the latter one means "sinlessness," I would argue that it certainly does, since the whole process of atoning is to ensure that a community remains in such a state.

Ju 9,16 & 19: Abimelech invokes the aid of the kinsmen of his Shechemite mother and with their financial help puts to death his seventy step brothers with the exception of the youngest, Jotham (9,1-5). The killing seems to have been done according to ritual prescriptions--"upon one stone"--so as to avoid the guilt involved in the shedding of blood (cf. 1Sam 14,33ff.; 2Kg 10-11; see G. F. Moore, A Critical and Exegetical Commentary on Judges, pp. 242-43). Thereupon, Abimelech was made king by the citizens of Shechem and Bethmillo. At the end of the parable of Jotham, the Shechemites are asked if they have acted "in truth and perfection" (ɔemet, tāmîm) in making Abimelech king and with the house of Jerubbaal (vs. 16;19). If not, and the presumption is that they did not, then they were accursed (vs. 20). God sends an evil spirit between Abimelech and the Shechemites so "that the violence done to the seventy sons of Jerubbaal might come and their blood be laid upon Abimelech their brother, who slew them, and upon the men of Shechem, who strengthened his hands to slay his brothers" (vs. 24). I would suggest that "tamîm" here means "purity" in the sense of not violating the rules and obligations of kinship and bloodshed. The RSV translation--"honor"--is too abstract and moralistic in the modern sense.

Gn 20,5f.: Chap. 20 is attributed to E and is a variant of Gn 12,10-20 (J) and 26,6-11 (J). In contrast to Gn 12, the theme of guilt plays a central role in this story (cf. G. von Rad, Genesis, A Commentary, p. 225). Abimelech's taking of Sarah constituted a fatal danger (vs. 3--"behold, you are a dead man") since he had violated a marriage, although unwittingly. He protests to Yahweh that his people are "righteous" (ṣaddîq) and that he had acted "with perfection of heart" (tōm lēbab) and "cleanness of hand" (nīqyon kap; cf. Ps 26,6; 73,13; Ex 25,29; 37,16-- passages which show the ritual character of the term). The danger to the king and community is removed by restoration of Sarah and the intercessory prayer of the prophet, i.e., Abraham, and is an understanding of prophecy ascribed to theEElohist (von Rad, ibid., p. 223-24). There is another and, it seems to me, more traditional way by which the unwitting sin was righted and which the Elohist has woven into the story, namely, vs. 16. The thousand pieces of silver given to Abraham were a "covering" (kāsût) of the eyes to all who are with Sarah and her "being made right" (ykḥ) before all. The exact meaning of the former expression is unclear (according to von Rad "undoubtedly a legal term," ibid., p. 224); here again the distinction between a "legal" and "cultic" procedure seems to me to be on shaky grounds. I would, therefore, suggest that "perfection of heart" here has the connotation of "cleanness or purity" in the sense that no conscious violation of a taboo was intended and is analogous in meaning to the ritual term "cleanness of hand." The objective violation of taboo was righted by means of monetary compensation (vs. 16). The statement of 2Sam 15,11 could be interpreted in the same way as implying no conscious intention of violating their loyalty to David, which was undoubtedly sanctioned by ritual procedures.

Gn 6,9; 17,1; 25,27: The context of these passages is of no help. At most one can advance some conjectures on the basis of our suggestions thus far. That Noah is "îsh saddîq tāmîm" is probably to be seen as a contrast to the continual wickedness of men on earth which is exemplified by the intercourse of the sons of God with the daughters of men. Given the fact that the cultic view of the world concerns itself with the setting of boundaries between what is clean and unclean, the sacred/holy and profane, etc., Gn 6,1-4 constitutes a break down in the "order" of the universe, and Noah alone emerges as an exception who did not violate these boundaries and hence maintained "justice" and "purity/wholeness." Ascribed to P, 17-1-14 is a variant of the covenant with Abraham (15,7-21) and what is stressed in comparison is the circumcision. To walk before God and be "perfect" could be interpreted as conduct which is "pure" according to priestly prescriptions (cf. Lv 26). In Gn 25,27, the parallel items in the comparison between Esau and Jacob are: "man who knows hunting"--"perfect man (îsh tām)," and "man of the field"--"one who dwells in tents." It is commonly recognized that the comparison is between the "roving and more uncultured hunter" and the "more civilized Israelites" (von Rad, ibid., pp. 260f.). From this has followed quite fanciful interpretations of "tām": von Rad--"means actually belonging to the solidarity of community life with its moral regulations, a solidarity that the hunter does not know . . . " (ibid., p. 261); E. A. Speiser--"The over-all contrast, then, is between the aggressive hunter and the reflective semi-nomad," (The Anchor Bible Genesis, p. 195, note 27). I would suggest that the contrast is between the occupation and life of a hunter which was considered "unclean" and that of a shepherd which was deemed "clean/pure" (cf. Gn 46,34: " . . . every shepherd is an abomination (tôᶜebāh) to the Egyptians").

    Job: In the prologue (Chaps. 1-2), Job is described as a man who was "perfect (tām) and upright (yaŝar), one who feared God and turned away from evil" (1,1; 1,8; 2,3). The specific act of piety that is mentioned is that Job had his sons "purified" (yᵉqaddᵉŝem) and offered burned offerings for their inadvertent sins (1,5).

    In the dialogue (Chaps. 3-31), Job's claims to perfection are described with terms which belong to the realm of ritual purity--clean, pure, innocent, etc.:[23]

> "Is not your fear of God your confidence,
> and the integrity (tom) of your ways your hope", (4,6).
> "Think now, who that was innocent (naqî) ever perished?
> Or where were the upright (yᵉsarîm) cut off", (4,7).

> "Can mortal man be righteous (yiṣdāq) before God,
> Can a man be pure (yithar) before his Maker", (4,17).

> "if you are pure (zak) and upright (yaŝar),
> surely then he will rouse himself for you", (8,6).

> "Behold, God will not reject a blameless man (tām),
> nor take the hand of evildoers", (8,20).

> "Though I am innocent (ᵓeṣdaq), my own mouth would
> condemn me; though I am blameless (tām), he would
> prove me perverse", (9,20).
> "I am blameless (tām); . . . " (9,21).

> "I become afraid of all my suffering,
> for I know thou wilt not hold me innocent (tᵉnaqqēnî)",
> (9,28).

---

[23]Translation is that of the Revised Standard Version.

114

"For you say, 'My doctrine is pure (zak),
and I am clean (bar) in God's eyes", (11,4),[24]

"Surely then you will lift up your face without
blemish (mimmûm); . . . ". (11,15).

" . . . a just (saddîq) and blameless man (tāmîm),
am a laughingstock", (12,4c).

"Who can bring a clean thing (ṭāhôr) out of an
unclean (miṭṭāmē);
There is not one", (14,4).

"What is man, that he can be clean (yizkeh)?
Or he that is born of a woman, that he can be
righteous (yiṣdaq)?" (15,14)
"Behold, God puts no trust in his holy ones,
and the heavens are not clean (zakkû) in his sight;
how much less one who is abominable (niteᶜāb) and
corrupt (neʾĕlāḥ), . . . ", (15,15-16a).

"My face is red with weeping, and on my eyelids is
deep darkness;
although there is no violence (hāmās) in my hands,
and my prayer is pure (zakkah)", (16,17).

"How then can man be righteous (yiṣdaq) before God?
How can he who is born of woman be clean (yizkeh)?",
(25,4; cf. 15,15f. above).

"Far be it from me to say that you are right (ʾaṣdîq);
till I die I will not put away my integrity (tom)
from me", (27,5).

In the discourses of Elihu (Chaps. 32-37), Job is charged
with the same claims to being "clean", "pure" and "innocent."

"You say, 'I am clean (zak), without transgression;
I am pure (hap), there is no iniquity in me. . . . ".
(33,9).

Given the way in which the terms expressing the distinction
between "clean" and "unclean" ("abomination," "corruption") is
woven with terms such as "righteous/just" and "upright," it
would be false to deny the ritual or cultic character of Job's
"perfection" (M. H. Pope: "Taken together they indicate the peak
of moral perfection"--i.e., the terms tam and yasar--The Anchor
Bible Job, p. 7). In fact, the Akkadian parallels to Job stress
this ritual character of the righteousness of the sufferer; he
protests that he was being treated:

"Like one who did not offer a libation to a god,
And at meal-time did not invoke a goddess,
Who did not bow his face and did not know reverence,
In whose mouth prayer and supplication ceased
For whom the holiday had been eliminated, the eššešu
    festival had been curtailed,
Who became negligent, despised their images,
Who did not teach his people religion and reverence,
Who did not remember his god, although eating his
    food,

---

[24]M. H. Pope emends this passage to read: "You say, 'My
doctrine is pure.' You are clean in your own eyes" (ibid., p.
80). Pope explains: "The Job of the Dialogue does not know that
God reckons him as just; this is his complaint, that God treats
him as the wicked ought to be (and often are not) treated" (ibid.,
p. 81, note on 4b).

Who forsook his goddess and did not offer her a
   libation;
Nay, worse than one who became proud and forgot his
   (divine) lord,
Who swore frivolously in the name of his honourable
   deity - like such a one have I become!
Yet I myself was thinking only of prayer and suppli-
   cation:
Supplication was my concern, sacrifice my rule;
The day of the worship of the gods was my delight,
The day of my goddess' procession was my profit and
   wealth.
Veneration of the king was my joy,
And I enjoyed music in his honor.
I taught my land to observe the divine ordinances,
To honor the name of the goddess I instructed my
   people.
The king's majesty I equated to that of a god,
And reverence for the (royal) palace I inculcated
   in the troops.
Oh that I only knew that these are well pleasing
   to a god!"
("I will praise the Lord of Wisdom", ANET, cols. II,
12-33; pp. 434-35; translator: R. H. Pfeiffer.)

   The sufferer is healed through purification (ibid., IIIA,
24-28), the removal of his trespasses (ibid., IIIA, 58) and the
exorcism of the demons of sickness. In the end he praises Marduk
and offers incense, gifts and libations (ibid., IV,35-41). This
is perhaps as good a description as we have of what is meant by
the term "perfection" in the Old Testament. M. H. Pope incorrectly states: "The Mesopotamian stresses his ritual piety, Job
his ethical probity" (ibid., p. LIX). Another Akkadian text is
an acrostic poem which reads: "I, Saggil-kinam-ubbib, incanta-
tion priest, worship god and king" and the name means "O Saggil
(i.e., Marduk's temple) declare the righteous one pure." The
dialogue runs in terms quite similar to Job:

   "Have I withheld the meal-oblation? (No), I have
      prayed to the gods,
   I have presented the prescribed sacrifices to the
      goddess . . . " (ANET, V,54-55, p. 439).

   "They walk on a lucky path those who do not seek
      [a god],
   Those who devoutly pray to [a goddess] become poor
      and weak.
   In my childhood I [investigated] the mind of the god,
   In humility and piety have I searched for the goddess:
   (And yet) a corvee without profit I bear like a yoke;"
   (ibid., VII,70-74).

   "You have rejected the truth, you have despised the
      decree of the god.
   Not to observe the ordinances of the god was the wish
      of your soul,
   The correct purifications of the goddess you have
      [neglected]," (ibid., VIII,79-81).

   We observe here the same stress on ritual piety and its
close tie to concepts of obedience to divine decrees and ordinances. It is clear that one ought not to separate the "ritual"
and "moral" in this thought world.

   In light of this background, an aspect of the story of Job
receives some illumination. By afflicting Job with a skin

disease which spread throughout (a crucial criterion for distinguishing between a skin ailment which was clean and unclean in Lv 13), Job had been rendered unclean in the eyes of the community. In the LXX, instead of "in the ashes" of the MT (2,8), we have "epi tēs koprias" (on a dunghill) and adds "outside the city"--all indicative of his unclean state. Yet Job, contrary to traditional beliefs, held that he was "clean/pure," "righteous," "upright" and "perfect" when his external malady had already pronounced him unclean or imperfect. Hence--

"If I am wicked, woe to me! If I am righteous, I can
   lift up my head,
for I am filled with disgrace and look upon my
   affliction (10,15).

"He has made me a byword of the peoples,
and I am one before whom men spit." (117,6)

"He has put my brethren far from me,
and my acquaintances are wholly estranged from me.
. . . I have become an alien in their eyes" (19,13 & 15c).

"They abhor me (ticǎbûnî), they keep aloof from me;
they do not hesitate to spit at the sight of me"
(30,10).

One who is reckoned unclean stands outside the protection of the sacral community and is thus victimized by his enemies and other outcasts, and this seems to be the import of Chap. 30. We find the same idea expressed in Ps 38 (a lament), although the Psalmist holds to the traditional views of Job's comforters that his sickness was due to his sins and his only recourse was confession and prayer for God's aid:

"There is no soundness (ᵓên mᵉtōm) in my flesh
      because of thy indignation
there is no health in my bones
      because of my sin" (38,3; cf. vs. 7).

"My friends and companions stand aloof from my plague,
      and my kinsmen stand afar off (38,11).
Those who seek my life lay their snares,
those who seek my hurt speak of ruin . . . " (38,12).

Contrary to the Job of the dialogue, the psalmist:

"Yea, I am like a man who does not hear,
in whose mouth are no rebukes" (38,14; cf. Ps 41).

The same victimization by enemies and ill-wishers is also expressed in the Akkadian parallels:

"While the grave was still open they took possession
      of my jewels,
Before I was dead the weeping (for me) was ended.
All my land said, "How sad!" (alternative translation
         is "How has he been mistreated").

My ill-wisher heard it, and countenance shone
      (with joy);
They brought the good news to the woman who was my
      ill-wisher, and her spirit was delighted".
("I will praise the Lord of Wisdom", ibid., II
reverse, 49-53; pp. 435-36).

"The god brought me scarcity instead of wealth;
A cripple above, a fool in front,
Have stolen my necklace, and I have been brought low"
(A Dialogue about Human Misery, ibid., VII,75-77).
"As if he were a thief, they (i.e., the gods) mistreat

a wretched man,
They bestow slander on him, they plot murder
 against him,
Disloyally they bring every evil upon him because
 he lacks protection; . . . "
(ibid., XXVI,283-85).

Another aspect worth noticing in Job, in view of the warnings against fornication in association with exhortations to
"perfection" in the Testaments of the Twelve Patriarchs, is the
importance that Job lays in the recitation of his past behaviour
on his sinlessness in this respect (Chap. 31 in the form of 16
oaths):

"I have made a covenant with my eyes;
how then could I look upon a virgin?" (31,1).
"If my step has turned aside from the way,
and my heart has gone after my eyes,
and if any spot (m'ûm) has cleaved to my hands;
then let me sow, and another eat; . . . " (31,7f.)
"If my heart has been enticed to a woman,
and I have lain in wait at my neighbour's door;
then let my wife grind for another,
and let others bow down upon her.
For that would be a heinous crime;[25]
that would be an iniquity to be punished by the
 judges;
for that would be a fire which consumes upto Abaddon,
and it would burn to the root all my increase"
(31,9-12).

This could have served as a key text for some of the Testaments. Expressions such as "to see all things in the uprightness
of heart" (TestIss 4,6), "perfection of eyes" (ibid., 3,4),
"right mind sees right" (TestB 3,2), etc., are analogous statements to Job 31,7 and 31,1. They imply intention and behaviour
which is fully in accordance with religious prescriptions (perhaps the term "religious" could avoid the false distinction
between cultic and moral in this respect), within a religious
world view which is concerned with distinctions between clean and
unclean/abomination, pure and impure, and sacred and profane.

In terms of the history of morals/ethics, I think, that a
case could be made that morals are essentially abstractions (de-
contextualized applications) of the ancient understanding of
taboo, a world organized and differentiated by concepts of clean
and unclean, sacred and profane, which provide the boundaries for
communal existence--of what is permissible and what is not. The
Psalms and Proverbs give us numerous examples of such generalized
or abstracted usage of the term "perfection"/"wholeness," which
has become the basis for a moralistic interpretation of the term.
One such example will suffice, in which the Law is praised with
such "abstractions":

---

[25]M. H. Pope translates verse 11a: "For that were licen-
tiousness." His note on the translation is instructive: "This
word (zimmah) is used regularly of lewdness, indecent and dis-
gusting sexual conduct. A cognate of this word is used in
Ugaritic in reference to some shameful misdeed committed by the
slave girls at a divine feast, an act so repulsive that Baal himself stood up and spat in the midst of the assembly of the gods!"
(ibid., p. 203, note on 11a.).

118

"The law of the Lord is perfect (t^{e}mîmāh)
    reviving the soul;
the testimony of the Lord is sure (ne'ĕmānāh)
    making wise the simple;
the precepts of the Lord are right (y^{e}šārîm)
    rejoicing the heart;
the commandment of the Lord is pure (bārāh)
    enlightening the eyes;
the fear of the Lord is clean (t^{e}hôrāh)
    enduring for ever;
the ordinances of the Lord are true ('ĕmet)
    and righteous altogether."
(Ps 19,7-9)

PART II

THE SUPERIORITY OF JESUS OVER THE INTERMEDIARIES
AND EXEMPLARS OF PERFECTION

<u>Introduction</u> to the interpretation of the main themes and
arguments of Hebrews.

It is not perchance that the author advances his arguments
through a series of comparisons both explicit and implicit. To
list these is at the same time to point to some of the major
themes of the writing:

1,4 τοσούτῳ κρείττων γενόμενος τῶν ἀγγέλων ὅσῳ διαφορώτερον
παρ' αὐτοὺς κεκληρονόμηκεν ὄνομα.

3,3 πλείονος γὰρ οὗτος δόξης παρὰ Μωυσῆν ἠξίωται καθ' ὅσον
πλείονα τιμὴν ἔχει τοῦ οἴκου ὁ κατασκευάσας αὐτόν.

7,6-7 ὁ δὲ μὴ γενεαλογούμενος ἐξ αὐτῶν δεδεκάτωκεν 'Αβραάμ,
καὶ τὸν ἔχοντα τὰς ἐπαγγελίας εὐλόγηκεν. χωρὶς δὲ πάσης
ἀντιλογίας τὸ ἔλαττον ὑπὸ τοῦ κρείττονος εὐλογεῖται.

7,19 οὐδὲν γὰρ ἐτελείωσεν ὁ νόμος, ἐπεισαγωγὴ δὲ κρείττονος
ἐλπίδος, δι' ἧς ἐγγίζομεν τῷ θεῷ.

7,22 κατὰ τοσοῦτο καὶ κρείττονος διαθήκης γέγονεν ἔγγυος
'Ιησοῦς.

8,6 νῦν δὲ διαφορωτέρας τέτυχεν λειτουργίας, ὅσῳ καὶ
κρείττονος ἐστιν διαθήκης μεσίτης, ἥτις ἐπὶ κρείττοσιν
ἐπαγγελίαις νενομοθέτηται.

9,11 Χριστὸς δὲ παραγενόμενος ἀρχιερεὺς τῶν γενομένων
ἀγαθῶν, διὰ τῆς μείζονος καὶ τελειοτέρας σκηνῆς . . .

9,13-14 εἰ γὰρ τὸ αἷμα τράγων καὶ ταύρων . . . πόσῳ μᾶλλον
τὸ αἷμα τοῦ Χριστοῦ . . .

9,23 ἀνάγκη οὖν τὰ μὲν ὑποδείγματα τῶν ἐν τοῖς οὐρανοῖς
τούτοις καθαρίζεσθαι, αὐτὰ δὲ τὰ ἐπουράνια κρείττοσιν
θυσίαις παρὰ ταύτας.

11,16 νῦν δὲ κρείττονος ὀρέγονται, τοῦτ' ἐστιν ἐπουρανίου.

11,39-40 καὶ οὗτοι πάντες μαρτυρηθέντες διὰ τῆς πίστεως οὐκ
ἐκομίσαντο τὴν ἐπαγγελίαν, τοῦ θεοῦ περὶ ἡμῶν κρεῖττόν τι
προβλεψαμένου, ἵνα μὴ χωρὶς ἡμῶν τελειωθῶσιν.

12,24 καὶ αἵματι ῥαντισμοῦ κρεῖττον λαλοῦντι παρὰ τὸν "Αβελ.

These comparisons are by no means exhaustive but emphatic
and characteristic in their use of comparative adjectives and
adverbs. They are illustrative of some of the principal themes
in Hebrews. In the first ten chapters, the author presents us
with three series of comparisons:

1) Jesus as the Son and heavenly Man with angels (1,1-2,18).

2) Jesus as Highpriest, Apostle and Son with Moses (3,1-6).

3) Jesus as the Highpriest according to the order of
   Melchizedek with Levi and Aaron (chaps. 5-7 and 8-10).

The overriding theme in each of these series is "perfection."
The subject matter can be summarily stated under the following
headings:

<u>Perfection as effected by Jesus</u>: Jesus effects the true
perfection in distinction from the Levitical priesthood and Law
(7,11 and 19). Perfected and called by God to the highpriesthood

according to the order of Melchizedek, he has passed through the heavens and is seated on the right hand of God in the inner sanctuary of the heavenly tabernacle (4,14; 5,4-10; 8,1-2; 10,19-20). His ministry and sacrifice (=death) is superior in that it is enacted on the better promises of a better covenant (chaps. 8-10). Perfection is the promise, that better thing which God saw before-hand (11,39-40); it is the arrival of that better hope by which we draw near to God, whereas the Law perfected nothing (7,19)--perfection is thus proximity or access to God.

Perfection of Jesus and the believer: Jesus has been perfected for ever through suffering (2,10; 5,9; 7,28). As the perfected Son, he is the leader (archēgos) of our salvation. Although the heavenly Man, he partook of flesh and blood like humans whom he is not ashamed to call "brethren" and whom he leads to glory as "sons" (2,10-18). He is able to aid and to sympathize with human weakness in that he himself was tempted, suffered and was perfected through suffering (2,18; 4,15; 5,8-10).

It is Christian faith and hope which procures such perfection, such access to God. Christians are sharers of Christ if they hold fast to faith and hope (3,7.14; 6,11-12); this faith is described as that which enables them to enter into God's sabbath/ seventh day rest (4,2-3.10) in contrast to the disbelief and disobedience which prevented those led by Moses from entering into God's rest (3,18-19; 4,6.11; cf. 3,12-13 and 17); hope is described as that safe and firm anchor of the soul which enters into the inside of the veil, where Jesus has entered as the "forerunner" (prodromos)--an eternal highpriest according to the order of Melchizedek (6,19-20), and as that better hope by which we draw near to God (7,19). Jesus is the one who effects such perfection by his entry into the heavenly sanctuary (=heaven; 4,14-16; 10,19ff.) and can thus rightly be called the leader (archēgos) and perfector (teleiōtēs) of faith (pistis)--12,1-2 which follows 11,39-40.

The latter points to another aspect of the general character of Hebrews, namely, the rationale for the transitions and sequence of themes: between 1,3 and 4 (comparison with angels); 2,4 and 5ff. (theme of the heavenly Man and the unexpected introduction of Jesus as highpriest in 2,17-18 and 3,1); 2,18 and 3,1-6 (why the comparison with Moses at this point? How does he fit in a sequence after the angels, heavenly Man, highpriest, apostle?); 4,13 and 14 (what has the theme of the sabbath rest got to do with Jesus as the highpriest who has passed through the

heavens?); what is the relationship of 4,12-13 with what precedes? 5,10 and 11 (propriety of the content of the exhortation);
does c. 11 start a new theme? the relationship between c. 11 and
12 and 13.

An answer to the question of the rationale behind these
series of comparisons, the particular character of the themes and
the transitions has already been partly anticipated in Pt.I above.
They belong to a single thought world and form a coherent whole.
We have elaborated in detail the character of such a thought
world in Philo (alongside other literature of Hellenistic Judaism) which makes plausible the themes, comparisons and transi
tions in Hebrews. In this thought world, the logos, wisdom,
angels, heavenly man, son, highpriest, mind, etc. have synonymous
titles and interchangeable functions as sustainers and agents of
creation, sources of knowledge and virtue, and mediators between
God and man (see above pp. 8-17). To this correspond two levels
of religious existence. The intermediary world mediates an inferior revelation and imperfect religious status (see above pp. 44-
45). The higher level or perfection constitutes an unmediated
and direct access to God and participation in the primary religious gifts and highest status. The exemplars of this perfection
were Moses, Isaac, Aaron, Levi, Melchizedek and the heavenly Man
(see above pp. 42-45; 68-72). It is our contention that the
readers addressed in Hebrews were Christians who operated within
such a frame of religious thought and which explains the series
of comparisons which we find in Hebrews and its close tie with
the theme of perfection (see above pp. 121-23). In primitive
Christianity the identification of Jesus with wisdom and logos
provided the basis for the conception of his preexistence, agency
in creation and divinity (Phil 2,6-11; 1Cor 8,6; Col 1,15-16; Jn
1,1-18). To those addressed in Hebrews, however, this would mean
that Jesus was a representative figure of the intermediary world
and could easily be identified with any one of them. Therefore,
the revelation and salvation which he mediates would be inferior
and a lower stage which could be surpassed on the path to perfection. Although it would be right and proper in this thought
world for those who fall short of perfection. As a result, the
central salvific conceptions and institutions of primitive Christianity as faith, hope, confidence, baptism, communal gatherings
and church regulations (cf. 3,6; 3,14; 3,11ff.; 6,1-3; 10,19-25;
11,1; 11,39-12,2; 13,17, etc.) become irrelevant for those who
are pressing towards the supreme goal of perfection (the secondary

character of some of which the author readily grants - 6,1-3).
The genius of the author of our writing lies in his use of the
Christology of Jesus' suffering, death and exaltation as the
"Son" to reinterpret this frame of religious thought. The revelation through the Son is shown to be superior to his predeces-
sors (1,1-2); he has a more exalted status than the angels and
proven to be superior over them (1,2-2,4) as also over Moses
(3,1-6), Levi and Aaron (c. 5-7; 8-10). He is indeed the heavenly Man, but in contrast to the traditional depiction, partakes in
flesh and blood, is perfected through suffering, in order to be a
merciful and sympathetic highpriest according to the order of
Melchizedek (2,5ff.; 4,14-16; 5,6-10). It is precisely by his
suffering, death and exaltation that he himself was perfected and
prepared the path to perfection, namely, the way into the Holy of
Holies (= upper reaches of the heavens, cf. 7,26; 8,5; 9,23-24,
etc.), a direct access to God (see above the statement on themes,
pp. 121-22). This sequence of comparisons and themes makes a
coherent whole in the thought world with which he was dealing.

Furthermore, the particular characteristics of perfection in
this thought world provide a clue to the particular themes and to
the peculiarities in the transitions in Hebrews. We list these
briefly at this point and we will elaborate on them in the suc-
ceeding sections:

(1) The intermediary world (logos, wisdom, angels, etc.)
mediates an inferior revelation and imperfect religious
status - cf. Hb 1,1-2; 1,4-2,4 (see above pp. 42-45 for
documentation of this and the following).

(2) Perfection means rising above the intermediary world and
unmediated access to God - cf. Hb 4,14-16; 6,19-20; 7,18-19;
10,19-20.

(3) Perfection is characterized by sinlessness without
involuntary errors, wholly cleansed minds, state of full
knowledge - cf. Hb 4,15; 7,26; 7,28; 9,9; 9,14; 9,28; 10,1-
4/11-18; 10,26; 12,1.

(4) The perfect are incorporeal, worshipping souls, whereas
the imperfect are burdened with bodies, corruptible, Adamic,
composite of body and soul - cf. Hb 2,5-18; especially
2,14ff.

(5) The perfect have the status of "sonship" to God (they
are not the sons of the logos or any intermediary) and the
status of the "first-born" - cf. Hb 1,5-6; 2,10-13; 12,23-24.

(6) The perfect do not need instruction, exhortation or

admonition - cf. Hb 5,11ff. (see above pp. 68-78 and also
for the following).

(7) Perfection is characterized by the seventh day rest of
God - cf. Hb 3,7-4,13.

(8) Perfection is characterized by the quality of the
seventh - ever virgin and motherless - cf. Hb 7,3.

(9) Inside the Holy of Holies, the highpriest Aaron is
neither man nor God but a minister (leitourgos) and perfect -
cf. Hb 8-10 (see further Chap. 6).

Accordingly, the transition between 1,3 and 4 is understandable
given a thought world in which the traditional Christology, i.e.,
Jesus' identity with wisdom and logos, could lead to his being
identified with the intermediary world of angels and this in
spite of the exalted terminology in 1,2-3. The introduction of
Jesus as highpriest in 2,17-18 and into 3,1-6 in the comparison
with Moses is perfectly understandable in a thought world in
which the highpriest is the logos, Moses is logos, highpriest and
archangel. Besides, Moses, Aaron, Levi, Melchizedek and the
heavenly Man are the primary exemplars of perfection. The understanding of perfection as the sabbath rest of God and entry into
the Holy of Holies (=upper-heavens) explains the surprising transition between 4,13 and 14. Similarly the content of the exhortation in 5,11ff. belongs intrinsically in this conceptual world
(see above item (6) on pp.124f.). We would also argue against the
view that we have an entirely new theme or themes in chapters 11-
13. It is a crucial part of the author's reinterpretation of
this thought world to show that it is precisely Christian faith
and hope which procures perfection (see delineation of themes on
p. 122). Noteworthy is the concluding statement of chapter 11
(39-40) and its tie with 12,1ff. We interpret the author to be
saying that whereas there were previous exemplars of faith in the
history of the Hebrews, they did not obtain the promise, that
better thing which God foresaw, namely, perfection. It is faith
which enables one to enter into God's sabbath rest (cf. 4,2-3;
4,10f, etc.) and it is hope which enters into the inside of the
veil, where Jesus has entered as the "forerunner" (prodromos)--an
eternal highpriest according to the order of Melchizedek (6,19-
20). Thus Jesus is indeed the leader and perfector of faith
(12,1-2). It is through Christian hope and faith, according to
author's reinterpretation, that we obtain perfection.

In comparison to the role which Christology plays in the
author's reinterpretation of this frame of religious thought and

of such concepts of Christian existence, such as faith and hope,
the role of eschatology is primarily paraenetic and very terse in
expression by comparison with other traditions of early Christian
apocalyptic (e.g., 1Thess 4-5; 2Thess; Mk 13 and Rev). We have
compared earlier the themes of perfection and intermediary world
of angels in Jewish apocalyptic with Philo and in a preliminary
way with Hebrews. We have shown that the presence of intermediaries is not occasioned by an emerging concept of the transcendence of God which distances him from the world nor does the presence of angels create a problem of access or immediacy to God
(contra Bousset-Gressmann). Their presence and role in Judaism
in general and in apocalyptic in particular are marks of divine
beneficence and favour. In the case of the thought world of the
reader of Hebrews, it would be a mark of imperfection, although a
useful and necessary accommodation to the weakness of men (see
above pp. 45f., 93-94). Furthermore there is no correlation in
apocalyptic between immediacy and perfection. It describes a
state of religious purity and full/total compliance to religious
beliefs and obligations (both moral and cultic) of a particular
community. We also noted the absence of the characteristic
vocabulary associated with perfection (in the Old Testament and
apocalyptic) in both Philo and Hebrews (see above pp. 83-110;
especially 93-96 and 110).

The people addressed in Hebrews, accordingly, were not in
the danger of relapsing into a less taxing Judaism which promised
inferior salvific benefits than Christianity, nor were they in a
state of post-apostolic fatigue, as some have characterized it,
but on the contrary their "neglect" (2,3) of Christianity was
occasioned by a particular tradition of Judaism which promised
much more--perfection and immediacy to God without intervening
mediators and the highest of religious status, like that of Aaron
and Moses.

The following sections will elaborate in greater detail our
interpretation of some of the major themes in Hebrews as outlined
above (pp. 121-25). It will do so by bringing to bear in specific instances the tradition in regard to intermediaries and perfection, which has been elaborated in the preceding chapters,
where an understanding of this tradition illuminates the terminology and arguments of Hebrews, their sequence as well as their
coherence in the framework of a single thought world.

CHAPTER FOUR

JESUS AND THE ANGELS (HEBREWS 1,1-2,4)

Introduction: It is clear that the basic thrust of the
argument in this section is to demonstrate the superiority of
Jesus as "Son" over the angels (1,4ff.; 2,1-4). This comparison
with the angels also appears in Hb 2,5; 16. Commentators have
expressed surprise not only at the comparison itself but also at
the way in which the comparison is introduced in 1,1-3. The comparisons involve that between the Son and the prophets in 1,1-2,
and between the Son and the angels in 1,4-14 and 2,1-4. And if
Jesus is all that which 1,1-3 describe him to be, then the elaborate argument that follows in 1,4ff. as to his superiority over
the angels has seemed unusual (see below f.n. 15, pp.145f.). The
earlier attempts to see here some kind of heresy resulting from
a Gnostic cult of angels or an angel-Christology have been aban-
doned (e.g., Spicq, Michel, Windisch). An alternative is that
proposed by Michel that we have here a necessary feature of
apocalyptic enthronization. However, his assumption of the
existence or knowledge of the scenario of an ancient ceremony of
enthronement in Judaism of the period is unproved and besides how
the enthronement of the Son of Man in 1Enoch (45,3; 51,3; 55,4,
etc.--all references to sitting on the throne on the day of
judgement, a connection never made in Hebrews) could call for a
comparison with angels and the necessity of proving Jesus' superiority over the angels remains unclear (see below pp. 145ff.).

A second and related issue of interpretation in this section
concerns the background and function of the concepts and themes
utilized by the author in his argument. For example, it is readily admitted by Spicq and Michel that the terms "apaugasma,"
"charaktēr" and "hypostatis" come from the thought world of Hellenistic Judaism. But "klēronomos" is an eschatological and
messianic concept (see below p. 135) "di'hou" expresses the "Biblical tradition of God's creation through his word" since philosophical presuppositions are foreign to Hebrews (see below f.n. 9,
p. 139). This tendency to consider the Old Testament and Apocalyptic background as legitimate and to minimize the Hellenistic
Jewish elements in Hebrews on the part of interpreters has been
called into question by E. G. Grässer (p. 167). The more important interpretative issue, however, has not received sufficient

notice. Given the clear recognition that we have formulations
which were current in Hellenistic Judaism (e.g., "apaugasma,"
"charaktēr," "hypostatis") as well as those for which the author
is dependent on earlier Christian traditions (e.g., title "Son,"
"in these last days," use of Ps 2 and 110), the question of their
interrelationship both as to historical context and religious
issues involved would seem to be one which needs to be answered
for an adequate interpretation of Hebrews. The explanation to
which both Spicq and Michel subscribe, namely, that the author
was familiar with the religious language of the Hellenistic syna-
gogue and that these are merely surface phenomena which leave the
author's thinking unaffected in its essentials is far too general
an explanation to clarify the historical situation of Hebrews.
The function of these two elements and how they engage each other
remain unclear in their commentaries both for this section and
for the rest of Hebrews.

On both these points we intend to show how the tradition
regarding the intermediaries and perfection is the one with which
the writing is dealing and which explains in this particular context the following:

(1) The surprising sequence of comparisons between Jesus as
"Son" with the prophets in 1,1-2, and with the angels in 1,4ff.
and 2,1-4. Why, inspite of the characterization of the Son and
his role with such terminology as is found in 1,2-3, there was a
need to prove his superiority over the angels and prophets, and
the superiority of the revelation in the Son over that through
the prophets and angels.

(2) That many of the terms and concepts which the author
uses in his argument--such as "polymerōs," "polytropōs," "klēronomos," "di' hou . . . ," "apaugasma," "charaktēr," "hypostasis,"
"onoma"--belong to the above named tradition and that once this
is recognized their meaning and significance for the author's
argument can be seen in a new light.

(3) The primitive Christian traditions (humiliation-exaltation Christology--3b; title "Son," scriptural proof texts--Ps 2;
110; 2Sam 7,14) which the author has utilized and modified to
subject the tradition regarding intermediaries and perfection to
reinterpretation so as to avert the religious threat it presented
for Christian claims. It was this threat which determined the
character and course of the author's argument and the sequence of
comparisons both here and in the subsequent sections of Hebrews.

We have chosen to follow the author's own order of the

arguments and to focus on the specific aspects mentioned above
where we can document and substantiate the contentions of the
thesis.

Imperfection of the Multiplicity and Manifoldness of Revelation in the Old Testament

In view of the significance of the comparisons in Hebrews'
argument (see above pp. 121ff.), the character of the comparison
involved in the opening statement takes us directly into the
heart of the tradition regarding intermediaries and perfection.
The writing begins with a comparison between the revelation given
through the prophets and that given through the Son. The elements of the comparison are:

ἐν τοῖς προφήταις	ἐν υἱῷ
πάλαι	ἐπ' ἐσχάτου τῶν ἡμερῶν τούτων
πολυμερῶς κ. πολυτρόπως	---

In respect to the degree of comparison intended, much depends on
the interpretation of the latter two terms. There is agreement
that the revelation "in Son" is final and eschatological in character ("in the last of these days"--cf. 9,9; 1Pet 1,20; Hermas,
Sim 9,12.3). Whether this implies a "progressive" revelation
within a schema of promise and fulfillment (Bruce, Montefiore) or
the incomplete, inconclusive and inferior character of the revelation in the Old Testament (Michel, Spicq) is disputed. The
evidence is ambiguous and depends largely on the choice of meaning of "polymer$\bar{o}$s" and "polytrop$\bar{o}$s." On the one hand, we have a
positive understanding of these and related terms:[1]

Jos Ant 10,142: ταῦτα μὲν οὖν ἱκανῶς ἐμφανίσαι δυνάμενα τὴν τοῦ
θεοῦ φύσιν τοῖς ἀγνοοῦσιν εἰρήκαμεν, ὅτι ποικίλη τέ ἐστι
καὶ πολύτροπος . . . (context refers to the surety of
divine prophesy.)

Wis Sol 7,22: ἔστιν γὰρ ἐν αὐτῇ πνεῦμα νοερόν, ἅγιον, μονογενές,
πολυμερές, λεπτόν, εὐκίνητον . . . (= attributes of
wisdom).

---

[1]F. F. Bruse, pp. 2-3; H. Montefiore, pp. 33-34; O. Michel,
p. 93: "diese Vielheit und Verschiedenheit ist jetzt nicht mehr
ein Zeichen für den Reichtum Gottes, sondern für die Unabgesch-
lossenheit und Unvollständigkeit der prophetischen Fassungskraft
(7,33)." C. Spicq, II, p. 1: "La révélation faite aux pères et
la révélation faite par le Fils s'opposent comme l'imparfait et
le transitoire au parfait et au définitif." Windisch, Michel and
Spicq cite examples for "polymer$\bar{o}$s" and "polytropos" from Maximus
Tyrius, Wisdom of Solomon, Philo, Josephus, and 4Maccabees without noticing that the evidence is contradictory and imply positive as well as negative meanings. Their judgement on the nature
of the comparison involved seems to have to relation to the evidence cited!

130

Eph 3,10: ἵνα γνωρισθῇ νῦν ταῖς ἀρχαῖς καὶ ταῖς ἐξουσίαις ἐν
τοῖς ἐπουρανίοις διὰ τῆς ἐκκλησίας ἡ πολυποίκιλος σοφία
τοῦ θεοῦ . . . (chapter 3 speaks of the revelation of
the apocalyptic mystery, and wisdom has the same connotation as mystery in this context.)

On the other hand, these terms have a decidedly negative
connotation in the schema of perfection and imperfection in
Philo:

Ebr 85: τοιγάρτοι καὶ θεοπρόπος Μωυσῆς διὰ τῆς τῶν κατὰ τὸν
νεὼν δημιουργίας ἱερῶν τὴν ἐν ἀμφοτέροις τελειότητα
διαδείξει. οὐ γὰρ ἀπερισκέπτως ἡμῖν τὴν κιβωτὸν ἔνδοθέν
τε καὶ ἔξωθεν χρυσῷ περιαμπίσχει, οὐδὲ στολὰς τῷ
ἀρχιερεῖ διττὰς ἀναδίδωσιν, οὐδὲ βωμοὺς δύο, . . .
βουλόμενος διὰ συμβόλων τούτων τὰς καθ᾽ ἑκάτερων εἶδος
ἀρετὰς παραστῆσαι.

86: τὸν γὰρ σοφὸν κἄν τοῖς κατὰ ψυχὴν ἔνδον ἀοράτοις κἄν
τοῖς ἔξω περιφαινομένοις δεῖ τῇ παντὸς τιμιωτέρα χρυσοῦ
φρονήσει κεκοσμῆσθαι, καὶ ὁπότε μὲν τῶν ἀνθρωπείων
σπουδασμάτων ὑποκεχώρηκε τὸ ὄν θεραπεύων μόνον, τὴν
ἀποίκιλον ἀληθείας ἐνδύεσθαι στολήν, ἧς οὐδὲν ἐφάψεται
θνητόν . . . , ὁπότε δὲ μέτεισι πρὸς πολιτείαν, τὴν μὲν
ἔνδον ἀποτίθεσθαι, ποικιλωτάτην δὲ καὶ ὀφθῆναι
θαυμασιωτάτην ἑτέραν ἀναλαμβάνειν. πολύτροπος γὰρ ὧν ὁ
βίος ποικιλωτάτου δεῖται τὴν σοφίαν τοῦ πηδαλιουχήσοντος
κυβερνήτου.

87: οὗτος κατὰ μὲν τὸν περιφανῆ βωμὸν ἤ βίον καὶ δορᾶς καὶ
σαρκῶν καὶ αἵματος καὶ πάντων ὅσα περὶ σῶμα δόξει
πολλὴν ποιεῖσθαι πρόνοιαν, . . . κατὰ δὲ τὸν ἔνδον
πᾶσιν ἀναίματος, ἀσάρκοις, ἀσωμάτοις, τοῖς ἐκ λογισμοῦ
μόνοις χρήσεται, ἅ λιβανωτῷ καὶ τοῖς ἐπιθυμιωμένοις
ἀπεικάζεται.

For the context of this passage, see above pp. 51ff. Jacob is an
example of obedience to both parents and when he reaches perfection exchanges hearing for sight and becomes Israel, i.e., vision
of God (82). Perfection is also depicted as Sarah who is "with
out mother" (amētōr) and self-taught Isaac; as Sarah who soars
above all bodily forms and exults with joy in God (60-62) and as
those who pass over the mother's biddings and adhere to the
father's and are judged worthy of highest honour--the priesthood
(65). Here the symbolism of the temple is adduced to describe
the twofold perfection of Jacob or two types of virtue (85). The
"sophos"/highpriest must be adorned with understanding more precious than gold and when he has withdrawn from human pursuits and
worships the Existent alone, he must put on the undecorated robe
of truth which has no concourse with things mortal. When he
passes into the realm of political life he must put off this
inner robe and put on another "most varied/decorated." For
(earthly) life (bios) is manifold (polytropos) and needs a helms-
man with wisdom of the most varied kind (poikilōtatou)--86. When
he is at the visible altar of life he will seem to be much con-

cerned with skin, flesh, blood and all things surrounding the
body. At the inner altar he deals with only what is bloodless,
fleshless, bodiless, that which is alone born of reason. Therefore, "poikilos" and "polytropos" characterize the state of imperfection which is embroiled in earthly--political life--a life
concerned with flesh, blood and body, symbolized by the decorated
robe of the highpriest with which he serves outside the Holy of
Holies. Perfection is the opposite--withdrawal from human pursuits, exclusive worship of God, symbolized by the undecorated
robe of the highpriest in his service inside the Holy of Holies.

Ebr 36: τῆς μὲν οὖν φιλομήτορος ταῖς πολλῶν δόξαις ὑπεικούσης
καὶ κατὰ τὰς πολυτρόπους τοῦ βίου ζηλώσεις παντοδαπὰς
μεταβαλλούσης ἰδέας Αἰγυπτίου Πρωτέως τὸν τρόπον . . .

The type of children which loves the mother are characterized by
their submission to the opinions of the multitude and changeable
form according to the manifold (polytropos) desires of life, like
the Egyptian Proteus.

Plant 44: . . . ὁ δὲ (οὐδὲν διαφέρει) τοῦ πολυμιγοῦς καὶ
γεωδεστέρου σώματος, ἀπλάστου καὶ ἀπλῆς φύσεως ἀμέτοχος,
. . . πολυτρόπῳ δὲ καὶ ἐκ παντοίων συνηρημένη καὶ
πεπλασμένη διαθέσει χρώμενος.

The discussion is on Gn 2,8 and speaks of the "moulded" man. In
contrast to him, the man who is stamped with the spirit (Gn 2,7)
which is according to the image of God differs in nothing from
the tree which bears the fruit of immortal life, whereas the
"moulded" man differs in nothing from the composite and earthly
body and has a manifold (polytropos) disposition knitted and
moulded out of all sorts of things. As we have seen above, this
distinction between the two types of man corresponds to the distinction between perfection and imperfection (see above pp. 38-
40). To this may be compared 4Macc 1,25: ἐν τῇ ἡδονῇ δὲ ἔνεστιν
καὶ κακοήθης διάθεσις, πολυτροπωτάτη πάντων οὖσα τῶν παθῶν . . .

Som ii,10: δυεῖν δὴ θιάσων ἡγεμόνας εἰσάγει Μωυσῆς, τοῦ μὲν
γενναίου τὸν αὐτομαθῆ καὶ αὐτοδίδακτον Ἰσαάκ--ἀναγράφει
γὰρ αὐτὸν <ἀπὸ> γαλακτιζόμενον, ἀπαλαῖς καὶ γαλακτώδεσι
νηπίαις τε καὶ παιδικαῖς τροφαῖς οὐ δικαιοῦντα χρῆσθαι
τὸ παράπαν, ἀλλ' εὐτόνοις καὶ τελείαις, . . . τοῦ δὲ
εἴκοντος καὶ εὐενδότου τὸν Ἰωσήφ. 11: οὗτος γὰρ οὐκ
ἀλογεῖ μὲν τῶν κατὰ ψυχὴν ἀρετῶν, προμηθεῖται δὲ καὶ τῆς
τοῦ σώματος εὐσταθείας, ἐφίεται <δὲ> καὶ τῆς τῶν ἐκτὸς
εὐπορίας. ἀνθέλκεται δὲ εἰκότως πολλὰ τέλη τοῦ βίου
προτεθειμένος, καὶ ἀντισπώμενος ὑφ' ἑκάστου σείεται καὶ
κλονεῖται μὴ δυνάμενος στηριχθῆναι. . . . 14: τοιοῦτος
μὲν δὴ κύκλος εἱλεῖται περὶ τὴν πολύτροπον ψυχὴν
ἀϊδίου πολέμου . . .

In this second book on the Dreams, Philo introduces the third
type of dreams which, in contrast to the first which originates
with God and the second which is divinely inspired, is obscure

132

and enigmatic (1-4). The main examples of such dreams are those
of Joseph, Pharaoh, and his chief butler and baker. There are
two companies whose leaders are Isaac and Joseph. The leader of
the noble band is Isaac--self-learnt and self-taught, does not
use at all the soft, milky food for infants but the strong food
for the perfect/grown (i.e., perfection). Joseph is not uncon-
cerned for the virtues of the soul, but is thoughtful for the
well-being of the body and external things. Since he sets before
himself many ends in life, he is drawn in different directions,
shaken, and driven to confusion, unable to find fixity, etc.
Such is the cycle of unending warfare which revolves around the
manifold (polytropos) soul.

Mig 152: . . . παγκάλως δὲ καὶ εὐθυβόλως τὴν τοῦ φαύλου ψυχὴν
ἐπίμικτον καλεῖ. συνηρημένη γὰρ καὶ συμπεφορημένη καὶ
μιγὰς ὄντως ἐκ πλειόνων καὶ μαχομένων δοξῶν, μία μὲν
οὖσα ἀριθμῷ, μυρίας δὲ τῷ πολυτρόπῳ.

153: διὸ καὶ τῷ ἐπίμικτος πρόσκειται πολύς. ὁ μὲν γὰρ πρὸς
ἓν μόνον ἀφορῶν ἁπλοῦς καὶ ἀμιγὴς καὶ λεῖος ὄντως, ὁ δὲ
πολλὰ τέλη τοῦ βίου προτιθέμενος πολὺς καὶ μιγὰς καὶ
δασὺς ἀληθείᾳ. . . .

154: διὰ τὸν ἐπίμικτον καὶ δασὺν τοῦτον ὄχλον . . .
ὠκυδρομῆσαι δυνάμενος ὁ νοῦς, . . . καὶ τρισὶν
ἡμέραις διαδέξασθαι τὸν ἀρετῆς κλῆρον . . . τεσσαράκοντα
ἐτῶν ἀριθμόν, μῆκος τοσούτου χρόνου, τρίβεται τὴν ἐν
κύκλῳ περιάγων καὶ ἀλώμενος ἕνεκα τοῦ πολυτρόπου, τὴν
ἐπ᾽ εὐθείας ἀνυσιμωτάτην οὖσαν δέον.

Migration 148-75 is an interpretation of Gn 12,4 and sets forth
Abraham's path to perfection (see above pp. 37; 49-50). Lot's
accompaniment of Abraham shows that he is yet a beginner in the
contemplation of divine things and unformed and wavering (150).
Lot like the "mixed multitude" of Ex 12,38 is a hindrance to
progress (151). The soul of the wicked man is called "mixed,"
knitted, brought together and in fact a mixture of many discord-
ant opinions (cf. above Plant 44), one in number but myriad in
manifoldness (polytropos). The one who aims alone at some one
thing is truly simple/perfect (haplous), unmixed and smooth (Gn
27,11). But the one with many ends in life is many, mixed, and
rough (152-53). Compare to this Som ii,10-14 above. The mind,
on account of this mixed and rough crowd (= Egypt, realm of the
body), which is able to speed in three days and receive the
inheritance of virtue (i.e., perfection), instead for forty long
years wanders and circles the bodily realm of Egypt, on account
of manifoldness. It ought to have taken the straight and
speediest path (154).

These examples will suffice to show that such terms as
"polymeros," "polytropos" and "poikilos" are technical terms

which describe a state of imperfection in the context of this
tradition regarding intermediaries and perfection.[2] That this is
the thought world which Hebrews is dealing with becomes evident
from the numerous instances where themes and concerns of Hebrews
appear in this context. This imperfection is characterized by a
life embroiled in this world of flesh, blood and body which in
its manifold (polytropos) character requires a corresponding
wisdom--the most varied (poikilōtatos)--a crucial theme in Hb 2,
esp. vs. 14; it is symbolized by the decorated robe (poikilōtates)
of the highpriest with which he serves outside the Holy of Holies
(Ebr 85-87; perfection in Hebrews is access into the Holy of
Holies, c. 8-10); by the changeable and manifold (polytropos)
desires of life (Ebr 36); by the manifold (polytropos) disposition of the "moulded man" (Gn 2,8), who represents imperfection,
incapable of sharing in the not-moulded and simple/perfect (haplē)
nature (Plant 44; cf. 4Macc 1,25; we will show below that such a
tradition underlies Hb 2); by the manifold (polytropos) soul
which has many ends in life, is drawn in different directions,
shaken, driven to confusion and unable to find fixity (Som ii,10-
14; the opposite term is "bebaios"--a term associated with hope
and confidence in Hb 3,6; 6,19; and the principle of reality in
3,14; in Philo, the term "bebaios" describes the stability and
firmness of the logos and the mind--QG IV,53; QE II,3); by the
forty years of wandering in the wilderness on account of manifoldness (polytropos = mixed multitude of Ex 12,38)--a central
theme in Hb 3,7-4,13 (Mig 152-54). Perfection, on the other
hand, is represented by Sarah who is "without mother" (amētōr)--
cf. Hb 7,2; by the highpriest/sophos dressed in the undecorated
(apoikilos) robe of truth, worshipping the Existent alone, un-
touched by mortality, and having dealing with only that which is
bloodless, fleshless and bodiless (Ebr 85-87; cf. Hb 2,14; 8-10);
by the man made according to the image of God = tree of life
(Plant 44); by Isaac, self-learnt and self-taught, who does not
use the milky food of infants but the strong food of the perfect/

---

[2]The prime example of such earthly-political wisdom is
Joseph, cf. Jos 32: Joseph's coat is an appropriate representa-
tion of the varied (poikilos) and manifold (polytropos) character
of political life (politeia) which is subject of myriad changes;
Quod Det 6: he follows a dogma woven of different things, very
varied (poikilos) and complex (polyplokos), re. his coat of many
colours; he is the introducer of labyrinthus and hard to disen-
tangle opinion (doxa) and deals more with politics (politeia) than
with truth in that he combines the goods of external world, body
and soul--cf. 28; Conf 71: Joseph = varied (poikilos) pride of
life.

full grown (Som ii,10-14; the same theme in Hb 5,11ff.); by one who aims at one thing and is simple/perfect (haplous), unmixed and smooth; by entry into the promised land, here described as the receiving of the inheritance of virtue, instead of wandering forty years in the wilderness (Mig 152-54; cf. Hb 3,7-4,13).[3]

The language and the themes, therefore, manifestly belong to a single coherent thought world both here and in Hebrews. "Polymerōs" and "polytropōs" are technical terms which describe the inferiority and imperfection of the revelation through prophets/angels in the Old Testament (i.e., its manifold--multiple character) in contrast to the singular character of the revelation in the Son ("in Son"--without the article and emphatic in its position in the sentence). It should be borne in mind that imperfection does not mean something bad or evil in this tradition. It is an accommodation on the part of God towards those unable yet to reach the highest religious status, namely, perfection (see above pp. 45f.; 93f., e.g., QE II,13, Som i,232 - p. 37). The positive meaning of these terms in Josephus and Wisdom of Solomon has its roots in Stoicism in which the one indestructible being, whether fire or Zeus, undergoes changes in the process of creation and its many manifestations (cf. DL VII,135-37; 142; 147; SVF I,87; II,1009; 1021). On the other hand, Philonic usage has its roots in middle Platonism whose kinship to Hebrews is well known, e.g.:

Maximus Tyrius XI, 7a: τῇ τοῦ ἀνθρώπου ψυχῇ δύο ὀργάνων ὄντων πρὸς σύνεσιν, τοῦ μὲν ἁπλοῦ, ὃν καλοῦμεν νοῦν, τοῦ δὲ ποικίλου καὶ πολυμεροῦς καὶ πολυτρόπου, ἃς αἰσθήσεις καλοῦμεν . . .

The statements in Josephus and Wisdom (see above p. 129) would appear quite perverse in the thinking of middle Platonism.

Heir of the Universe

It is generally recognized that the participation of the Son

---

[3]Philo also uses the term "poikilos" in a positive sense to describe the robe which the highpriest wears outside the holy of holies and which represents the varied character of the cosmos (cf. Spec Leg i,95; Mig 102; Som i,207; Fug 10). Negative sense, apart from passages we have discussed, by and large describes the evils of pleasure (cf. Sac 23; Quod Det 157; Op 165; Abr 148; Gig 18; Leg All ii,75f.; iii,61; ii,107, etc.). The positive use in the description of the cosmos (= highpriest's decorated robe) does not contradict the perfection which is associated with the simple and unmixed character of God. Philo is obviously not a gnostic. One can find in Philo more general usage of these terms, e.g., thought in many forms (Mos ii,289); sickness in many forms (Virt 5); nature's many sided skill (Mig 85); variety of melodies (Post 104), etc.

in creation and the terminology which describes his relationship
to God ("apaugasma," "charaktēr," "hypostasis") come from the
wisdom-logos speculation of hellenized Judaism (Wis Sol, Philo,
etc.). But that the Son is the heir of all things is understood
by some commentators as an eschatological and messianic concept
(Michel on the basis of Rom 4,13; Ps 2,8; Gal 4,7; Rom 8,17--a
liturgical tradition older than Hebrews--p. 94; Spicq on the
basis of Gal 4,7; Mt 21,38; Dan 7,13f.; Mt 28,18 II,5). However,
the concept of sonship and inheritance is not absent in Philo and
other literature of Hellenistic Judaism and provide, in the context of the traditions with which we are dealing, a better clue
to the themes and concerns of the writer.[4] We leave aside the
question whether we have a hymn here or not. It is not a point
to which we can add further illumination. It is the specifics of
the content, which differ from the prologue of John, Col 1,15-20,
Phil 2,5-11 and 1Tim 3,16, with which we are concerned, and especially how it could have called for a comparison with angels and
the necessity to prove Jesus' superiority over them as well as
the subsequent comparison with Moses, etc.

Mos i,155: γεραίρει θεὸς τὸν μέγιστον καὶ τελεώτατον ἀντιδοὺς
            πλοῦτον αὐτῷ. οὗτος δ᾽ ἐστὶν ὁ τῆς συμπάσης γῆς καὶ
            θαλάττης καὶ ποταμῶν καὶ τῶν ἄλλων ὅσα στοιχεῖα καὶ
            συγκρίματα. κοινωνὸν γὰρ ἀξιώσας ἀναφανῆναι τῆς ἑαυτοῦ
            λήξεως ἀνῆκε πάντα τὸν κόσμον ὡς κληρονόμῳ κτῆσιν
            ἁρμόζουσαν.

   156:     τοιγαροῦν ὑπήκουεν ὡς δεσπότῃ τῶν στοιχείων ἕκαστον
            ἀλλάτον ἣν εἶχε δύναμιν ταῖς προστάξεσιν ὑπεῖκον. καὶ
            θαυμαστὸν ἴσως οὐδέν, εἰ γὰρ κατὰ τὴν παροιμίαν "κοινὰ
            τὰ φίλων," φίλος δὲ ὁ προφήτης ἀνείρηται θεοῦ, κατὰ τὸ
            ἀκόλουθον μετέχοι ἂν αὐτοῦ καὶ τῆς κτήσεως, καθ᾽ ὃ
            χρειῶδες.

   157:     . . . κοσμοπολίτης γάρ ἐστιν, ἧς χάριν αἰτίας οὐδεμιᾷ
            τῶν κατὰ τὴν οἰκουμένην πόλεων ἐνεγράφη, δεόντως, οὐ
            μέρος χώρας ἀλλ᾽ ὅλον τὸν κόσμον κλῆρον λαβών.

   158:     τί δ᾽; οὐχὶ καὶ μείζονος τῆς πρὸς τὸν πατέρα τῶν ὅλων
            καὶ ποιητὴν κοινωνίας ἀπέλαυσε προσρήσεως τῆς αὐτῆς
            ἀξιωθείς; ὠνομάσθη γὰρ ὅλου τοῦ ἔθνους θεὸς καὶ βασιλεύς.
            εἴς τε τὸν γνόφον, ἔνθα ἦν ὁ θεός, εἰσελθεῖν λέγεται,
            τουτέστιν εἰς τὴν ἀειδῆ καὶ ἀόρατον καὶ ἀσώματον τῶν
            ὄντων παραδειγματικὴν οὐσίαν, καὶ ἀθέατα φύσει θνητῇ
            κατανοῶν . . .

---

[4] Cf. Joseph and Asenath XII (56), 20-22: ἰδοὺ γὰρ πάντα τὰ
δώματα τοῦ πατρός μου Πεντεφρῆ ἃ δέδωκέ μοι εἰς κληρονομίαν πρόσ-
καιρα εἰσὶ καὶ ἀφανῆ, τὰ δὲ δώματα τῆς σῆς κληρονομίας κύριε,
ἄφθαρτα εἰσὶ καὶ αἰώνια. Sibylline Oracles, Prooimion, 84-87:
οἱ δὲ θεὸν τιμῶντες ἀληθινὸν ἀέναόν τε ζωὴν κληρονομοῦσι, τὸν
αἰῶνος χρόνον αὐτοὶ οἰκοῦντες παραδείσου ὁμῶς ἐριθηλέα κῆπον,
δαινύμενοι γλυκὺν ἄρτον ἀπ᾽ οὐρανοῦ ἀστερόεντος. In Philo, as is
to be expected, the highest form of inheritance is to inherit God
himself (cf. Som i,159; Fug 102--see above pp. 34-35).

136

The context of the passage speaks of Moses' appointment to kingship and rule (148ff.), his virtues and nobility (kalokagathia)
and despisement of earthly wealth for the treasures of kingly
virtues (148-54). God rewarded him with the greatest and best
wealth of all, namely, the possession of the whole world as heir,
a sharer of God's possessions (155). Therefore, the elements
(stoicheia) obey him as master and submit to his commands. If
according to the proverb "the possession of friends are in common" (Aristotle), and the prophet is called friend of God, it
would follow that he shares God's possessions (156). He is a
cosmopolitan and is not enrolled in any city in the inhabited
world (oikoumenē) and received as his portion (klēros) the whole
world and not a piece of land (157). And furthermore, he enjoyed
greater partnership (koinōnia) with God in that he was deemed
worthy of the same title--he was named God and King of the whole
race. He entered into the darkness (gnophos), that is the eternal, invisible, incorporeal and archetypal essence of all existing things and saw what cannot be seen by mortal nature (158).
He is the form of perfect virtue (eidos teleion aretēs) and
paradigm (paradeigma) for all to imitate (158-59). He is reason
(logikos) and the law in person (nomos empsychos)--162.[5]

Conf 74: See above p. 53. Self-learnt kind Isaac alone inherits
   (klēronomein) from the Father "things that are sub-
   stantial/basic realities" (πράγματα ὑφεστηκότα καὶ ὄντως
   ὑπαρκτά).[6]

QG IV,153: . . . And (Scripture) in another passage call him
   (i.e., Abraham) "forefather" and not "firstborn" inheriting all from his divine Father and being without share in
   a mother or female line. (Marcus: Loeb)

The passage is an interpretation of Gn 25,8 and contrasts Abraham
with Isaac who is "firstborn" and inherits all things from God.

Plant 69: Μωυσῆς δὲ οὕτως περίβλεπτον καὶ περιμάχητον ἡγεῖται
   σοφίαν, ὥστε οὐ μόνον τὸν σύμπαντα κόσμον ἀξιόχρεω
   κλῆρον αὐτῆς ἀλλὰ καὶ τὸν τῶν ὅλων ἡγεμόνα νομίζειν.

The term "inheritance" in Ex 15,17-18 is the subject of discussion
in Plant 54-72. God is the special lot of those wise souls of
keenest vision (58) and the special lot of the tribe of Levi (Dt
10,9; Nu 18,20; passage will be discussed in Chap. 6.) who represents the perfectly cleansed and purified mind which has renounced
all things of creation and drawn nigh to God alone (62-64). Such

---

[5]For the background of the concept "nomos empsychos," see
E. R. Goodenough, "The Political Philosophy of Hellenistic Kingship," Yale Classical Studies 1 (1928), 53-102.

[6]Cf. H. Koester, TWNT VIII,582.

too is the privilege of Wisdom who is heir of not only of the whole world but of God himself (cf. Som i,159 and Fug 102--see above pp. 34-35).

Virt 52: δείγματα γάρ ἐστι τῆς συνεχοῦς καὶ ἀδιαστάτου καλοκάγαθίας, ἣν ἀσύγχυτον ἐνεσφραγίσατο τῇ ψυχῇ χαρακτῆρι θείῳ τυπωθείσῃ.

The subject is philanthropy of which Moses, the prophet of the laws, is the greatest lover and paradigm (paradeigma) and archetypal model (graphē archetypos). There are one or two things which he accomplished at the end of his life. These are proofs of the constant and unbroken nobility (kalokagathia) which he imprinted on his soul which was moulded/impressed with a divine stamp/character.

It is not only that the writer of Hebrews builds his picture of Jesus out of elements of such a tradition, but has precisely to argue the case for the superiority of Jesus with such a tradition. Here Moses who is Logos, archangel, highpriest, king and prophet is the supreme example of perfection (see above pp. 71-72), the perfect from of virtue, the paradigm to be imitated by all who strive for perfection. His supreme status is indicated in the fact that he is heir to the whole world, the elements obey him and are subject to his commands, he is the maker of the archetypes (cf. Leg All iii,102), and above all he has the title "God" and "king" and entered into the eternal essence and saw what no mortal can see (Ex 20,21)--Mos i,155-58. The divine "character" is engraved in his soul (Virt 52). It is Isaac, "first-born," the highest type of perfection (self-learnt), who inherits all from God--the substantial realities (Conf 74; QG IV, 153). Wisdom inherits the whole world and it is probably a Philonic twist to consider God himself as the highest inheritance (Plant 62-64; 69; Fug 102; Som i,159). It is within this tradition that one can understand the assertion on the part of the author that it is Jesus as the Son who is heir of all things, through whom the universe was made, who is the reflection and stamp/character of God's "underlying/basic reality" (hypostasis).[7] He bears the title "God" (1,8), "firstborn" (1,6), "Lord" (1,10) and is both God and king (1,8-9). Thereby the author of Hebrews has set the stage for the comparison of Jesus with Moses, who bears these honours and titles, and which forms the explicit theme in chapters 3-4. The polemic in Hb 12,18ff. against Moses who enters into the "gnophos" (Ex 20,21) has such a tradition in

---

[7]Cf. H. Koester, TWNT VIII, 571-88; esp. 584-88 on Hb 1,1; 3,14 and 11,1.

mind. Jesus the heir of all things is also the one to whom the "world to come" is subject (2,5) and not to "angels." (In Mos i,156, since Moses is the heir of the whole cosmos, the elements are subject to his commands.) In leading many "sons" to glory he partakes in flesh and blood. In contrast, in Quis Her 66: ". . . incorporeal natures (asōmatoi physeis) are heirs of intelligible things."[8]

Agent of Creation

The sequential correspondence between being heir of all things and participation in the creative process in Philo (Mos i,156) and Hebrews is striking as well. Whereas it is well known that the logos and wisdom have a role in creation in the traditions of Hellenistic Judaism and a similar role is attributed to

---

[8] A similar tradition is probably at the basis of Rom 4. Paul's interpretation of Gn 17,17 in Rm 4,19-21 is very similar to that in Philo: QG III,55--". . . Rightly did he laugh in his joy over the promise, being filled with great hope and in the expectation that it would be fulfilled, and because he had clearly received a vision, through which he knew more certainly Him who always stands firm . . . " (interpretation of Gn 17,17; cf. Rom 4,18.20); QG III,56--". . . . Perhaps too he is not in a state of doubt but being struck with amazement at the excessivenss of the gift, says, 'Behold, our body has passed (its prime) and has gone beyond the age of begetting. But to God all things are possible, even to change old age into youth, and to bring one who has no seed or fruit into the begetting and fruitfulness.' And so if a centenarian and (a woman) of ninety years produce children, the element of ordinary events is removed, and only divine power and grace clearly appear" (interpretation of Gn 17,17; cf. Rom 4,19-21; Hb 11,11-12); QG IV,17--"That the divine words are deeds and powers is clear from the preceding, for there is no impossibility for the Deity. But the rebuke would seem to indicate praise rather than personal blame according to natural expectation . . . But Abraham was delivered and, as it were, escaped rebuke and reprobation, being secured by an unswerving and inflexible conviction of faith, for to him who has faith in God all uncertainty is alien" (interpretation of Gn 18,13-14; cf. Rom 4, 19-21). For the significance of the concept of "grace" in Philo, see above pp. 76-77. The phrase "the one who calls things that do not exist into existence" in Rm 4,17 is a commonplace in Philo (cf. Leg All iii,10; Mig 183; Mut 46; Mos ii,267; esp. Spec Leg iv,187: τὰ γὰρ μὴ ὄντα ἐκάλεσεν εἰς τὸ εἶναι . . . ; Virt 130, etc.; cf. 2Macc 7,28; Hb 11,2). That Abraham is heir of the cosmos also belongs to this thought world. There is little basis for considering this as eschatological and messianic as do Michel (p. 93) and Spicq (I, p. 5). The same argument can be made for Gal 4,7 which is undergirded by an allegorical interpretation in 4,21ff. which is similar to that of Philo (see references in E. Burton, ICC). Mt 21,38 is an allegorization of a motif of the story in a parable (see Jeremias, The Parables of Jesus, pp. 72-74) and has no relation to the tradition with which we are dealing in Rom 4 and Gal 4. Such is also the case with Mt 28,18 which has nothing to do with inheritance or for that matter Dan 7,13ff., as Spicq asserts (I, p. 5).

Jesus elsewhere in the New Testament (1Cor 8,6; Col 1,16; Jn 1,3), it is not clearly recognized that the language in such descriptions has its origin in the discussion on "causes" (aitiai) in hellenistic philosophy (see above note on pp. 18ff.).[9]

The point of departure is usually Aristotle's theory of the four causes (Phys 194b,16ff.; first 10 chapters of Metaphysics) which was adapted and modified in middle Platonism and Stoicism. The evidence (see above pp.13-20) may be schematized as shown on page 140 below.

In middle Platonism, the three "causes"--God, matter, forms/ideas--seem to represent a standard doctrine (Albinus, Timaeus Locri, Apuleius) and the Aristotelian final cause was assimilated in the formal/instrumental cause. The latter is the intelligible world of "ideas" which serves as the paradigm/pattern (paradeigma) for creation, i.e., the formation of matter which is without form and quality. Although Philo (Cher 125) gives here the four causes, it is modified by the middle Platonic doctrine of the intelligible world of ideas/forms as the pattern/paradigm for the creation of the sense perceptible world. The intelligible world of ideas is identified by Philo with the logos (Op 25).

Stoic modifications: The Stoics recognized two principles (see above pp. 18-20), namely, the active (logos, God) and passive (matter), the former being inherent in the latter. They are both material causes (sōmata) and in fact all causes are material (sōmatika--SVF I,98; II,336, 340, 341). Although the same language of causes is used (dia ho, ex hēs--cf. SVF I,89; II,316), there is ultimately a single cause (material) (SVF II,341),

---

[9]Michel explains "di' hou" as equivalent to the Hebrew "b^e"--(p. 96, f.n. 1); Spicq thinks that philosophical presuppositions are foreign to Hebrews and one ought to evoque the Biblical tradition of God's creation through his word (II, p. 6). Bultmann in his treatment of the prologue of John in his commentary denies that Logos is an intermediary and has no reference to the language of "causes" in Jn 1,3 (ET pp. 36-38). E. Lohse in his commentary on Colossians 1,15-20 gives a rich sampling of parallels and points to the Stoic formulations as the background of Col 1,16 and 17. He does not distinguish between the differences in the Stoic and middle Platonic formulations and lumps them all together and incorrectly evaluates the evidence: "It was impossible to identify the God of Israel with nature, and the faith of Israel could not be dissolved into a pantheistic world view" (Hermeneia, p. 50). Philo who uses middle Platonic formulations and identifies God with "nature" does not dissolve the God of Israel into pantheism (cf. Fug 172; see above the note on pp. 18-20). Furthermore, Lohse makes no mention that we are dealing here with the theory of "causes," which are stated in standard formulations, and mistakenly calls the succession of prepositions as "almost a play on words" (Hermeneia, p. 49).

Middle-Platonic modifications[10]

Aristotle	Philo	Albinus	Timaeus Locri	Apuleius
ἀρχὴ τῆς κινήσεως	τὸ αἴτιον – ὑφ᾿ οὗ – θεός	πρῶτος θεός/νοῦς – ὑπό τινος – πατήρ – ἀρχή	θεός/νοῦς – ἀρχή	deus
ὕλη – ἐξ οὗ	ὕλη – ἐξ οὗ – τιθήνη – μήτηρ – τροφός	ὕλη – ἐκ τινος – τιθήνη – μήτηρ – ἐκμαγεῖον – δεξαμενός – ἀποτύπωμα	ὕλα – τιθήνα – μάτηρ – ἐκμαγεῖον – μόρφωσις – δοχήμων	materia – informis – nec – qualis
τὸ τί ἦν εἶναι – οὐσία – παράδειγμα – λόγος – τὸ τί ἦν εἶναι	τὸ ἐργαλεῖον – δι᾿ οὗ – παράδειγμα – ἀρχέτυπος – λόγος – ὄργανον – σφραγίς – ἰδέα – κόσμος νοητός – νόημα	ἡ ἰδέα – πρὸς ὅ – παράδειγμα – οὐσία – μέτρον – πρὸς ὅ – νοητός	ἡ ἰδέα – ἀγένητος – παράδειγμα – μένουσα – νοητόν	forma = "idea" – exemplum rerum – nec corporalis – simplex – aeterna
τὸ οὗ ἕνεκα – ἀγαθόν – τέλος	ἡ αἰτία – δι᾿ ὅ – ἀγαθότης			

[10]Aristotle: Metaph 983a,24-32; 1013a,24-35; Phys 194b,16-195a,26; Philo: Cher 125; Ebr 61; cf. Fug 12; Albinus: chaps. 8-10; Timaeus Locri: chaps. 1-2; Apuleius, De Platone et eius Dogmate, I,V and VI.

namely, God/body. Examples of such Stoic formulations are:

De Mundo: ἀρχαῖος μὲν οὖν τις λόγος καὶ πάτριός ἐστι πᾶσιν
    ἀνθρώποις ὡς ἐκ θεοῦ πάντα καὶ διὰ θεοῦ ἡμῖν συνέστηκεν
    . . . (397β, 14-15).

Marcus Aurelius 4,23: πᾶν μοι καρπός, ὃ φέρουσιν αἱ σαὶ ὧραι,
    ὧ φύσις, ἐκ σοῦ πάντα, ἐν σοὶ πάντα, εἰς σὲ πάντα.

It is probable that Jewish monotheism found the Stoic formulation more suitable in its emphasis on a single cause, although
it would have undoubtedly denied its bodily character. In this
respect, Hb 2,10, Rom 11,36 and 1Cor 8,6a seem to reproduce such
a monotheistic formula:

Rom 11,36: ὅτι ἐξ αὐτοῦ καὶ δι' αὐτοῦ καὶ εἰς αὐτὸν τὰ
    πάντα.

1Cor 8,6a: εἷς θεὸς ὁ πατήρ, ἐξ οὗ τὰ πάντα
    καὶ ἡμεῖς εἰς αὐτόν

Hb 2,10: (θεός) δι' ὃν τὰ πάντα καὶ δι' οὗ τὰ πάντα

In these two statements we observe the coalescence of the causes
into one, i.e., God. On the other hand, the christology influenced by the speculations on the logos and sophia introduce a
second cause and these formulas are influenced by middle Platonic
formulations:

Hb 1,2: δι' οὗ καὶ ἐποίησεν τοὺς αἰῶνας

Jn 1,3: πάντα δι' αὐτοῦ ἐγένετο

Col 1,16: ἐν αὐτῷ ἐκτίσθη τὰ πάντα . . .
    τὰ πάντα δι' αὐτοῦ καὶ εἰς αὐτὸν ἔκτισται. . . .

    17: τὰ πάντα ἐν αὐτῷ συνέστηκεν . . .

1Cor 8,6b: εἷς κύριος 'Ιησοῦς Χριστός, δι' οὗ τὰ πάντα
    καὶ ἡμεῖς δι' αὐτοῦ.

The formulations in Rom 11,36, 1Cor 8,6a and Hb 2,10 would have
been considered a gross error in middle Platonism and explicitly
so by Philo (see Cher 124-25). It is possible that Paul in his
argument with the Corinthians wants to underline the fact that
all causes, including the material (ex hou), are ultimately one
and that Christians recognize only a single principle, namely, the
monotheistic, and for this purpose has adapted a monotheistic
formula (8,6a) and appended a different christological one which
becomes awkward in this juxtaposition between a strictly monotheistic formula which recognizes only a single cause and a logos/
wisdom christology, which implies a second. Perhaps he intends to
control the implications of such a wisdom christology in Corinth
by this adapted monotheistic principle, in that one who has par-
taken of wisdom has risen above matter, and activity in this
realm has no consequence. Paul argues on the contrary that the
monotheistic principle implies that all realms belong to God (ex
hou ta panta), including the material.

142

Furthermore, the difference and variety in the formulations
in Hebrews, John and Colossians precludes the view that these
are liturgical or confessional in character (contra Michel).
These are theological statements from the world of hellenized
Judaism which certainly was not of one mind even on this point.

In the participation of the intermediary world of logos--
sophia in creation, it is significant that Moses and the "first
born," "eldest son," "man" have the highest privilege, that is
to create the archetypes and forms (Leg All iii,102; Conf 63; see
above p. 14). And "first born," "order of the son," "sons of
God" describe the highest status (see above pp. 40-42). The significance of Hebrew's ascription of this status of "sonship" to
Jesus exclusively and its denial to the angels or Moses is understandable in the context of this tradition. We will discuss this
further in the context of Hb 3,1-6.

Reflection and Stamp of God

That the terms "apaugasma," "charactēr" and "hypostasis"
come from the realm of hellenized Judaism is commonly acknowl-
edged, the main evidence for the two former terms being Philo and
Wisdom of Solomon, e.g.:[11]

Wis Sol 7,22: ἔστιν γὰρ ἐν αὐτῇ (i.e., σοφία) πνεῦμα--νοερόν,
ἅγιον, μονογενές, πολυμερές, λεπτόν, εὐκίνητον, τρανόν,
ἀμόλυντον, σαφές.

23 ἀπήμαντον, φιλάγαθον, ἐξύ, ἀκώλυτον, εὐεργετικόν,
φιλάνθρωπον, βέβαιον, ἀσφαλές, ἀμέριμνον, παντοδύναμον,
πανεπίσκοπον, καὶ διὰ πάντων χωροῦν πνευμάτων, νοερῶν,
καθαρῶν, λεπτοτάτων.

24: πάσης γὰρ κινήσεως κινητικώτερον σοφία, διήκει δὲ καὶ
χωρεῖ διὰ πάντων διὰ τὴν καθαρότητα.

25: ἀτμὶς γάρ ἐστιν τῆς τοῦ θεοῦ δυνάμεως καὶ ἀπόρροια
τῆς τοῦ παντοκράτορος δόξης εἰλικρινής διὰ τοῦτο οὐδὲν
μεμιαμμένον εἰς αὐτὴν παρεμπίπτει.

26: ἀπαύγασμα γάρ ἐστιν φωτὸς ἀιδίου καὶ ἔσοπτρον
ἀκηλίδωτον τῆς τοῦ θεοῦ ἐνεργείας καὶ εἰκὼν τῆς
ἀγαθότητος αὐτοῦ.[12]

QG I,57: For in a certain sense the wisdom of the world was a
mirror of the powers of God, in accordance with which it
became perfect and this universe is governed and managed
(interpretation of Gn 3,24).

Spec Leg iv,123: τὸ μὲν αἷμα δι' ἣν εἶπον αἰτίαν ὅτι οὐσία
ψυχῆς ἐστίν--οὐχὶ τῆς νοερᾶς καὶ λογικῆς ἀλλὰ τῆς
αἰσθητικῆς . . . ἐκείνης γὰρ οὐσία πνεῦμα θεῖον . . .

---

[11]For the background and meaning of the term "hypostasis,"
see H. Koester, TWNT VIII, 571-88.

[12]For Stoic and Philonic parallels to this passage, see
J. A. F. Gregg, The Wisdom of Solomon, 72-76.

τῆς μακαρίας καὶ τρισμακαρίας φύσεως <u>ἀπαύγασμα</u>-- . . .
(cf. Op 146; Plant 50--kosmos = aisthētos oikos theou,
<u>apaugasma</u> hagiōn, mimēma archetypou).

Virt 52: (see above p. 137) Moses has the "divine character"
engraved on his soul.

Plant 18: . . . ὁ δὲ μέγας Μωυσῆς οὐδενὶ τῶν γεγονότων <u>τῆς</u>
<u>λογικῆς ψυχῆς τὸ εἶδος</u> ὡμοίωσεν, ἀλλ᾽ εἶπεν αὐτὴν τοῦ
θείου καὶ ἀοράτου πνεύματος ἐκείνου δόκιμον εἶναι
νόμισμα σημειωθὲν καὶ τυπωθὲν <u>σφραγῖδι θεοῦ</u>, <u>ἧς ὁ</u>
<u>χαρακτήρ ἐστιν ὁ ἀΐδιος λόγος</u>.

Leg All iii,95: . . . λεκτέον οὖν ὅτι καὶ τοῦτο <u>τὸ σχῆμα τῇ ψυχῇ</u>
<u>ἐντετύπωκεν ὁ θεὸς</u> νομίσματος δοκίμου τρόπον. τίς οὖν
ἐστιν ὁ <u>χαρακτήρ</u> . . . <u>ὁ λόγος αὐτοῦ</u> . . .

These examples will suffice to show that both the <u>logos</u> and <u>wis-</u>
<u>dom</u> are described by such terms in their relationship to God in
Philo and Wisdom of Solomon as well as the "son" in Hebrews. The
use of such imagery from the world of sculpture and coinage is
common in the cosmology of middle Platonic writers, e.g., <u>Albinus</u>:

ἐπεὶ γὰρ τῶν κατὰ φύσιν αἰσθητῶν καὶ κατὰ μέρος ὡρισμένα
τινὰ δεῖ <u>παραδείγματα εἶναι τὰς ἰδέας</u>, ὧν καὶ τὰς ἐπιστήμας
γίνεσθαι καὶ τοὺς ὅρους. παρὰ πάντας γὰρ ἀνθρώπους ἄνθρωπόν
τινα νοεῖσθαι καὶ παρὰ πάντας ἵππους ἵππον καὶ κοινῶς παρὰ
τὰ ζῷα ζῷον ἀγένητον καὶ ἄφθαρτον ὃν τρόπον <u>σφραγῖδος μιᾶς</u>
<u>ἐκμαγεῖα</u> γίνεται <u>πολλὰ</u> καὶ ἑνὸς ἀνδρὸς <u>εἰκόνες</u> μυρίαι ἐπὶ
μυρίαις, τῆς <u>ἰδέας</u> οὔσης αἰτίας ἀρχὴν τοῦ εἶναι ἕκαστον
τοιοῦτον, οἷον αὐτῇ ὑπάρχει. ἀναγκαῖον καὶ τὸ κάλλιστον
κατασκεύασμα τὸν κόσμον <u>ὑπὸ τοῦ θεοῦ</u> δεδημιουργῆσθαι πρός
τινα <u>ἰδέαν</u> κόσμου ἀποβλέποντος, <u>παράδειγμα</u> ὑπάρχουσαν
τοῦδε τοῦ κόσμου ὡς ἂν ἀπεικονισμένου ἀπ᾽ ἐκείνης . . .
(12,1-9).

It ought to be reiterated here that such terminology should not
be understood as technical or in a substantive sense, but rather
they describe sets of relationships in the realm of both cosmology and psychology. Hence the same terms can be used to describe
the logos, wisdom, the rational mind, the cosmos, etc. (see above
pp. 21f. and 27-28). In the same circle of thought belongs the
idea of supporting the world, governance and management (see
above QG I,57; pp. 13ff., especially Plant 8-10 "achthophorein").
The intermediary world of logos and sophia have such creative and
preservative roles. The idea seems to be a commonplace in philosophical handbooks and treatises, e.g., De Mundo:

λέγεται δὲ καὶ ἑτέρως <u>κόσμος</u> ἡ τῶν ὅλων <u>τάξις</u> τε καὶ
<u>διακόσμησις, ὑπὸ θεοῦ τε καὶ διὰ θεὸν φυλαττομένη</u>
(391β,11-12).

<u>σωτὴρ</u> μὲν γὰρ ὄντως <u>ἁπάντων</u> ἐστὶ καὶ <u>γενέτωρ</u> τῶν
ὁπωσδήποτε κατὰ τόνδε τὸν κόσμον συντελουμένων <u>ὁ</u>
<u>θεός</u> . . . (397β,20-23).

κρεῖττον οὖν ὑπολαβεῖν, ὃ καὶ πρέπον ἐστὶ καὶ θεῷ
μάλιστα ἁρμόζον, ὡς ἡ ἐν οὐρανῷ δύναμις ἱδρυμένη καὶ
τοῖς πλεῖστον ἀφεστηκόσιν, ὡς ἕνι γε εἰπεῖν, καὶ
<u>σύμπασιν αἰτία γίνεται σωτηρίας</u> . . . (398α, 2-5).
Cf. 400b,7-10; Seneca, Ep 31,10.

144

The examples in Philo in which "pherein" has the sense of "bringing into existence" has a striking resemblance to Hebrews in
formulation, although the meaning in Hebrews is most probably
that of sustaining and preserving (Quis Her 36: ὁ τὰ μὴ ὄντα
φέρων καὶ τὰ πάντα γεννῶν (i.e., θεός); Mut 192: τῷ τῆς ψυχῆς
φέροντι καὶ αὔξοντι καὶ πληροῦντι καρποὺς θεῷ; 256: πάντα φέρων
σπουδαῖα ὁ θεός).[13]

Christology of Humiliation and Exaltation (Hb 1,3b)

On this point see H. Koester, "The Structure and Criteria of
Early Christian Beliefs," Trajectories, pp. 219-23. We wish to
draw attention only to some aspects pertinent to the thesis. The
author of Hebrews introduces here a primitive Christological
tradition of the exaltation of the Son (Acts 2,33-34; Eph 1,20-23;
Mk 16,19; Col 3,1) on the basis of Ps 110,1 which originally had
no reference to exaltation (cf. Mk 12,35-37 and par.; 1Cor 15,
25).[14] The psalm was probably adapted for such a Christology of
exaltation whose origins probably lie in mythical traditions
regarding wisdom (e.g., 1Enoch 42) and the destiny of the righteous sufferer within this tradition (cf. Wis Sol 2,13:
(ὁ δίκαιος) ἐπαγγέλεται γνῶσιν ἔχειν θεοῦ καὶ παῖδα κυρίου ἑαυτὸν
ὀνομάζει; 2,16 . . . καὶ ἀλαζονεύεται πατέρα θεόν; 2,18 εἰ γάρ
ἐστιν ὁ δίκαιος υἱὸς θεοῦ, ἀντιλήψεται αὐτοῦ καὶ ῥύσεται αὐτὸν ἐκ
χειρὸς ἀνθεστηκότων; 4,10 εὐάρεστος θεῷ γενόμενος ἠγαπήθη καὶ ζῶν
μεταξὺ ἁμαρτωλῶν μετετέθη (i.e., Enoch); 5,5 πῶς κατελογίσθη ἐν
υἱοῖς θεοῦ καὶ ἐν ἁγίοις ὁ κλῆρος αὐτοῦ ἐστιν; 5,15 δίκαιοι δὲ
εἰς τὸν αἰῶνα ζῶσιν, καὶ ἐν κυρίῳ ὁ μισθὸς αὐτῶν, καὶ ἡ φροντὶς
αὐτῶν παρὰ ὑψίστῳ. 5,16 διὰ τοῦτο λήμψονται τὸ βασίλειον τῆς
εὐπρεπείας καὶ τὸ διάδημα τοῦ κάλλους ἐκ χειρὸς κυρίου . . .).
Noteworthy is the importance of the status of "son" in the Wisdom
of Solomon, which provides the background for understanding the
significance of this title in Philo and Hebrews. The language is
strongly reminiscent of the Gospel of John (cf. 1,12. 14. 18;
5,18, etc.). That the righteous are numbered among the "sons of
God" and have their lot among the "holy ones" is probably a reference to their belonging to the angelic world (cf. Hb 12,22-23).
The translation of Enoch is held up as an example of one "beloved"

---

[13]Cf. Hermas, Sim 9,14.5-6: ἄκουε, φησί, τὸ ὄνομα τοῦ υἱοῦ
τοῦ θεοῦ μέγα ἐστι καὶ ἀχώρητον καὶ τὸν κόσμον ὅλον βαστάζει. εἰ
οὖν πᾶσα ἡ κτίσις διὰ τοῦ υἱοῦ τοῦ θεοῦ βαστάζεται, . . .

[14]Cf. F. Hahn, The Titles of Jesus in Christology, pp. 129-
33.

although living among sinners. The kingdom and the crown belong
to the righteous and they live forever (cf. Jn 3,35f.). They
have the knowledge of God and the title of son (cf. Jn 1,18; Hb
1,1-2).

With this primitive Christological tradition, the author has
combined the tradition of the sacrificial death of Jesus (i.e.,
for the forgiveness of sins--Hb 1,3; 2,9. 17; c. 8-10; cf. 2Pet
1,9; Hermas, Sim 5,6.2). Such a combination is not to be found
in either Phil 2,5-11 or the prologue of John, or 1Tim 3,16 and
is barely hinted at in Col 1,20, if at all. For in this Christological scheme the death of Jesus marks the lowest point of
humiliation. It is with such a Christology that the author subjects to reinterpretation the tradition regarding intermediaries
and perfection with which he was faced.

Jesus' Superiority over the Angels

Verse 4 introduces the first explicit comparison in the
writing (see above pp. 121ff.) and is seen as both surprising and
sudden by commentators. The need to establish the superiority of
the son over the angels at such length after vs. 2-3 has seemed
unusual. Various hypotheses have been advanced to account for it.
The older attempts to find here a gnostic cult of angels (Col
2,8.18--an argument really from one unknown to another) or an
angel-Christology (the evidence for it being mainly second century literature--Justin, Dial 34,2; Slavic Josephus 11,175; Hermas) has been rejected.[15] Spicq attempts an explanation in terms

---

[15]Windisch flatly states: "Der Sohn ist göttlichen Wesens
und Mittler der Gesamten Welt--und Heilsgeschichte . . . daher
natürlich über die Engel hoch erhaben . . . " (underlining my
own; p. 9). He denies that Hebrews combats a gnostic false doctrine (p. 17). Moffat, on the other hand, holds that "enthronement exhibits (v. 4) the superiority of the Son to the angels,"
and on the other hand, "the sudden transition to a comparison between the Son and the angels implies that something is before the
writer's mind. . . . undue deference to angels . . . or . . .
some contemporary belief about angels and revelation? Probably
the latter, though this does not emerge till 2,2" (underlining my
own; pp. 8-9). Michel similarly states: "In der Erhöhung tritt
der Sohn die Weltherrschaft an. . . . Der Übergang des Vergleich
Sohn-Engel ist unvermittelt und fällt immer wieder auf" (p. 106).
His own view is that: "Oder ist die Vorstellung der apokalyp-
tischen Inthronisation so mächtig, dass der Hintergrund der Engelwelt notwendig hervortreten muss? Dan 7,9-10 und äethHen 71,7-10
zeigen, wie himmlische Inthronisation des Menschensohnes und
Präsentation der Engelwelt notwendig zueinander gehören . . .
Dann wäre keine gedankliche Abstraktion, sondern eine lebendige
apokalyptische Anschauung die Ursache des Vergleiches zwischen
Engel und Christus in Hebr 1-2" (underlining my own; p. 132).
Spicq states: "Le lecteur moderne ne peut qu'etre étonné et de

146

of the right of angels as mediators of revelation to glory. For
this he provides no documentation and how it illuminates the connection between vs. 2-3 and 4ff. is unclear. Michel's explanation in terms of a necessary feature of apocalyptic enthronization (Dan 7,9-10; 1Enoch 71,7-10) fails to notice that angels
form the retinue of the heavenly court and any attempt to show
the superiority of the Son of Man over the angels is completely
absent. More serious is the fact that the enthronization of the
Son of Man is consistently associated with the scene of judge-
ment--i.e., the day of judgement--45,3; 51,3; 55,4, etc. This is
a connection never made by Hebrews. One must attempt an explanation, not in a piecemeal fashion--a verse at a time, but in terms
of the sequence of comparisons both in this chapter and ahead.

It is our contention that in the thought world which the
author was dealing with, the Christology presupposed by the
author which identified Jesus with the logos/sophia was itself the
source of the problem. Here, as we have demonstrated above (pp.
8-30), logos, wisdom, son, heavenly man, angels, highpriest, etc.
constitute the intermediary world in which these titles of status
are synonymous and their functions as mediators interchangeable.
The exaltation of the son does not in itself prove his superiority over the angels or any other figure of the intermediary world.
In fact, wisdom sits beside God's throne in the holy heavens, a
throne of glory (Wis Sol 9,4: δός μοι τὴν τῶν σῶν θρόνων
πάρεδρον σοφίαν. 9,10: ἐξαπόστειλον αὐτὴν ἐξ ἁγίων οὐρανῶν καὶ
ἀπὸ θρόνου δόξης σου πέμψον αὐτήν, . . .). In Ezekiel the
Tragedian, Moses sits on God's throne in a dream which is a prophecy of his future lordship over heaven and earth (Eus PE IX,
29,440a-c). Similarly, in Philo, Moses has the same exalted
status (see above pp. 71-72).

The author of Hebrews comes to terms with such a tradition
first of all by proving Jesus' superiority over the angelic world
and assigning to him alone the prerogative of sitting beside God.
Nor is the transition of the comparison of the son with prophets
to that with angels sudden or surprising in this context. The

---

la nécessité d'établir l'infériorité des anges par rapport au
Fils de Dieu, et du peu de rigueur critique de la démonstration
biblique. Mais, selon la tradition, les anges étaient censés
avoir transmis a Israel et édicté la Loi divine . . . Cette
médiation était pour eux un titre de gloire. Il fallait donc
établir que malgre leur dignité, ces princes du ciel étaient bien
inférieurs au Christ" (underlining my own; II, p. 14).

prophet is equated with the logos and angels by Philo (see above pp. 16-17) as well as with the true priest (see above p. 63) and his role is that of a "hermeneus" of God (cf. De Mundo 391a: the soul by means of philosophy takes the ruling mind as a guide καὶ θείῳ ψυχῆς ὄμματι τὰ θεῖα καταλαβοῦσα, τοῖς τε ἀνθρώποις προφητεύουσα). See further Abr 113; Congr 170; Quod Det 40; Plutarch, Def. Orac. 416f. Furthermore, the author has set the stage for the comparison with Moses in these opening statements (see above pp. 134-38) whose formulation ascribes to Jesus titles, descriptions and honours which were ascribed to Moses in the tradition with which he was dealing.

The superiority of the son over the angels is proven by citation of scripture (vs. 5-13). Some of these the author undoubtedly took over from the tradition of the church and which originally had a messianic import: Ps 2,7 (cf. 1QSa 2,11; Ps Sol 17,26; Acts 4,26-27; Rev 2,27; 12,5; 19,15); 2Sam 7,14 (cf. 4QF1; 2Cor 6,18; Rev 21,7) and Ps 110 (cf. Mk 12,35-37 par.; 1Cor 15,25; Acts 2,33-34; Eph 1,20-23; Col 3,1; Mk 16,19). The view that these passages describe a scenario of the exaltation and enthronement of the son (Michel, Spicq) seems dubious and the evidence given does not support the view that the schema of such an ancient ceremony was current in the Judaism of the period. That a variety of figures had the honour of sitting beside or on God's throne is well known (wisdom in the Wis Sol 9,4; 9,10; Moses in Ezekiel the Tragedian--Eus PE IX,29.440; the Elect One and Son of Man as judge in 1Enoch 45,3; 51,3; 55,4; 61,8; 79,27-29; Metatron in 3Enoch 48c.1ff.). The author of Hebrews himself provides the clue as to the basis of these citations, namely, the honour and status of the son as evidenced by his "name." What is in view is not a single name but a series--"son," "first born," "God," and "Lord." The meaning of "name" in this context is not the Semitic one[16] but that which was current in the Hellenistic world in the sense of honourific titles. The highest title is undoubtedly "God" and this is the title given to Moses who is the heir of the cosmos. He is "king" and "God" (see above pp. 134-38). It is the "first born" who inherits all things from the father (QG IV,153; see above p. 136). In this tradition the status of sonship/son of God is the highest and represents perfection. Those unfit to be called by such a name are to place themselves under the Logos who bears a similar series of titles (see above pp. 31-

---

[16]Cf. Bousset-Gressmann, Die Religion des Judentums, pp. 349f.

148

34; Conf 145-48):

Conf 146: κἂν μηδέπω μέντοι τυγχάνῃ τις ἀξιόχρεως ὢν υἱὸς θεοῦ
προσαγορεύεσθαι, σπουδαζέτω κοσμεῖσθαι κατὰ τὸν
πρωτόγονον αὐτοῦ λόγον, τὸν ἀγγέλων πρεσβύτατον, ὡς
ἂν ἀρχάγγελον, πολυώνυμον ὑπάρχοντα. καὶ γὰρ ἀρχὴ
καὶ ὄνομα θεοῦ καὶ λόγος καὶ ὁ κατ᾽ εἰκόνα ἄνθρωπος
καὶ ὁ ὁρῶν, ᾽Ισραήλ, προσαγορεύεται. (Cf. Leg All i,43)

We need only remind at this point that Moses is logos, archangel,
bears the name "god," and "the man according to the image" and
"Israel" (the one who sees) are representatives of perfection.
The same kind of tradition has influenced the description in
Colossians 1,15-20 (εἰκὼν τοῦ θεοῦ; πρωτότοκος πάσης κτίσεως; ὅς
ἐστιν ἀρχή, πρωτότοκος ἐκ τῶν νεκρῶν).[17] Further examples will
demonstrate the continuing influence of similar traditions in
Christological formulations of the later church:

Justin, Dial 34,2: ὁ γὰρ Χριστὸς βασιλεὺς καὶ ἱερεὺς καὶ θεὸς
καὶ κύριος καὶ ἄγγελος καὶ ἄνθρωπος καὶ ἀρχιστράτηγος
καὶ λίθος καὶ παιδίον . . .

61,1: . . . ὅτι ἀρχὴν πρὸ πάντων τῶν κτισμάτων ὁ θεὸς
γεγέννηκα δυναμίν τινα ἐξ ἑαυτοῦ λογικήν, ἥτις καὶ δόξα
κυρίου ὑπὸ τοῦ πνεύματος τοῦ ἁγίου καλεῖται, ποτὲ δὲ
υἱός, ποτὲ δὲ σοφία, ποτὲ δὲ ἄγγελος, ποτὲ δὲ θεός, ποτὲ
δὲ κύριος καὶ λόγος, ποτὲ δὲ ἀρχιστράτηγον . . .
(Cf. 56,4; 56,10; 58,3; 59,1; 60,1, etc.)[18]

Apostolic Constitutions 8,12,7: σὺ γὰρ εἶ ἡ ἄναρχος γνῶσις, ἡ
ἀΐδιος ὅρασις, ἡ ἀγγένητος ἀκοή, ἡ ἀδίδακτος σοφία,
ὁ πρῶτος τῇ φύσει καὶ μόνος τῷ εἶναι καὶ κρείττων
παντὸς ἀριθμοῦ, ὁ τὰ πάντα ἐκ τοῦ μὴ ὄντος εἰς τὸ εἶναι
παραγαγὼν διὰ τοῦ μονογενοῦς σου υἱοῦ, αὐτὸν δὲ πρὸ
πάντων αἰώνων γεννήσας βουλήσει καὶ δυνάμει καὶ ἀγαθό-
τητι ἀμεσιτεύτως, υἱὸν μονογενῆ, λόγον θεόν, σοφίαν
ζῶσαν, πρωτότοκον πάσης κτίσεως, ἄγγελον τῆς μεγάλης
βουλῆς σου, ἀρχίερεα σόν, βασιλέα δὲ καὶ κύριον πάσης
νοητῆς καὶ αἰσθητῆς φύσεως, τὸν πρὸ πάντων, δι᾽ οὗ τὰ
πάντα.[19]

The almost exact similarity in vocabulary and ideas to Philo is
obvious in both these writings. The precise background for the

_____

[17]For Colossians see Lohse's commentary for a rich presentation of sources on the terminology--ET translation in the
Hermeneia series.

[18]In Joseph and Asenath, the angel who appears to Asenath is
described as: ἄνθρωπος ἐκ τοῦ οὐρανοῦ; ὁ θεῖος ἄγγελος; ὁ ἀρχιστράτηγος κυρίου τοῦ θεοῦ (14; 15). Most probably the archangel
Michael.

[19]The evidence we have presented in thesis so far, perhaps,
illuminates the nature of the tradition which led to the angel-
christology in the second century onwards. Jesus' identity with
the logos and sophia meant that he was also the archangel and
chief of them--Michael. The evidence is presented in detail by
Joseph Barbel, Christos Angelos: Die Anschauung von Christus als
Bote und Engel in der gelehrten und volkstümlichen Literatur des
christlichen Altertums. J. Danielou presents the evidence in a
straightforward manner in: The Theology of Jewish Christianity,
Chapter 4.

piling of such honourific names and titles is the hellenistic
idea of the "many named" (polyonymos) deity, which is explicitly
stated by Philo in Conf 146 (cf. Leg All i,43), e.g., Cleanthes,
Hymn to Zeus: line 1 - κύδιστ' ἀθανάτων, πολυώνυμε, παγκρατὲς
αἰεί . . .

De Mundo 401a,13ff.: εἷς δὲ ὢν πολυώνυμός ἐστι, κατονομαζόμενος
     τοῖς πάθεσι πᾶσιν ἅπερ αὐτὸς νεοχμοῖ. There follows a
     long list of titles.

In the context of the thought world with which the author
was faced, it was urgent for him to prove the superiority of
Jesus over the angels since the intermediary world's revelation
and salvific benefits were inferior and imperfect and the exemplars of perfection in the sense of unmediated access to God were
above all Moses and the Highpriest. In the author's proof, it is
Jesus who bears the high titles of honour--"son," "first born,"
"God" and "Lord,"--the angels were to worship the first born (cf.
Phil 2,10f.; Asc Is 11,23; Rev 5,8ff.),[20] they are changeable
into spirits/winds and fire (cf. 4Ezra 8,21), whereas the son is
God and Lord, and remain forever in contrast to passing away of
his creation. The angels are mere ministering spirits (cf.
Philo, Virt 74; Enoch 15,1ff.; TestL 3,5; Jub 2,2; 15,27; Midrash
Tehillim 104,442) at the service of Christians. A very similar
view is expressed by Philo:

Gig 12: τῶν οὖν ψυχῶν αἱ μὲν πρὸς σώματα κατέβησαν, αἱ δὲ οὐδενὶ
    τῶν γῆς μορίων ἠξίωσάν ποτε συνενεχθῆναι. ταύταις
    ἀφιερωθείσαις καὶ τῆς τοῦ πατρὸς θεραπείας περιεχομέναις
    ὑπηρέτισι καὶ διακόνοις ὁ δημιουργὸς εἴωθε χρῆσθαι πρὸς
    τὴν τῶν θνητῶν ἐπιστασίαν. (These souls are angels, as
    he explicitly states in 16.)

QE II,13: (see above p. 37)
This view of angels in Hebrews and Philo stands in marked contrast to their important role in Judaism of the period and especially in apocalyptic (see above pp. 83-96).[21]

---

[20]The term "first born" is basically an honourific title
ascribed to different things: in Rabbinics to the Torah, Adam,
Jacob, Israel, Messiah (see Michel, pp. 113-14; W. Michaelis in
TDNT VI, 837-76); in Philo to the logos (Quis Her 117; Conf 146;
Agr 51; Som i,215); to wisdom (QG IV,97--"first born mother of
all things"); to anthropos (Conf 63); to Isaac (Conf 74; QG IV,
153); Levi (Sac 19); in Philo it is equivalent to the title "
"eldest" (presbytatos) which is ascribed to the logos, Moses, etc.
(cf. Conf 146; Quis Her 205); in the Orphic Hymns it is ascribed
to different deities, e.g., "physis" (10,5--among whose other
titles are: divine all mother, pilot, all luminous (panaugēs),
"pantokrateira," pure, self-fathered (autopatōr), without father
(apatōr), etc.; cf. 25,2; 52,6; 30,2; 12,10).

[21]Windisch is more accurate than Michel in his evaluation of
the angelology of Hebrews: "Seine Engellehre ist die orthodox-

Inferiority of the Revelation through Angels/Prophets

The exhortation in 2,1-4 contrasts ὁ δι᾿ ἀγγέλων λαληθεὶς τηλικαύτη σωτηρία . . . λαλεῖσθαι διὰ τοῦ κυρίου. The word spoken through the angels is the same as that spoken through the prophets in 1,1. In Philo (see above pp. 146f.) as well as in Josephus, angels, prophets, messengers, envoys, etc. were deemed identical in accordance with hellenistic usage, e.g.,

Jos Ant 15,136: ἃ γὰρ ὁμολογεῖται παρανομώτατα τοῖς τε ῞Ελλησιν καὶ τοῖς βαρβάροις, ταῦτα ἔπραξαν εἰς τοὺς ἡμετέρους πρέσβεις, ἀποσφάξαντες αὐτούς, τῶν μὲν ῾Ελλήνων ἱεροὺς καὶ ἀσύλους εἶναι τοὺς κήρυκας φαμένων, ἡμῶν δὲ τὰ κάλλιστα τῶν δογμάτων καὶ τὰ ὁσιώτατα τῶν ἐν τοῖς νόμοις δι᾿ ἀγγέλων παρὰ τοῦ θεοῦ μαθόντων. τοῦτο γὰρ τὸ ὄνομα καὶ ἀνθρώποις θεὸν εἰς ἐμφάνειαν ἄγειν καὶ πολεμίους πολεμίοις διαλλάττειν δύναται.22

The point that Josephus makes (in this speech of Herod) is that Greeks, barbarians and Jews hold ambassadors, heralds and angels inviolable. It is through angels that the Jews have learnt the best doctrines and holiest things in the law. It is this "name" which makes God manifest to men and reconciles enemies. To kill them is the greatest of impiety (137). Philo expresses the same idea of the inviolability of angels in almost identical terms:

Gig 16: . . . ὥσπερ γὰρ ἀγαθοὺς δαίμονας καὶ κακοὺς λέγουσιν οἱ πολλοὶ καὶ ψυχὰς ὁμοίως, οὕτως καὶ ἀγγέλους τοὺς μὲν τῆς προσρήσεως ἀξίους πρεσβευτάς τινας ἀνθρώπων πρὸς θεὸν καὶ θεοῦ πρὸς ἀνθρώπους ἱεροὺς καὶ ἀσύλους διὰ τὴν ἀνυπαίτιον καὶ παγκάλην ταύτην ὑπηρεσίαν . . .

Abr 115: . . . (ἄγγελοι) . . . , ἱεραὶ καὶ θεῖαι φύσεις, ὑποδιά-κονοι καὶ ὕπαρχοι τοῦ πρώτου θεοῦ, δι᾿ ὧν οἷα πρεσβευτῶν ὅσα ἂν θελήσῃ τῷ γένει ἡμῶν προθεσπίσαι διαγγέλει. Cf. Plato, Symp 202E; Phaedo 64A, 67E.

Apart from Josephus, the idea that the revelation at Sinai and the law were given through the angels is found in Gal 3,19 and

---

jüdische und philonische, nicht die gnostisch-apokalyptische. Die These, dass Hebr eine gnostisierende Irrlehre bekämpfe, ist also wenig wahrscheinlich" (p. 17). Michel, on the other hand, states: "Der Hebr ist in seiner Engellehre sehr viel unkomplizierter, apokalyptischer als etwa Paulus" (p. 133). In the New Testament as a whole, G. Kittel points out that: "The active participation of angels seems to be most strongly assumed in relation to events of the last time" (TDNT I,83). Cf. Lk 13,8f.; iThess 4,16; 2Thess 1,7, etc. For angels as spiritual beings, see Bousset-Gressmann, Die Religion des Judentums, p. 321.

22 The footnote on this passage in the Loeb edition cites three other examples which identify angels with the highpriest and prophets: "in the LXX of Malachi ii,7 the high priest as in-terpreter of the Torah, is called ἄγγελον τοῦ κυρίου"; "Hecataeus of Abdera (ap. Diodorus x1.3) speaks of the high priest as ἄγγελον τῶν τοῦ θεοῦ προσταγμάτων"; "in the Midrash Wayyiqra Rabba . . . states that 'the prophets were called mal'akīm (= ἄγγελοι).'"

Acts 7,35.38 and 53. The validity of such mediation is recognized by Hebrews, Acts and Paul (cf. Gal 3,21).[23] The same is of course true in Philo, except that mediation through the angels, logos, wisdom, etc. is inferior and imperfect in comparison to that which is directly from God (see above pp. 42-45). Given the fact that Moses and Aaron are exemplars of such perfection, there is no hint at all in Philo that the revelation at Sinai was given through the angels, on the contrary, Moses saw there what no mortal can see, namely God (Mos i,158--see above p. 135). Most probably this idea of the superiority of unmediated revelation lies behind the enigmatic statement in Gal 3,20. The author of Hebrews used such a tradition of angelic mediation of the law to point out that all Old Testament revelation is through mediation of prophets/angels (1,1ff.) and inferior to that given through the Son or Lord who is superior to the angels/prophets. These arguments which he is developing here are directed ultimately at the tradition which saw Moses and Highpriest Aaron/Levi as exemplars of unmediated perfection.

The salvation spoken by the Lord was confirmed by hearers and attested by God through signs, wonders, powerful acts and allotments of the spirit--a widespread understanding of the divine attestation of the Christian message in the New Testament (Rm 15,18-19; 2Cor 12,12; Mk 16,17.20; Acts 2,22).

Summary and Conclusions

The course of the author's arguments and formulations have in view a particular tradition of Judaism of which Philo is the principal example. He begins with two technical terms from this thought world which describe the revelation through the prophets/angels as "in many parts" (polymerōs) and "manifold" (polytropōs) and hence inferior to the singular and definitive revelation through the Son (Philo, Ebr 85-87; 36; Plant 44; Som ii,10; Mig 152 versus the positive understanding of the terms in Jos Ant 10, 142 and Wis Sol 7,22; cf. 4Macc 1,25; Maximus Tyrius XI,7a). He concludes this section with an exhortation which utilizes a tradition of the angelic mediation of the Law (Jos Ant 15,136; Gal 3,19; Acts 7,35.38 and 53; cf. Philo Gig 16; Abr 115) and sets it in comparison with the superiority of the salvation through the

---

[23]The meaning of the term "bebaios" in Hb 2,2 is probably juridical, i.e., in the sense of being legally valid (see examples from papyrii in Moulton and Milligan). Cf. Philo, Mos ii,22; 2Pet 1,19; Plato, Tim 49b and Phaedo 90c.

Lord, which is described in traditional Christian terms for the divine attestation of the message. The opening statements regarding the Son, despite their similarity to the prologue of John, Col 1,15ff., Rm 11,36 and 1Cor 8,6, are distinctive in their vocabulary and ideas. It is generally recognized that the language used to describe the Son, such as "apaugasma," "charaktēr" of God's "hypostasis," are to be found in Philo and Wisdom of Solomon. What has not been recognized is that they follow closely themes of a tradition which form a coherent whole here as well as in the rest of the writing.

"Polymerōs," "polytropōs" and "poikilōs" are technical terms which describe a state of imperfection, namely, in middle Platonic terms the realm of sense perception in contrast to the singular (haplous) realm of the mind or intelligible world (Maximus Tyrius XI,7a). In Philo, this imperfection is characterized by a life (polytropos) embroiled in the world of flesh, blood and body (a crucial theme in Hb 2) and symbolized by the decorated robe (poikilōtatēs) of the highpriest with which he serves outside the Holy of Holies (Ebr 85-87; perfection in Hebrews is access into the Holy of Holies--c.8-10); by the changeable and manifold (polytropos) desires of life (Ebr 36); by the manifold (polytropos) disposition of the "moulded man" (Gn 2,8)--cf. 4Macc 1,25; by the manifold (polytropos) soul which has many ends in life, is drawn in different directions, shaken, driven to confusion and unable to find fixity (Som ii,10-14; the opposite term is "bebaios"--a term associated with hope and confidence in Hb 3,6, 6,19 and the principle of reality in 3,14; in Philo, the term "bebaios" describes the stability and firmness of the logos and the mind--QG IV,53; QE II,3); by the forty years of wandering in the wilderness on account of manifoldness (polytropos = mixed multitude of Ex 12,38)--a central theme in Hb 3,7-4,13 (Mig 152-54). Perfection on the other hand is characterized by Sarah who is "without mother" (amētor)--cf. Hb 7,2; by the highpriest/sophos when he has withdrawn from human pursuits, worships the Existent alone wearing the undecorated (apoikilos) robe of truth, having no concourse with things mortal and dealing only with that which is bloodless, fleshless and bodiless (Ebr 85-87; cf. Hb 2,14; 8-10); by the man made according to the image of God (Plant 44); by Isaac who does not use milky food but strong food of the perfect/full grown (Som ii,10-14; the same theme in Hb 5,11ff.); by the one who aims at one thing and is truly perfect/simple (haplous); by entry into the promised land = inheritance of

virtue (Mig 152-54; cf. Hb 3,7-4,13). The language and the
themes, therefore, manifestly belong to a single coherent thought
world both here and in Hebrews.

Specifically, in the context of this tradition regarding
perfection, the author has to argue the case for the superiority
of Jesus over and against the intermediary world of angels,
logos, wisdom, etc. with whom Jesus was identified and especially
Moses who was the supreme exemplar of perfection. Moses is indeed the Logos, archangel, highpriest, king and prophet (Mut 103;
Mig 83; 122; Quis Her 205-06; QG IV,8; Som ii,231; Gig 48-52,
etc.); he is heir of the whole world, the elements are subject to
him, he stands in closest partnership with God and his titles
"God" and "king" exemplify this relationship (Mos i,155-58); the
divine "charaktēr" is engraved in his soul (Virt 52); he is the
maker of the archetypes (Leg All iii,102).

The status of sonship is another term which characterizes
perfection and the highest religious claim of dignity (see above
pp. 40-42; Wis Sol 2,13.16.18; 5,5; Jn 1,12.14.18; 5,18). The
"first born" Isaac inherits all from God, namely, the realities
(Conf 74; QG IV,153; cf. Plant 69). Moses, the "first born,"
"eldest son," "man" create the archetypes and forms (Leg All iii,
102; Conf 63). The author of Hebrews follows precisely these
themes in his description of Jesus as the Son and attempts to
prove that Jesus is uniquely the one who has these attributes and
titles, and specifically denies the title "son" to the angels,
although he undoubtedly knew that in the Old Testament (LXX) the
angels are called sons of God, and also denies this title to
Moses (3,1-6). Jesus is thus the Son who is heir of all things,
through whom the universe was made, who is the reflection and
stamp of God's reality.

The author's choice of scriptural proof for the superiority
of Jesus over the angelic world has in view the honourific titles
of Moses which has at its basis the tradition of ascribing numerous titles ("many names") to Greek deities (cf. Philo, Conf 146;
Cleanthes, Hymn to Zeus 1; De Mundo 401a,13ff.; Justin, Dial
34,2; Apostolic Constitutions 8,12.7, etc.). The author specifically states that it is the "name" which proves the superiority
of Jesus over the angels (1,4). Jesus is Son, God, First Born,
Lord and by implication King (1,5-13). Some of these scriptural
proofs he undoubtedly took over from the tradition of the church
(esp. Ps 2; 110; 2Sam 7,14) and probably added the others on his
own.

In the context of this tradition, in which the intermediary world has synonymous titles and interchangeable functions, in which angels and prophets are identical, and on account of the fact that they mediate an imperfect revelation and religious status of a lower order, the transition of the comparison of Jesus with the prophets (1,1) to that with angels (1,4ff.) is quite understandable. Jesus' identity with logos and wisdom in primitive Christianity was itself the basis of the problem, in that he could be identified with a series of intermediary figures, as was true later in the church (see above pp. 148f.). It is the same identity with logos and sophia which forms the background of the christology of humiliation and exaltation which is presupposed by the author. It was therefore crucial for the author to show that Jesus is superior over all intermediaries and the salvation which he effected is superior as well. The titles and prerogatives of Moses, who is the exemplar of perfection, are ascribed to Jesus alone and thereby the author has already prepared in this chapter his preliminary proof of Jesus' superiority over Moses (explicitly in 3,1ff.) as well. This is indirectly driven home in his comparison in 2,1-4, where he uses the tradition of angelic mediation of the Law vis-a-vis the salvation effected by the Lord. On the other hand, according to Philo, Moses saw at Sinai what no mortal can see, and it is this tradition which bears the polemical brunt of the author in 12,18ff. (Mos i,158).

Furthermore, the author has used the primitive Christian Christology of the humiliation and exaltation of the Son as the criterion for his reinterpretation of this tradition (see above pp. 144-45). He has linked this humiliation with the sacrificial character of Jesus' death--the cleansing of sins (1,3; 2,9 & 17; c.8-10). In this respect he has achieved a combination of themes which were originally distinct and separate. That Jesus' death was sacrificial in character does not appear in Phil 2,6-11, 1Tim 3,16, Jn 1,1-18, and is barely hinted at in Col 1,20. His death was understood in this Christological scheme as the lowest point of humiliation. The eschatological character of the revelation in the Son (1,2) remains a rubric as does the futurity of salvation in 1,14 (cf. 9,28). It is this combination of the Christology of humiliation and exaltation with the tradition of the sacrificial death of Jesus which will prove to be the decisive criterion in the author's reinterpretation of the tradition.

CHAPTER FIVE

JESUS AND MOSES (HEBREWS 3,1-6)

Introduction: The passage is an explicit attempt to prove
the superiority of Jesus over Moses (πλείων δόξα κ. τινή, πιστὸς
ὡς υἱός - ὡς θεράπων). The reason for this comparison and how it
fits the context, in terms of what precedes and what follows, is
a basic issue of interpretation. Windisch denies the possibility
of a "false doctrine" which plays off Moses against Christ as
messengers of God since it could not have been disposed with so
few words. Rather it is a "positive Schriftweisheit" which is
parallel to the theme in 1,1-14--"Jesus greater than the Angels"
and "Jesus greater than Moses." Spicq goes one step further and
argues that the comparison is only literary and not real, and
that since the author has proven Jesus to be superior to the
angels, it would be superfluous to establish the superiority of
Jesus over Moses. His real explanation is a dogmatic one: "la
simple supériorité du Fils sur le législateur hébreu et sur
Josué." Whereas the Rabbinic interpretation of Nu 12,7 (Sifre
103) is alluded to by the commentators, Michel considers this
passage to be a "midrash" on Nu 12,7. However, he does not carry
through this proposal in the actual exegesis of the passage so as
to show how the formal characteristics and content of the "midrash" illuminate the specific content and argument of the passage. The remark of rabbi Jose ben Chalafta on Nu 12,7: "God
calls Moses 'faithful in all His house,' and thereby he ranked
higher than all the ministering angels themselves," does not explain why Jesus should be compared to either the angels or Moses.
Such midrashic traditions have not been shown to underlie 1,1-14
and certainly not 1,1-4. It does not explain the form or content
of the comparison in 3,3 and 4. That in Rabbinic tradition the
priests are "s^{e}lûḥîm" of God (StrB ad. loc.) is of little help
since the highpriesthood of Jesus is not elaborated in Hebrews in
these terms (e.g., 2:16-18; 4,14-16) in the immediate context or
later (chaps. 7-10).[1]

---

[1]Windisch, p. 28--the way he poses the issue in terms of
"false doctrine" is a misunderstanding of the religious situation
of early Christianity as a competing sect in the Mediterranean
world in which the issues were not dogmatic but of relative
claims and counter-claims of religious sects; Spicq II, p. 62;

Commentators have found it difficult to explain how this passage fits the context. The appearance of Jesus as highpriest in 2,17 has seemed unusual (Moffat: "Jesus is suddenly . . . called archiereus" (p. 37); "The introduction of the peirasmoi of Jesus (v. 18) is as abrupt as the introduction of the archiereus idea, but is thrown out by way of anticipation"--p. 39); according to Michel vs. 17f. sets forth a new thesis by means of the "Stichwort"--highpriest--taken up in 4,14 and elaborated from 5,1-10 onwards (p. 135). Its appropriateness in 3,1 is equally unclear. At most a literary explanation is forthcoming in terms of anticipatory hints given by the author. In terms of content and themes, explanations are of the most general kind. For example, Spicq following Vaganay,[2] sees 2,17f. as the statement of the theme of Jesus' highpriesthood, 3,1-6--faithful, 5,1-10--compassionate, in between a long paranesis (3,7-4,13--a midrash on Ps 95). This leads Spicq to misconstrue the theme of 3,1-6 as the superiority of Jesus as "pistos," whereas the point is that both Jesus and Moses are "pistoi" (ὡς καὶ Μωϋσῆς), but that Jesus has a superior <u>status</u> as Son over against Moses as servant.[3]

In terms of these issues of interpretation, we will show that the tradition regarding intermediaries and perfection enables us to explain the following:

(1) How this comparison with Moses fits the progression of themes and belongs to the same coherent thought world we have been unfolding. That it is not an isolated piece and the polemical issues are not being disposed of in a few words. The issues are real and the comparison is not merely a literary device to speak of the superiority or excellence of Jesus.

Michel, pp. 170-71. Moffat only vaguely refers to the possibility of "Jewish veneration of Moses" (Sifre, 110)--p. 41; Montefiore: "The stress on Jesus' <u>full humanity</u> makes it necessary to prove that he is superior to Moses, since Moses was admitted to be superior to all other men. Philo, <u>rhapsodising</u> on Moses, <u>even</u> calls him a high priest . . . but there is no reason to suppose that our writer has this particular <u>extravagance</u> in mind" (underlining my own, p. 71). This is an example of an unhistorical approach towards early Christianity, namely, all New Testament claims about Jesus are true and Judaism is false!

[2]Cf. Spicq II, pp. 62-63.

[3]Spicq: "La personnalité du Fils incarné est si haute que sa fidélité est d'une qualité bien supérieure à celle du médiateur de l'ancienne Alliance" (II, p. 63). This simply misses the most obvious meaning of vs. 2 (hōs kai Mōusēs). In fact the section is titled by Spicq: "La fidélité du Christ est supérieure à celle de Moise (iii, 1-6)" (p. 63).

(2) That the form and content of the argument belong in this tradition--highpriesthood, "homologia," heavenly call, etc., and the appropriateness of vs. 4, which commentators have not been able to fit within the argument.

Perfection and Highpriesthood of Moses

The appropriateness of this comparison with Moses can be understood because in this tradition Moses is the supreme exemplar of perfection (see above pp. 63-68). The author has already prepared for this comparison in 1,1-2,4, where the titles and prerogatives of Moses have been attributed to Jesus (see above pp. 134-38). The introduction of the title Highpriest in 2,17 and 3,1 is not surprising since in this tradition the heavenly Man, Son, Highpriest Aaron, Melchizedek and Levi are exemplars of perfection (see above pp. 38-40; 40-42; 58-63) and Moses is the supreme exemplary highpriest and "anthrōpos" (as we shall present below), and the thematics of perfection can be elaborated in terms of any of these intermediaries and exemplary religious figures (see above pp. 46-48). What follows in 3,7-4,13, belongs to this tradition in which perfection is entry into the promised land and the seventh day rest of God (see above pp. 132-34; esp. Mig 152-54; p. 77).[4]

In the tradition of the highpriesthood of Moses, there appear themes and motifs which will begin to clarify the rationale for this comparison as well as its connection with other

---

[4]Moffat denies that "any explicit antithesis to Moses is implied in archierea, for although Philo invested Moses with highpriestly honour . . . this is never prominent, and it is never worked out in Hebrews" (p. 41-42). Not only is the highpriesthood of Moses repeatedly introduced by Philo, it forms a long section in his life of Moses. The latter objection misunderstands the character of this tradition in which religious themes such as perfection can be elaborated and worked out in terms of any intermediary or exemplar. One uses them as is opportune and on the basis of where one can make his best case. Hebrews follows exactly this procedure in his argument. Furthermore, we have shown in 1,1-2,4 and will do so here, namely, the significance of the Moses tradition in Hebrews. Spicq cites Philo, Mos i,3; ii,2-5; 66; 187; 292; Praem 53; Sac 138, but without comment (II, 65). He prefers to see here the understanding of the highpriest as a Shaliah of the community (Berakoth., v. 5; Rosh ha Shanah iv, 9) since it harmonizes better the meaning of apostle and highpriest (II, 65). This is a direct contradiction of Hb 5,5--Jesus is highpriest called by God, and the highpriesthood of Jesus is not elaborated in Hebrews in terms of his being a representative of the church before God. Michel is hard to follow since he seems to exhaust all possibilities; he sees connections with Philo, apocalypticism and esoteric gnosis (pp. 165-67).

158

aspects of Hebrews. The following passages are chosen for this purpose:

Mos ii,67: τοιγαροῦν μετ' ὀλίγων ἄλλων φιλόθεός τε καὶ θεοφιλὴς
ἐγένετο, καταπνευσθεὶς ὑπ' ἔρωτος οὐρανίου καὶ
διαφερόντως <u>τιμήσας τὸν ἡγεμόνα τοῦ παντὸς</u> καὶ <u>ἀντι</u>-
<u>τιμηθεὶς</u> ὑπ' αὐτοῦ, <u>τιμὴ</u> δ' ἁρμόττουσα σοφῷ <u>θεραπεύειν</u>
τὸ πρὸς ἀλήθειαν ὄν, <u>ἱερωσύνη</u> δὲ <u>θεραπείαν</u> ἐπιτετήδευκε
θεοῦ. . . .

68: ἔδει δὲ πρότερον ὥσπερ τὴν <u>ψυχὴν</u> καὶ τὸ <u>σῶμα</u>
<u>καθαρεῦσαι</u>, μηδενὸς πάθους προσαψάμενον, ἀλλ' ἀγνεύσαντα
ἀπὸ πάντων ὅσα τῆς θνητῆς ἐστι φύσεως . . .

Sections 66-186 discuss the priesthood of Moses. Perfected in
piety and virtue, he loved God and was loved by Him as few others
and he <u>honoured the Ruler of All</u> and <u>was honoured in return</u> by
Him; the <u>service</u> (therapeuein) of the Being Who truly Is being a
fitting <u>honour</u> for the wiseman and <u>priesthood</u> which has as its
business the <u>service</u> (therapeia) of God (66-67). It was necessary that his soul and body be cleansed, having nothing to do
with passions, but <u>purified from everything mortal</u> (68). This
is exemplified by his forty days without eating and drinking,
and the beauty of his countenance when he descended from the
"highest," "most holy," "inaccessible" and "unapproachable" place
(69-70; cf. 1Tim 6,16). Here he learnt of his priestly duties
and saw the incorporeal forms of the corporeal tabernacle (74-
76):

75: προσῆκον γὰρ ἦν <u>τῷ ὡς ἀληθῶς ἀρχιερεῖ</u> καὶ τὴν τοῦ <u>ἱεροῦ</u>
<u>κατασκευὴν</u> ἐπιτραπῆναι . . .

Praem 56: τέτρατον δ' <u>ἀρχιερωσύνην</u>, δι' ἧς προφητεύων ἐπιστη-
μονικῶς <u>θεραπεύσει τὸ ὄν</u> καὶ τὰς ὑπὲρ τῶν ὑπηκόων
κατορθούντων μὲν εὐχαριστίας, εἰ δὲ διαμαρτάνοιεν,
εὐχὰς καὶ ἱκεσίας <u>ἱλασκόμενος</u> ποιήσεται.

The topic of the treatise is on privilege and <u>honour</u> (pronomia,
timē) versus punishment (kolasis) arranged under a series--indi-
viduals, houses, cities, etc. (7). The two triads of perfection
are introduced--Enos (hope); Enoch (repentance); Noah (justice);
Abraham (perfect through instruction/teaching-faith); Isaac
(self-learnt and self-taught--joy) and Jacob (perfect through
practice--vision of God). Abraham and his faith are described
in the following manner:

Praem 30: ὅτῳ δ' ἐξεγένετο πάντα μὲν <u>σώματα</u> πάντα δ' <u>ἀσώματα</u>
ὑπεριδεῖν καὶ ὑπερκῦψαι, μόνῳ δ' <u>ἐπερείσασθαι καὶ</u>
<u>στηρίσασθαι θεῷ μετ'</u> ἰσχυρογνώμονος λογισμοῦ καὶ
<u>ἀκλινοῦς καὶ βεβαιοτάτης πίστεως</u>, εὐδαίμων καὶ τρισ-
μακάριος οὗτος ὡς ἀληθῶς (cf. Hb 3,6.14; 6,19).

But above all stands Moses as the winner of the holy contests
with his fourfold prizes of kingship, legislation, prophecy and
<u>highpriesthood</u> (52-55). This last is described as <u>service</u>

(therapeuein) to the One Who Exists, thanksgiving for right
conduct and prayers and supplications for propitiation, in case
of sin (56).

Gig 52: ὁρᾷς ὅτι οὐδὲ ὁ ἀρχιερεὺς λόγος ἐνδιατρίβειν ἀεὶ καὶ
ἐνσχολάζειν τοῖς ἁγίοις δόγμασι δυνάμενος ἄδειαν ἔσχηκεν
ἀνὰ πάντα καιρὸν πρὸς αὐτὰ φοιτᾶν, ἀλλ' ἅπαξ δι'
ἐνιαυτοῦ μόλις; . . .

53: ὥστε οὖν ἐν μὲν τοῖς πολλοῖς, τουτέστι τοῖς πολλὰ τοῦ
βίου τέλη προτεθειμένοις, οὐ καταμένει τὸ θεῖον πνεῦμα
. . . μόνῳ δὲ ἀνθρώπων εἴδει ἑνὶ παραγίνεται, ὁ πάντα
ἀπαμφιασάμενον τὰ ἐν γενέσει καὶ τὸ ἐσωτάτω
καταπέτασμα καὶ προκάλυμμα τῆς δόξης καὶ γυμνῇ τῇ

54: διανοίᾳ πρὸς θεὸν ἀφίξεται. οὕτως καὶ Μωυσῆς ἔξω τῆς
παρεμβολῆς καὶ τοῦ σωματικοῦ παντὸς στρατοπέδου πήξας
τὴν ἑαυτοῦ σκηνήν, τουτέστι τὴν γνώμην ἱδρυσάμενος
ἀκλινῆ, προσκυνεῖν τὸν θεὸν ἄρχεται καὶ εἰς τὸν
γνόφον, τὸν ἀειδῆ χῶρον, εἰσελθὼν αὐτοῦ καταμένει
τελούμενος τὰς ἱερωτάτας τελετάς. γίνεται δὲ οὐ μόνον
μύστης, ἀλλὰ καὶ ἱεροφάντης ὀργίων καὶ διδάσκαλος
θείων, ἃ τοῖς ὦτα κεκαθαρμένοις ὑφηγήσεται.

The context of the passage is a discussion of Gn 6,3. Whereas
the divine spirit dwells only temporarily among the mass of men
(20) on account of its fleshly nature (28-29), it abides in Moses
on account of his stability (Nu 14,44; Dt 5,31--a classic text
for the perfection of Moses, see Sac 8 quoted on p. 63 above;
"stasis," "bebaiotēs," etc. 48-49). Not even the highpriest
Logos (Aaron), though able, is allowed to enter the Holy of
Holies (here interpreted as "holy doctrines") all the time but
barely once a year (52). Among the majority who set many ends
in life, the spirit does not abide (a characteristic of imperfection, see above pp. 131-32). But only one type of men, namely,
those who have disrobed themselves of all created things, the
innermost veil (katapetasma--that which separates the Holy of
Holies from the outside) and covering of opinion, will come to
God with naked mind (i.e., enter into the Holy of Holies). Such
a man is Moses who pitched his tent outside the camp (Ex 33,7),
i.e., the realm of the body, and enters into the darkness
(gnophos--see above Mos i,158, pp.135f.) to worship God and be
initiated into the mysteries of priesthood. In other words,
entry into the Holy of Holies, pitching the tent outside the
camp, entry into the darkness of Mt. Sinai are symbolically
equivalent descriptions of access and immediacy to God--perfec-
tion. What hinders is the realm of body and flesh symbolized by
the veil that separates the Holy of Holies from the realm of
creation.[5]

---

[5]On the psychic level, it is the soul unencumbered by the
senses--the realm of body and flesh--which then turns to God.

160

Post 173: . . . τρίτην δὲ καὶ τελεωτέραν δεκάδος ἑβδομάδα ἀπὸ
τούτου μέχρι Μωυσῆ τοῦ πάντα σοφοῦ παρήκουσαν.
ἕβδομος γὰρ ἀπὸ 'Αβρααμ οὗτός ἐστιν, οὐκέτι κατὰ τὸν
ἔξω τῶν ἁγίων κύκλον οἷα μύστης εἰλούμενος, ἀλλ' ὥσπερ
ἱεροφάντης ἐν τοῖς ἀδύτοις ποιούμενος τὰς διατριβάς.

The immediate context of the discussion is Gn 4,25--"another
seed"--how Seth is different from Abel. Abel having left mortality has transferred to a better nature, Seth being a seed of
human virtue will never leave the race of men, but will receive
enlargement--to the perfect ten (Noah)--second and better one to
another ten ("pistos" Abraham)--a third and more perfect than
ten, namely, seven from Abraham to Moses, wise in all things.
His perfection lies in that he does not like the others roam outside the Holies seeking initiation, but dwells as the Hierophant
in the inner shrine (= Holy of Holies, cf. Mos ii,176 and 178).
Cf. Sac 130.

   At this preliminary point, certain aspects become clear.
Priesthood or highpriesthood is a matter of privilege and honour
(timē) and a mark of perfection. The same point is at issue in
3,1.3--Jesus is the highpriest and has greater glory/honour than
Moses. It is the same tradition which underlies the formulation
of the argument in Hb 5:

   5:4: καὶ οὐχ ἑαυτῷ τις λαμβάνει τὴν τιμήν, ἀλλὰ καλούμενος
          ὑπὸ τοῦ θεοῦ, καθώσπερ καὶ 'Ααρών. οὕτως καὶ ὁ Χριστὸς
          οὐχ ἑαυτὸν ἐδόξασεν γενηθῆναι ἀρχιερέα . . .

   5:9-10: καὶ τελειωθεὶς . . . προσαγορευθεὶς ὑπὸ τοῦ
           θεοῦ ἀρχιερεὺς κατὰ τὴν τάξιν Μελχισέδεκ.

Another significant dimension of the priesthood and perfection of Moses is his complete purification from the realm of body
and flesh, everything mortal. Such is also the characteriztic of
the heavenly "anthrōpos" (see above pp.26f.; 29f.; 40; 76) as well
as Aaron, Levi and Moses in their perfection. This is symbolized
by entry and abiding in the Holy of Holies, when Moses pitches
his tent outside the camp or when he goes up on Sinai and enters
the darkness--i.e., immediacy and access to God. This is the
predominant theme in Hb 7-10 and apart from these chapters one
notes the polemic in 12,18 and the reinterpretation of the theme
in 13,13. It is against such a background, as we will show
below (c. 7), that 2,5-18 and esp. 14-18 can best be understood.
That the "katapetasma" which separates the Holy of Holies from
the outside represents the realm of body and flesh underlies and
explains the enigmatic statement in Hb 10,20 διὰ τοῦ καταπετάσ-

---

The "katapetasma"/"prokalumma" is the symbol of the soul in its
inward and outward dimensions--cf. Mut 43-44.

ματος, τοῦτ' ἔστιν τῆς σαρκὸς αὐτοῦ, which is followed by an il-
lusion to Nu 12,7: "great priest upon the house of God." In
other words, Jesus passed out of the realm of flesh when he entered the Holy of Holies at his death (cf. 9,11-12) and continues
to be the highpriest in the heavenly tabernacle.[6]

The tie between 3,1-6 and 2, esp. 17-18 can be seen in the
function of Moses as highpriest to effect propitiation through
prayers and supplication. This function is of course given to
Jesus alone in Hebrews. Moses has his abiding place in the Holy
of Holies, a teacher and hierophant of matters divine. Here he
performs his "therapeia" of God. Hebrews as we shall see reduces
the status of "therapōn" below that of Son and assigns to Moses a
lesser role as "witness" of the divine words rather than its preeminent teacher and master of the cult.

Anthropos-Moses and His Call Above

The opening description of Christians as "partakers of the
heavenly call" receives perfunctory attention from commentators
and the usual reference is to Phil 3,14. It amounts to explain-
ing one unknown by another. Michel vaguely refers to "the origin
and goal of Christianity" (p. 171). Spicq, so full of Philo,
makes the incredible remark: "Il se réfère à I,1; II,3,10 et
contient une légère opposition à Israël dont les destinées
étaient terrestres" (II, p. 64). This needs closer attention

---

[6]That this is so, that Jesus' participation in flesh and
blood (2,14.16.17) was only temporary and part of his work on
earth, seems to be verified by 5,7: "who in the days of his
flesh"--seems to imply that this is no longer so; 10,5ff.: that
God prepared a body for him for the final sacrifice. And once
that is done, that is the sacrifice of the body, Jesus enters into the Holy of Holies and his sacrifice opens the way for others
to follow (10:19ff.). This would also fit the fact that in Hebrews there is no resurrection of Jesus and in what sense the
author understood the only reference in 6,2 is unclear. This is
no more "gnostic" than Philo--where creation is good and the
source of the problem is the confusion of the Creator with creation; that the ultimate good and destiny of man is God alone,
to know Him and serve Him. There is no dualism between an evil
world and the divine, only a distinction between the imperfection
of the world in comparison with the perfection of the Creator.
There are no end of passages in Philo, where the positive educative role of the senses and world is stressed and whose task is
to educate men for the knowledge and vision of God. It is the
inversion of this hierarchy between God and creation which lies
at the root of the problem. In the same way, Jesus was trained
to perfection in his earthly life through suffering (5,7-10).
The theology of Hebrews is more complex since he is reinterpret-
ing these traditions in terms of the threat it posed to the
claims of primitive Christianity.

162

since the description is unparalleled elsewhere in the NT (except
probably Phil 3,14) and the term "partakers" appears in 3,14;
5,13; 6,4; 7,13; 12,8 and in the immediate context in 2,14.[7]
Furthermore, one has to ask what relevance such an appeal has in
this particular context, in view of its unique formulation. In
fact as we will show it belongs to the tradition regarding Moses
as the exemplary "anthrōpos" who has the privilege of being called to the presence of God--a mark of perfection. It illuminates
further the connection of this passage to chap. 2.

Mut 125: τὸν δὲ ἀρχιπροφήτην συμβέβηκεν εἶναι πολυώνυμον.
          ὁπότε μὲν γὰρ τοὺς χρησμῳδουμένους χρησμοὺς ἑρμηνεύων
          ὑφηγεῖται, προσαγορεύεται Μωυσῆς, ὁπότε δ᾽ εὐχόμενος
          εὐλογεῖ τὸν λεών, ἄνθρωπος θεοῦ, ἡνίκα δὲ Αἴγυπτος τὰς
          ὑπὲρ τῶν ἀσεβηθέντων δίκας ἐκτίνει, τοῦ βασιλεύοντος
          τῆς χώρας Φαραὼ θεός.

   126:   διὰ τί δέ; ὅτι τὸ μὲν νόμους μεταγράφειν ἐπ᾽ ὠφελείᾳ
          τῶν ἐντευξομένων ψηλαφῶντός ἐστι καὶ διὰ χειρὸς
          ἔχοντος ἀεὶ τὰ θεῖα καὶ ἀνακεκλημένου ὑπὸ τοῦ θεσπιῳδοῦ
          νομοθέτου καὶ εἰληφότος παρ᾽ αὐτοῦ μεγάλην δωρεάν,
          ἑρμηνείαν καὶ προφητείαν νόμων ἱερῶν. μεταληφθεὶς
          γὰρ Μωυσῆς καλεῖται λῆμμα, δύναται δὲ καὶ ψηλάφημα . . .

The context is a discussion of Gn 17,5 (60-129), the subject
being the meaning of the change of names of various OT personalities. Moses stands out preeminent since he has many names
(a tradition which we have argued is used by the author to prove
the superiority of Jesus over the angels in 1,4ff. and this is a
further instance which shows that the titles and prerogatives of
Moses have been transferred to Jesus in chap. 1--see above esp.
pp. 146-49). He is Moses, man of God and God of Pharoah. The

_____

[7]Cf. TDNT III, 487-93; it is clear that the usage, especially in Paul, is a technical term for God's call to salvation
(ibid., p. 489). If, however, one observes the data on "klesis"
(ibid., pp. 491-92), then clearly Hb 3,1 and Phil 3,14 are ex-
ceptional, in their terminology: "participants of the heavenly
call," "the prize of the call above." At this point we cannot
enter into the interpretation of Phil 3,14, but there seems
little doubt in my mind that we are dealing in this section with
a very similar tradition, namely, perfection. The unusual terminology itself points in this direction: "koinōnia," "symmorphi-
zein," "teleios," "symmimetai," "typos," "politeuma en ouranois,"
etc. The difficulty lies in the fact that Paul transforms and
restates the language of his opponents so drastically in terms of
his own religious conceptions, so as to render them virtually un-
recognizable. It comes to mind that a way to get at the theology
of Paul would be to establish these patterns of restatement and
transformations which would give us a clue to the major religious
themes in the structure of his thinking. And thereby would ena-
ble us to differentiate his thinking from that of his opponents.
It seems this is precisely what H. Koester has done in his review
of U. Wilckens, Weisheit und Torheit (Gnomon 33 (1961), 590-95).

reason for the first being that legislation is the work of one
who is ever handling things divine (pselaphon), called up (Ex
24,1) and receives from Him the great gift of interpretation and
prophecy of divine laws (used synonymously by Philo--cf. Praem
55). Translated Moses can mean both "receiving" and "handling"
(the etymological basis for this is unclear).[8]

Plant 26-27: (for text and analysis see above pp. 65f.).

QE II,46: (for text and analysis see above pp. 66-67).

These texts have as their basis either God's call to Moses
to come to the top of Sinai (Ex 24,1; 24,16b) or His communication with him in the tent of witness (Lv 1,1; Nu 12). They concern Moses' receiving of the laws and rules of cult. This call
above (anaklēsis) is described as second birth, divine birth,
without mother, having God alone for its father, in accordance
with the ever virginal nature of the seventh, differing from the
earth-born moulded-man in that it is without body (QE II,46 on
Ex 24,16b). In other words, it is another term for perfection.
Similarly, in Plant 23, the call above (anakeklēsthai, anō
kaleisthai) is the mark of the "anthrōpos" made after God's image, namely, the mind of man and of which Moses is the supreme
exemplar, superior to Bezalel who also shares in this call (Ex
31,2). In Mut 125-27 he is the "anthrōpos" of God--who has no
kinship with creation--an allusion to blessing of Levi in Dt 33,9
(127; cf. Fug 89). It now becomes clear how the discussion about
"anthrōpos" in chap. 2 is tied to the thematics of perfection and
exemplified here in the honour and glory of the priesthood of
Moses and his call above as the perfect "anthrōpos." Again we
note the character of the perfection of the "anthrōpos" as without body or kinship with creation (cf. Hb 2,14).

The author of Hebrews has made Jesus the highpriest and
perfect man, instead of Moses. Therefore, "adelphoi" and
"hagioi," although traditional terms for Christians, receive in
this context (cf. 2,11-14) along with "partakers of the call to
heaven" (cf. 11,16; 12,22) a different nuance, namely the call to
participate in perfection (cf. 2,10; 6,1). Cf. 2,14. And they
will do so not by looking to Moses or Aaron, but to Jesus as
their exemplar, their highpriest, who has entered into heaven

---

[8]This unusual term, not attested in the LXX, which describes
Moses' receiving of the law when he was called up to Sinai is
used in Hb 12,18 and points to the fact that it is such tradition
which is bearing the brunt of the author's polemic in 12,18ff.
(cf. Gig 54--p. 159 above; Mos i,158--p. 135 above).

itself (9,24). This becomes, of course, the burden of the
paranesis in 3,7ff.

Apart from such a tradition, the connection and coherence of
chaps. 1-3 as well as what follows would remain unclear and the
relevance of 3:1-6 enigmatic.

At this point we postpone the discussion of the tradition of
"participation" (metochos-metechein-koinōnia-koinōnein, etc.)
since it is crucial to the understanding of how one participates
in perfection and can be best elaborated in the context of the
discussion of the corelationship between the perfection of Jesus
and the perfection of the believer. The meaning of faith and
hope in Hebrews (3,6b) can also be best illuminated at that
point. Here we draw attention to the following: Moses enjoyed
greater partnership (meizōn koinōnia) with God in that he was
deemed worthy of the same title--God and King--he entered into
the "gnophos," etc. (Mos i,158; see above pp. 135f.). The "moulded
Man" does not participate in the simple/perfect nature (ametochos
haplēs physews--Plant 44; see above p. 131). Isaac the "first
born" is without share in a mother or female line (i.e., amētōr;
QG IV,153; see above p. 136).

Perfection of Moses as "Pistos"

Given the tradition with which we are dealing, it should not
surprise us that the call above of Moses and his faithfulness
belong together as marks of his perfection, and that Nu 12 would
serve as an important proof text in this tradition. It speaks of
God's direct communication with Moses and that Moses saw the
glory of God (LXX 12,8: kai tēn doxan kuriou eiden).

Leg All iii,100: ἔστι δέ τις τελεώτερος καὶ μᾶλλον κεκαθαρμένος
νοῦς τὰ μεγάλα μυστήρια μυηθείς, ὅστις οὐκ ἀπὸ τῶν
γεγονότων τὸ αἴτιον γνωρίζει, ὡς ἂν ἀπὸ σκιᾶς τὸ μένον,
ἀλλ᾽ ὑπερκύψας τὸ γενητὸν ἔμφασιν ἐναργῆ τοῦ ἀγενήτου
λαμβάνει, ὡς ἀπ᾽ αὐτοῦ αὐτὸν καταλαμβάνειν καὶ τὴν
σκιὰν αὐτοῦ, ὅπερ ἦν τόν τε λόγον καὶ τόνδε τὸν κόσμον.

101: οὗτός ἐστι Μωυσῆς ὁ λέγων "ἐμφάνισόν μοι σαυτόν, γνωστῶς
ἴδω σε" (Ex 33,13) . . . διὰ τοῦτο Μωυσῆν ἀνακέκληκε καὶ
ἐλάλησεν αὐτῷ ὁ θεός.

102: καὶ Βεσελεὴλ ἀνακέκληκεν, ἀλλ᾽ οὐχ ὁμοίως, ἀλλὰ τὸν μὲν
τὴν ἔμφασιν τοῦ θεοῦ λαμβάνοντα ἀπ᾽ αὐτοῦ τοῦ αἰτίου, τὸν
δὲ ὥσπερ ἀπὸ σκιᾶς τῶν γενομένων τὸν τεχνίτην ἐξ
ἐπιλογισμοῦ κατανοοῦντα. διὰ τοῦθ᾽ εὑρήσεις τὴν σκηνὴν
καὶ τὰ σκεύη πάντα αὐτῆς πρότερον μὲν ὑπὸ Μωυσέως, αὖθις
δ᾽ ὑπὸ Βεσελεὴλ κατασκευαζόμενα. Μωυσῆς μὲν γὰρ τὰ
ἀρχέτυπα τεχνιτεύει, Βεσελεὴλ δὲ τὰ τούτων μιμήματα,
χρῆται μὲν γὰρ Μωυσῆς ὑφηγητῇ τῷ θεῷ,

103: . . . (Ex 25,40), Βεσελεὴλ δὲ Μωυσεῖ, καὶ εἰκότως, καὶ
γὰρ ὅτε Ἀαρὼν ὁ λόγος καὶ Μιριὰμ ἡ αἴσθησις ἐπανίσταν-
ται, ῥητῶς ἀκούουσιν ὅτι, "ἐὰν γένηται προφήτης κυρίῳ, ἐν

ὁράματι αὐτῷ γνωσθήσεται" καὶ ἐν σκιᾷ ὁ θεός, οὐκ
ἐναργῶς, Μωυσεῖ δέ, ὅστις "πιστὸς ἐν ὅλῳ τῷ οἴκῳ στόμα
κατὰ στόμα λαλήσει, ἐν εἴδει καὶ οὐ δι᾽ αἰνιγμάτων"
(Nu 12,6-8).

The context of the passage is the discussion of Gn 3,14-15. The
cursing of the serpent without an opportunity for defence is explained by the fact that the serpent = pleasure is bad in itself.
This calls forth a series of counter examples of those deemed
good without any manifest reason (65ff.; 77ff.). Such is Bezalel,
who is called up by God (anakalein) and given wisdom and knowledge and made the artificer and architect of the tabernacle
(= soul) without previous mention of any praise or worthy deed
(95). The clue to his "charaktēr" lies in the interpretation of
his name = shadow (skia), and God's shadow is the Logos, the
archetypal pattern for creation, e.g., Gn 1,27 (95-96). It is
through the works of creation and reason (epilogizesthai) that he
comes to the knowledge of God (97-99). But there is a more perfect and more cleansed mind which knows God from Himself, that is
without the mediation of the Logos or creation and knows the
Logos and the world directly from God (100). This is Moses and
his request--Ex 33,13 (101). This is why God called up Moses and
spoke to him. This call is superior to Bezalel's since Moses'
knowledge of God is direct and Bezalel's indirect through reasoning. Moses makes the archetypes, Bezalel the copies/imitations
of the tabernacle (cf. Som i,206). Moses has God for his
teacher, Bezalel's teacher is Moses. Furthermore when Aaron =
Logos and Miriam = Sense Perception rose in rebellion, they were
expressly told by God that a prophet knows God "through the
shadow" (en skia, i.e., the Logos) but to Moses "faithful in the
whole house, he will speak mouth to mouth." (Nu 12,6-8) Therefore to be "called up," and "faithful" are marks of perfection,
and perfection means direct knowledge of God, immediacy to God
(cf. Plant 26-27; pp. 65f. above). Two other passages make the
same point:

Leg All iii,204: ἔφασαν δέ τινες, ὡς ἀνοίκειον ἦν ὀμνύσαι,
        ὁ ὅρκος γὰρ πίστεως ἕνεκα παραλαμβάνεται, πιστὸς δὲ
        μόνος ὁ θεὸς καὶ εἴ τις θεῷ φίλος, καθάπερ Μωυσῆς λέγεται
        "πιστὸς ἐν παντὶ τῷ οἴκῳ" γεγενῆσθαι . . .

Leg All iii,228: . . . "Ἀβραάμ γε τοι ἐπίστευσε τῷ θεῷ, καὶ
        δίκαιος ἐνομίσθη" (Gn 16,6), καὶ Μωυσῆς ἄρχει μαρτυρού-
        μενος ὅτι ἐστι "πιστὸς ἐν ὅλῳ τῷ οἴκῳ" . . .

Both these comments on Moses are incidental in their context and
are left unelaborated. But they make clear that to be "pistos"
is a mark of excellence--only God and his friend, such as Moses,
are "pistoi" and this is superior to the belief (pisteuein) of

Abraham.

Vis-a-vis this tradition, the christology of humiliation and exaltation which has its basis in the identification of Jesus with Sophia and Logos, itself constitutes the root of the problem in that to have the Logos or Sophia as one's Lord and Master means imperfection. To be perfect, one must reach or attain the same status as the Logos and thereby have direct/immediate access to God. In this tradition, Moses among others exemplifies the type of person who has attained this perfection as the highpriest, anthrōpos, faithful, and the one called up. The author therefore has to prove that Jesus as highpriest is superior to Moses and procures perfection for the Christian, namely the same status as himself (cf. 2,10-18).

Homologia and the Argument from Creation

Commentators have found it difficult to explain the logic of the author's proof of Jesus' superiority over Moses in vs. 3-6a. The difficulty lies in vs. 4 where one expects the maker of the house to be the Son. But that would not solve the difficulty either, since how can one be the maker/founder of the house and at the same time the son in it? Hence, it is popular to speak of two proofs, vs. 3 and 5-6 (Moffat followed by Montefiore). Vs. 4 is considered an edifying aside (Windisch, Moffat, Spicq). Michel is able to make three theses out of it (see p. 176). We do not see making theses out of apparent inconsistencies as a solution. There is nothing in the way the author states his argument to warrant the view that vs. 4 is an aside. It is clearly an explanation of vs. 3 and he expects us to follow the progression of this brief argument from 3-6.[9]

---

[9]It is Windisch's view that vs. 4 is a "Zwischengedanke" that is followed by most commentators and the expectation that following vs. 3 one would expect the Son to be the maker or founder of the house (p. 29). This has led commentators into considerable difficulties in attempting to explain how both Jesus and God could be the maker or founder of the house (understood by most as the church). One finds dogmatic explanations: "No distinction can be made between the Father and the Son in this regard. . . ." (Bruce, p. 57); forced explanations: "The author then adds an edifying aside, in v. 4, to explain how the 'oikos' was God's (v. 2 "autou"), though Jesus had specially founded it" (Moffat, p. 42; underlining my own); "Some scholars, however, understand this passage to mean that it was God who founded his household, not Jesus; but this is incorrect, since our author wished to contrast Moses not with God, but with Jesus. After all, Jesus did found the church" (Montefiore, p. 72; underlining my own). Spicq sees a "messianic nuance" inspired by Zech 6,12--the connection completely misses me--a "profound theological thought"

We find a solution to this difficulty in the tradition
regarding "homologia." We offer it as an alternative to that
proposed by Bornkamm and Kaesemann (see summary in Michel, pp.
172-75). The usage in Hebrews seems much less technical than
proposed: "confession of hope" (10,23); "they confessed that
they were strangers and sojourners on earth" (11,13) and 13,15 in
the sense of praise. The discussion shows that a great deal has
to be hypothesized in order to speak of a definite creed which is
being elaborated in Hebrews, be it baptismal or cultic. In any
case, there is little that we can contribute to the discussion
along these lines.

The first thing that helps towards clarification is an
understanding of the form of the comparative argument. It is not
a one-to-one comparison, but a comparison from analogy. It
establishes a relation of proportion by means of an analogous
comparison.

Spec Leg i,275: ὅσῳ γάρ, οἶμαι, λίθων μὲν εἰκαίων ἀμείνων
χρυσός, τὰ δ᾽ ἐν ἀδύτοις τῶν ἐκτὸς ἁγιώτερα, τοσούτῳ
κρείττων ἡ διὰ τῶν ἐπιθυμιωμένων εὐχαριστία τῆς διὰ
τῶν ἐναίμων.

The translation in Loeb is accurate in respect to form: "For as
gold is better than casual stones and all in the inner shrine
more sacred than what stands outside, so and in the same measure
is the thankoffering of incense superior to that of the blood of
beasts." Obviously, thankoffering of incense is not gold or
things in the inner shrine, nor is blood of beast stones and
things outside the inner shrine.

Sob 5: ὅσῳ τοίνυν ψυχὴ σώματος κρείττων, τοσούτῳ καὶ νοῦς
ὀφθαλμῶν ἀμείνων.

Following the pattern of the previous translation: "As the soul
is better than the body, so and in the same measure the mind is
better than the eyes." The relationship that the mind is a part
of the soul and eyes are part of the body is not intrinsic to the
form of the comparison.

So much for the obvious and the puzzlement why commentators
should expect in a similar formulation as in vs. 3 a one-to-one
relationship, that Jesus is the maker or Moses is the house!
Verse 4 is obviously an explication of the other side of the
analogy which is not intrinsic to the form but used when there is
a significant correlationship as in Sob 5 (above). Therefore
restated after this explication in vs. 4, the statement in vs. 3

whose aim is "to make acceptable to the readers the inferiority
of Moses and the Old Testament" (II, pp. 67-68).

would read: Jesus is worthy of more glory than Moses in the same
measure as God has more honour than the universe he created. It
does not mean that Jesus is God and Moses is a part of creation,
the correlation is a more complex one: that is, between God--
creation--Jesus--Moses. This type of comparison has its basis in
the use of the doctrine of creation as the formula for religious
comparison, i.e., comparison of topics of religious interest.
And in these instances the correlative analogies are not
perfunctory.

Op. 140: τοιοῦτος μὲν ὁ πρῶτος ἄνθρωπος κατά τε σῶμα καὶ ψυχὴν
γεγενῆσθαί μοι δοκεῖ, τούς τε νῦν ὄντας καὶ τοὺς πρὸ
ἡμῶν διενεγκὼν ἅπαντας. ἡ μὲν γὰρ ἡμετέρα γένεσις ἐξ
ἀνθρώπων, τὸν δὲ θεὸς ἐδημιούργησεν, ἐφ' ὅσον δὲ
κρείττων ὁ ποιῶν ἐπὶ τοσοῦτον καὶ τὸ γινόμενον ἄμεινον.

Mig 193: ὁ μὲν γὰρ ἡμέτερος νοῦς οὐ δεδημιούργηκε τὸ σῶμα, ἀλλ'
ἔστιν ἔργον ἑτέρου, διὸ καὶ περιέχεται ὡς ἐν ἀγγείῳ τῷ
σώματι. ὁ δὲ τῶν ὅλων νοῦς τὸ πᾶν γεγέννηκε, τὸ
πεποιηκὸς δὲ τοῦ γενομένου κρεῖττον . . .

In both these instances, the formula of the relationship between
creator and creation is invoked to prove in the first instance
the superiority of the "first man" who was created directly by
God in contrast to all others who have their genesis from other
men. In the second instance, the difference between the human
mind which is contained in a body, whereas God, the Mind of the
universe has made all things and cannot be contained by that
which he has made, since the creator is better than its creation.
In the same manner, the argument of Hebrews proceeds by postulat-
ing the superior honour of the creator over its creation and in-
voking the theological principle that God is the creator of all
things. We have yet to establish the significance of the invocation of this theological principle which will clarify the heart
of the argument. We turn therefore to the tradition of
"homologia."

Post 175: νήφοντος μὲν γὰρ ἔργον λογισμοῦ καὶ (σώφρονος) τὸν
θεὸν ὁμολογεῖν ποιητὴν καὶ πατέρα τοῦ παντός. . . .

The confession is set in contrast to the mad and drunken doctrine
(dogma) that man or his mind is the author of all things (e.g.,
Gn 19,32--the desire of Lot's daughters to have children by Mind,
their father). The confession is of God as the creator and
father of the All.

Cher 106: τοιούτου κατασκευασθέντος οἴκου παρὰ τῷ θνητῷ γένει,
χρηστῶν ἐλπίδων τἀπίγεια πάντα ἀναπλησθήσεται κάθοδον
δυνάμεων θεοῦ προσδοκήσαντα . . .

107: χαίρει δ' ἐπ' οὐδενὶ μᾶλλον ἢ κεκαθαρμένη διάνοια ἢ
τῷ δεσπότῃ ἔχειν τὸν ἡγεμόνα πάντων ὁμολογεῖν, τὸ γὰρ
δουλεύειν θεῷ μέγιστον αὔχημα . . .

108: . . . "καὶ ἡ γῆ οὐ πραθήσεται εἰς βεβαίωσιν, ἐμὴ γάρ
ἐστι πᾶσα ἡ γῆ, διότι προσήλυτοι καὶ πάροικοι ὑμεῖς ἐστε
ἐναντίον ἐμοῦ" (Lv 25,23). ἆρ᾽ οὐκ ἐναργέστατα

109: παρίστησιν, ὅτι κτήσει μὲν τὰ πάντα θεοῦ, χρήσει δὲ
μόνον γενέσεώς ἐστι; . . .

124: πάντων οὖν ἀνομολογημένων θεοῦ κτημάτων . . .

125: ὅτι ὁ θεὸς αἴτιον, οὐκ ὄργανον, τὸ δὲ γινόμενον δι᾽
ὀργάνου μὲν ὑπὸ δὲ αἰτίου πάντως γίνεται . . .

The second part of this treatise is an interpretation of Gn 4,1
(40ff.). Eve is sense perception and Cain represents the human
mind in its mistaken conception that all things are its possession rather than God's (64-65). After disproving such a viewpoint it turns to a discussion that "all things are His possessions" (83ff.) with an interpretation of Nu 28,2. From 98 the
discussion turns to the soul as the "house" of God on earth which
is made fit by preliminary encyclical education (101-105). When
such a house is prepared among mortals, the entire earth is
filled with good hopes in expectation of the descent of the
powers of God (i.e., laws). The cleansed mind rejoices in
nothing more than in confessing that it has as its master the
Ruler of All. For to be the servant of God (douleuein) is the
greatest boast, more precious than freedom, wealth or power. The
oracle in Lv 25,23 ("strangers," "sojourners," cf. Hb 11,13) is
the clearest proof that all things are God's possession. 109-23
is an elaboration of Lv 25,23 and 124 returns to the confession
that all things are God's possessions. Gn 4,1 is picked up again
with a discussion of the error of Eve's statement that she begat
"through God" (dia tou theou) whereas God is the cause (aition),
the one by whom (hypo hou).

The basic "homologia" therefore is of God as creator, father,
master, ruler of all things; all things are his possession. It
is the basis of hope and service to Him is the greatest boast.
On our part we prepare ourselves to be his house through
"paideia." The confession is the confession of such a prepared
house, a cleansed mind. We see the same constellation of themes
in our passage, the "homologia," the affirmation that "the one
who made all things is God," that we are "his house" if we hold
to the "boast of hope," and the linking of the affirmation of God
as creator with the formula of the "cause"--hypo tinos. This
isn't over by subtle as one will notice the role such formulas
play in 1,2 (see above pp. 138-42) and 2,10-11. That is, the
doctrine of creation, or more specifically the "aitia" play a
very important role in this tradition and its arguments. And
this is not peripheral since the themes of perfection, immediacy

or direct access to God, and status, are constructed in terms of
God as creator, his Logos/Sophia, types of souls, etc. That is
the link we have shown above between the intermediary world and
patterns of perfection. That this is so can be documented further. We will show below that the "house" is both cosmic and
psychic in this tradition (cf. Hb 3,4 and 3,6). That we prepare
to be God's house through "paideia," we will show as belonging
to the tradition of "participation" (metochos, etc.).

Ebr 106: δείκνυσι δ', ὡς γ' ἐμοὶ δοκεῖ, τὸ γεγονὸς πᾶν,
οὐρανόν, γῆν . . . , ἑκάστῳ γὰρ αὐτῶν ὁ τὰς τῆς ψυχῆς
ἐνεργείας πρὸς θεὸν τείνας καὶ παρ' αὐτοῦ μόνου τὰς
ὠφελείας ἐπελπίζων δεόντως ἂν εἴποι, (παρ') οὐδενὸς
λήψομαι τῶν σῶν . . . ἀλλὰ πάντα παρὰ τοῦ μόνου σοφοῦ
τὰς αὐτοῦ χαριστηρίους δυνάμεις πάντῃ τείναντας καὶ
διὰ τούτων ὠφελοῦντος.

107: ὁ μὲν οὖν τοῦ ὄντος ὁρατικὸς τὸν αἴτιον ἐπιστάμενος
τὰ ὢν ἐστιν αἴτιος δεύτερα μετ' ἐκεῖνον τετίμηκεν
ὁμολογῶν ἀκολακεύτως τὰ προσόντα αὐτοῖς. ἡ δὲ ὁμολογία
δικαιοτάτη, παρ' ὑμῶν μὲν οὐδέν, παρὰ δὲ τοῦ θεοῦ
λήψομαι, οὐ κτήματα τὰ πάντα, δι' ὑμῶν δὲ ἴσως,
ὄργανα . . .

The immediate context of the discussion is on Dt 21,20 (the dis-
obedient son) who is compared to the worshippers of the golden
calf (Ex 32,17-19; 93-99). There follow counter examples, a
uniquitous technique of Philo, Gn 14,22-23 being the one which
is commented on in this passage. It is seen as a reference to
the entire creation, and the one who hopes for aid from God alone
would rightly say that he receives nothing from creation (list
follows) but all from the Only Wise (God) who extends his bene-
ficent powers and provides aid through them (cf. Cher 106 above).
The one who has vision of the existent (i.e., perfection) and
knows the Cause gives secondary honours to things of which He is
the Cause confessing without flattery what is due to them. But
the most just confession is of God, the possessor of all (cf.
Cher 109 above). Creation can at most be considered "dia hymōn"
--"organa" (cf. Cher 125 above). Only the man who lacks compre-
hension thinks that things in the world are causes (108)--again
the typical counter theme.

It is possible that Hb 3,4 is introduced to guard against
this counter theme, in that it makes clear that Jesus is not the
creator/maker of the house, but as is clear in 1,2, the one
"through whom." He is the creature of God like the Logos,
Sophia, "first born," etc.--faithful to the one who made him
(3,2)--the importation of Nicene theology is misleading (cf.

Prov 8,22; Sir 24,8; Wis Sol 7,22, etc.).[10] We note here again
the themes of <u>hope</u>, the <u>confession of God</u> as creator and <u>cause</u>
and <u>possessor of all things</u>. This is repetitious, but it is
necessary to show that Cher 106-25 is not a freak instance. For
the same purpose we quote two further passages.

Leg All iii,28: . . . ὁ γὰρ ἀποδιδράσκων θεὸν καταφεύγει εἰς
ἑαυτόν.

29: δυοῖν γὰρ ὄντων τοῦ τε τῶν ὅλων νοῦ, ὅς ἐστι θεός, καὶ
τοῦ ἰδίου, ὁ μὲν φεύγων ἀπὸ τοῦ καθ' αὑτὸν καταφεύγει
ἐπὶ τὸν συμπάντων - ὁ γὰρ νοῦν τὸν ἴδιον ἀπολείπων
<u>ὁμολογεῖ</u> μηδὲν εἶναι τὰ κατὰ τὸν ἀνθρώπινον νοῦν, <u>ἅπαντα</u>
<u>δὲ προσάπτει</u> θεῷ . . . (interpretation of Gn 3,8 - "in
the midst of the wood of the garden" = midst of the
human mind).

Agr 128: . . . εἰσί τινες οἱ τὸ εὐσεβὲς ἐν τῷ <u>πάντα</u> φάσκειν
<u>ὑπὸ θεοῦ</u> γενέσθαι, τά τε καλὰ καὶ τὰ ἐναντία . . .

129: . . . ἔδει γὰρ μὴ φῦραι καὶ συγχέαι <u>πάντων</u> ἀθρόως
ἀποφήναντας <u>αἴτιον</u>, ἀλλὰ μετὰ διαστολῆς <u>μόνων ὁμολογῆσαι</u>
<u>τῶν ἀγαθῶν</u>. (Interpretation of Gn 4,7--to make the
right distinction and confess that God is the Cause of
only good things and not to make the mistake in thinking
that "all things" includes the bad.)

Sac 3: . . . ὁπότε δὲ <u>τὴν πρὸς τὸ αἴτιον ὁμολογίαν</u> ἐγγένησε,
τὴν πρὸς τὸν δοκησίσοφον νοῦν ἐξέλιπε. (Interpretation
of Gn 4,2: Cain is the opinion which attributes all
things to the human mind, Abel, the God-loving doctrine
(dogma)--that which <u>confesses</u> the Cause--cf. Cher 64-65).

We need to elaborate one further dimension of this tradition, namely, that such a "homologia" is a <u>mark of perfection</u> and
we would thereby have shown in this particular case as well that
it forms a coherent part of the tradition regarding intermediaries and exemplars of perfection.

Leg All i,82: . . . ὅτι ὁ μὲν 'Ιούδας ὁ <u>ἐξομολογητικὸς</u> τρόπος
<u>ἄυλός</u> ἐστι καὶ <u>ἀσώματος</u>, καὶ γὰρ αὐτὸ τοὔνομα τὸ τῆς
<u>ἐξομολογήσεως</u> ἐμφαίνει τὴν ἐκτὸς ἑαυτοῦ <u>ὁμολογίαν</u>, ὅταν
γὰρ ἐκβῇ ὁ νοῦς ἑαυτοῦ καὶ ἑαυτὸν ἀνενέγκῃ θεῷ, ὥσπερ
ὁ γέλως 'Ισαάκ, τηνικαῦτα <u>ὁμολογίαν τὴν πρὸς τὸν ὄντα</u>

---

[10]The phrase "the one who made him" can be understood either
in the sense "the one who appointed him" to the office of apostle
and highpriest (Mk 3,14; 1Sam 12,6) or in the sense of maker or
creator (Dt 32,15; Ps 95,6; Is 17,7). That the Logos is a part
of creation--see Philo, Leg All iii,175 and Wolfson, I, pp. 226-
40. Logos is "first born" (protogonos)--Agr 51, see above p. 10;
identification of the Logos with the intelligible world which was
the first act of God's creation--see Op 24; 36. It is difficult
to see how in the monotheism of Philo, Logos, Sophia or any of
the intermediaries can be anything else than creatures of God and
the closest relationship that one can have to the Creator is to
be preeminently his "son" (see below Congr 177, p. 172). The
meaning of the terms "first born," "only begotten", etc. is a
claim to such preeminence, since any of God's creatures can claim
to be his children (see f.n. 20, p. 149).

172

ποιεται, ἕως δὲ ἑαυτὸν ὑποτίθεται ὡς <u>αἴτιόν</u> τινος, μακρὰν
ἀφέστηκε τοῦ παραχωρεῖν θεῷ καὶ <u>ὁμολογεῖν</u> αὐτῷ, καὶ αὐτὸ
γὰρ τοῦτο <u>τὸ ἐξομολογεῖσθαι</u> νοητέον ὅτι <u>ἔργον</u> ἐστὶν <u>οὐχὶ</u>
<u>τῆς ψυχῆς</u>, <u>ἀλλὰ</u> τοῦ φαίνοντος αὐτῇ <u>θεοῦ</u> τὸ εὐχάριστον.
<u>ἄυλος</u> μὲν δὴ <u>ὁ ἐξομολογούμενος</u> ᾿Ιούδας.

83: τῷ δὲ ἐκ πόνου προεληλυθότι ᾿Ισσάχαρ δεῖ καὶ <u>ὕλης</u>
<u>σωματικῆς</u>, . . .

The passage (79-84) is an interpretation of Gn 2,12--ruby and
green stone--Judah is the symbol of the <u>confessing disposition</u>
(ruby) and Issachar (green stone) of the one working at good
deeds and making progress through labour (80; 82; 83). The characteristics of the confessing type are: <u>without matter</u> and <u>body</u>
(a mark of perfection--see above pp. 160-61); the confession
which takes him out of himself, the mind which goes out of itself
and offers itself to God, <u>just like Isaac</u> (exemplar of perfection
--see above pp. 53-58), then only is it <u>confessing the Existent</u>;
as long as one considers himself (mind, here soul) the <u>cause</u> of
anything, it is far from <u>confessing God</u>; <u>confession</u> is not the
<u>work</u> of the soul but <u>of God</u>. In contrast, Issachar the progres-
sing type needs a physical body. In other words, the one who is
able to make the true "homologia" of God as the Cause is perfect.

Congr 177: ἐνθένδε μοι δοκεῖ τις τῶν φοιτητῶν Μωυσέως . . .
Σαλομῶν . . . (Prov 3,11-12). οὕτως ἆρα ἡ ἐπίπληξις καὶ
νουθεσία καλὸν νενόμισται, ὥστε <u>δι᾿ αὐτῆς ἡ πρὸς θεὸν</u>
<u>ὁμολογία</u> συγγένεια γίνεται. <u>τί γὰρ οἰκειότερον υἱῷ</u>
<u>πατρὸς ἢ υἱοῦ πατρί</u>;

The immediate context is the interpretation of Gn 16,6 ("and she
afflicted her") as "admonition" (nouthesia) and various texts
with the term "affliction" (Ex 12,8; 25,23-25; Dt 8,2-3) are
discussed, the last being our passage which quotes <u>Prov 3.11-12</u>.
This shows that reproach and <u>admonition</u> are considered good. So
that through it (nouthesia), the <u>confession of God</u> becomes <u>kin-</u>
<u>ship</u>. <u>For what is more closely related than a father to a son</u>,
<u>or a son to a father</u>? In this tradition sonship to God is a mark
of perfection (see above pp. 40-42; 153). Confession of God
procures such a status of perfection. For this reason, the title
"son" is denied to Moses in Hb 3,5-6 or, in other words, the
superiority of Jesus is proven in terms of his exclusive sonship
to God, a title which was also denied the angels in 1,4ff. (See
above.) We shall show in the next chapter that this tradition
underlies Hb 12,1-11 and the concept of how one becomes a
"metochos Christou" (3,14; 3,1; 12,8-9, etc.).

Therefore, to prove the superiority of Jesus over Moses, the
author of Hebrews has drawn from both the form and content of
this tradition. It is a comparative argument from analogy, where

the significance of the analogy, if any, is not intrinsic to the
form. Its significance derives from the invocation of the theological principle that God as creator is superior to his creation
and the religious worth of anything depends on its position in
the hierarchy of creation--thus the first man created directly by
God is superior to all others who have their origin in other men,
the Mind (God) is superior to the human mind, and human mind is
superior to the body, etc. The intrinsic significance of this
theological principle for the author's argument lies in the tradition of "homologia."

Once the character of this tradition is grasped, it becomes
clear that 3,4 is not an aside but the centre of the argument.
What is at issue is the status of Jesus and Moses in the scheme
of creation, which is only a different modulation of the question
of perfection, namely who is or are the exemplars of perfection.
It is a question of the status of Jesus and Moses in relation to
the "one who made him"/them, the Creator. Both are "faithful"
(a mark of perfection) to the Creator in the realm of creation
("in his house," note the parallelism in vs. 4 "house"--"the All"
= universe). But, the author argues, Jesus is worthy of more
glory than Moses in the same measure as the Creator has more
honour than the house He made, i.e., creation, the universe.
This is made clear in vs. 4, where the author states that every
house is made by a "cause" (hypo tinos), and God is the creator
of All. And in relation to God, in the universe (= house), Moses
is only a "servant," but Jesus is "son," i.e., the status of
Jesus is higher than Moses. This latter attempt by the author to
contrast "son" with "servant" (therapōn) is his own proof on the
basis of Nu 12,7 and is a novel distinction.[11]

---

[11]We have already noted that the priesthood of Moses is described as service (therapeia, therapeuein) to God, a privilege
with which God has honoured him (Mos ii,67, see above p. 158;
Praem 56, see above p. 158).   It is a widely used term for
the worship and service of gods.   In Aristotle, the true purpose
of human life is "ton theon therapeuein kai theorein" (Eth Eud
VII,15. 1249b). Similarly, Philo in Som i,35 considers the service to God as man's special privilege beside all other creatures.
It is the prize of Isaac and Rebecca and which Jacob obtains only
at the end, i.e., it is a mark of perfection (Fug 47). Earlier
it is described as the best prize of men (40), this type of person (therapeutikon genos) is a sacred offering to God, conse-
crated for the great highpriesthood to God alone (42). Those who
are truly men are chosen for such a service (Spec Leg i,303). It
is lordlier than any lordship and more royal than any sovereignty
(Spec Leg iv,147). In the Wisdom of Solomon, wisdom delivered
from troubles those that served her (10,9); and she entered into
the soul of the one who served the Lord, i.e., Moses (10,16); the
priesthood of Aaron and his intercession (Nu 16,41ff.) shows that

174

In the author's reformulation of the "homologia," it is no longer Moses who is the supreme exemplar of perfection in his highpriesthood and "service" (therapeuein) of God, in his high call and faithfulness, marks of "honour" he has received from God, but Jesus the Son who has more glory-honour than him. The basic "homologia" of God as Creator of All remains, the conflict is one status among intermediaries and exemplars of perfection. And hence also for lives of those who pattern themselves according to one or the other. This forms the live context of the author's reinterpretation of the tradition which made primitive Christianity appear second best!

Cosmic--Psychic and Cultic House

We have assumed so far that the "house" refers to the universe, taking our clue from vs. 4, and that it fits the "homologia" of God as creator. On the other hand, Moffat, Spicq and Michel taking their clue from vs. 6 understand the "house" as a reference to the church. And they run into difficulties with vs. 4 as we have seen and the apparent inconsistency of how one can be both founder and "son" in the house he has founded seems to have escaped them. The difficulty of such an interpretation becomes even more visible when one notices that in 10,21 where Nu 12,7 is again alluded to, the house of God is clearly the heavenly tabernacle and not the Christian church. It is the same as saying that Jesus has gone to the upper extremity of heaven, i.e., the very presence of God (7,26; 8,1-2). When Michel tries to reconcile these by pointing that like Qumran the church is conceived here as the temple or house of God (1QS 8,5ff.; 9,6; Mk 14,58; 1Cor 3,16; 6,19; 2Cor 6,16), apart from the difficulty of interpreting these NT passages, he makes it difficult to understand how in the rest of Hebrews, Jesus who has his dwelling as Son and Highpriest in heavenly tabernacle (4,14; 9,11; 9,24; 10,19-21, etc.), can be the Son and Highpriest in the temple-church! The other possibility of considering "house" as the people of God, Israel (Spicq) does not fit 3,4 or 10,21 or 3,5

---

he is "therapōn" of God (18,21). 4Macc the youngest describes his martyred brothers as "servants" (therapontai) of God and as "practicers of piety" (asketai eusebeias)--12,11. These examples will suffice to show the consistency with which this term was used in hellenistic Judaism to describe the honour and excellence of serving God. There was no distinction drawn between this term and "son" (cf. Wis Sol 2,18). According to Spicq: "En conservant ce terme, Hébr réagit sans doute contre l'exaggération du midrasch (Tehill. sur Ps II,12) appelant Moïse" son of the house (II, p. 68; underlining my own).

(Moses then would be a witness of what will be spoken among the people of Israel!).[12] The plain fact is that in Hebrews Jesus has entered into the heavenly tabernacle, the house of God, the heavens, the true Holy of Holies, etc., having effected perfection, being himself perfected and opening a way for Christians here on earth to follow having him as their pioneer, forerunner and exemplar. The Christians are here on earth and Jesus is in heaven and occasionally the author, following traditional eschatological rubrics of primitive Christianity, speaks of his return in judgement (9,28; 10,25--mainly as warnings). There is no way that I can see by which Hebrews could have spoken of Jesus as Son "upon" the people of God, the church on earth.

We, therefore, have in 3,4 the "house" as the universe (ta panta), in 10,21 as the heavenly tabernacle--the highest reaches of the heavens (7,26), the right hand of the throne of God in the heavens (8,1; 1,3); the heaven itself (10,24). How then do we become the "house of God"? The author himself answers this question in the "if" clause which follows. We will discuss the meaning of faith and hope in the next chapter, what we want to explain here is the meaning of "house" in vs. 6. In the tradition with which we are dealing, "house" is understood as both cosmic and psychic, just as the tabernacle and temple are symbols of both. The following passages will illustrate and show how this belongs to the same tradition.

Cher 127:   μετελθὼν οὖν ἀπὸ τῶν ἐν μέρει κατασκευῶν ἴδε τὴν
μεγίστην οἰκίαν ἢ πόλιν, τόνδε τὸν κόσμον, εὑρήσεις γὰρ
αἴτιον μὲν αὐτοῦ τὸν θεὸν ὑφ' οὖ γέγονεν, ὕλην δὲ τὰ
τέσσαρα στοιχεῖα ἐξ ὧν συνεκράθη, ὄργανον δὲ λόγον θεοῦ
δι' οὖ κατεσκευάσθη . . .

For discussion of the context, see above pp. 168-69. In 106 the "house" is the soul of man, here it is the "cosmos," whose "cause" is God "by whom" it has been made. It is the same kind of argument as in Hebrews (as we have shown above) and same kind of parallelism as between 3,4 and 3,6. According to Hebrews, we

---

[12]Michel, pp. 177-79: It is supposedly an apocalyptic mystery that the community of the new covenant has the promise to be the house of God and this is supported by the passage cited. This is very confusing since earlier in the context of vs. 2, Michel cites the Targums to interpret "house" as possibly the tabernacle, the community of Israel or the palace of God (p. 175). It is not clear how one has moved from Targummic traditions in vs. 2 to apocalyptic mystery in vs. 6! Cf. Spicq II, pp. 66-67: not content with Hebrews, Spicq adds his own comparison--"L'Église étant supérieure à Israël, son fondateur a plus de gloire que le chef du peuple hébreux" (67). There is no basis in the text for this, since both Moses and Jesus are in the same "house of God" in vs. 5-6.

become God's house by preparing our souls with faith and hope.
And it is this faith and hope that links our souls with heaven,
the heavenly tabernacle: κρατῆσαι τῆς προκειμένης ἐλπίδος, ἣν
ὡς ἄγκυραν ἔχομεν τῆς ψυχῆς ἀσφαλῆ τε καὶ βεβαίαν καὶ εἰσερχομέ-
νην εἰς τὸ ἐσώτερον τοῦ καταπετάσματος, ὅπου πρόδρομος ὑπὲρ ἡμῶν
εἰσῆλθεν ᾿Ιησοῦς . . . (Hb 6,18-20). That is how we become God's
house. As we shall show below and can point to now, the language
associated with faith and hope (e.g., bebaia) clearly comes from
this tradition (see above Praem 30--p. 158).

Som i,149: . . . σπούδαζε οὖν, ὦ ψυχή, θεοῦ οἶκος γενέσθαι,
    ἱερὸν ἄγιον, (ἐν)διαίτημα κάλλιστον, ἴσως γάρ, ἴσως ὂν
    ὁ κόσμος ἄπας, καὶ σὺ οἰκοδεσπότην σχήσεις ἐπιμελούμενον
    τῆς ἰδίας οἰκίας, ὡς εὐερκεστάτη καὶ ἀπήμων εἰσαεί
    διαφυλάττοιτο.

For the context of this passage and its place in the tradition of
perfection, see above p. 35 and p. 43. Such a soul which
becomes God's house and holy temple is perfect. And this is seen
in consonance with the fact that God is the master of the household of the entire world. In other words, the bid to become the
house of God (Hb 3,6) is a bid to perfection.

Plant 48: . . . ὅτι τὰ σπέρματα καὶ τὰς ῥίζας ἁπάντων καθεὶς
    ὁ θεὸς αἴτιός ἐστι τοῦ τὸ μέγιστον ἀναβλαστῆσαι φυτόν,
    τόνδε τὸν κόσμον . . .

    50: . . . τὸ τὸν κόσμον εὐτρεπῆ καὶ ἕτοιμον αἰσθητὸν
    οἶκον εἶναι θεοῦ, τὸ κατειργάσθαι καὶ μὴ ἀγένητον εἶναι,
    ὡς ᾠήθησαν τινες, τὸ "ἀγίασμα" οἶον ἀγίων ἀπαύγασμα,
    μίμημα ἀρχετύπου . . .

The immediate context of the passage is the interpretation of Ex
15,17-18. God who sets the seeds and roots of all things is the
cause of the greatest growing plant, this cosmos. Moses prays
that we may be planted in this world and live a life in consonance with nature. This sense perceptible world is the house of
God, a "sanctuary" (Ex 15,18), an effulgence (apaugasma) of the
Holies (i.e., noetic tabernacle--as we have noted Moses is its
maker, see above pp. 164f.), an imitation of the archetype.

These passages will suffice[13] to show that in this tradition,
the "house" is both cosmic and psychic, the argument is set forth
in terms of "causes," as in Hb 3,4 and that to be God's house is
perfection--a totally cleansed mind or soul--and Hebrews has
reinterpreted this tradition to argue that we become God's house
through Christian faith and hope, and it is a soul conditioned by
faith and hope which links us to God, or in the words of Hebrews,
hope enters into the Holy of Holies (inside the veil where Jesus

---

[13]See further: Sob 62-66; Leg All iii,99; Congr 116; Post 5;
Som i,185ff.; Praem 123.

has entered as our forerunner--3,6; 6,18-20). The house of God
is the heavenly tabernacle (the noetic house, world, heaven, etc.
--cf. Hb 10,21; 8,2; 9,1ff.; 9,11, etc.). The distinction between noetic and aisthetic is a further differentiation along
Platonic lines of the cosmos.[14] This diagram amy help clarify:

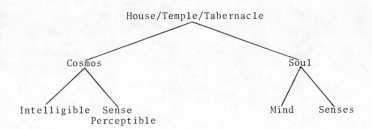

A Note on "Apostle"

The various explanations are summarized in Michel (pp. 171-
72). At best we have the Rabbinic tradition in which priests are
"s^{e}lûḥîm" of God (StrB, ad. loc.). The terminology is rare in
literature of hellenistic Judaism (TDNT I, pp. 413-14). The purpose of this note is to draw attention to another tradition,
which to my knowledge has not received the attention of scholars,
in this respect, and which could provide a clue to this enigmatic
title. It is the tradition regarding "metator-metatron." The
evidence in the Rabbinic tradition is discussed and analysed by
G. F. Moore, "Intermediaries in Jewish Theology," HTR 15 (1922),
pp. 62-85. In the Palestinian midrash, it speaks of God as one
who goes before hand: "With his finger he (God) was a metatron
to Moses and showed him the whole land of Israel. . . ." (Sifre
on Dt 32,49, sec. 338); ". . . that the voice of God was made a
metatron over the waters" (Bereshith Rabbah 5,4--on Gn 1,9, it is
an answer to the question how the waters found their way into the
ocean); "And not only that, but in the desert I go before them as
metator--'The Lord goeth before them by day' (Ex 13,21) . . . "
(Midrash Tanhuma, Parashah Ki Tissa (Ex 34,27)--quoted from Aruk);
to these is to be compared a later midrash--". . . God said to
Israel, when you were worthy of it, I myself was made a messenger
(shaliḥ) for you. . . . (Ex 13,21); but now that you are not
worthy, I turn you over to a messenger (shaliḥ) . . . (Ex 23,20).
. . ." (Shemoth Rabbah on Ex 23,20). From such examples, Moore
concludes: "In all the context requires some such general sense
as 'one who leads or shows the way, one who goes in advance'"
(p. 64). Translated into Greek, the appropriate terms would certainly be "apostolos" and "prodromos" and probably also
"archēgos"/"archēgetēs." In the Babylonia Talmud, metatron is an
angel, e.g.: A heretic quotes Ex 24,1 and asks the question--
"Why not unto me? The Rabbi replied: It means metatron . . .
(Ex 23,21) . . . we do not accept him even as a precursor . . . .
(Ex 33,15)" (Sanhedrin 386; the term "precursor" is a Persian
loan word). After a review of such examples, Moore concludes:

---

[14] In the traditions of wisdom, for her dwelling in man's
soul--see Wis Sol 7,27; 10,15 and 1,4. For the cosmic meaning of
the "house of God"--see 1Baruch 3,24-29.

"Metator thus had an evolution closely parallel to the English 'harbinger'; 'One sent on before to purvey lodgings for an army, a royal train, etc.; . . . a pioneer who prepares the way. One that goes before and announces the approach of some one; a fore-runner.'" (p. 66, underlining my own). Moore goes on to show that the angel is Michael.

This fits so well with the usage of the terms in Hebrews, that one can hypothesize that "apostolos," "prodromos" and "archēgos" mean one and the same thing (Hb 2,10; 3,1; 6,20; 12,2). But what relation does this have to the tradition with which we are dealing? My own work here is not complete, but some hypotheses are in order. That it is the title of an angel or of God, depending on who is performing the function of "pioneer"--"fore-runner." In Justin, the title "apostolos" appears in conjunction with "angel" for Christ (Apol I,63.5.10.14; cf. 12.9) and we have already noted that behind the practice of listing many titles lies the tradition of the "many named" deity, the titles being honourific (see above pp. 148-49 and 162). We have observed the similarity between Philo and Justin in these lists of titles. But Philo never uses the titles "apostolos" or "prodromos" anywhere that we know of. It is possible, however, that in Mos i, 166 we have a hint of such a tradition:

> νεφέλη γὰρ εἰς εὐμεγέθη κίονα σχηματισθεῖσα προήει
> τῆς πληθύος . . . ἀλλ᾽ ἀπλανεστάτῳ ἕπεσθαι ἡγεμόνι
> ὁδοῦ. τάχα μέντοι καὶ τῶν ὑπάρχων τις ἦν τοῦ μεγάλου
> βασιλέως, ἀφανὴς ἄγγελος, ἐγκατειλημμένος τῇ νεφέλῃ
> προηγητήρ, ὃν οὐ θέμις σώματος ὀφθαλμοῖς ὁρᾶσθαι.

This is an interpretation of Ex 13,1. In Mig 171, which is an interpretation of Ex 24,1 and 33,15, Moses prays that God may be his guide (hēgemōn) on the way which leads to Himself. This is of course a mark of perfection. Abraham as long as he is short of perfection has the Logos as his guide (Ex 23,20f.; Mig 174) but when he reaches full knowledge, they are coequal in their pace and become attendants of God who leads (Mig 175--see above pp. 37ff.). In Agr 51, the Logos-Firstborn Son is the viceroy of the Great King (God)--cf. Mos i,166. The basic idea is of course the "leadership" (hegemōn) of either the Logos or God. Only in Mos i,166 is there the idea of "going before hand" (prohegetēr), but it is associated with "angel" and "leader." While this isn't adequate proof for the existence of the "metator" tradition in Philo, at least the hints are there, and the hypothesis that it exist in the traditions of hellenistic Judaism can be made.

The traditions in Jewish mysticism are intriguingly similar: R. Bahya ben Asher in his commentary on Ex 23,21 through etymo-logical interpretation of meṭaṭron deduces that "Metatron is the lord of all beings of lower rank, for all the host above and below are in his authority and under his power; and he is an envoy (messenger) of Him who is over him, and higher than he is He who gave him dominion over the universe and appointed him lord of His house and manager of all His possessions" (Moore's para-phrase, ibid., p. 68; underlining my own). This is the same as the picture of Moses in Philo, as we have seen above. Doctrine of Meṭaṭron in Zohar: "He is first of the creations of God; to him God gave dominion over all the hosts; servant of God, the senior of his house, ruling over all; his name is like his master's; he is created in his image and likeness. He is a priest of the Most High, etc." (Moore, ibid., footnote 84). What could be closer than the traditions regarding the Logos and Moses, etc. in Philo! The relations between Jewish mysticism and tradi-tions of hellenistic Judaism certainly merit much closer attention.

Summary and Conclusions

The view that no polemical situation is involved (Windisch, Spicq, Michel and others) has led the commentators to deal with this passage in isolation. No satisfactory rationale has been advanced as to the appropriateness of this comparison with Moses or how it fits in the progression of themes. At most a literary explanation is forthcoming in terms of anticipatory hints in 2,17-18 and 3,1, the actual subject matter of the priesthood of Jesus only beginning in 4,14ff. (Michel, Spicq following Vaganay.) As to whether any particular traditions are involved in the content of the comparison, most refer to the midrash on Nu 12,7 (Sifre 103--that Moses ranked higher than the ministering angels). Michel who proposes that this passage is an actual "midrash" never carries it forth in his actual exegesis in terms of either the form or content of the passage.

It is our argument that this comparison both in form and content belongs in the tradition regarding intermediaries and exemplars of perfection. Moses is the supreme exemplar and it was necessary for the author to prove Jesus' superiority over Moses. We have shown in 1,1-2,4 that the author had already prepared for this explicit comparison with Moses by attributing to Jesus the titles and prerogatives of Moses (see above pp. 134-38). For this particular passage it is the tradition of the high-priesthood and perfection of Moses which enables us to understand the content of this comparison as well as its contextual coherence.

The priesthood of Moses (Mos ii,67-68; Praem 65; Gig 52-54; Post 173) was an honour (timē) which he received from God (the same concept in Hb 5,4. 9-10; cf. 3,1.) and a mark of perfection. The business of this priesthood was the service (therapeia) of God, thanksgiving for the right conduct of his subjects and prayers and supplications for propitiation in the case of sin (cf. Hb 2,18). His abiding place is inside the Holy of Holies in contrast to Logos-Aaron who was permitted entry only once a year and this was the mark of his perfection--i.e., his continual access and immediacy to God (a principal theme in Hb 7-10). This is also symbolized by his pitching the tent outside the camp (i.e., realm of the body)--a theme applied to Jesus and the Christians in Hb 13,;3--and his entry into the darkness (gnophos) on Sinai (cf. the author's polemic in 12,18ff.). Another characteristic of his priesthood was his complete purification from the realm of creation, flesh and body. Such was also the mark of perfection of the heavenly "anthropos," Levi and Aaron (see above

pp. 26f.; 29-30; 40; 76). This partly explains the tie of the
theme of priesthood with chap. 2 of Hebrews, esp. vs. 14 and 16-
18. The inner veil of the temple (katapetasma) which is a symbol
of the separation of the Holy of Holies (God) from the outside
world of body and flesh explains the enigmatic statement in Hb
10,20, namely, that Jesus has passed out (or through, in terms of
the spatial metaphor) of the realm of flesh when he entered into
the Holy of Holies at his death (cf. 9,11-12). Furthermore,
Moses is a teacher and hierophant of divine things. Hebrews
reduces his status as "therapōn" and assigns him a lesser role as
"witness" of the divine words (see above f.n. 11, p. 173).

The perfection of Moses was exemplified by his many titles--
Moses, God, anthrōpos of God--and his call above (Mut 125-26;
Plant 26-27; QE II,46). This "call above" was a second/divine
birth, without mother (cf. Hb 7,3), virginal seventh and, in contrast to the earth-born moulded-man, without body. The "call
above" is the mark of the perfect "anthropos" made after God's
image. It thereby becomes quite clear how this comparison with
Moses is a modulation of the thematic of perfection and why it
appropriately follows the discussion concerning the heavenly
"anthropos" in chap. 2. The author of Hebrews has assigned the
honour of such a priesthood and perfect manhood to Jesus and made
the "call above" (call to heaven) applicable to all Christians.
For them it is not Moses but Jesus who is the exemplary highpriest who has entered into heaven itself (symbolized by the Holy
of Holies)--cf. Hb 9,24. What follows in the paranesis (3,7ff.)
is another theme of perfection as the seventh day rest of God and
entry into the promised land (see above pp. 132-34 and p. 77).
Apart from this tradition, the coherence of themes both in general
and in details in these chapters would remain unexplained and the
relevance of 3,1-6 in this context enigmatic.

It is not surprising that the call above and the faithfulness (pistos) of Moses belong together as marks of his perfection
(Leg All iii,1000. 204. 228). As the more perfect and cleansed
mind than Bezalel's, his call above is superior in that he knows
God directly without the mediation of the Logos or creation; he
is the maker of the archetypes (Bezalel makes the copies). The
further proof of this perfection being that while God speaks to
prophets through the Logos, he speaks to Moses, "faithful in all
his house," mouth to mouth. God and Moses alone are faithful and
Moses' faithfulness is superior to Abraham's believing.

It is evident that the primitive Christology of humiliation

and exaltation which has its basis in the identification of Jesus with the Logos/Sophia would be a problem in this tradition. To be a follower of Jesus or to acknowledge him as lord would mean that the Christian isn't perfect. It is Moses, Aaron, Levi, Melchizedek, the heavenly "anthrōpos" and similar paradigms who are the exemplars of perfection. It was therefore imperative for the author of Hebrews to show that Jesus did attain perfection in terms of this tradition and did procure for Christians the same status as himself (cf. 2,10-18). It is within this larger thematic context that the author's proof of Jesus' superiority over Moses must be placed. It is a particular modulation of the larger thematic of intermediaries and perfection.

The actual argument in the comparison (3,3-6) and its logic become clear, we have seen, once we understand the character of such comparisons within this tradition. It is a comparison from analogy in which the analogy does not bear a one-to-one relationship with the comparison itself. The analogy becomes significant in one particular instance where the comparison of God with his creation is invoked in the analogy (e.g., Op 140; Mig 193). The significance of the comparison in this passage (Hb 3,3-6) is further heightened by the entry of the tradition of homologia in this context. The basic "homologia" is of God as Creator (Father, Master, Ruler) of All and that all things are His possessions. It is the basis of hope and service to Him is the greatest boast of man. A significant feature of this "homologia" of God as Creator is the explication of it in terms of the theory of causes, namely, that God is the Cause, the "hyph' hou" of creation (Cher 106-27; Ebr 106-07; Leg All iii,28; Agr 128-29; Sac 3). The same combination of features appear in this passage in Hebrews: "homologia," "God is the one who made all things," He is the cause (hypo tinos), boast of hope. The explication of "causes" plays an important role in this tradition as well as Hebrews (cf. 1,2--see above pp. 138-42; 2,10-11). In fact, as it has now become clear to me, the thematics of the intermediary world and perfection are constructed in terms of the schema of creation. One's status and degree of perfection depend on how high one stands or is able to rise in the hierarchy between God and creation (simply another formulation of perfection as access and immediacy to God).

Therefore, it is fitting, that the one who can truly make this homologia of God as Cause is perfect (Leg All i,82-83). The characteristic of this type of person (here the exemplar is Judah)

is that he is <u>without matter</u> and <u>body</u>, and just like <u>Isaac</u> (i.e.,
perfection). Such a confession brings one in closest kinship
(suggeneia) with God, namely that of being a "son" (Congr 177).
Accordingly, sonship to God in this tradition is a mark of perfection.

What is, therefore, at issue in this comparison in Hebrews
is the status of Jesus and Moses in the schema of creation. Once
this is grasped, the logic of this comparison becomes clear and
vs. 4 understandable. Instead of being an after-thought, it is
the heart of the argument. Jesus and Moses are both faithful to
their Maker ("to the one who made him") in the realm of the universe ("house" = "panta"--vs. 4). But, the author argues, Jesus
is worthy of more glory than Moses in the same measure as the
Creator has more honour than his house = universe/creation.
Every house has a "cause" (hypo tinos) and God is the Maker of
All. And in His creation = house, Moses has the status of a
<u>servant</u> (as scripture says--Nu 12,7) but Jesus has the status of
<u>Son</u> (as scripture says--1,4ff.). The title "son" would therefore
obviously be denied to both the angels and Moses. The basic
homologia of God as Creator remains, but within it, it is no
longer Moses who is the supreme exemplar of perfection in his
honour as highpriest, in his service (therapeia) to God, in his
call above, perfect manhood and faithfulness, but Jesus who as
Son and highpriest has more glory than Moses.

The difficulty of considering the <u>house</u> as the church is
evident from the fact that in Hebrews Jesus is Son and highpriest
in the "house of God," namely the heavenly tabernacle (Nu 12,7
quoted again in 10,21; cf. 4,14; 9,11.24; 10; 10-21). It does
not fit 3,4 and makes nonsense out of 3,5, since it would imply
that Moses is witness of things which will be spoken in the
church. For clearly the house in which Jesus is Son is the same
house in which Moses is servant. In our interpretation, there is
no difficulty in understanding 3,4 and 10,21, since the "house"
is the universe and heavenly tabernacle is heaven itself/the
highest reaches of the heavens (7,26; 9,24). What needs explain-
ing therefore is vs. 6: "we are God's house if. . . ." In the
tradition of intermediaries and perfection the "house" is both
<u>cosmic</u> and <u>psychic</u> and <u>to be God's house means to be perfect</u>.
(Cher 106; 127; Som i,149; Plant 48-50). In Hebrews we become
God's house through <u>hope</u> (3,6) and this hope enters inside the
Holy of Holies where Jesus has entered as our forerunner (6,18-
20). That is <u>why</u> the author can say that faith is the

reality (hypostasis) of things hoped for, because conditioned by
Christian faith and hope the soul is in contact with God, i.e.,
it has access to the heavenly Holy of Holies (Hb 11,1; 10,20-23).
Contact with God is the ultimate goal of faith and hope (Hb 11),
and it is Christian faith and hope which is perfect in this
sense or is in the process of being perfected through paranesis
(12,1ff.). This latter interpretation of faith and hope is preliminary at this point and will be elaborated further when we
deal with the perfection of the believer.

CHAPTER SIX

JESUS, MELCHIZEDEK, LEVI AND AARON (HEBREWS 7,1-28)

Introduction: From the perspective of the tradition with
which we are dealing, one can see that in this series of comparisons what is being disputed is the exemplary character of the
perfection of Levi and Aaron, and hence the need to establish the
inferiority of this order of priesthood and that this priesthood
cannot procure perfection for its followers (vs. 11, 19, 26, 28).
The arguments in vs. 20-28 are elaborated further in chapters 8-
10 and can be best dealt with in that connection, namely, the
interpretation of the cult in terms of perfection. In other
words, what we expect to find here are thematics from the tradition of intermediaries and perfection. We note, accordingly, the
following aspects in the author's argument:

(1) The fact that the author has to argue that the Levitic-
Aaronide priesthood is inferior to the priesthood of Melchizedek,
and that it is Jesus who belongs to the order of Melchizedek,
leads us to suspect--from our previous knowledge of the way the
author deals with this tradition--that such a claim was originally made for the Levitic priesthood, i.e., Levi-Aaron are priests
according to the order of Melchizedek.

(2) The argument of such superiority on the basis of who
gives and receives tithes (note the numerous repetitions of this
point in vs. 4-9), and which has seemed curious to commentators,
needs an explanation as to how it fits in the argument concerning
perfection, i.e., how it leads up to and makes comprehensible the
argument in vs. 11ff.

(3) We have the curious phenomenon that Melchizedek is a
priest who remains forever (vs. 3) and so also Jesus who belongs
to the same order (vs. 16-17). On a literal level, it would seem
we have two eternal priests in heaven! The argument here from
"taxis," as we shall see provides a clue, as does the related
understanding of "exemplars" in this tradition.

(4) Closely related to the above, is the author's argument
that Levitic-Aaronide priests are mortal men, sinful, or stated
differently, they are beset with "weakness" (astheneia). Whereas, Melchizedek like the son of God is eternal, and Jesus like
Melchizedek is without sin and eternal, in comparison with "men
who die," "men who have weakness" (vs. 3, 8, 16-18, 23-28; cf.

5,2-3; 4,15). Obviously, this must relate to the understanding of perfection.

(5) Finally, how do the themes of "covenant," "legislation" and "oath" relate to the argument concerning Levitic-Aaronide perfection (vs. 11, 20-22, 28)?

We intend to show that the tradition of intermediaries and perfection can explain how these various and even curious aspects of the author's argument are coherent and that it illuminates the purpose and thrust of the argument.

The attempt to understand this chapter in terms of apocalyptic messianic expectations (Michel), which seems to be supported by Qumran and especially 11Q Melchizedek, is an alternative. However, it has serious deficiencies, since in Hebrews we do not have the concept of a battle in the end times in which God intervenes through "annointed" figures, priest, or prince or Melchizedek, or the dualism of angelic hosts against the hosts of Belial.[1] We have already shown above the difference in the conception about intermediaries and perfection between apocalyptic traditions and that which we find in Philo, and in a preliminary way, in Hebrews (Chapter 3 above). It is difficult to conceive of an "annointed" figure or Melchizedek coming from Qumran with a list of titles of Greek gods (Hb 7,3). In his TDNT article, in the space of a couple of lines Michel states: "In spite of these lofty statements Melchizedek is only a shadow and reflection of the Son of God (aphōmoiōmenos, 7:3)." (The underlining is my own.) I fail to see how "aphōmoiōmenos" could possibly mean shadow or reflection. Michel then proceeds to say: "Melchizedek implies the dissolving of the Jewish Law and cultus. He is one and at the same time person, intimation and order, primal history and eschatological history, the divine plan of salvation and human fulfilment (teleiosis)" (TDNT IV, p. 570). Apart from the contradiction between these two statements, I do not know of any apocalyptic figure who could be described in such terms.

The connection between traditions about Melchizedek in Gnostic writings and Hebrews seem to be even more tenuous. That

---

[1] On the problem of even accenting the role and function of "annointed" figures in the literature of Qumran or to see any development in it, see M. de Jonge, "The Role of Intermediaries in God's Final Intervention in the Future According to the Qumran Scrolls," Studies on the Jewish Background of the New Testament (O. Michel et alia), pp. 44-63. The choice of the term "intermediaries" is unfortunate in our view since by it he wanted a "neutral word" instead of "messiah" or "Messiah." It would have been much better to simply use "annointed," as he actually does in the rest of the article.

Milchizedek discharges his office at the middle of the earth and
then is buried there (Melchizedek fragment in Slavic Enoch) and
that he ministers at the tomb of Adam and carries his body to
the hill of Calvary and receives his highpriestly office as the
second highpriest after Adam and before the third, Christ (Book
of Adam--see TDNT IV, p. 570--footnote 8), and such traditions
seem extremely remote from the themes and arguments in Hb 7. On
this point we are dependent on Michel's presentation and have not
been able to examine the gnostic traditions on our own.

Perfection and the "Taxis" of Eternal Priesthood

It is the tradition of the perfection of Levi, Aaron and
Melchizedek which lies at the basis of this chapter. For its
character and place in the tradition of perfection, see above pp.
58-63 and summary chart on pp. 70-71. We draw attention to certain features pertinent to Hb 7.

"Taxis" of immortality: We notice that one of the emphatic
points in Hb 7, is that Jesus and Melchizedek are not men like
the Levites and Aaronides who die, but priests who are immortal
and remain as such forever--

7,3: ἀπάτωρ, ἀμήτωρ, ἀγενεαλόγητος, μήτε ἀρχὴν ἡμερῶν μήτε
ζωῆς τέλος ἔχων, ἀφωμοιωμένος δὲ τῷ υἱῷ τοῦ θεοῦ, μένει
ἱερεὺς εἰς τὸ διηνεκές.

7,8: καὶ ὧδε μὲν δεκάτας ἀποθνήσκοντες ἄνθρωποι
λαμβάνουσιν, ἐκεῖ δὲ μαρτυρούμενος ὅτι ζῆ.

7,15-16: . . . εἰ κατὰ τὴν ὁμοιότητα Μελχισέδεκ ἀνίσταται
ἱερεὺς ἕτερος, ὃς οὐ κατὰ νόμον ἐντολῆς σαρκίνης γέγονεν
ἀλλὰ κατὰ δύναμιν ζωῆς ἀκαταλύτου.

7,23-24: καὶ οἱ μὲν πλείονές εἰσι γεγονότες ἱερεῖς διὰ τὸ
θανάτῳ κωλύεσθαι παραμένειν, ὁ δὲ διὰ τὸ μένειν αὐτὸν
εἰς τὸν αἰῶνα ἀπαράβατον ἔχει ἱερωσύνην . . .

7,28: ὁ νόμος γὰρ ἀνθρώπους καθίστησιν ἀρχιερεῖς ἔχοντας
ἀσθένειαν, ὁ λόγος δὲ τῆς ὁρκωμοσίας τῆς μετὰ τὸν νόμον
υἱὸν εἰς τὸν αἰῶνα τετελειωμένον.[2]

---

[2]The way commentators have divided up this chapter, in
effect, makes it impossible to discover the coherence of the author's argument and the tie between the themes. It is highly
artificial and has hardly any relation to the content. Both
Michel and Spicq divide this chapter into: 7,1-3; 4-10; 11-14;
15-19; 20-22; 23-25; 26-28. Again when 7,3 is considered a poem
from the realm of Hellenistic Judaism (Michel sees such influence
of Hellenistic Judaism thus far only in 1,3; 4,12-13; and 7,3;
p. 259), it is used as means to argue that it was only adopted
and left unelaborated by the author (Windisch p. 63; Michel p.
256). We do not find that the attempt to find a poetic "Vorlage"
in 7,3 and 16 helpful in understanding either the form or content
of this chapter. See the latest attempt in Gerd Thiessen, Untersuchungen zum Hebräerbrief, pp. 20-25.

In <u>Som ii,231-35</u> (see above pp. 58f.), the highpriest (Aaron) is
perfect when he enters the Holy of Holies and there he is <u>nei-
ther man nor God</u>, but belongs to the <u>middle "taxis."</u> He is related to <u>mortality</u> by birth, and to <u>immortality</u> by being <u>made
like</u> the Unbegotten (i.e., God; "<u>oikeioumenos</u> tōi agenetōi").
Outside the Holy of Holies he is in the realm of <u>body and flesh</u>,
an exemplar of one making progress towards perfection. Similarly, in <u>Quis Her 84</u> (see above p. 59), the priest when he
enters the Holy of Holies is <u>not man or human</u> but <u>divine</u>. In
<u>Sac 120</u> (see above pp. 60-61), the clearest proof of Levi's per-
fection is that he has taken refuge in God having left dealings
with <u>created things</u>. In other words, the priest who exemplifies
the closest proximity to God (to enter the Holy of Holies)
belongs to a particular "taxis" which is above that of body,
flesh, mortal men, and he belongs to it by becoming or being like
exemplary figures of such perfection (see below pp. pp. 203ff.).
This is precisely the form of the argument in Hb 7,3 and 7,15-16.
Melchizedek is a priest forever since he is <u>like the son of God</u>
(aphōmoiōmenos). And in this tradition, to be a son of God is to
be perfect (see above pp. 43 and 44). Jesus is a priest forever
since he is "according to the <u>likeness</u> of Melchizedek" (note that
he has substituted "taxis" with "homoiotēs"), or "according to
the power of indestructible life." The substitution of "taxis"
with "homoiotēs" is completely in accord with the tradition with
which we are dealing. And it becomes clear why the immortality
of Jesus and Melchizedek is so emphatically established--it is
the mark of the perfect priest in this tradition. The author,
when he argues that Ps 110,4 speaks of a different order of
priesthood than that of Aaron, states his case in terms of the
fact that Jesus "partook" of the tribe of Judah (cf. 2,14-17; we
will discuss the concept of "metechein" in the next chapter), but
<u>what makes it far more clear</u> is that Jesus is a priest <u>like</u> Mel-
chizedek, namely, in that he is immortal (vs. 11-16; "perisso-
teron eti katakēlon estin"). On the other hand, he denies that
Levitic-Aaronide priests participate in such immortality, they
are sinful men, beset by weakness and subject to death. And this
is evident, according to the author, in their sacrificial offerings for their own sins before they act as priests for the people
(vs. 27; cf. 5,1-3). It was essential for the author to prove
that Levi and Aaron do not belong to the "taxis" of the eternal
priesthood of Melchizedek (on this more in the next section
below).

This counter argument is not based on the historical fact that Levites and Aaronides die, for that matter Jesus also died and the author does not argue in terms of his resurrection. That he rose bodily would not have been of much help in the context of this tradition--that would mean that he has fallen from heaven into the realm of body and flesh (cf. Quis Her 84, above p. 59). It is with a Christology of his exaltation that one can reasonably argue in the context of this tradition and to which it has the closest affinity. What is crucial is the "taxis" to which one belongs, i.e., it is an issue about perfection and who can procure perfection for his followers (cf. vs. 11, 19, 25, 28). The argument about the mortality and sinfulness of Levi and Aaron are the author's scriptural proofs that in fact they did not attain the perfection claimed for them in this tradition.

What then is "taxis"? Obviously, it is a term which belongs to the tradition of perfection. It denotes a status or class in the hierarchical order between God and his creation. Closer to God and further from the world of creation (flesh, body, etc.) mean higher the "taxis." And to be close to God is to be like Him and one of the marks is immortality. In this monotheistic tradition, one cannot become God (the highpriest in the Holy of Holies is neither man nor God--but in between--and that is why the question of intermediaries is a significant one); the closest relationship one can have with God is to be "his" son, not the son of one of his intermediaries (cf. Conf 145-48, see above p. 32; Congr 177, pp. 172-73 above). Isaac exemplifies such perfection in that he belongs to the "taxis" of Son (pp. 40f. above --Som i,173). There are three classes of men--the perfect, middle and the wicked ("genos," "taxis," etc., see above Quis Her 45-47, p. 39). These examples will suffice here and we will meet many more examples of it below. The point is that the "taxis" of perfection is exemplified by various religious figures--Moses, Aaron, Levi, Melchizedek, Isaac, etc., and the theme of perfection is modulated in terms of the exigencies of the biblical stories or narratives about these characters.[3] Here, of course, we

---

[3]One can group most of the usage of the term "taxis" in Philo into two. One, "taxis" in the sense of order versus disorder. Second, "taxis" in the sense of class or status in a hierarchical scheme--i.e., in terms of perfection and imperfection. In this second group, apart from the ones quoted in this chapter, we note the following: Abr 124-25:--there are three "taxeis" of human characters (ethon), the best worships the Existent alone, the next best is introduced and made known to the Father by his beneficial power--God and the third by the kingly

are dealing with priest and priesthood. In terms of this tradition, what is important about these figures is not their historical character, that they lived and died and have a biography, but
that they exemplify models of existence which can be emulated and
participated in. They are dispositions of the soul, characters,
types and virtues (see above pp. 46-48). One does not have to be
a priest to share in the perfection of Aaron or Levi (see Quis
Her 82, p. 60 above). This explains the apparently curious fact,
that Melchizedek is an eternal highpriest and Jesus is an eternal
highpriest. The author of Hebrews has accepted this exemplary
character of the perfection of the priesthood of Melchizedek because by exegeting this Genesis passage he can make the best case
for the superiority of Jesus' priesthood over that of Aaron and
Levi. It is in this context, that we can understand the author's
contention in vs. 28 that Jesus is the son perfected and appointed highpriest for ever and he procures the same status for Christians (2,10-18), and that underlines his preeminent salvific significance for the Christian community whose claims were endan-
gered by the confrontation with this tradition in which Moses,
Aaron and Levi were the exemplars of perfection. It is in this
larger scope that the argument about genealogy or not having a
genealogy has its significance.

Congr 43: καὶ Ναχὼρ μέντοι, ὁ ἀδελφὸς ᾿Αβραάμ, ἔχει δύο
γυναῖκας, ἀστήν τε καὶ παλλακήν, ὄνομα δὲ τῆς μὲν ἀστῆς
Μελχά, ῾Ρουμὰ δὲ τῆς παλλακίδος.

44: ἀλλ᾿ οὐχ ἱστορικὴ γενεαλογία ταῦτ᾿ ἐστὶν ἀναγραφεῖσα
παρὰ τῷ σοφῷ νομοθέτῃ - μηδεὶς τοῦτ᾿ εὖ φρονῶν
ὑπονοήσειεν, - ἀλλὰ πραγμάτων ψυχὴν ὠφελῆσαι δυναμένων
διὰ συμβόλων ἀνάπτυξις. τὰ δ᾿ ὀνόματα μεταβαλόντες εἰς
τὴν ἡμετέραν διάλεκτον εἰσόμεθα τὴν ὑπόσχεσιν ἀληθῆ.
(This followed by etymological interpretation of the
names in the same way as Hb 7,2; the context of this passage is the discussion of patriarchs who had two wives
like Abraham--Sarah and Hagar--the latter representing
the lower encyclical education.)

Abr 31: οὕτως δ᾿ ἀποσεμνύει τὸν φιλάρετον, ὥστε καὶ γενεαλογῶν
αὐτὸν οὔ, καθάπερ ἔθος ἐπὶ τῶν ἄλλων . . . ἀλλά τινων
ἀρετῶν, μόνον οὐχὶ βοῶν ἄντικρυς, ὅτι οἰκία καὶ συγγένεια

---

power--Lord. They represent, therefore, "taxies" of perfection
in terms of immediacy and distance. Mig 196--Samuel is the type
of disposition (tropos) which is placed (tachtheis) in the best
"taxis" beside God (para theoi). Abr 19--Enoch was translated and
placed in the better "taxei." Som i,152--The practisers are in
the middle of the two extremities of Olympus and Hades, drawn in
opposite directions until God bestows the prizes on the better
"taxei" and destroys the opposite. Congr 108--the soul which ex-
periences the "release" (aphesis), perfect freedom of the soul
(Lv 25,9ff.), the holy Logos honoured and gave it an immortal
heritage (athanatos kleros), the "taxin" in the immortal race.

καὶ πατρὶς οὐδεμία ἐστιν ἑτέρα σοφῷ ὅτι μὴ ἀρεταὶ καὶ
αἱ κατ' ἀρετὰς πράξεις (the reference is to Noah and the
passage is followed by the quotation of Gn 6,9; the con
text is the presentation of the first triad of patriarchs
whose virtues are inscribed in the holy scriptures and
who are the unwritten laws 4-5).

The significance of scripture does not lie in recounting the stories or biographies of past men; their contemporary and eternal
significance lies in that they are models or exemplars for human
existence. They are "facts of nature," "types of good men,"
"virtues" which are immortal and hence of significance for contemporary men (see above pp. 72-73).   Genealogy in this sense
is not a matter of history but a revelation through symbols of
facts which are able to benefit the soul. Not to have a genealogy is to receive great praise, for such a one is truly immortal.
Instead of a genealogy such a one has a list of virtues. The
etymological interpretation of Melchizedek's name and the list
that follows in 7,3 is precisely a list of virtues which prove
that indeed he is an immortal exemplar of perfect priesthood. We
have already met some of the terms--such as "without mother"--as
characterizations in this tradition of perfection (e.g., Sarah,
Ebr 82, see above p. 130).[4] It is for this reason that the
author considers the genealogical fact that Jesus arose from the
tribe of Judah less significant than that he is a priest accord
ing to _likeness_ of Melchizedek, i.e., immortal. Belonging to the
tribe of Judah would not as such prove that, it only serves to
prove that scripture in the Psalms, after the Law, spoke of a
priest according to the order of Melchizedek (Ps 110,4) who is
not "according to the order of Aaron" (vs. 11ff.), namely, Jesus.
Furthermore, Jesus is the heavenly man who "partook" of flesh and

---

[4]To be "without father" or "without mother" are attributes
of Greek gods (see Windisch, Moffat, Spicq and Michel). The original implication was that the gods descended from a single sex.
Later it seems it was seen as a characteristic of the unbegotten
or self-begotten character of divinity, e.g., "physis" in Orphic
Hymns 10,10 is "autopator," "apator." Hence, God is without
father and without mother (see Apoc Abr 17,9--quoted in Michel,
p. 261). Philo never applies such a characterization to God.
But to beings lower than God and never "without father," since
there is nothing in existence apart from God which is not created.
"Without mother" in Philo implies that one has no part in creation, the female aspect (thus Sarah, wisdom, seven, etc. are
male), and belongs to God alone, and hence shares in God's immortal and perfect nature (see Quis Her 216; 62; Mos ii,210; QG IV,
145; 68). In Hb 7,3, the implication is obviously that Melchizedek has no human genealogy, but is like the son of God related
to God alone and without a part in the world of flesh and blood--
creation.

blood for a particular purpose (2,14-17), and this is further
described in genealogical terms as "partaking" of the tribe of
Judah. In his real identity and being, he is the Logos, the
heavenly man, the Son of God. The reason for all this proof of
his superiority is, of course, that such claims could also be
made by Moses, Aaron, Levi and others in this tradition.

"Taxis" of sinlessness/without weakness

At one's closest proximity to God or to be in such a state
of perfection implies that one has left the world of creation, of
body and flesh, that one has left mortality behind, and is with
out sin--a point that has reappeared again and again as we have
examined this tradition (cf. Albinus, Chap 18, see below f.n. 10,
p. 209). Hence, it is no surprise that such a list occurs of
Jesus' sinlessness as highpriest (vs. 27). What is to be noted,
and this is what marks the particular understanding of sinlessness in this tradition, is that it is equivalent to being "separated from sinners," "higher than the heavens" (i.e., in the
presence of God, inside the heavenly Holy of Holies) and being
sinful is equivalent to having "weakness" (astheneia--vs. 28; cf.
5,2). Weakness is what characterizes this world of creation and
God is one who is without weakness. This is an important concept
in the author's Christology and needs to be clarified further
(cf. Cher 90; Quod Deus 52; Sac 94ff.; 139). Here we only call
attention to the fact that in this tradition the highpriest/
priest is without intentional and unintentional sins and that
such a state is a mark of perfection (Fug 102; Som i,148; see
above pp. 34-35).

Virt 176: . . . ἀνάμνησις, ἧς ἀδελφὸν καὶ συγγενέστατον τὸ
μετανοεῖν ἐστιν, οὐκ ἐν τῇ πρώτῃ καὶ ἀνωτάτω τεταγμένον
τάξει, ἀλλ' ἐν τῇ μετὰ ταύτην φερόμενον δευτερεῖα.

177: τὸ μὲν γὰρ μηδὲν συνόλως ἁμαρτεῖν ἴδιον θεοῦ τάχα δὲ
καὶ θείου ἀνδρός, . . . (175-186 is a discussion of
repentance, probably a missionary sermon, since it gives
a great deal of attention to proselytes and the monotheistic creed. Cf. Hb 6,1--where "repentance" is part
of the list of what is to be left behind on the way to
perfection). Complete sinlessness is peculiar to God and
possibly a divine man and this is the first and highest
"taxis."

Spec Leg i,230: . . . ὅτι ὁ πρὸς ἀλήθειαν ἀρχιερεὺς καὶ μὴ
ψευδώνυμος ἀμέτοχος ἁμαρτημάτων ἐστιν, . . . (interpretation of Lv 4,3).

Spec Leg iii,134: . . . τῶν μὲν ἑκουσίων ἀδικημάτων αὐτὸ μόνον
ἰδιώτας καθαρεύειν ἐφεῖσθω, λεγέτω δ' εἰ βούλεταί τις
καὶ τοὺς ἄλλους ἱερεῖς, ἀμφοτέρων δ' ἑκουσίων τε καὶ
ἀκουσίων κατὰ τὸν ἐξαίρετον λόγον τὸν ἀρχιερέα.

135: προσάπτεσθαι γὰρ αὐτῷ <u>μιάσματος</u> τὸ σύνολον οὐ
θεμιτόν, . . . (an allegorical interpretation of why the unintentional homicide may not return from exile in the city of refuge till the death of the highpriest, namely, since the highpriest is free from both intentional and unintentional sin).

Fug 108: λέγομεν γὰρ τὸν ἀρχιερέα <u>οὐκ ἄνθρωπον ἀλλὰ λόγον θεῖον</u> εἶναι πάντων οὐχ ἑκουσίων μόνον ἀλλὰ καὶ ἀκουσίων ἀδικημάτων ἀμέτοχον.

109: οὔτε γὰρ ἐπὶ πατρί, τῷ νῷ, οὔτε ἐπὶ μητρί, τῇ αἰσθήσει, φησὶν αὐτὸν Μωυσῆς δύνασθαι <u>μιαίνεσθαι</u>, διότι, οἶμαι, <u>γονέων ἀφθάρτων καὶ καθαρωτάτων ἔλαχεν</u>, <u>πατρὸς μὲν θεοῦ</u>, ὃς καὶ τῶν συμπάντων ἐστὶ πατήρ, <u>μητρὸς δὲ σοφίας</u>, δι' ἧς τὰ ὅλα ἦλθεν εἰς γένεσιν. (Context is the same as above, the interpretation of Nu 35,25.)

Som ii,185: ὁ δὲ ἀρχιερεὺς ἄμωμός ἐστιν, ὁλόκληρος, ἀνὴρ παρθένου . . . (the context is the contrast between the cupbearer of Pharoah and the cupbearer of God, the High-priest Logos).[5]

These passages will suffice to show that in this tradition the highpriest in his perfection is sinless. The author of Hebrews describes the sinlessness of Jesus as highpriest in similar terms, and points out on the basis of the OT that neither Aaron nor Levi could be considered perfect in these terms since they are represented as making sacrifices for their own sins before offering sacrifices for the people (7,27; 5,1-3).

"Taxis" of the Teacher and Guardian of the Laws and Covenants

A point that needs clarification in Hb 7 is how the author's argument about law and covenant fits in this context. We are concerned here with the following passages:

7,11: εἰ μὲν οὖν τελείωσις διὰ τῆς Λευιτικῆς ἱερωσύνης ἦν, ὁ λαὸς γὰρ ἐπ' αὐτῆς νενομοθέτηται . . .

7,18: ἀθέτεσις μὲν γὰρ γίνεται προαγούσης ἐντολῆς διὰ τὸ αὐτῆς ἀσθενὲς καὶ ἀνωφελές, (19) οὐδὲν γὰρ ἐτελείωσεν ὁ νόμος . . .

---

[5]The idea of the sinlessness of the perfect probably has its background in the Stoic view that the wise man who lives in complete harmony with God is sinless. See SVF III, 163.12; 148.19; Festugière, Personal Religion among the Greeks, p. 107. Völker thinks that Philo is unclear at this point and cites Spec Leg i, 252, Fug 157 and Mut 36 (pp. 337-40). When carefully examined we see that he has misunderstood these passages. Spec Leg i,152 speaks of the perfect "in that he is mortal," whereas full perfection as we have seen implies reaching beyond the realm of flesh and blood and quite possible for man (see above p. 60--Quis Her 82). The answer to Mut 36 is given by Philo himself in 34 and 37-39. That it is not impossible to find the kind which pleases God. That the wise man exists and we who are evil fail to see him and he shuns our company, e.g., Enoch. Völker incorrectly concludes: "So sagt unser Alexandriner des öfteren mit Nachdruck und Entschiedenheit, dass es sündlose Menschen überhaupt nicht gebe . . ." (p. 339).

194

7,20: καὶ καθ' ὅσον οὐ χωρὶς ὀρκωμοσίας . . .
7,22: κατὰ τοσοῦτο καὶ κρείττονος διαθήκης γέγομεν ἔγγυος
      Ἰησοῦς.
7,28: ὁ νόμος . . . ὁ λόγος δὲ τῆς ὀρκωμοσίας τῆς μετὰ τὸν
      νόμον . . .

The author's argument in vs. 11-18 is rather straightforward.
The law here is the commandment concerning the genealogical
descent of priests from the Levitic-Aaronide line. To paraphrase
these verses--if perfection could be procured through the Levitic
priesthood, for the people have received legislation concerning
the Levitic priesthood[6] (i.e., concerning their genealogical
descent), what need could there be to speak of the rise of another priest according to the order of Melchizedek and not according
to the order of Aaron? For when there is a change of priesthood
there is of necessity a change in the law (i.e., concerning genealogical descent). For concerning whom these things are spoken,
partook of a different tribe, from which no one has served the
altar. For it is evident, that our Lord has arisen from the
tribe of Judah, and Moses said nothing about priests from this
tribe. And this becomes even more clear, if another priest has
arisen according to the likeness of Melchizedek, who (traces his
genealogy) not according to the law of the commandment which
deals with physical descent, but whose real genealogy is traced
in accordance to the power of indestructible life. For it is the
witness of scripture that "you are a priest forever according to
the order of Melchizedek." For there is the setting aside of the
previous commandment concerning genealogical descent on account
of its weakness and uselessness (it deals with the realm of body
and flesh--of mortality and imperfection).

This paraphrase is based on our understanding of the tradition concerning the "taxis," genealogy and immortality of the
perfect priest, which we have discussed so far. From vs. 19, the
author generalizes about the law, oath and covenant. The law
perfected nothing, since it deals with the realm of body and

---

[6]There has been unnecessary speculation on the meaning of
"epi autēs" in 7,11b. Most follow Bauer's lexicon and understand
the phrase as "on the basis of" the Levitic priesthood (Windisch,
Moffat, Spicq, Michel). Hence, some consider it a parenthetical
remark which would fit better after vs. 12 (Moffat, Spicq). It
is simply a variant of "peri" with the genitive which is frequent
in Philo in connection with the passive of the verb--nomothetein.
For example, Spec Leg ii,35: ταῦτα μὲν ἐπ' ἀνθρώπων, ἐπὶ δὲ
κτηνῶν τάδε νομοθετεῖται. It simply means that people have received legislation concerning the Levitic priesthood. What kind
of legislation depends on one's interpretation of the larger context of the argument.

flesh which is characterized by sin and weakness (a point made
with considerable vigour in chaps. 8ff.--cf. 9,8-10; 9,13f.).
And against the law is contrasted the "word of oath"--Ps 110,4,
and a better covenant. The basic issue in all this is about perfection and one can easily surmise that this argument about the
weakness and uselessness of the law and inferiority of the covenant must have something to do with the tradition of the perfection of the Levitic-Aaronide priesthood.

Quod Det 62: . . . ἢ οὐχ ὁρᾷς ὅτι τὴν τῶν ἁγίων διατήρησίν τε
καὶ φυλακὴν οὐ τοῖς ἐπιτυχοῦσιν ὁ νομοθέτης ἀλλὰ τοῖς τὰς
γνώμας ἱερωτάτοις Λευίταις ἐπιτρέπει;

63: καὶ οὐδ' ἅπασιν ἐξεγένετο τοῖς ἱκέταις γενέσθαι φύλαξιν
ἱερῶν, ἀλλ' εἴ τινες ἀριθμὸν πεντηκοστὸν ἔλαχον ἄφεσιν
καὶ ἐλευθερίαν παντελῆ . . . προκηρύττοντα.

64: οὐκοῦν τῷ μὲν ἡμίσει τὴν τελειότητα - τέλειος γὰρ ὁ
πεντηκοστὸς λόγος, ὁ δὲ τῶν πέντε καὶ εἴκοσιν ἥμισυ
μέρος - ἐνεργεῖν ἐπιτρέπει καὶ δρᾶν τὰ ἅγια . . . τῷ δὲ
τελείῳ μηκέτι πονεῖν, τὰ δ' ὅσα ἐκ μελέτης καὶ πόνου
περιεποιήσατο φυλάττειν, μὴ γὰρ γενοίμην ἀσκητὴς ὢν μὴ
φύλαξ αὖθις.

65: ἡ μὲν οὖν ἄσκησις μέσον, οὐ τέλειον, γίνεται γὰρ ἐν οὐ
τελείαις μὲν ἀκρότητος δὲ ἐφιεμέναις ψυχαῖς, ἡ δὲ φυλακὴ
παντελές . . .

66: οὗτος δὲ πρότερον ὅτε ἐγυμνάζετο μαθητὴς ἦν διδάσκοντος
ἑτέρου, ὁπότε δὲ ἱκανὸς φυλάττειν ἐγένετο, διδασκάλου
δύναμιν καὶ τάξιν ἔλαχε . . . ὥστε ὁ μὲν τοῦ ἀστείου
νοῦς φύλαξ καὶ ταμίας τῶν ἀρετῆς δογμάτων, ὁ δὲ ἀδελφὸς
αὐτοῦ λόγος λειτουργήσει τοῖς παιδείαν μετιοῦσι διεξιὼν
τὰ σοφίας δόγματά τε καὶ θεωρήματα.

67: διὸ καὶ Μωυσῆς ἐν ταῖς εὐλογίαις Λευὶ πολλὰ καὶ θαυμάσια
προειπὼν ἐπιφέρει (Dt 33,9-10) . . .

68: οὐκοῦν ὅτι καὶ λόγων καὶ διαθήκης θεοῦ φύλαξ ὁ ἀστεῖός
ἐστιν, ἐναργῶς παρίστησι, καὶ μὴν ὅτι δικαιωμάτων καὶ
νόμων ἑρμηνεὺς καὶ ὑφηγητὴς ἄριστος . . .

The context of the passage is the interpretation of Gn 4,9--"Am I
my brother's keeper." Life indeed would be wretched if Cain was
the guardian of his brother's good. Rather the Levites have been
entrusted with the keeping and guardianship of holy things. They
are the most holy in their thinking and their excellence is seen
in the fact that the whole world is not worthy to be their portion but God alone to whom their ministry is exclusively devoted.
It is not to everyone that this guardianship of holy things is
given but only to those who have received by lot the number 50
(a symbol of perfection), which represents release and perfect
freedom (followed by quotation of Nu 8,24-26). As long as the
Levites are 25 (years old) they are half of perfection and charged
to engage in holy actions, the perfect do not labour but guard
what they have acquired by toil and exercise. Practice is half
way and not perfect, and it takes place in souls which are not

perfect but striving to reach the summit. <u>Guardianship is per-
fect</u>. When <u>in training</u> earlier, <u>he is a disciple while someone
else is the teacher</u>, but when he became a guardian, <u>he received
the "taxis" and power of the teacher</u> (i.e., a mark of perfection,
cf. <u>Hb 5,11-6,1</u>, it is the same kind of tradition which underlies
that passage--i.e., the tradition of paideia). At this level of
perfection, the Levite's (or any cultured man--"asteios"--for
whom Levi can be an exemplar of perfection; note the typical
generalizing that Philo engages in as he interprets the scripture, i.e., they are meant to be applicable to all who can follow
a particular paradigm) mind is the guardian and treasurer of the
dogmas of virtue and his speech/logos <u>ministers to those seeking
education</u> (that leads to perfection) by pursuing the doctrines
and principles of wisdom. It is for this reason (i.e., their
role as "educators" to perfection) that Moses pronounces on Levi
the many and marvellous <u>blessings</u> (quotes Dt 33,9-10) which
clearly show that he is the <u>guardian of the words and covenant of
God</u>, the <u>best interpreter and instructor of the ordinances and
laws</u>, etc.

It is in the context of such a tradition, and its affinity
to 5,11ff. is obvious, that one can understand that, when the
author is arguing about perfection through the Levitic-Aaronide
priesthood, he must state at the same time that the law perfected
nothing and Jesus is the guarantee of a better covenant. Because
it is by instruction through the laws and covenant--they are the
doctrines and principles of wisdom--that one makes progress towards perfection or when one is perfect, one becomes like Levi
the teacher and interpreter of the words and covenant of God (cf.
<u>5,12</u>). Levitic perfection is therefore to belong to the "taxis"
of the teacher of the laws and covenant. These are the wonderful
blessings of Levi.

> Hb 5,12: καὶ γὰρ ὀφείλοντες εἶναι <u>διδάσκαλοι</u> διὰ τὸν
> χρόνον, πάλιν χρείαν ἔχετε <u>τοῦ διδάσκειν</u> ὑμᾶς <u>τινα</u> τὰ
> στοιχεῖα τῆς ἀρχῆς <u>τῶν λογίων τοῦ θεοῦ</u> . . .

So that even at this preliminary point one can see that
Hb 5-6 and 7 are not disconnnected units but coherent parts of
the tradition of perfection. Furthermore, the discussion on law
and covenant in this chapter as well as in 8-10 pertains to the
priesthood and cult.

> Congr 131: τοῦτον τὸν τρόπον καὶ <u>τὰ νομοθετικῆς</u> τῆς παρὰ
> ἀνθρώποις κατεβλήθη <u>σπέρματα</u> . . . (Ex 2,1-2)
> 132: οὗτός ἐστι Μωυσῆς, ὁ καθαρώτατος νοῦς, ὁ ἀστεῖος
> ὄντως, ὁ <u>νομοθετικὴν</u> ὁμοῦ καὶ προφητείαν ἐνθουσιώσῃ καὶ
> θεοφορήτῳ σοφίᾳ λαβών, <u>ὃς γένος ὢν τῆς Λευιτικῆς φυλῆς</u>

καὶ τὰ πρὸς πατρὸς καὶ τὰ πρὸς μητρὸς ἀμφιθαλὴς τῆς
ἀληθείας ἔχεται.

133: μέγιστον δὲ ἐπάγγελμα τοῦ γενάρχου τῆς φυλῆς ἐστι
ταύτης, θαρρεῖ γὰρ λέγειν, ὅτι αὐτός μοι μόνος ἐστι
θεὸς τιμητέος . . .

134: μεγάλης καὶ ὑπερφυοῦς ψυχῆς τὸ αὔχημα, γένεσιν
ὑπερκύπτειν καὶ τοὺς ὅρους αὐτῆς ὑπερβάλλειν καὶ μόνου
τοῦ ἀγενήτου περιέχεσθαι κατὰ τὰς ἱερὰς ὑφηγήσεις, ἐν
αἷς διείρηται "ἔχεσθαι αὐτοῦ". τοιγάρτοι τοῖς ἐχομένοις
καὶ ἀδιαστάτως θεραπεύουσιν ἀντιδίδωσι κλῆρον αὐτόν.
ἐγγῦαται δέ μου τὴν ὑπόσχεσιν λόγιον, ἐν ᾧ λέγεται,
"κύριος αὐτὸς κλῆρος αὐτοῦ."

The context is a discussion on the false pride of some teachers
who attribute the progress of a gifted pupil to themselves. Such
are represented by Hagar who is said "to have in the womb" in
contrast to Rebecca who "receives in the womb" (127-30). This
leads to a digression on the birth of Moses (Ex 2,1-2; "she receives in her womb"). This is the way the art of legislation
was sown among men. Moses, the most pure mind and the truly
noble, received the art of legislation and prophecy by the inspiration of divine wisdom, and is the descendant of the tribe of
Levi on both the father's and mother's side thereby having a
double portion of truth. The greatest profession of the founder
of the tribe (Levi) is that he must honour God alone rather than
any part of the universe--a list follows (earth, sea, rivers,
etc.). The boast of such a great and exalted soul is to rise
over creation and pass beyond its boundaries and to hold fast to
the Uncreated in accordance to the sacred instructions--"to hold
on to Him" (Dt 30,20). Therefore to those who hold on to Him and
serve Him unceasingly he gives Himself as their portion in return.
And this word of promise is guaranteed in the saying--"the Lord
is his portion" (i.e., Levi's--Dt 10,9).

We observe that the art of legislation is a mark of the
excellence of the Levites. And Moses the archetypal legislator
(cf. Virt 70) traces his genealogy from the Levites. So that
when Hebrews speaks of the law, covenant, genealogy, perfection,
the Levites, in this chapter, the shadow of Moses is always there.
How could one read vs. 19 and 22 and 28 without thinking about
Moses? Given the character of this tradition of exemplars of perfection, the author in showing the inferiority of the Levites has
done the same for Moses as well. And the excellence of the
Levites who are the teachers and guardians of the laws and covenants, who lead others to perfection by instruction, is that they
rise above creation and hold on to God alone and He alone is their

portion. This is their boast.[7] Such immediacy to God is of
course perfection. The author of Hebrews uses the same language
--to hold fast, to grasp, boast, etc.--to characterize Christian
faith and hope (3,6; 3,14; 4,14; 6,18; 10,23) which procures the
same immediacy to God for Christians--i.e., the perfecting of
faith (11,39-12,2). Similarly, in this tradition, such proximity
to God--to have Him as one's portion--is the highest form of the
covenant.

Mut 58: . . . εἴδη μὲν διαθήκης ἐστι πάμπολλα χάριτας καὶ δωρεὰς
τοῖς ἀξίοις ἀπονέμοντα, τὸ δ' ἀνώτατον γένος διαθηκῶν
αὐτὸς ἐγώ εἰμι. . . .

59: τοῖς μὲν γὰρ δι' ἑτέρων τὰς εὐεργεσίας εἴωθε προτείνειν
ὁ θεός, γῆς, ὕδατος . . . τοῖς δὲ δι' ἑαυτοῦ μόνου,
κλῆρον ἀποφήνας τῶν λαμβανόντων ἑαυτόν, οὓς εὐθέως καὶ
προσρήσεως ἑτέρας ἠξίωσε.

The passage is an interpretation of Gn 17,4 and the climax of
which, namely, Abraham's perfection, is his change of name in
17,5 which is quoted at the end of the passage. The description
of the highest type of covenant is almost identical to Congr 133-
34. To some God extends his beneficence through the world of
creation, to others through Himself alone, showing Himself to be
their portion. The differentiation is between mediation and unmediated access to God. In other words, the highest type of
covenant, God himself, God as our portion alone, the typical mark
of the excellence of Levi, is simply another theme of perfection.
So that when Hebrews represents Jesus as the guarantee of a better covenant, it is the same as saying that Jesus procures perfection rather than the Levitic priesthood, its laws and its
covenants, and it is the same as saying that this is a new covenant enacted on better promises--it is not like the covenant
which God made with the patriarchs (Abraham, Moses, Levi, etc.),
but here God places the law in the minds and hearts of men, so
that there is no necessity for instruction of one's fellow citizen or brethren for all will know God (i.e., no need for a Levitic
priesthood; Hb 8,6-12)--and it is a covenant which establishes
entry into the presence of God--inside the true heavenly Holy of
Holies (Hb 9,15-24). Note the language of promise and guarantee
in Congr 134. The same point, that God himself is the archetypal
covenant is made in QG III,42.

---

[7]Probably a similar tradition bears the brunt of Paul's
polemic in 2Cor 10-13. The frequency with which he opposes the
view of the exaltation of the mind, its rising above the realm of
flesh and weakness, its boast in this respect and in respect to
genealogy, etc., does point in this direction and would merit
further investigation (10,3-6; 11,22ff.; 12,6-10; 13,3-4, etc.).

One further passage will suffice to show that the exercise
of legislative power is an exercise of divine power and it characterizes the perfection of Levitic priesthood.

Sac 131: . . . τῶν γὰρ περὶ τὸν θεὸν δυνάμεων ἀρίστων πασῶν
μία οὖσα ταῖς ἄλλαις ἰσότιμος ἡ νομοθετικὴ - νομοθέτης
γὰρ καὶ πηγὴ νόμων αὐτός, ἀφ' οὗ πάντες οἱ κατὰ μέρος
νομοθέται - διχῇ πέφυκε τέμνεσθαι, τῇ μὲν εἰς εὐεργεσίαν
κατορθούντων, τῇ δὲ εἰς κόλασιν ἁμαρτανόντων.

132: τοῦ μὲν οὖν προτέρου τμήματος ὑπερέτης ὁ Λευίτης ἐστί,
τὰς γὰρ λειτουργίας ἁπάσας ἀναδέχεται, ὅσαι πρὸς
ἱερωσύνην ἀναφέρονται τέλειαν, καθ' ἣν διασυνίσταται
καὶ γνωρίζεται τὸ θνητὸν θεῷ, ἢ δι' ὁλοκαυτωμάτων ἢ διὰ
σωτηρίων ἢ διὰ μετανοίας ἁμαρτημάτων . . .

The passage is an alternative interpretation of Lv 25,32 (127ff.)
and meant only for mature ears. The Levites exercise the best of
the powers of God--legislation--and that too only its beneficial
side for those who act correctly. He undertakes all the services
that pertain to the perfect priesthood in that he acts as a mediator between mortality and God through burnt offering, peace
offerings and repentance of sins. Just earlier (130), Moses is
described as their leader (hēgemōn), general (stratēgos), highpriest, prophet and friend of God--the reference being to Ex 32,
26ff. So that in this tradition, Moses, Levi and Aaron belong
together as exemplars of perfection.[8]

"Taxis" of Melchizedek

We have dealt with a crucial dimension of the argument,
namely, that Jesus like Melchizedek is an immortal and therefore
eternal highpriest (para one above). We have left the interpretation of Gn 14,17ff. till this point since it becomes comprehensible against the background of the tradition of the perfect
highpriesthood or priesthood of Levi-Aaron. On the tradition of
the perfection of Melchizedek--see above pp. 61-62. He is the

---

[8]We did not see any need to deal with the question of "oath"
at any length at this point, since the similarity between Philo
and Hebrews at this point is well known. Observations on our part
will be more appropriate with 6,13-20. We only draw attention to
the fact that the author's argument in 7,20-22 has as its basis
the principle that matters in dispute are settled by an oath (Som
i,12; Dec 86, etc.) and in this case totally certain since it is
God's oath. The author has for the sake of his argument introduced a novel distinction between the law and oath (vs. 19-20;
28), since in this tradition there is no distinction drawn between
God's words, laws and covenants, they are correlative terms (Leg
All iii,204; Sac 93; Wis Sol 12,21; 18,22). This also enables us
to understand the connection between vs. 19-22, which otherwise
seems quite abrupt. In this tradition one can speak of the law,
oath and covenant in the same breath!

Logos, God's own priest, and has God for his portion (just like
Levi and Moses--see above Leg All iii,79-82). Like Isaac--who
belongs to the order of the son of God (cf. Som i,173; QG IV,153,
etc., see above p. 44)--his priesthood is described as self-
learnt and self-taught, which is the same thing as saying that
he needs no instruction (see above p. 74 --"Perfection and
Paraenesis"), and belongs to the "taxis" of the teacher. Abraham, while still under the "rod" of paideia (Lv 27,32), i.e.,
still progressing towards perfection, pays him the tithe (Congr
99, see above pp. 61-62). Similarly, in Congr 105 (see above
p. 60), the perfect priest rises above the nine parts of the world
and honours the Tenth (God) and continually offers the tithe to
the One who is alone and eternally Tenth (cf. Hb 7,26--"higher
than the heavens"). In other words, who pays tithe to whom differentiates the progresser from the perfect. When one pays tithe
to the intermediary (Melchizedek-Logos), he is under the disci-
plinary rod of education and still progressing towards perfection. When one pays tithe to God, he is the perfect priest. It
is this argument which is being applied in Hb 7,4-10, and the
same principle is expressed clearly in vs. 7 in terms of blessing.
The author's argument is somewhat of a tour-de-force, when he
argues that Levi could be considered to have paid tithe to Melchizedek in that he was potentially in the seed of Abraham when
the latter paid the tithe to Melchizedek (vs. 9-10). This proof
was undoubtedly necessitated by the fact that Levi-Aaron and
Melchizedek are exemplars of perfect priesthood and the author
could assume that Melchizedek's perfection would be granted in
this tradition and all that he needed to show was that Levi is
inferior to Melchizedek.

There is more involved in the author's choice of Melchizedek
and the Genesis passage for his counter argument. The etymological interpretation, which is the same as in Leg All iii,79 (see
above p. 61), is not merely decorative, they are the prizes of
the priesthood of Levi (i.e., peace and eternal priesthood). And
secondly, in this tradition, Levites are priests who receive
tithes on the basis of this same Genesis passage. That is, they
are priests according to the order of Melchizedek:

Ebr 65: εἰσι δέ τινες, οἱ τῶν μητρῴων ὑπερορῶντες περιέχονται
παντὶ σθένει τῶν πατρῴων, οὓς καὶ τῆς μεγίστης τιμῆς,
ἱερωσύνης, ὁ ὀρθὸς λόγος ἠξίωσε. . . .

74: ἆρ' οὐχὶ καὶ οὗτος ἀνδροφόνος παρὰ πολλοῖς ἂν εἶναι
νομισθείη, . . . ; ἀλλὰ παρά γε θεῷ τῷ πανηγεμόνι καὶ
πατρὶ μυρίων ἐπαίνων καὶ ἐγκωμίων καὶ ἀναφαιρέτων ἄθλων,

ἀξιωθήσεται, τὰ δ᾽ <u>ἆθλα μεγάλα καὶ ἀδελφά, εἰρήνη καὶ</u>
<u>ἱερωσύνη</u> (Nu 25,13).

75: . . . ἀλλὰ τὸ πρεσβύτατον τῶν αἰτίων τὸ πρὸς ἀλήθειαν
θεραπείας καὶ τῆς ἀνωτάτω τιμῆς ἀξιώσαντα μόνον <u>τὴν</u>
<u>ἱερωσύνης λαβεῖν τάξιν</u> θαυμαστὸν καὶ <u>περιμάχητον</u>.

One of the symbolic meanings of wine is folly which is caused by
lack of education (apaideusia) and this is illustrated by Dt 21,
18-21. There are four types of children, who obey one or the
other or both or neither. These passages (65-76) discuss the
type which uses as its ally the father--right reason--and is
accused by the mother--custom, politics and demagogue (65-68).
They are deemed worthy of the <u>highest honour--priesthood</u>. There
follows a series of texts which are interpreted in various other
contexts in Philo to speak of the perfection of Levi--Ex 32,27-
29 (66-71); Dt 33,9 (72); Nu 25,7-8 (73-74)--all implying in
general that Levites have rejected this world of creation for the
sake of ministry to God alone. Such a one would be considered a
murderer (Ex 32,27ff.) by the multitude, but by God worthy of
myriads of praise and songs of honour and of great prizes,
namely, <u>peace</u> and <u>priesthood</u> (74). The latter refer to <u>Nu 25,</u>
<u>12-13</u>:

οὕτως εἶπόν ʹΙδοὺ ἐγὼ δίδωμι αὐτῷ <u>διαθήκην εἰρήνης</u>,
καὶ ἔσται αὐτῷ καὶ τῷ σπέρματι αὐτοῦ μετʹ αὐτὸν
<u>διαθήκη ἱερατείας αἰωνία</u>

The one who considers the One who is truly the Eldest of the
causes alone worthy of the highest honour and service receives
the "<u>taxis</u>" of priesthood, which is a marvellous honour worth
every effort.

The author of Hebrews has used the Melchizedek passage from
Genesis to show that it is Jesus who has received the covenant of
peace and the covenant of eternal priesthood, for such is the
etymological significance of "king of Salem" and the fact that
Melchizedek has no genealogy and the prophecy of Ps 110,4. However, his argument had one difficulty, namely, in this tradition,
Levi is a priest like Melchizedek and the Genesis passage was
proof text for his receiving the tithe.

τὰ γὰρ τοῦ πολέμου ἀριστεῖα δίδωσι τῷ ἱερεῖ καὶ τὰς
τῆς νίκης ἀπαρχάς. ἱεροπρεπεστάτη δὲ καὶ ἁγιωτάτη
πασῶν ἀπαρχῶν ἡ δεκάτη διὰ τὸ παντέλειον εἶναι τὸν
ἀριθμόν, ἀφʹ οὗ καὶ τοῖς ἱερεῦσι καὶ νεωκόροις αἱ
δεκάται προστάξει νόμου καρπῶν καὶ θρεμμάτων ἀποδί-
δονται, <u>ἀρξαντος τῆς ἀπαρχῆς</u> ʹΑβραάμ, <u>ὃς καὶ τοῦ</u>
<u>γένους ἀρχηγέτης ἐστίν</u>. (Unidentified passage from
Philo--from Harris, pp. 71-72.)

The passage most probably belongs to QG on Gn 14,18, which is lost
in the Armenian (see the note in the Loeb edition). In this passage, Levites are ranked with Melchizedek and the origin of the

tithe is traced to Abraham's giving of the tithe to Melchizedek.
It is for this reason that the author tries to prove that, on the
contrary, Levi gave tithes to Melchizedek since he was in Abraham's loins at this juncture.

Tithe/Tenth in the Schema of Perfection

This point can be dealt with briefly since the character of
the argument in Hebrews is already clear from Congr 99 and 105
(see above pp. 199-200). A few supportive texts will suffice to
show that such an argument is commonplace in this tradition concerning perfection.

Post 173:   See above p. 160.

Leg All i,15:   οἵ τε ἐντὸς δεκάδος ἀριθμοὶ ἢ γεννῶνται ἢ γεννῶσι
τοὺς ἐντὸς δεκάδος καὶ αὐτήν, ἡ δὲ ἑβδομὰς οὔτε γεννᾷ
τινα τῶν ἐντὸς δεκάδος ἀριθμῶν οὔτε γεννᾶται ὑπό τινος.
παρὸ μυθεύοντες οἱ Πυθαγόρειοι τῇ ἀειπαρθένῳ καὶ ἀμήτορι
αὐτὴν ἀπεικάζουσιν, ὅτι οὔτε ἀπεκυήθη οὔτε ἀποτέξεται.
(Interpretation of Gn 2,2--on the number seven).

Mut 2:   . . . προκοπῆς μὲν γὰρ δεκάς, ἑκατοντὰς δὲ τελειότητος
σύμβολον.   (Interpretation of Gn 17,1. Self-taught
Isaac represents hundred = perfection; and the priests
receive a hundred = first fruits from non-priests of the
Levitic tribe who give a tenth of their tenth and the
latter represent, therefore, progress). Cf. Spec Leg
i,156-57.

Mut 228:   οὐ διὰ τοῦτο καὶ ὁ Ἀβραὰμ ἐπὶ τῆς Σοδομιτῶν ἀπωλείας
ἀρξάμενος ἀπὸ πεντηκοντάδος εἰς δεκάδα τελευτᾷ, ποντιώ-
μενος καὶ ἱκετεύων, ἵν᾽, εἰ μὴ εὑρίσκοιτο ἐν γενέσει ἡ
παντελὴς εἰς ἐλευθερίαν ἄφεσις, ἧς σύμβολον ὁ πεντηκοστὸς
λόγος ἱερός (Lv 25,10), ἡ μέση παιδεία παραληφθῇ δεκάδι
παραριθμουμένη . . . (The two texts in view are Gn 18,
24f. and Lv 25,10; 50 represents the perfect release to
freedom and 10 as the lower education--i.e., progress).
The same exact point with the same texts in Sac 122.

Post 97:   ἡ δὲ ῥάβδος παιδείας σύμβολον, ἄνευ γὰρ τοῦ δυσωπηθῆναι
περὶ ἐνίων ἐπιπληχθῆναι νουθεσίαν ἐνδέξασθαι καὶ
σωφρονισμὸν ἀμήχανον. δεκὰς δὲ τῆς κατὰ προκοπὴν
τελειώσεως πίστις, ἀφ᾽ ἧς ὅσιον ἀπάρχεσθαι τῷ τάξαντι,
τῷ παιδεύσαντι, τῷ τὰ ἐλπισθέντα τελεσφορήσαντι.
(Interpretation of Lv 27,32-33)

To these compare Congr 105 (p. 60 above). What might be confusing is that ten/tithe is a symbol of progress through education
(paideia), whereas perfection is represented by the number seven,
hundred, or fifty. On the other hand, ten is the symbol of God
(Congr 105; cf. 94; 106; 107). In Congr 99, Abraham as progres-
ser--under the rod of paideia--gives tithe to Melchizedek, the
perfect priest. The explanation for this lies in grasping that
this system of numerology establishes proportional relationships
and in itself is no clue to the level of the hierarchy between
God and his creation where it belongs. It depends where it is

being applied. This is exactly parallel to the use of plastic
imagery in Philo (eikōn) which has misled scholars (see above
pp. 20-30), who have not observed its comparative usage. What
is clear is the principle involved in this comparative usage, the
one who gives the tithe stands below and is inferior to the one
who receives the tithe (cf. Spec Leg i,156-57). The point as to
this proportional application is explicitly made in the sequel
to Post 173:

Post 174: τὸ μὲν γὰρ πέρας τῆς κατὰ Σὴθ ἐπιστήμης ἀρχὴ τοῦ
δικαίου γέγονε Νῶε, τὴν δὲ τούτου τελείωσιν Ἀβραὰμ
ἄρχεται παιδεύεσθαι, ἡ δὲ ἀκροτάτη τοῦδε σοφία Μωυσέως
ἐστὶν ἡ ἄσκησις ἡ πρώτη.

This is a crucial point if one is not to be confused in his
reading of Philo. Ten is a perfect number, but seven is more
perfect than ten, as is also the case with fifty and hundred.
There are the perfect and the more perfect. It depends where in
the hierarchy the discussion is taking place. The highest level
of perfection is always immediacy to God.

Perfection as Approaching and Drawing Near God

At the most generalized level, one could say that perfection
is immediacy to God (see above pp. 75-76). And we have seen how
it underlies the various modulations of the theme of perfection.
Here we intend to show that the specific formulation of this in
terms of "approaching" or "drawing near" God is the same in this
tradition as in Hebrews.[9] In Hebrews we draw attention to the
following passages:

4,16: προσερχώμεθα οὖν μετὰ παρρησίας τῷ θρόνῳ τῆς χάριτος,
ἵνα λάβωμεν ἔλεος καὶ χάριν εὕρωμεν εἰς εὔκαιρον
βοήθειαν.

7,19: οὐδὲν γὰρ ἐτελείωσεν ὁ νόμος, ἐπεισαγωγὴ δὲ
κρείττονος ἐλπίδος, δι᾽ ἧς ἐγγίζομεν τῷ θεῷ.

7,25: ὅθεν καὶ σῴζειν εἰς τὸ παντελὲς δύναται τοὺς
προσερχομένους δι᾽ αὐτοῦ τῷ θεῷ . . .

10,1: σκιὰν γὰρ ἔχων ὁ νόμος . . . οὐδέποτε δύναται τοὺς
προσερχομένους τελειῶσαι.

10,22: προσερχώμεθα μετὰ ἀληθινῆς καρδίας ἐν πληροφορίᾳ
πίστεως . . .

11,6: χωρὶς δὲ πίστεως ἀδύνατον εὐαρεστῆσαι, πιστεῦσαι γὰρ
δεῖ τὸν προσερχόμενον (τῷ) θεῷ

12,18: οὐ γὰρ προσεληλύθατε ψηλαφωμένῳ

12,22: ἀλλὰ προσεληλύθατε Σιὼν ὄρει καὶ πόλει θεοῦ ζῶντος,
Ἰερουσαλὴμ ἐπουρανίῳ . . .

---

[9] On the Test Dan 6,1, see above pp. 87-92 and esp. 89-90.
In the Rabbinic tradition, neither the presence of angels nor the
plurality of heavens create any problem of distance from God. On
this point see Moore, Judaism, I, pp. 368-69 and Chap. V.

We note that such a commonplace religious theme is absent elsewhere in the NT, with the exception probably of Eph 2,18, 3,12,
and 1Pet 3,18. This is of course true of most of that with which
we have been dealing with in Hebrews. The point of significance
is that "to approach" or "to draw near" to God is to be made
perfect (7,19; 10,1). Where God is can be expressed either as
inside the heavenly Holy of Holies (4,16; 7,25; 10,1.22) or very
generally as in 11,6 or the heavenly Jerusalem, Mt. Zion, the
city of the living God (12,22). The polemic is of course against
Sinai which figures so prominently in the tradition of the perfection of Moses. And it is Christian faith, hope and confidence
which enables such approach or drawing near God (see above our
preliminary remarks on this--pp. 182-83).

What the following passages will show is that to approach
and draw near God, to become like Him (7,3), to have faith and
hope (7,19; 10,22; 11,6), to receive His covenant, Logos and law
(7,22; 28), etc. are only different ways of stating the theme of
perfection and enables us to understand how they follow each
other so abruptly in Hebrews (e.g., how does 7,19 connect with
20-22 and with the question of priesthood; we have already shown
the coherence of these elements in the tradition and here it will
be confirmed further).

QG IV,122:   . . . She gave birth to the model of character who
is by nature self-taught. . . . And (scripture) confirms
the perfection in all things of him who is born by saying, not that he was born in the old age, but after the
old age, of his father; that is, not in length of time
but as if to say that nothing in mortal life is untem-
poral but only that which comes after mortality and is
not corruptible. For it belongs peculiarly to the incorruptible soul which has been removed from its corporeal
nature and has been fitted to the incorporeal ruler (and)
sovereign of joys to sow gladness, for the race without
sorrow approaches and is near God." (Interpretation of
Gn 24,36; Marcus: Loeb.)

The passage speaks of the perfection of Isaac, the self-taught
type, incorruptible soul, which has withdrawn from corporeal
nature, "has been fitted" (probably--oikeiousthai--and better
translated as "has been made like") to God and it is his peculiar
privilege to approach and be near God (clearly--proserchesthai
and eggizein--as well shall see from other passages).

We note the same connection between perfection and drawing
near/approach to God in Hb 7,19 and 10,1. To be near God is to
be made like Him or to be like an exemplar of such proximity--it
is in this sense that Isaac who belongs to the "taxis" of the
"son of God" is a "model of character" (Marcus, f.n. h--"typon

ēthōn). As we have pointed out above this is the tradition which
underlies Hb 7,3 and 15--Melchizedek is like the son of God and
Jesus is like Melchizedek and that is why they are immortal and
priests forever, just as Isaac here is the "incorruptible soul."
This is confirmed by two further passages.

Op 144: . . . συγγενής τε καὶ ἀγχίσπορος ὢν τοῦ ἡγεμόνος, ἄτε
δὴ πολλοῦ ῥυέντος εἰς αὐτὸν τοῦ θείου πνεύματος, πάντα
καὶ λέγειν καὶ πράττειν ἐσπούδαζεν εἰς ἀρέσκειαν τοῦ
πατρὸς καὶ βασιλέως, ἑπόμενος κατ' ἴχνος αὐτῷ ταῖς ὁδοῖς,
ἃς λεωφόρους ἀνατέμνουσιν ἀρεταί, διότι μόναις ψυχαῖς
θέμις προσέρχεσθαι τέλος ἡγουμέναις τὴν πρὸς τὸν
γεννήσαντα θεὸν ἐξομοίωσιν.

The passage speaks of the first man, the ancestor of the human
race, made of body and soul, etc. (134ff.), made directly by God
and hence superior to all other men (140), the only citizen of
the world (142), which was earlier peopled by natures rational,
divine, without body and intelligible and some with bodies like
the stars. Holding concourse with such, the first man lived in
unmixed happiness (143-44). Being a <u>kin</u> and close relative of
God, since the divine spirit flowed into him with fullness, in
all that he spoke and did he was eager <u>to please</u> God, following
Him step by step on the lofty highways cut open by the virtues,
<u>because to approach God is lawful only for souls which consider
that the ultimate end of life is to be like God their Maker</u>.

We have observed earlier, that given the monotheism of this
tradition, the closest one can come to God is to be His son, i.e.,
in terms of a metaphor of relationship. Therefore, when Jesus
saves the Christians who approach God through him (7,25), he
gives them the same status as himself--sons of God and his brothers (2,10-13), he opens the way into the Holy of Holies (10,19-
22), they are perfected as he was perfected as "son" (2,10-13;
5,8-10; 7,28). We observe also that pleasing God is associated
with approaching Him as in Hb 11,6. Though the term here is
"areskeia," "euarestein" is used often by Philo to describe the
goal of human existence (cf. Praem 24; QG I,85; IV,88; cf. Wis
Sol 8,9-10.18).

Som ii,223: ἀλλὰ γὰρ τοσαύτη περὶ τὸ θεῖόν ἐστιν ὑπερβολὴ τοῦ
βεβαίου, ὥστε καὶ ταῖς ἐπιλελεγμέναις φύσεσιν ἐχυρότητος,
ὡς ἀρίστου κτήματος, μεταδίδωσιν. αὐτίκα γέ τοι τὴν
πλήρη χαρίτων διαθήκην ἑαυτοῦ - νόμος δ' ἐστὶ καὶ λόγος
τῶν ὄντων πρεσβύτατος - ὡς ἂν ἐπὶ βάσεως τῆς τοῦ δικαίου
ψυχῆς ἄγαλμα θεοειδὲς ἱδρύσεσθαι παγίως φησίν . . .

227: . . . καὶ Μωυσεῖ μέντοι θεοπρόπιον τοιόνδε, "σὺ
αὐτοῦ στῆθι μετ' ἐμοῦ," δι' οὗ τὰ λεχθέντα ἀμφω παρίσταται, τό τε μὴ κλίνεσθαι τὸν ἀστεῖον καὶ ἡ τοῦ ὄντος περὶ
πάντα βεβαιότης.

228: καὶ γὰρ τῷ ὄντι τὸ τῷ θεῷ <u>συνεγγίζον οἰκειοῦται</u> κατὰ τὸ ἄτρεπτον αὐτοστατοῦν, καὶ ἡρεμήσας ὁ νοῦς, ἡλίκον ἐστὶν ἀγαθὸν ἠρεμία, σαφῶς ἔγνω . . . ὑπέλαβεν, ὅτι ἢ <u>θεῷ μόνῳ</u> προσκεκλήρωται ἢ <u>τῇ μεταξὺ φύσει θνητοῦ καὶ ἀθανάτου γένους</u>.

For the context of this passage and what follows--the perfection of the highpriest--see above pp. 58-59. God shares with chosen natures from the abundance of his stability. He <u>establishes</u> firmly the <u>covenant</u> = <u>law</u> = <u>Logos</u> as if on the pedestal of the soul as a god-like image (223). There follow examples--Noah (Gn 9,11), Abraham (Gn 18,22)--and then <u>Moses</u> (Dt 5,31). It shows the two aspects, that the praiseworthy man does not swerve and the complete <u>stability</u> of God. For the <u>one who draws near to God becomes like</u> the Existent on account of his immutable self-standing. Such <u>rest</u> belongs either to God alone or to a nature which is between the mortal and immortal kind. Such is Moses (Dt 5,5) and the highpriest inside the Holy of Holies (see above pp. 187-88) who becomes like the Unbegotten God.

What this passage clarifies further is that the <u>Logos</u>, the <u>law</u> and the <u>covenant</u> are equivalent and are the source of our share in God's stability (<u>bebaios</u>) and we do so by <u>drawing near to God</u> and <u>becoming like Him</u>. This is exemplified in the highest degree by Moses (the next passage will make this clear) and by the highpriest inside the Holy of Holies, where he like Moses is neither man nor God, but a nature in between the two and immortal. In other words, all this is another description of perfection. This explains the connection between Hb 7,19 and 20ff. What the author of Hebrews has done is that he has replaced the law and covenant and reason (logos in man) with Christian faith and hope, which then become the source of the stability of the soul and make for our approach and drawing near to God. Though not exact, the same conceptualization is clearly indicated in Hb 6,19-20 and in briefer form in 7,19. So also 10,19ff. The exemplar of this is no longer Moses, Levi or Aaron, but Jesus. It is for this reason that we have the language of "bebaios" associated with faith and hope in Hebrews (cf. 3,6; 3,14; 6,19; 10,23--note "akline" and Som ii,227). It is for the same reason that he found the text of the new covenant in Jeremiah useful for his argument since it speaks of another covenant and here the laws are placed in the minds and hearts of men and for which there is no need for Levitic instruction. It is therefore the <u>better</u> covenant of which Jesus is the surety and Christian hope is the <u>better</u> hope, for we shall see that faith, hope and stability are associated quite frequently in this tradition.

Post 23: . . . συμβαίνει γὰρ τὸ (μὲν) τῷ ἑστῶτι πλησιάζον
ἠρεμίας διὰ πόθον ὁμοιότητος ἐφίεσθαι. τὸ μὲν οὖν
ἀκλινῶς ἐστιν ὁ θεός ἐστι, τὸ δὲ κινητὸν ἡ γένεσις, ὥστε
ὁ μὲν προσιὼν θεῷ στάσεως ἐφίεται . . .

26: ἐλπὶς μὲν γὰρ τῶν ἀγαθῶν οὖσα προσδοκία ἐκ τοῦ
φιλοδώρου θεοῦ τὴν διάνοιαν ἀρτᾷ . . .

27: . . . Ἀβραὰμ δὲ ὁ σοφὸς ἐπειδὴ ἔστηκε, συνεγγίζει τῷ
ἑστῶτι θεῷ, λέγει γὰρ ὅτι "ἑστὼς ἦν ἔναντι κυρίου καὶ
ἐγγίσας εἶπεν" (Gn 18,22-23). ὄντως γὰρ ἀτρέπτω ψυχῇ
πρὸς τὸν ἄτρεπτον θεὸν μόνῃ πρόσοδός ἐστιν, καὶ ἡ τούτον
διακειμένη τὸν τρόπον ἐγγὺς ὡς ἀληθῶς ἵσταται δυνάμεως
θείας.

28: τό γε μὴν χρησθὲν τῷ πανσόφῳ Μωυσῇ λόγιον ἐναργέστατα
δηλοῖ τὴν περὶ τὸν σπουδαῖον βεβαιοτάτην εὐστάθειαν . . .
(Dt 5,31), ἐξ οὗ δύο παρίσταται, ἓν μὲν ὅτι τὸ ὂν τὰ ἄλλα
κινοῦν καὶ τρέπον ἀκίνητόν τε καὶ ἄτρεπτον, ἕτερον δ' ὅτι
τῆς ἑαυτοῦ φύσεως, ἠρεμίας, τῷ σπουδαίῳ μεταδίδωσιν. . . .

30: ὅταν μὲν οὖν πρὸς τὸ ἴδιον ἀγαθὸν καλῇ, "σὺ μετ' ἐμοῦ
στῆθι" φησίν . . . ὅταν δὲ πρὸς τὸ οἰκεῖον γενέσεως
ἔρχηται, ὀρθότατα ἐρεῖ, "ἐγὼ μετὰ σοῦ καταβήσομαι."
(I.e., Gn 46,4)

The immediate context is a discussion of the instability of Cain
who goes into the land called "tossing" (salos)--i.e., Nod.   On
the other hand, it is a principle, that proximity to something
stable leads to a desire for rest (ēremia) because of the desire
to be like it (pothos homiotētos).   God is unswervingly (aklinōs)
stable, and the one who draws near him desires stability (stasis).
In contrast the foolish man bears the curse of Dt 28,65-66 ("has
no rest"--anapauein--and "your life is hanging before your eyes").
Hence also the saying in Dt 21,23--which means that instead of
hanging on God this one hangs on his body, a wooden mass, and
gives up hope for desire.   For hope being an expectation of good
things hangs upon the bountiful God.   The examples of such stability and proximity are Abraham, the wise man, who draws near God
who stands, since he stands (Gn 18,22-23).   For only to a soul
which is truly unchanging is there access/approach (prosodos) to
the Unchanging God and such a disposition (tropos--note the characteristic generalizing application) truly stands near the divine
power (Lord in Gn 18,22).   This is of course less than perfection
since Moses stands beside God himself, beyond and above his
powers (see above pp. 71f.--Sac 5-8; Quod Deus 109-10).   Hence the
clearest example is Moses (Dt 5,31) which shows, that God is the
Unmoved Mover (an Aristotelian formulation) and that He shares
His own nature with Moses, the "spoudaios," namely, His rest.
This perfection of the Moses type is clarified further.   For when
God calls someone to his own peculiar good he makes the statement
in Dt 5,31.   But to the progresser Jacob, still in affinity to
the world of creation, he speaks the word in the Gn 46,4 ("I will

go down with you"--Jacob is still one who is in movement).

This passage states as a principle the correlation between proximity and likeness which is the basis of the argument in Hb 7,3 and 15-17. The stability of God is here interpreted as "rest" (ēremia, anapauein) and this is what He shares with the perfect (cf. Hb 4,10--Christians share in God's own rest). It is by faith and hope, in Hebrews, that Christians have such proximity (7,19; 10,22) and enter into God's rest (3,12.19; 4,2-3, etc.). In Hb 11,1, the author has reformulated such a statement as--"hope is the expectation of good things" (Post 26)--to argue that Christian faith in fact is the stable reality (hypostasis) of hope of good things (cf. 9,11--Christ is the highpriest of good things which have already come into existence) since it accomplishes the Christian's proximity to God (10,19-22; 12,22--"you have come"--the perfect tense; 6,19-20; 7,19, etc.). As we have stated above, it is for this reason that the language of stability is associated in Hebrews with faith and hope. For the remainder, the passage confirms that here we are dealing with a variation of the theme of perfection--i.e., approach and pro- ximity to God. It should be noted that Abraham's proximity to one of God's powers is inferior (as is Jacob) to Moses who stands beside God Himself. Perfection, in other words, is unmediated access or approach. Though in 7,25, it would seem that the author thinks of Jesus as a mediator--"through him"--in every other case it is a matter of direct approach to God which Jesus has procured by his sacrifice and entry into the Holy of Holies (4,16; 6,19-20; 10,19ff.). In the next chapter we will examine further the extent to which the author has modified primitive Christian soteriology. Even at this point it is clear that sal- vation must imply the same status of "sonship" (2,10ff.), direct and immediate access to God (10,19ff.), and Jesus is described as our "forerunner" and exemplar of perfect faith (6,20; 12,1ff.).

Two further passages, which belong at the level of progress rather than perfection, will show terminological similarity with Hebrews, and we will only quote them briefly:

Mig 57: οὐκοῦν ὅτι καὶ πρὸς βοήθειαν δύναμις ἀρωγὸς εὐτρεπὴς ἐφεδρεύει παρὰ θεῷ καὶ αὐτὸς ὁ ἡγεμὼν ἐγγυτέρω πρόσεισιν ἐπ' ὠφελείᾳ τῶν ἀξίων ὠφελεῖσθαι, δεδήλωται. . . .

59: οὗτος ὁ ὅρος ἐστὶ τοῦ μεγάλου λεώ, τὸ τῷ θεῷ συνεγγίζειν ἢ "ᾧ θεὸς συνεγγίζει." (Interpretation of Dt 4,6-7; context--Abraham as progresser--53ff.; cf. Hb 4,16.)

Praem 84: . . . κἂν εἰ πύθοιτό τις, ποῖον ἔθνος μέγα, . . . ἀποκρίνασθαι, ᾧ ὁ θεός ἐστιν ἐπήκοος ἱεροπρεπεστάτων εὐχῶν καὶ ταῖς ἀπὸ καθαροῦ τοῦ συνειδότος κατακλήσεσι συνεγγίζων. (Interpretation of Dt 4,7; cf. Hb 10,22.)

Cf. further Plant 64--perfection of Levitic mind, and Mig 132--
Abraham draws near to God through faith.[10]

Summary and Conclusions

Hebrews 7 is a coherent whole and not a series of unrelated
arguments. It should be seen within the framework of the series
of comparisons in chapters 1-7. We have shown to a large extent
that the tradition of intermediaries and perfection enables us to
see that the themes in these chapters are different aspects of
the same tradition and fit together in the progression of the
author's argument. Specifically, it is the tradition of the perfection of Levi, Aaron and Melchizedek as exemplars of perfect
priesthood which lies at the basis of this chapter, just as the
tradition of the perfection of Moses stands at the basis of
3,1-6.

An emphatic point in the author's argument is that Melchizedek and Jesus are immortal and therefore priests forever in
contrast to the Levites and Aaronides who are mortal men, sinful
and beset with weakness (vss. 3,8, 15-16, 23-24, 28). The reason
for this argument lies in the fact that such immortality is the
mark of the perfect priest in this tradition. The priest/high-
priest is perfect in the Holy of Holies, belongs to the middle
"taxis" in that he is neither God nor man, but divine, having
left all dealings with the world of creation (Som ii,231-35; Quis
Her 84; Sac 120). He belongs to this "taxis" by virtue of the
principle that what is close to God becomes like Him. And in a

---

[10]The background of this tradition of perfection, of
approach and becoming like God, is obviously Platonic. Cf.
Theaetetus, 176a-b; Republic 613a; Phaedo 82a-b, etc. Most illu-
minating in this respect is Albinus, Chap. 28, from which we
quote some close parallels: . . . διὸ καὶ πειρᾶσθαι χρὴ(ναι)
ἐνθένδε ἐκεῖσε φεύγειν ὅτι τάχιστα, φυγὴ δὲ ὁμοίωσις θεῷ κατὰ τὸ
δυνατόν. . . . τὴν δὲ θεῷ ἑπομένην τε καὶ εἰκασμένην ψυχήν . . .
ἀκόλουθον οὖν τῇ ἀρχῇ τὸ τέλος εἴη ἂν τὸ ἐξομοιωθῆναι θεῷ, θεῷ
δηλονότι τῷ ἐπουρανίῳ, μὴ τῷ μὰ Δία ὑπερουρανίῳ, ὃς οὐκ ἀρετὴν
ἔχει, ἀμείνων δ᾽ ἐστι ταύτης . . . Perfection in this tradition
is to rise above the normal range of morality and virtues, though
these are a part of the training and preparation of the soul, and
be made like God as far as is possible for humans--hence "epoura-
nios" or "hyperouranios"--cf. Hb 7,26. At the end of the chapter, the author speaks of the cleansing of the spirit (daimon) in
man through school learning. In Phaedo 82b, no soul can attain
the divine nature which is not absolutely pure when it leaves the
body and this is attained by the practice of philosophy. For a
more general discussion of this theme, see Festugière, Personal
Religion among the Greeks, Chap. VII. On the relation between
flight, becoming like God and perfection, see Philo Fug 63; 88-
89; 96-99; Sac 120 (see above p. 60) and Hb 6,19.

monotheistic tradition, the closest kinship one can have with
God is to belong to the "taxis" of the son of God, which is perfection (Conf 145-48; Som i,173; Congr 177). This is the basis
of the argument in 7,3 and 15-16. Melchizedek and Jesus belong
to the "taxis" of such proximity to God, and are therefore immortal. On the other hand, the author argues that the Levitic-
Aaronide priests are not perfect since they are mortal, sinful
and beset with weakness, which is evidenced by the fact that the
OT represents them as offering sacrifices for their own sins
(7,27; 5,1-3).

That they are mortal men is not a matter of historical
observation in the author's argument. For Jesus also died and
there is no argument here on the basis of the resurrection. In
this tradition a bodily resurrection would have implied imperfection, a fall to the realm of flesh and blood, rather than perfection and immortality. The argument is on the basis of "taxis."
"Taxis" is the class or status in the hierarchical order between
God and his creation. The highest "taxis" or perfection is
exemplified in this tradition by various religious figures--
Moses, Aaron, Levi, Melchizedek, Isaac and others, and the theme
of perfection is modulated according to the exigencies of the
biblical narrative. Apart from their personal historical destiny,
their real significance for contemporary men lies in the fact
that they exemplify types of men (typos, taxis, paradeigma, etc.),
souls, dispositions (tropos, diathesis, etc.), virtues, which
constitute their immortal aspect and significance (see above pp.
46-48). This explains the curious fact that both Melchizedek
and Jesus are immortal and priests forever in Hb 7. The author
accepted the exemplary significance of Melchizedek since on this
basis he could prove from the OT (Ps 110,4 and Gn 14,17-20) the
superiority of Jesus over Levi and Aaron.

It is in terms of such a tradition that one can understand
the argument from genealogy in Hb 7,3 and 11-18. It has not been
clearly recognized that in vs. 11-18 we have such an argument.
Genealogy in this tradition is not primarily a matter of history
and biography, but about "facts of nature," "types of men,"
things which can benefit the soul. And not to have a genealogy
is a matter of great praise since it underlines the immortality
of such a type, namely, its virtue (Congr 43; Abr 31). Such is
Melchizedek who is without genealogy, i.e., without human descent,
and therefore truly immortal and eternal priest. That Jesus
traces his genealogy to the tribe of Judah (7,13-14) is only a

partial proof that he belongs to a different "taxis" than Aaron's. What is more significant, according to the author, is that he is like Melchizedek and therefore also immortal and eternal priest (7,15-16), which the matter of historical genealogy would not necessarily prove.

Related to the above, is the understanding in this tradition that perfection, proximity to God, implies separation from the realm of flesh and blood, mortality and weakness, and stated differently sinlessness. It is the highest "taxis," peculiar to God and divine men. The highpriest in this tradition is free fom both intentional and unintentional sins (Virt 176-77; Spec Leg i,230; iii,134-35; Fug 108-109; Som ii,185). In Hb 7,26, the author describes the sinless perfection of Jesus as priest in similar terms. Noteworthy is the understanding of sin as weakness and the description of sinlessness as "separated from sinners," "higher than the heavens" (cf. Albinus, Chap. 18 and f.n. 10, p. 209). This is the precise understanding of sinlessness in this tradition. Probably, the same view underlies the description of the highpriest in Wis Sol 18,21 as "amemptos." The author's counter argument is that this contradicts the depiction of the Levitic-Aaronide priest in the O.T.

When the author argues that perfection did not come through the Levitic priesthood (7,11-18), that the law perfected nothing (7,19) and that Jesus is the guarantee of a better covenant (7,20-22), these are not unrelated themes in this chapter, but have their basis in the tradition of the perfection of the Levites and Aaronides. They were entrusted with the keeping and guardianship of the words, laws and covenant of God. The perfect Levites belong to the "taxis" of the teacher (cf. Hb 5,12) and lead others to perfection by instructing them in the doctrines and principles of wisdom (= words, laws and covenant of God). In other words, perfection comes through the "paideia" of the Levitic-Aaronide priesthood who are the teachers and guardians of the laws and covenant of God (Quod Det 62-68). The art of legislation is a mark of the perfection of the Levites and Moses who traces his genealogy from them is the archetypal legislator. The perfection of the Levites as legislators is characterized by their boast of rising above the world of creation and its boundaries (cf. Hb 7,26--"higher than the heavens") and their exclusive adherence to God alone (Congr 131-34; Sac 131-32). When Hebrews uses the same language--"to hold fast," "to grasp," "boast," etc. (3,6; 3,14; 4,14; 6,18; 10,23)--to characterize

Christian faith and hope, he has thereby replaced the laws and covenant as the means to perfection with faith and hope. Instead of the law, there is the "better hope," and instead of the covenant, there is the "better covenant." It is these which lead to proximity to God (7,19-22). Related to this is the fact that, in this tradition, the highest form of the covenant is God himself, in that he becomes our portion (Mut 58-59; QG III,42). When, therefore, Hebrews represents Jesus as the guarantee of a better covenant, it is the same as saying that he procures perfection rather than the Levitic priesthood, laws and covenant. The author found the new covenant (in the very fact that it is called new) in Jeremiah 31,31-34, a useful text for his counter argument, since it also speaks of God's placing the laws in men's minds and hearts and that there is no need for instruction (a mark in this tradition of perfection--cf. Hb 5,11ff.), which I think implies for the author that there is no need for Levitic instruction. It is a covenant which establishes entry into the true heavenly Holy of Holies (8,6-12; 9,15-24).

It is in the context of the thematics of the perfection of the Levitic-Aaronide priesthood that one must set the argument concerning Melchizedek and Gn 14. In this tradition he is the Logos, God's own priest, has God for his portion (like Levi and Moses), and like Isaac--who belongs to the "taxis" of son of God --self-taught and self-learnt, i.e., the "taxis" of the teacher (Leg All iii,79-82). Abraham, while still a progresser under the rod of paideia, paid him tithes (Congr 99). Whereas, the perfect priest rises above the nine parts of the universe and pays tithe to the Tenth, God (Congr 105). In other words, who pays tithes to whom differentiates the progresser from the perfect. While one pays tithe to the intermediary Logos-priest Melchizedek, he is still a progresser, but when one pays tithe to God the Tenth, he is a perfect priest. The one who pays is inferior to the recipient. This is the principle in the argument of the author in Hb 7,4-10, and is explicitly stated in vs. 7 in terms of who blesses whom. Further, this explains the inherent connection between this argument and what follows in 7,11ff. They are part and parcel of the theme of perfection. The Genesis passage was undoubtedly chosen also because of the fact that it was used in this tradition as the basis of the Levites receiving the tithes (unidentified QG passage), which means that they were priests of the order of Melchizedek. And the etymology of Melchizedek has its significance in the fact that the Levites received from God the prize of the <u>covenant of peace</u> and <u>covenant of eternal priesthood</u> (Ebr 65-75, ref. to Nu 25,12-13).

A singularly important modulation of the theme of perfection is that, at the most generalized level, it implies immediacy to God. One of its specific formulations is in terms of <u>"approaching" and "drawing near"</u> God (4,16; 7,19; 7,25; 10,1; 10,22; 11,6; 12,18-22). There is a very rich level of association between Hebrews and the tradition at this point (QG IV,122; Op 144; Som ii,223-28; Post 23-30; Mig 57-59; Praem 84). We will summarize first the different aspects of the tradition:

(a) It is the privilege of the perfect, characterized by an incorruptible soul, withdrawal from corporeal nature, etc., to approach and be near God. The exemplars ("model of character") are Isaac, Moses and the highpriest in the Holy of Holies.

(b) To be close to God is to become like Him, to share in His nature--"stability," "rest." The source of such stability and rest are the logos=covenant=law which God firmly establishes in the soul. The ultimate goal of life is to be like God.

(c) As progressers, Abraham and Jacob do not reach the highest level of proximity or stability. Such ultimate nearness and stability is exemplified by Moses.

(d) Approach and nearness to God is associated with pleasing God, a clean conscience, and God's help (boetheia)--cf. Hb 4,16; 10,22; 11,6; Praem 24; QG I,85; IV,88; Wis Sol 8,9-10 and 18.

(e) On the contrary, the fool has no rest and replaces hope with passionate desire. Hope is the expectation of good things and hangs on the bountiful God.

In Hebrews, we have the association of proximity with perfection (7,19; 10,1). That such proximity implies likeness to God or to exemplars of such likeness is the basis of the argument in 7,3 and 15-16. The closest likeness, in terms of kinship, that one can have to God is to be His son. Hence to approach God and be saved implies that Jesus must be the perfected son and Christians have the same status--sons of God and brothers of Jesus (2,10-13; 5,8-10; 7,25 and 28). And his priesthood provides for such immediacy and approach to God (7,25; 10,19-22). Hebrews, furthermore, has replaced the law and covenant as the basis of approach, nearness and participation in God's stability or rest with Christian faith and hope which is anchored in the soul (6,19-20; 7,19; 10,19ff.). It is for this reason that the language of stability is associated with faith and hope in Hebrews (3,6; 3,14; 6,19; 10,23). He has reformulated the under-

standing of faith and hope as the expectation of good things
in such a way that Christian faith and hope are actually the
basis of perfection. Faith is therefore the stable reality
(hypostasis) of things hoped for (11,1; 9,11--the good things
have already come into existence). It is faith which enables
one to enter into God's own rest (3,12; 3,19; 4,2-3; 4,10). It
is faith and hope which have accomplished the approach and nearness to God (10,19-22; 12,22--"you have come"; 6,19-20; 7,19).

In conclusion, one could say that all this is really an
extended commentary on Wis Sol 6,18-19:

> ἀγάπη δὲ τήρησις νόμων αὐτῆς,
> προσοχὴ δὲ νόμων βεβαίωσις ἀφθαρσίας,
> ἀφθαρσία δὲ ἐγγὺς εἶναι ποιεῖ θεοῦ.

CHAPTER SEVEN

THE PERFECTION OF JESUS (Hb 2,5-18; 4,14-5,10)

Introduction: The recognition that in Hb 2,5-10 we have
formulations from the realm of primitive Christian apocalyptic
(vs. 5-9; 14b-15) as well as the language of Hellenism (vs. 10-
11) has led both Michel and Spicq to divide this section into two
parts--vs. 5-9 and 10ff. For Michel vs. 17 constitutes the
introduction to a new theme. In terms of content, Michel and
Spicq accent the apocalyptic elements and consider them to be the
clue to the author's concern and the language of Hellenism as
embroidery. Hence for Michel, the motivation for vs. 5-9 lies
in either a veiled protest against the view that this aeon has
been handed over to the angels or the devil (Det 32,8 LXX; Gal
4,3; Hermas, Vis 3,4,1) or an antithesis to an angel-Christ cult.
And that it is Christ as the apocalyptic "Son of Man" who has the
promise of world rule (1Cor 15,27; p. 136). Spicq on a similar
vein considers the author to be arguing against the view that the
world and the natural elements are subject to the angels rather
than to men (Dt 32,8 LXX; 1Enoch 89,70-76, etc.; II, p. 30) and
that Jesus is the apocalyptic "Son of Man" (Mk 13,36, etc.;
II, p. 31).

In contrast, we have the view of Kaesemann, for whom vs. 10
is crucial, that underlying this section is the gnostic myth of
the "Urmensch"--the redeemed redeemer (perfected and sanctified),
the pre-existence of the redeemed sons and their identity with
the redeemer (the idea of "suggeneia"), earthly existence as
enslavement to powers antagonistic to God and life in the body
as imprisonment (vs. 14-15; see Michel, pp. 135-36 for summary
and discussion).

Both these contrasting interpretations share the common
assumption that there is no real polemical situation in Hebrews
and hence they seek for a singular theological point of view in
the writing, whether apocalyptic or gnostic. This has led these
commentators to stress one or the other of the religious traditions one finds in Hebrews at the cost of the neglect or under-
estimation of the other features. For the difficulties of a
gnostic interpretation of this chapter, see Michel, pp. 135-36
and 143 (that there is no evidence in Hebrews of the pre-
existence of the sons or their identity with the preexistent

redeemer in a naturalistic sense, etc.). To this one could add
that vs. 5-9 and 14b-15 are quite straightforward pieces of early
Christian apocalyptic with no gnostic tendencies and that fur-
thermore the rest of Hebrews does not elaborate on these themes.
Similarly, the hellenistic parallels for vs. 10-11 (mostly from
Philo) do not support the gnostic thesis. I do not see how
Philo can be used for a gnostic religious viewpoint.

On the other hand, the attempts to interpret this chapter
exclusively from the perspective of apocalyptic breaks down in
vs. 10-11 and does not illuminate the coherence of the author's
argument--Michel has to divie the chapter into three units: vs.
5-9; 10-16; 17-18. There is no sound basis for such a division
of the chapter in that the theme concerning the angels occurs in
vs. 5 and 16 and themes from primitive Christian apocalyptic in
vs. 5-9 and 14-15. Clearly it is a coherent unit in the author's
argument and a satisfactory interpretation must explicate this
coherence. The artificial character of Michel's interpretation
is evident from the numerous and even curious history of religions explanations that he has to introduce in order to maintain
a consistently apocalyptic viewpoint in vs. 10ff. For example:
that vs. 12-13 are both "doxological" and "soteriological" and
that in the doxology one finds hellenistic statements on the All
and creator of All (p. 143); that it is in the "style of revelation" in which the revealer presents himself as the intercessor
(Vorbeter) for the community and reveals his solidarity with them
and that this is a "cultic unity" between the revealer and the
children God has given him (p. 134); that the concept "Herzog
ihres Heiles" (vs. 10) belongs to the predications of the "hellenistic community" (p. 143) and that vs. 10 is an "Ausdruck auch
einer orientalisch-hellenistischen Erlösererwartung" (p. 144).
The only evidence for all this is the "Son of Man" in Daniel and
Enoch which somehow gets connected with Acts 5,31 and 7,35. Such
a history of religions picture for Hb 2 is quite doubtful and
introduces categories whose validity has not been established and
the documentation hardly bears the weight of such hypothetically
conceived traditions.

Although Spicq provides numerous lexical parallels, his
interpretation of vs. 10ff. is subsumed under such broad dogmatic
formulations that it does not illuminate the questions of history: "Comment et pourquoi le Christ a-t-il souffert? . . . Si
Dieu a abaissé le Christ au-dessous des anges par l'incarnation
et la mort, c'est parce qu'il devait être non seulement roi, mais

prêtre-sauveur, et expier les péchés de l'humanité" (II, p. 29).

We intend to show that the tradition of intermediaries and perfection can explain the coherence of the chapter itself as well as its contextual rationale, the character of the religious issue in focus, and the author's reinterpretation which is the locus of the engagement of the traditions which the commentators have characterized as apocalyptic and hellenistic.

The Context

The themes in this chapter concerning angels, highpriest, the heavenly man who did not originally partake of flesh and blood, and perfection belong together. We have already shown the connection between these themes and 3,1-6, where Moses as the perfect highpriest, the perfect man and the one called above has, in the author's reinterpretation, been replaced by Jesus, who is proven to be superior to Moses (see above the summary of chap. 5, esp. pp. 179-80). The particular theme in this chapter which belongs to this tradition is that of the perfection of the heavenly man who does not partake of flesh and blood and the angelic characterization of the perfection of men. This forms the context for the polemical thrust in the author's argument in vs. 5 and 16 and they are an integral part of the argument concerning perfection and intermediaries.

The Heavenly Man and Angels in the Schema of Perfection

We have shown that perfection in this tradition implies unmediated access to God. On the other hand when one reaches perfection his status is equal to that of the intermediaries. For example, Moses in his perfection is the Logos, archangel, man of God, highpriest, prophet, the one called above, etc. When Abraham is perfect he is added to the angels = people of God (Sac 5, see above pp. 63ff.). The angels are "sons of God" and Moses calls excellent men (i.e., perfect men) "sons of God" and wicked men "bodies" (QG I,92, see above p. 41). In other words the destiny of the perfect is angelic existence and status and with this the author of Hebrews is in agreement--12,22-24. In this particular instance his contention with the tradition lies at a different point. The Christian belief that the earthly Jesus, the man of flesh and blood, is the basis of salvation would have implied in this tradition imperfection rather than perfection/ salvation. The perfect heavenly man is incorporeal, immortal and without any share (ametochos) in corruptible and earthly essence

(cf. the language of Hb 2,14; for the character of the distinction between the earthly and heavenly man and its relation to the
tradition of perfection, see above chap. 1, section C and p. 40).
For the author of Hebrews, therefore, it was essential to connect
the earthly Jesus of flesh and blood--his suffering and death--
with the accomplishment of perfection/salvation (2,10). In terms
of this tradition, it would have been necessary to show that
Jesus himself became perfect in such a state of earthly existence
--since that would have been under question--and accomplished
perfection/salvation for others. This is precisely the thrust of
the author's reinterpretation of the tradition in this chapter.

The Human Situation--Flesh, Blood and Imperfection

That perfection and immediacy to God implies rising above
the realm of body, flesh and blood (earthly existence) we have
already met in numerous contexts and needs no further proof. We
draw attention here to another set of statements which describe
the human situation of imperfection in Hebrews: τοῖς πειραζομέ-
νοις (2,18; 4,15); ταῖς ἀσθενείαις ἡμῶν (4,15; 5,2; 7,28); τοῖς
ἀγνοοῦσιν καὶ πλανωμένοις (5,2); ἀποθνήσκοντες ἄνθρωποι (7,8.23).
These terms describe the human state of sin/imperfection, as the
context of these passages clearly show, with the exception of
4,15 where the author has introduced a novel distinction--that
Jesus shared in human weakness and temptation, but without sin.
The terminology is clearly from the realm of hellenistic Judaism
and in Philo it describes the human state of imperfection.

In <u>Philo</u>, God does not share in weakness (ametochon
astheneias) and true rest belongs to Him alone (Cher 90). Whereas disquiet is peculiar to human weakness (anthrōpinē astheneia),
God is free from all irrational passions of the soul and bodily
parts (Quod Deus 52). Man and creation in contrast to the excellence of God suffer from natural weakness (physikē astheneia)--
Quod Deus 80; Sepc Leg i,293. Whereas perfection, which is proximity and assimilation to God, implies detachment and separation
from the realm of mortality, flesh, blood, passions and weakness
(cf. the language in <u>Hb 7,26</u>). Wandering (planasthai) is opposite to the way of wisdom and good sense (phronēsis) which leads
to ἀπάθειαν ἀντὶ παθῶν καὶ ἀντὶ ἀγνοίας ἐπιστήμην καὶ ἀντὶ κακῶν
ἀγαθά (Plant 97-98). "Aphesis" (Lv 25,9ff.) represents the perfect freedom of the soul which has shaken off the wandering (planasthai) of the past and has found harbour in the nature which
does not wander (i.e., God; Congr 108). The highpriest who is

not perfect may be bodily inside the Holy of Holies, but his soul
is wandering (planasthai) outside (Quis Her 82). Philo corrects
the mistaken notion that the term "planets" might lead to, for no
occupant of the heaven which partakes (metechein) of the divine
nature wanders (planasthai)--Decal 104. Joseph is a negative
exemplar of such wandering--the true man (Logos) finds him wandering on the way (Gn 37,15) and since he is sunk in the hollows
of the body and senses he is found wandering instead of progressing, the mark of a man who does not submit to learning (Quod Det
10; 17ff.; cf. Fug 127ff.). Similarly, Israel's wandering in the
wilderness is a mark of its imperfection (Mig 154, see above p.
132). Ignorance (agnoia) is a pathos of the soul which destroys
its power of hearing and seeing and is the cause of all sins
(aitia pantōn hamartēmatōn; Ebr 154-61). The chief cause of
ignorance is flesh and assimilation (oikeiōsis) to it. It is the
foundation of "agnoias" and "amathias" (Gig 29-30). Some of the
characteristics of the uncultured city of Cain are "agnoia,"
"apaideusia," and "amathia" (Post 52).

Thus Hebrews shares with this tradition the understanding
of sin and imperfection as the realm of flesh and blood, human
weakness, ignorance, wandering, trial and temptation. Once the
character of the tradition with which he was faced is grasped,
the bold and revolutionary character of his reinterpretation
become evident. He has drawn upon primitive Christian apocalyptic to reaffirm that Jesus is superior to all intermediaries--the
age to come and all things, including the angels (an issue which
could not have arisen in the realm of apocalyptic), will be subject to him (vs. 5-9; cf. 1Cor 15,27; Eph 1,22)--as the "man."
Then his reinterpretation takes the bold step of arguing in the
language of the tradition of intermediaries and perfection that
Jesus' suffering and death were a divinely appropriate path to
his own perfection and that thereby he became the cause of the
perfection/salvation of others (2,10ff.; 5,7-10; note the language of "causes"). The bold and revolutionary thesis of the
author of Hebrews, which we shall now elaborate upon, is that
Jesus has entered and participated in the realm of imperfection
(flesh, blood and temptation) and has accomplished perfection
within this realm and thereby has opened the way for others to
participate in perfection within this realm of creation and not
outside of it. In this respect the author has overcome a duality
in the tradition with which he was dealing.

The Unity of Creation and the Problem of Perfection

Hb 5,11: ὅ τε γὰρ ἁγιάζων καὶ οἱ ἁγιαζόμενοι ἐξ ἑνὸς πάντες δι' ἣν αἰτίαν οὐκ ἐπαισχύνεται ἀδελφοὺς αὐτοὺς καλεῖν . . .

Hb 2,14a: ἐπεὶ οὖν τὰ παιδία κεκοινώνηκεν αἵματος καὶ σαρκός, καὶ αὐτὸς παραπλησίως μετέσχεν τῶν αὐτῶν . . .

It hardly needs assertion that Philo is not a gnostic in the sense that the world of creation is not evil. For Philo the world of nature shares in God's perfection, in its unity and harmony (Op 35; 171). The dualism is Platonic--the intelligible and sense perceptible--and hierarchically ordered. Perfection implies proximity to God in this hierarchy. At the same time Philo affirms the unity and brotherhood of all creation without reconciling the intrinsic dualism which such a hierarchically ordered world implies.

Decal 64: πᾶσαν οὖν τὴν τοιαύτην τερθρείαν ἀπωσάμενοι <u>τοὺς ἀδελφοὺς φύσει</u> μὴ προσκυνῶμεν, εἰ καὶ καθαρωτέρας καὶ ἀθανατωτέρας οὐσίας ἔλαχον - <u>ἀδελφὰ δ' ἀλλήλων τὰ γενόμενα καθὸ γέγονεν</u>, ἐπεὶ καὶ πατὴρ ἁπάντων <u>εἷς</u> ὁ ποιητὴς τῶν ὅλων ἐστίν . . . (Context is the interpretation of the first commandment and denunciation of polytheism.)

Spec Leg i,208: ἡ δὲ εἰς μέλη τοῦ ζῴου διανομὴ δηλοῖ, ἤτοι ὡς <u>ἓν τὰ πάντα</u> ἢ ὅτι <u>ἐξ ἑνός</u> τε καὶ <u>εἰς ἕν</u> . . . (Interpretation of the division of the burnt offering--a Stoic formulation which Philo clearly indicates as referring to "conflagration" and "reconstruction"--his own interpretation being that it refers to the different powers of God.)

De Mundo 396b,20-23: . . . τὸ παρὰ τῷ σκοτεινῷ λεγόμενον Ἡρακλείτῳ, "συνάψιες ὅλα καὶ οὐχ ὅλα, συμφερόμενον διαφερόμενον, συνᾷδον διᾷδον, καὶ <u>ἐκ πάντων ἓν καὶ ἐξ ἑνὸς πάντα</u>." (Context is the discussion of the harmony and union of the opposites--the opposing elements and qualities of the cosmos.)

The language in Hebrews 5,11, Philo and Pseudo-Aristotelian De Mundo clearly deals with the theory of "causes," or put differently, the doctrine of creation (see above pp. 138-42 and 169-70). Specifically, the formulation in these passages is Stoic and it asserts the unity and harmony of creation. Such cosmological theorizing was in a sense the heart of hellenistic philosophical religion, as can be seen from the role the Timaeus played in middle-Platonism. Its significance in the argument concerning intermediaries and perfection we have shown in chap. 5 above.

While Philo affirms the unity and brotherhood of all creation in Stoic terms, there remains an inner duality in his concept of religious perfection which requires that the world of sense perceptible creation (flesh, blood, senses, etc.)--the world of man--be left behind and overcome when one moves near to God. The imperfection of the world of man is keenly felt and perfeived and stands in contradiction to the affirmation of the unity and brotherhood of all creation. In contrast, the author of Hebrews in his reinterpretation of this tradition has located sanctification/perfection within the realm of man--Jesus is not ashamed to call men of flesh and blood his brothers and to participate in the human condition of imperfection (2,14). Salvation is wrought within the realm of human imperfection--flesh, blood, weakness, ignorance, wandering and temptation. It is to men of flesh and blood that the status of perfection--sons of God--is made possible. Whereas in Philo, "sons of God" are angels and perfect men and wicked men are "bodies." In Leg All ii,51, Levi in his perfection disclaims all human relationships--father, mother, brethren, children (Dt 33,9)--in order to have God alone for his portion (Dt 10,9). The author of Hebrews states the precise opposite, that God has claimed creation for his own--even flesh, blood, weakness and temptation--and opened for it the path to perfection even in that state. For it is faith and hope which link this imperfect world with God, i.e., the goal of religious perfection. In Spec Leg i,167, when one approaches the altar he must have no "pathos" in the soul, but must attempt to sanctify it completely (hagiazein) so that God may not turn away. The author of Hebres has located sanctification in the unity and brotherhood of creation. He has thereby overcome the inner duality in the understanding of creation and perfection in Philo by such reinterpretation.

In this respect, the author of Hebrews has maintained the integrity of the apocalyptic self-understanding of primitive Christianity that this world with its sins and imperfection does not separate it from God (= perfection in this tradition)--cf. Rom 8,31-39. Perhaps it is not reading in too much to admire the skill with which the author has used such apocalyptic traditions (vs. 5-9 and 14b-15) to reinterpret the tradition of intermediaries and perfection without such apocalypticism being the primary frame of his religious thought--as is evidenced by the fact that such themes are not elaborated by him in the writing. In this respect the author demonstrates the capacity of a hellenistically informed mind to grasp the religious self-understanding and intention of primitive Christianity and to translate it into an entirely different language context. Hebrews therefore provides the historical link which makes comprehensible the transi-

tion between primitive apocalyptic Christianity and Greek
theology.

The Suffering of Jesus and His Education unto Perfection

Hb 2,10: ἔπρεπεν γὰρ αὐτῷ, δι' ὃν τὰ πάντα καὶ δι' οὗ τὰ
πάντα . . . τὸν ἀρχηγὸν τῆς σωτηρίας αὐτῶν διὰ παθημάτων
τελειῶσαι.

5,8-9: καίπερ ὢν υἱός, ἔμαθεν ἀφ' ὧν ἔπαθεν τὴν ὑπακοήν,
καὶ τελειωθεὶς ἐγένετο πᾶσιν τοῖς ὑπακούουσιν αὐτῷ αἴτιος
σωτηρίας αἰωνίου . . .

7,28: . . . ὁ λόγος δὲ τῆς ὁρκωμοσίας τῆς μετὰ τὸν νόμον
υἱὸν εἰς τὸν αἰῶνα τετελειωμένον.

Undoubtedly in terms of this tradition, Jesus as the heavenly man
was perfect and did not partake of flesh and blood. But this was
contradicted by the fact that primitive Christian faith which
centred on the kerygma of the passion had its basis in the appearance of a human being on earth. The author of Hebrews argues
that the heavenly man Jesus participated in the realm of imperfection and attained perfection within it (2,14a). To this end
he has reinterpreted the suffering, temptation and death of Jesus
in terms of the understanding of suffering and temptation in this
tradition as the "paideia" which leads to perfection. This is
the tradition which underlies the formulation of such passages
as 2,10; 5,7-10 and 7,28.

Som ii,107: . . . καὶ ταῖς κατὰ μικρὸν ἐπανιὼν βελτιώσεσιν ὡς
ἐπὶ κορυφῆς τοῦ ἑαυτοῦ βίου καὶ τέλους ἱδρυθεὶς
ἀναφθέγξηται, ὁ παθὼν ἀκριβῶς ἔμαθεν, ὅτι "τοῦ θεοῦ"
ἐστιν (Gn 50,19), ἀλλ' οὐδενὸς ἔτι τῶν εἰς γένεσιν
ἡκόντων αἰσθητοῦ τὸ παράπαν . . . (The immediate context speaks of the change for the better in Joseph's
life when he gives up his idle visions, etc., 105ff.)

Quis Her 73: παθοῦσα δ' ὡς ἄφρων καὶ νήπιος παῖς ἔμαθον, ὡς
ἄμεινον ἦν ἄρα πάντων μὲν τούτων ὑπεξελθεῖν, ἑκάστου δὲ
τὰς δυνάμεις ἀναθεῖναι θεῷ . . . (The powers referred
to are the faculties of the body, senses and speech;
the passage is an interpretation of Gn 15,4 which is
understood as a call to the soul to leave behind the
body, sense, speech and self in order to inherit the
goods of God--68ff.)

Cf. Spec Leg iii,126 and iv,29.

These passages alone would suffice to show the character of
the tradition which has moulded such a passage as Hb 5,7-10.
Suffering is an education (paideia) which leads to progress/bet-
terment and in the end to perfection. That is, it is a thematic
in the tradition of perfection. And the tradition of intermediaries and perfection belongs within the larger tradition of Greek
paideia. This becomes indubitably clear in Wis Sol; 2 and 4
Maccabees.

Wis Sol 11,9-10: ὅτε γὰρ ἐπειράσθησαν, καίπερ ἐν ἐλέει
παιδευόμενοι, ἔγνωσαν πῶς μετ' ὀργῆς κρινόμενοι ἀσεβεῖς
ἐβασανίζοντο, τούτους μὲν γὰρ ὡς πατὴρ νουθετῶν
ἐδοκίμασας, ἐκείνους δὲ ὡς ἀπότομος βασιλεὺς καταδικάζων
ἐξήτασας.

Wis Sol 12,22: ἡμᾶς οὖν παιδεύων τοὺς ἐχθροὺς ἡμῶν ἐν μυριότητι
μαστιγοῖς, ἵνα σου τὴν ἀγαθότητα μεριμνῶμεν κρίνοντες,
κρινόμενοι δὲ προσδοκῶμεν ἔλεος.

2Macc 6,12: παρακαλῶ οὖν τοὺς ἐντυγχάνοντας τῇδε τῇ βίβλῳ μὴ
συστέλλεσθαι διὰ τὰς συμφοράς, λογίζεσθαι δὲ τὰς τιμωρίας
μὴ πρὸς ὄλεθρον, ἀλλὰ πρὸς παιδείαν τοῦ γένους ἡμῶν
εἶναι.

6,16: διόπερ οὐδέποτε μὲν τὸν ἔλεον ἀφ' ἡμῶν ἀφίστησιν,
παιδεύων δὲ μετὰ συμφορᾶς οὐκ ἐγκαταλείπει τὸν ἑαυτοῦ
λαόν. (These two passages from 2Macc come from the
Epitomist's prologue to the story of the martyrdom of
Eleazar and the seven brothers.)

6,27-28: διόπερ ἀνδρείως μὲν νῦν διαλλάξας τὸν βίον τοῦ
μὲν γήρως ἄξιος φανήσομαι, τοῖς δὲ νέοις ὑπόδειγμα
γενναῖον καταλελοιπὼς εἰς τὸ προθύμως καὶ γενναίως ὑπὲρ
τῶν σεμνῶν καὶ ἁγίων νόμων ἀπευθανατίζειν. (From the
speech of Eleazar prior to his martyrdom.)

6,31: καὶ οὗτος οὖν τοῦτον τὸν τρόπον μετήλλαξεν οὐ μόνον
τοῖς νέοις, ἀλλὰ καὶ τοῖς πλείστοις τοῦ ἔθνους τὸν
ἑαυτοῦ θάνατον ὑπόδειγμα γενναιότητος καὶ μνημόσυνον
ἀρετῆς καταλιπών. (The concluding comment of the author
on Eleazar's martyrdom.) Cf. 7,23; 10,4.

4Macc 10,10-11: ἡμεῖς μέν, ὦ μιαρώτατε τύραννε, διὰ παιδείαν καὶ
ἀρετὴν θεοῦ ταῦτα πάσχομεν, σὺ δὲ διὰ τὴν ἀσέβειαν καὶ
μιαιφονίαν ἀκαταλύτους καρτερήσεις βασάνους. (The concluding statement of the third brother just before his
death.) Cf. 11,2.

These selected passages illustrate the degree to which the
temptations/trials, suffering, misfortune and divine punishment
were interpreted in the literature of hellenistic Judaism in
terms of Greek paideia. The solution of the tragic poets to the
problem of innocent suffering was that such suffering educates
man and makes him better. "It is Zeus who has put men on the way
to wisdom by establishing as a valid law, 'By suffering they shall
win understanding.'" (Aeschylus, Agamemnon 176ff.; taken from
Festugière, Personal Religion Among the Greeks, p. 31.) In the
same way, the sufferings of Israel (Wis Sol) and the martyrs (2
and 4 Macc) are seen as educative whereas the punishment of the
impious is real torment. The relationship of God to his people
is like that between a father and a child, and the trials and
sufferings are for the purpose of edification (cf. Hb 12,1-11).
The martyrs are the exemplary/paradigmatic (hypodeigma) heroes of
Jewish religious piety and virtue. They have left an example for
the youth as well as the nation to follow. In brief, hellenistic-Jewish martyrology has assimilated the ideals of Greek
paideia.

It is precisely this tradition which has informed the
reinterpretation of the temptation, suffering and death of Jesus
on the part of the author of Hebrews. According to the author,
Jesus has entered and participated in the realm of imperfection--
flesh, blood, temptation/trial, suffering and death--and was perfected through this experience and has thereby opened the possibility of perfection for weak and mortal men who find their
existence caught in this human situation. In simpler terms, men
do not have to become supermen, like in Philo, to attain perfection. In the author's interpretation, it is Christian faith and
hope which is perfection. We will pursue this further in the
next chapter, we note here that this tradition of the paideia of
suffering is the one which has formed such passages as Hb 5,7-10;
12,1-11; 2,10; 7,28, etc.

Furthermore, it can be shown that the language in Hb 5,7 has
its origin in the tradition of hellenistic-Jewish prayer.

3Macc 1,16: τῶν δὲ ἱερέων ἐν πάσαις ταῖς ἐσθήσεσιν προσπεσόντων
καὶ δεομένων τοῦ μεγίστου θεοῦ βοηθεῖν τοῖς ἐνεστῶσιν
καὶ τὴν ὁρμὴν τοῦ κακῶς ἐπιβαλλομένου μεταθεῖναι κραυγῆς
τε μετὰ δακρύων τὸ ἱερὸν ἐμπλησάντων . . . (Describes
the prayer of the priests when Ptolemy Philopator decided
to enter the sanctuary.)

5,7: τὸν παντοκράτορα κύριον καὶ πάσης δυνάμεως
δυναστεύοντα, ἐλεήμονα θεὸν αὐτῶν καὶ πατέρα,
δυσκαταπαύστῳ βοῇ πάντες μετὰ δακρύων ἐπεκαλέσαντο
δεόμενοι . . . (Refers to the prayer of the Jews when
the king had decided to test their fate with elephants.)

5,25: οἱ δὲ Ἰουδαῖοι κατὰ τὸν ἀμερῆ ψυχουλκούμενοι
χρόνον πολύδακρυν ἱκετείαν ἐν μέλεσιν γοεροῖς τείνοντες
τὰς χεῖρας εἰς τὸν οὐρανὸν ἐδέοντο τοῦ μεγίστου θεοῦ
πάλιν αὐτοῖς βοηθῆσαι συντόμως. (The same context as
above.)

QG IV,233: . . . Similar to this was the way in which (God) had
pity on those whose souls were afflicted in Egypt--
(namely, those of) Israel, a name (meaning) "one who
sees." And by groaning and lamenting and crying aloud
with his voice no more than in his thoughts, he attained
to the salvation of God . . . (Interpretation of
Gn 27,39; Marcus: Loeb.)

Quod Deus 115: . . . κακωθεῖσα μὲν γὰρ καὶ στενάξασα ἔλεον
εὑρήσεις . . . (Philo's advice to the Joseph-like mind
which is a prisoner of passion.)

With the utilization of such traditions, the author of
Hebrews represents Jesus in 5,7ff. as the one who has achieved
salvation for himself (= perfection) through ardent prayer and
suffering, i.e., salvation from death and perfection through the
education of suffering. He ascended to heaven as the perfected
son and eternal highpriest like Melchizedek. Any satisfactory
interpretation of Hebrews must explain this odd feature, namely,

that Jesus himself need d to be saved/perfected. Vis-a-vis
Michel and Spicq, one must say that there is no basis in either
apocalyptic or early Christian tradition for such a viewpoint.
In this respect Kaesemann is quite correct in contending that
scholars have not yet advanced the interpretation of Hebrews
beyond his thesis that what underlies Hebrews is the gnostic myth
of the redeemed redeemer.

Jesus as the Sympathetic Highpriest (2,16-18; 4,14-5,3)

In the author's reinterpretation, Jesus' participation in
the realm of imperfection is given a further rationale along the
lines that it was a part of his education to perfection so that
he could be a highpriest who could be "merciful" and "sympathetic" to the human condition of imperfection. The radical
character of the author's reinterpretation becomes evident when
we contrast it with the understanding of "sympathy" in the tradition of perfection and in the broader field of hellenistic
Judaism.

Leg All iii,129-35: See above pp. 67-68. Moses in his
perfection is able to cut away all passions and to practice
"apatheia." Whereas Aaron, while still a progresser, practices
"metriopathein." Cf. Hb 5,2. Jos 26--Jacob, who represents
progress, states in his speech that he was trained in the ath-
letics of adversity and was trained in the moderation of feeling
(paideutheis metriopathein). To these may be compared the following passages from 4Macc.

4Macc 13,22: καὶ αὔξονται (i.e., the seven brothers) σφοδρότερον
    διὰ συντροφίας καὶ τῆς καθ᾽ ἡμέραν συνηθείας καὶ τῆς
    ἄλλης παιδείας καὶ τῆς ἡμετέρας ἐν νόμῳ θεοῦ ἀσκήσεως.

   13,23: οὕτως δὴ τοίνυν καθεστηκυίης συμπαθοῦς τῆς
    φιλαδελφίας οἱ ἑπτὰ ἀδελφοὶ συμπαθέστερον ἔσχον πρὸς
    ἀλλήλους.

   13,24: νόμῳ γὰρ τῷ αὐτῷ παιδευθέντες καὶ τὰς αὐτὰς
    ἐξασκήσαντες ἀρετὰς καὶ τῷ δικαίῳ συντραφέντες βίῳ
    μᾶλλον ἑαυτοὺς ἠγάπων.

   13,25: ἡ γὰρ ὁμοζηλία τῆς καλοκάγαθίας ἐπέτεινεν αὐτῶν
    τὴν πρὸς ἀλλήλους εὔνοιαν καὶ ὁμόνοιαν . . .

   14,1: προσέτι καὶ ἐπὶ τὸν αἰκισμὸν ἐποτρύνοντες, ὡς μὴ
    μόνον τῶν ἀλγηδόνων περιφρονῆσαι αὐτοὺς, ἀλλὰ καὶ τῶν
    τῆς φιλαδελφίας παθῶν κρατῆσαι.

This passage (13,19-14,20) has within it all the classic
concepts from the tradition of Greek paideia (as traced by
W. Jaeger--paideia, askēsis, aretē, kalokagathia, eunoia, homo-
noia, etc.) and could alone prove that 4Macc has as its larger
ideological structure the tradition of Greek paideia. It was to

show that the Jews had a culture (paideia of the law) of equal, if not superior, excellence (aretē) as the Greeks and their own exemplary cultural heroes both in the past and the present. For our specific purpose, we are interested in the concepts of sympathy and brotherhood in the tradition. Sympathy and brotherly love belong to the level of training and progress. But at the highest level of piety, exemplified in their martyrdom, their reason overcame the "pathos" of brotherly love. It implied exclusive devotion to their religion/God. In this respect, Philo and 4Macc are in complete agreement.

In contrast, in Hebrew's reinterpretation of this tradition, Jesus' entry into the realm of imperfection and his education to perfection through temptation and suffering, left an indelible mark even in his perfection, in that he continued to bear a "pathos" for his "brothers" who live in the realm of flesh and blood and of whom he is not ashamed. And the author argues that this is what makes him a superior highpriest in contrast to the perfect Moses or Aaron. This was undoubtedly a mark of the religious self-understanding of primitive Christianity and one marvels at the author's subtle grasp and ability to translate it into the framework of a different thought world. To underline the contrast in religious feeling, we quote:

4Macc 14,20: ἀλλ' οὐχὶ τὴν Ἀβραὰμ ὁμόψυχον τῶν νεανίσκων
             μητέρα μετενίκησεν συμπάθεια τέκνων.

Therefore the aid which Jesus provides is concerned not with angelic existence but with the imperfect children of Abraham whose life is in the realm of flesh and blood (2,14 and 16). He can help them because he has himself experienced the imperfection of this world without succumbing to them ("without sin"--4,15) and has attained salvation/perfection for himself within this world. The question then arises in what sense can Christians participate in perfection and in what sense is Jesus the "cause of eternal salvation."

CHAPTER EIGHT

THE PERFECTION OF THE BELIEVER: FAITH, HOPE
AND PARAENESIS IN HEBREWS

Introduction: At this point we cannot enter into this
question in detail. The passages under consideration are Hb 3,7-
4,13; 5,11-6,20; 10,19-39; 11-12; 13,9-15. We contend that these
passages have to be considered together to answer the question
how the believer becomes perfect in the understanding of Hebrews.
The key to the interpretation of these passages lies in the concept of "participation" and in the correlation between faith,
hope and paraenesis in the thought world of Hebrews. Perfection
in the thought world with which we are dealing means proximity
and access to God, and Jesus has accomplished this perfection at
least for himself. He is in the heavenly sanctuary as the Son
and eternal highpriest seated on the right hand of God. The author of Hebrews contends that this implies that Christians can
now have the same immediacy and access to God in that the way to
Holy of Holies is now open (4,14-16; 10,19ff., etc.). But Christians are here on earth in the realm of flesh and blood and
trials/temptations and the author does not propose that this will
be accomplished in the afterlife or in the eschatological future.
The author of Hebrews says that we can now become God's house
(3,6), that we can now enter into God's rest ("today"--4,7 and
11), that we can now approach the throne of grace (4,16), that we
have become participants of Christ (3,14), that we are already
enlightened, have tasted the gift of heaven, have become participants of the holy spirit, have tasted the word of God and the
powers of the age to come (6,4-5), that we can now approach and
enter the Holy of Holies (10,19-20), and that the good things of
which Christ is the highpriest have already arrived (9,11). Simply stated, perfection is possible for the Christian here and now.
And in each of these instances if one asks the question, as to
how this happens, the author consistently and unequivocally answers, in those cases where he does, that it is in Christian
faith and hope. And in the instances where he exhorts Christians
to hold on to faith and hope to the end or to the day of judgement, it is not a matter that at the end something more will be
added but a matter of retention of what the Christians already
have or can have. It is to this edge between what the Christians

227

already have or can have that the author's paraenesis is directed.

Christian Faith and Hope and the House of God

The basic outlines of our interpretation have already been anticipated, see above pp. 182-83 and 213-14. The basic thesis is that in the author's reinterpretation, faith and hope are what connect the Christian on earth with God in heaven. That is his perfection/aretē, his mode of existence. There were other exemplary heroes of faith in the culture of Israel but their faith was imperfect (11,39-40). It is the religious self-understanding which has arrived with Jesus--Christian faith--which is perfect and of which Jesus is the exemplar. The self-understanding of Christian faith which is exemplified in Jesus' own participation in imperfection and attainment of perfection is that the world of flesh and blood, trials and temptations does not separate the it from God (see Chapter 7 above). It is Jesus' own mode of existence, as an exemplary type of soul, which the Christian appropriates and which constitutes in himself as faith and hope. The Christian looks at Jesus as he runs the race of life and forms his own existence on the model exemplified in Jesus' own endurance and despisement of the shame of the cross in view of the joy of sitting on the right hand of God--i.e., perfection (12,1-4). In other words, primitive Christian soteriology has been reinterpreted by Hebrews in the language and concepts of the tradition of perfection. The key to all this is the concept of "participation" and the role of paraenesis in this tradition.

Paraenesis and Participation in Perfection

Hb 2,14: ἐπεὶ οὖν τὰ παιδία κεκοινώνηκεν αἵματος καὶ σαρκός, καὶ αὐτὸς παραπλησίως μετέσχεν τῶν αὐτῶν . . .

3,14: μέτοχοι γὰρ τοῦ Χριστοῦ γεγόναμεν, ἐάνπερ τὴν ἀρχὴν τῆς ὑποστάσεως μέχρι τέλους βεβαίαν κατάσχωμεν.

5,13: πᾶς γὰρ ὁ μετέχων γάλακτος ἄπειρος λόγου δικαιοσύνης, νήπιος γάρ ἐστιν.

6,4-5: ἀδύνατον γὰρ τοὺς ἅπαξ φωτισθέντας γευσαμένους τε τῆς δωρεᾶς τῆς ἐπουρανίου καὶ μετόχους γενηθέντας πνεύματος ἁγίου καὶ καλὸν γευσαμένους θεοῦ ῥῆμα δυνάμεις τε μέλλοντος αἰῶνος

12,8: εἰ δὲ χωρίς ἐστε παιδείας, ἧς μέτοχοι γεγόνασιν πάντες, ἄρα νόθοι καὶ οὐχ υἱοί ἐστε.

Apart from 2,14, the other passages are from the paraenetic sections of Hebrews. There must be an intrinsic connection between participation and paraenesis. They belong to the tradition of "paideia" and paraenesis in this context has the meaning of instruction of education. Christians are participants of the paideia of God (12,8) which gives them the status of "sons." It is Christian instruction which is the means of their participation in the Christian knowledge of God and Christ and the religious powers and benefits which pertain to such knowledge. Such religious instruction is the context of their progress from the status of children to that of the perfect--when they are teachers and no longer learners (5,11-6,20). It is through such paideutic paraenesis that they are participants of Christ--or put simply of Christianity, its religious self-understanding. The ultimate goal is to ground the believer in Christian faith and hope--not just any faith and hope--but faith and hope which as a mode of religious existence is moulded, formed and instructed by Jesus as the supreme exemplar of God's paideia. Such religious knowledge of God and Jesus is what makes faith and hope Christian faith and hope (which is perfect in comparison with other faiths and hopes--Hb 11). In other words, paraenesis in Hebrews is a mode of Christian paideia whose aim is to lead the Christians to the knowledge of God and the Christian "virtues" of faith and hope. This is the precise opposite of the view advanced that theology in Hebrews is at the service of paraenesis (Kaesemann, Michel and others). Put more simply, paraenesis in Hebrews has as its purpose to lead the learner to the knowledge of God and this knowledge informs and grounds their religious existence as faith and hope--and not the other way around. The description of Hebrews in 13,22 as a "logos parakleseōs" is therefore entirely correct.

The Evidence

Leg All ii,64: τρίτη γύμνωσίς ἐστιν ἡ μέση, καθ᾽ ἥν ὁ νοῦς ἄλογός ἐστι μήτε ἀρετῆς πω μήτε κακίας μετέχων. περὶ ταύτης ἐστὶν ὁ λόγος, ἧς καὶ ὁ νήπιος κοινωνεῖ . . .

The context of the passage is the interpretation of Gn 2,25 (53ff.) and that there are three kinds of nakedness--mind or soul which is completely free from passions and vices (= Moses, Ex 33,7--cf. Hb 13,13), soul/mind bereft of virtue (Gn 9,21), and the middle type--the mind which is not yet rational and does not partake of either virtue or vice, a type of which the child is a partaker, e.g., Gn 2,25. These are the three standard types of souls/minds/men--the perfect, the totally evil, and those who can still receive instruction/paideia. Cf. Hb 5,13.

Leg All iii,169: . . . (Ex 16,13-15; on the manna). ὁρᾷς τῆς ψυχῆς τροφὴν οἵα ἐστί, λόγος θεοῦ συνεχής, ἐοικὼς δρόσῳ κύκλῳ πᾶσαν περιειληφὼς καὶ μηδὲν μέρος ἀμέτοχον αὐτοῦ ἐῶν.

170: φαίνεται δ᾽ οὐ πανταχοῦ <u>ὁ λόγος</u> οὗτος, ἀλλ᾽ ἐπ᾽ ἐρήμου
παθῶν καὶ κακιῶν, καὶ ἔστι <u>λεπτὸς</u> νοῆσαί τε καὶ νοηθῆναι
καὶ σφόδρα <u>διαυγὴς</u> καὶ <u>καθαρὸς</u> ὁραθῆναι, καὶ ἔστιν ὡσεὶ
κόριον. φασὶ δὲ οἱ γεωπόνοι τὸ σπέρμα τοῦ κορίου
διαιρεθὲν εἰς ἄπειρα καὶ τμηθὲν καθ᾽ ἕκαστον τῶν μερῶν
καὶ τμημάτων σπαρὲν βλαστάνειν οὕτως, ὡς καὶ τὸ ὅλον
ἠδύνατο, τοιοῦτος καὶ <u>ὁ θεοῦ λόγος</u>, καὶ δι᾽ ὅλων <u>ὠφελητι-
κὸς</u> καὶ <u>διὰ παντὸς μέρους</u> καὶ <u>τοῦ τυχόντος</u>.

171: . . . παρὸ καὶ <u>λευκόν</u> ἐστι, τί γὰρ ἂν εἴη λαμπρότερον ἢ
τηλαυγέστερον <u>θείου λόγου</u>, <u>οὗ κατὰ μετουσίαν</u> καὶ τὰ ἄλλα
τὴν ἀχλὺν καὶ τὸν ζόφον ἀπελαύνει <u>φωτὸς κοινωνῆσαι
ψυχικοῦ</u> γλιχόμενα;

The context of this passage is the interpretation of Gn 3,14 (LXX
3,15) and that the food of the soul is heavenly--Ex 16,4 (161-
68). The present passage continues the interpretation with Ex
16,13-15. The <u>food of the soul</u> (manna) is the <u>Logos of God</u> which
is continuous and like dew. It encompasses the entire soul and
does not leave any portion <u>without a part</u> of itself. The description of the Logos which follows--fine, very clear, pure--is
like that of wisdom in Wis Sol 7,22ff. Like the coriander seed
it is infinitely divisible and yet can grow to a full plant and
is thus <u>beneficial as a whole</u>, <u>partially</u> and <u>incidentally</u>. It is
white, and there is nothing more brilliant or brighter than the
divine Logos. All other things by <u>partaking of it</u> drive out the
mist and darkness and desire to <u>become sharers</u> of the light of
the soul.

This is the paideutic function of the Logos for those who
are progressing and not yet perfect. The author of Hebrews using
similar language had to argue that "participants of Christ"
(3,14) are perfect--they attain the same status as Jesus, namely,
"sons" (12,8). In place of the paideia of the Logos of Philo,
in Hebrews it is the paideia of Christ in which Christians share.
The language of tasting, food and participation belong together
as in Hb 6,4-5, which is clearly a Christian elaboration of the
tradition of the manna as divine food and the Logos of God.

Such passages could be infinitely multiplied since they
permeate almost every page of Philo; it is the ideology which
provides the over-arching structure of Philo's thought. Cf. Post
124-69 (esp. 158); Quod Deus 140ff. (esp. 144). We turn to those
passages where the paraenetic function of the Logos of God is
more clearly indicated.

QG IV,51: (Gn 19,23-24) . . . But the <u>divine word</u> is an <u>example</u>
to future generations not to seek to do anything un-
worthy, (like) those cursed by calamities and burned by
fire, <u>in order that they may be admonished</u> by seeing the
sufferings of their fellows, . . . For if men saw this,
not with bodily eyes but rather with the mind they would
certainly be converted to virtue. (Marcus: Loeb)

QG III,30: (Gn 16,9) . . . Since the literal meaning is clear, the deeper meaning must be considered. <u>The divine Logos disciplines and admonishes the soul</u> which is able to receive healing, and turns it back to sovereign wisdom, lest being left without a mistress, it leap into absurd folly. And <u>he disciplines it</u>, not only that it may turn back to virtue but also submit itself under her hands, by which I mean under her powers. Now submission is of two forms. . . . The other is that which the <u>dominant Logos</u> enjoins, and rises from awe and reverence, such as <u>sons</u> feel toward <u>parents</u>, and <u>pupils</u> toward their <u>teachers</u>, and <u>youths</u> toward their <u>elders</u>. . . .
(Marcus: Loeb) Cf. III,28.

Mos i,325: ἔδει μὲν ὑμᾶς <u>ταῖς ἑτέρων</u> <u>πληγαῖς</u> <u>πεπαιδεῦσθαι</u>. φρονίμων γὰρ ἀνδρῶν μὴ ἀναμένειν, ἄχρις ἂν ἐπ' αὐτοὺς ἔλθῃ τὰ δεινά. νυνὶ δὲ <u>παραδείγματ'</u> ἔχοντες <u>οἰκεῖα τοὺς</u> <u>πατέρας</u>, οἳ κατεσκέψαντο τήνδε τὴν χώραν, καὶ τὰς ἐκείνων συμφορὰς καὶ τῶν συναπονοηθέντων--ἅπαντες γὰρ ἔξω δυοῖν ἀπώλοντο--, δέον μηδενὶ τῶν ὁμοίων συνεπιγράφεσθαι . . .
(From the speech of Moses in reaction to the request of the tribes of Reuben and Gad, who wished to settle in the Transjordan.)

328: τὴν δὲ <u>νουθεσίαν</u> πρᾴως ἐνεγκόντες ὡς <u>υἱοὶ γνήσιοι</u> σφόδρα εὔνου <u>πατρός</u> . . . (Philo's remark on the way the speech of Moses was received by the two tribes.)

Wis Sol 16,6: <u>εἰς νουθεσίαν</u> δὲ πρὸς ὀλίγον ἐταράχθησαν σύμβολον ἔχοντες σωτηρίας <u>εἰς ἀνάμνησιν ἐντολῆς νόμου σου.</u>
(Reference to the serpents in Nu 21.) Cf. 11,9-10; 12,2.

3Macc 2,5: σὺ (God) τοὺς ὑπερηφανίαν ἐργαζομένους Σοδομίτας διαδήλους ταῖς κακίαις γενομένους πυρὶ καὶ θείῳ κατέφλεξας <u>παράδειγμα τοῖς ἐπιγινομένοις</u> καταστήσας.
(From the prayer of the highpriest Simon.)

These passages clarify the meaning of paraenesis in this tradition. It is an aspect of "paideia" and a function of the Logos of God which is understood both as the divine and universal Reason as well as in its concrete manifestation in the inspired words of the OT. In particular, the stories and figures of the OT are understood as exemplary for contemporary men. They are not to be read only on the literal level but with eyes of the mind in order to discover their religious meaning and contemporary significance. The OT provides both positive as well as negative examples for religious piety. It is precisely this understanding which has formed and shaped the argument in Hb 3,7-4,13 and 1Cor 10,1-31. In both these passages, examples are taken from the OT to serve as paraeneses of warning, in 1Cor 10 against religious overconfidence and in Hb 3,7ff. as warning against "disbelief" and "disobedience" (note the repetition in 3,12; 3,19; 4,2; 4,3; 4,6; 4,11). In Hebrews, it is through faith that one is exhorted to enter into God's rest (= perfection). The understanding of this paraenetic ideology of the Logos of God also explains why we have this statement on the

Logos of God in Hb 4,12-13, for which there are numerous Philonic
examples, since it speaks of the penetrating and testing (elen-
chic) power of the Logos of God--its instructive and clarifying
power. The Logos of God instructs and admonishes us through
negative examples which serve to warn. The place of Hb 3,7-4,13
in its context becomes comprehensible once it is grasped that we
are dealing here with thematics and traditions of perfection.
The paraenesis of the Logos of God is for those who are on the
path of progress and have not yet reached perfection. They are
still pupils and children in need of instruction. They have not
reached the status of teachers (= perfection). The author of
Hebrews reminds his readers in these terms of the problem of remaining in imperfection for too long, since Christian faith and
hope are themselves the foundation of perfection (5,11ff.). It
becomes clear that the author of Hebrews understands himself as
a Christian teacher who has reached perfection--i.e., fully
grounded in Christian faith and hope as a man of flesh and blood
and beset with temptations--and his writing as a "word of exhortation." And his description of it as too brief is not incorrect
for such literature was consistently long winded (e.g., the
treatises of Philo). Such paraenetic literature consisted of
religious instruction (theology) and not just moral instructions
as we commonly assume.

That our interpretation of 1Cor 10 and Hebrews 3,7ff. is on
the mark can be proven by their own explicit statements:

1Cor 10,6: ταῦτα δὲ <u>τύποι</u> ἡμῶν ἐγενήθησαν, εἰς τὸ μὴ εἶναι
ἡμᾶς ἐπιθυμητὰς κακῶν, καθὼς κάκεῖνοι ἐπεθύμησαν.

10,11: ταῦτα δὲ <u>τυπικῶς</u> συνέβαινεν ἐκείνοις, ἐγράφη δὲ <u>πρὸς</u>
<u>νουθεσίαν ἡμῶν</u> ... .

Hb 4,11: σπουδάσωμεν οὖν εἰσελθεῖν εἰς ἐκείνην τὴν
κατάπαυσιν, ἵνα μὴ ἐν τῷ αὐτῷ τις <u>ὑποδείγματι</u> πέσῃ <u>τῆς</u>
<u>ἀπειθείας</u>.

The clue to the interpretation of Hb 3,14 lies in a passage like:

Abr 7: ἐπειδὴ τοίνυν <u>ἀρχὴ μετουσίας ἀγαθῶν ἐστιν ἐλπὶς</u> καὶ
ταύτην οἷα λεωφόρον ὁδὸν ἡ φιλάρετος ἀνατέμνει καὶ
ἀνοίγει ψυχὴ σπουδάζουσα τυχεῖν τοῦ πρὸς ἀλήθειαν
καλοῦ . . .

We therefore interpret Hb 3,14 to be saying that we become participants of Christ and remain so by holding on to the first principle of reality (hypostasis), namely, faith. It is in faith
that we enter into God's own rest (= perfection). And the wan-
derings (a decidedly negative symbol in this tradition) in the
wilderness and its fatalities should warn us against the dangers
of disbelief and disobedience. We should beware lest we fall

into the same example of disobedience (4,11). And the word of
God penetrates into the recesses of our being and lays bare the
basis of our existence--whether it is founded on the perfection
of Christian faith or the persistence of an evil heart of disbelief which leads to apostasy (3,12; 4,12-13). The scripture
(OT) serves this function of clarification and testing.

This tradition of participation and paraenesis, which is an
aspect of the tradition of intermediaries and perfection, is the
key to the interpretation of Hb 3,7-4,13; 5,11-6,20; 10,19-39;
11-12. We are unable to set forth in writing the details of the
interpretation of these passages at this point, but have hope-
fully got to the heart of the matter.

BIBLIOGRAPHY

Armstrong, A. H. An Introduction to Ancient Philosophy. Boston:
    Beacon Press, 1963.

_____. Plotinus. 6 vols. Loeb Classical Library. Cambridge:
    Harvard University Press, 1966- (in progress).

Arnim, Johannes von. Stoicorum veterum fragmenta. 4 vols.
    Stuttgart: Teubner, 1964.

Babbit, F. C. et al. Plutarch: Moralia. 15 vols. Loeb
    Classical Library. Cambridge: Harvard University Press,
    1927- (in progress).

Barbel, Joseph. Christos Angelos: Die Anschauung von Christus
    als Bote und Engel in der gelehrten und volkstümlichen
    Literatur des christlichen Altertums. Bonn: P. Hanstein,
    1941.

Bekker, I. Aristotelis Opera. Vols. 1, 2 (V. Rose. Fragments).
    Latin Translations Vol. 3, C. A. Brandis and H. Usener.
    Scholia Vol. 4, H. Bonitz. Index Aristotelicus Vol. 5.
    Berlin: Reimerum, 1831-1870.

Bousset, W. and Gressmann, H. Die Religion des Judentums im
    späthellenistischen Zeitalter. Handbuch zum Neuen Testament,
    21. Tübingen: J. C. B. Mohr (Paul Siebeck), 1966 (4th.
    edition).

Braun, Herbert. Qumran und das Neue Testament. 2 vols.
    Tübingen: J. C. B. Mohr (Paul Siebeck), 1966.

Bréhier, Émile. Les idées philosophique et religieuses de
    Philon d'Alexandrie. Étude de philosophie medieval, 8.
    Paris: Librarie Philosophique, 1925.

Brown, Raymond E. The Semitic Background of the Term "Mystery"
    in the New Testament. Philadelphia: Fortress Press, 1968.

Bruce, F. F. The Epistle to the Hebrews. The New International
    Commentary on the New Testament. Grand Rapids: Wm. B.
    Eerdmans, 1964.

Burnet, J. Platonis Opera. 5 vols. Scriptorum classicorum
    bibliotheca Oxoniensis. Oxford: Clarendon Press, 1953-56.

Charles, R. H. The Apocrypha and Pseudepigrapha of the Old
    Testament. 2 vols. Oxford: Clarendon Press, 1913.

_____. The Greek Versions of the Testaments of the Twelve
    Patriarchs. Oxford: Clarendon Press, 1908.

Cody, A. Heavenly Sanctuary and Liturgy in the Epistle to the
    Hebrews. St. Meinrad, Indiana, 1960.

Cohn, L. and Wendland, P. Philonis Alexandrini Opera quae
    supersunt. Vols. 1-6. J. Leisegang. Indices. Vol. 7, 1. 2.
    Berlin: Walter de Gruyter, 1896-1930.

Colson, F. H.; Whitaker, G. H.; and Earp, J. W. Philo. 10 vols.
    Loeb Classical Library. Cambridge: Harvard University
    Press, 1929-62.

Daniélou, J. The Theology of Jewish Christianity. Translated by
    J. A. Baker. Chicago: Regnery, 1964.

Diels, Hermann. Die Fragmente der Vorsokratiker. 3 vols.
    Berlin: Weidmannsche Buchhandlung, 1922 (4th. edition).

Drummond, James. Philo Judaeus or, The Jewish-Alexandrian
    Philosophy in its Development and Completion. 2 vols.
    London and Edinburg: T. & T. Clark, 1888.

Dupont-Sommer, A. The Essene Writings from Qumran. New York:
    Meridian Books, 1962.

Edlund, Conny. Das Auge der Einfalt: Eine Untersuchung zu
    MATT. 6,22-23 und LUK. 11,34-35. Acta Seminarii Neotesta-
    mentici Upsaliensis, 19. Lund: Gleerups, 1952.

Eltester, F. W. Eikon im Neuen Testament. Beihefte zur Zeit-
    schrift für die neutestamentliche Wissenschaft und die
    Kunde der älteren Kirche, 23. Berlin: Verlag Alfred Töpel-
    mann, 1958.

Festugière, A. J. Personal Religion Among the Greeks. Berkeley
    and Los Angeles: University of California Press, 1954.

_____. La Révélation D'Hermès Trismégiste. 4 vols. Études
    Bibliques. Paris: J Gabalda, 1950-1954.

Funk. F. X. Didascalia et Constitutiones Apostolorum. 2 vols.
    Paderborn: F. Schöningh, 1905.

Geffcken, J. Oracula sibyllana. Leipzig: J. C. Hinrichs, 1902.

Gifford, E. H. Eusebii Pamphilli Evangelicae Praeparationis.
    4 vols. Oxford: Oxford University Press, 1903.

Goodenough, Erwin R. By Light, Light. New Haven: Yale
    University Press, 1935.

_____. "The Political Philosophy of Hellenistic Kingship."
    Yale Classical Series, Vol. I. New Haven: Yale University
    Press, 1928.

_____. "Problems of Method in Studying Philo Judaeus."
    JBL 58(1939), 51-58.

Goodspeed, E. J. Die ältesten Apologeten. Göttingen: Vanden-
    hoeck & Ruprecht, 1914.

Grässer, Erich. Der Glaube im Hebräerbrief. Marburger
    Theologische Studien, 2. Marburg: N. G. Elwert Verlag,
    1965.

_____. "Der Hebräerbrief 1938 - 1963." ThR 30(1964), 138-236.

Gregg, J. A. F. The Wisdom of Solomon. Cambridge: Cambridge
    University Press, 1909.

Hadas, Moses. The Third and Fourth Books of Maccabees. Dropsie
    College Edition: Jewish Apocryphal Literature. New York:
    Harper and Brothers, 1953.

Hahn, Ferdinand. The Titles of Jesus in Christology; Their
    History in Early Christianity. Translated by Harold Knight
    and George Ogg. New York: World Publishing, 1969.

Haines, C. R. Marcus Aurelius Antoninus. Loeb Classical
    Library. Cambridge: Harvard University Press, 1930.

Hanhart, Robert. Maccabaeorum liber III. Septuaginta: Vetus
    Testamentum Graecum. Göttingen: Vandenhoeck & Ruprecht,
    1962.

Hermann, C. F. Platonis dialogi. Vol. 6. Leipzig: Teubner,
    1853.

Hicks, R. D. Diogenes Laertius. 2 vols. Loeb Classical Library. Cambridge: Harvard University Press, 1925.

Hobein, H. Maximi Tyrii: Philosophumena. Leipzig: Teubner, 1910.

Jaeger, Werner. Aristotle. Translated by R. Robinson. Oxford: Clarendon Press, 1948.

_____. Early Christianity and Greek Paideia. Oxford: Oxford University Press, 1961.

_____. Paideia: the Ideals of Greek Culture. 3 vols. Translated by Gilbert Highet. New York: Oxford University Press, 1939-44.

Jervell, Jacob. Imago Dei: Gn 1,26f im Spätjudentum, in der Gnosis und in den paulinischen Briefen. Forschungen zur Religion und Literatur des Alten und Neuen Testaments, 58. Göttingen: Vandenhoeck & Ruprecht, 1960.

Jonge, M. de. Testamenta XII Patriarcharum. Pseudepigrapha Veteris Testamenti Graece. Leiden: Brill, 1964.

Käsemann, Ernst. Das wandernde Gottesvolk. Forschungen zur Religion und Literatur des Alten und Neuen Testaments, 55. Göttingen: Vandenhoeck & Ruprecht, 1938.

Kappler, Werner. Maccabaeorum liber II. Septuaginta: Vetus Testamentum Graecum. Göttingen: Vandenhoeck & Ruprecht, 1959.

Kern, O. Orphicorum Fragmenta. Berlin: Weidmannsche Verlagsbuchhandlung, 1922.

Kittel, Gerhard. Theological Dictionary of the New Testament. Translated by Geoffrey W. Bromiley. Grand Rapids: Wm. B. Eerdmans, 1964-.

Köster, Helmut. "Die Auslegung der Abraham-Verheissung in Hb 6." Studien zur Theologie der alttestamentlichen Überlieferungen. G. von Rad Festschrift. Neukirchen Kreis Moers. Neukirchener Verlag, 1961.

_____. "'Outside the Camp:' Hebrews 13.9-14." HTR 55(1962), 299-315.

Lake, Kirsopp. The Apostolic Fathers. 2 vols. Loeb Classical Library. Cambridge: Harvard University Press, 1912-13.

Lohse, Eduard. Colossians and Philemon. Translated by William R. Poehlmann and Robert J. Karris. Edited by Helmut Köster. Hermeneia--A Critical and Historical Commentary on the Bible. Philadelphia: Fortress Press, 1971.

_____. Die Texte aus Qumran. München: Kösel Verlag, 1964.

Marcus, Ralph. Philo Supplement I and II. Loeb Classical Library. Cambridge: Harvard University Press, 1953.

Marrou, H. I. A History of Education in Antiquity. Translated by George Lamb. New York: Sheed and Ward, 1956.

Michel, Otto. Der Brief an die Hebräer. Kritisch-Exegetischer Kommentar über das Neue Testament. Göttingen: Vandenhoeck & Ruprecht, 1966 (12th. edition).

Michel, Otto; Safrai, S.; Déaut, R. Le.; Jonge, M. de.; Goudoever, J. van. Studies on the Jewish Background of the New Testament. Assen: Van Gorcum, 1969.

Moffat, James. A Critical and Exegetical Commentary on the Epistle to the Hebrews. The International Critical

Commentary. Edinburg: T. & T. Clark, 1924.

Montefiore, Hugh. The Epistle to the Hebrews. Harper's New Testament Commentaries. New York and Evanston: Harper and Row, 1964.

Moore, George Foot. A Critical and Exegetical Commentary on Judges. The International Critical Commentary. New York: Scribners, 1895.

_____. "Intermediaries in Jewish Theology." HTR 15(1922), 41-85.

_____. Judaism in the First Centuries of the Christian Era. The Age of the Tannaim. 3 vols. Cambridge: Harvard University Press, 1927-30.

Niese, B. Flavii Iosephi Opera. 7 vols. Berlin: Weidmannsche Verlagsbuchhandlung, 1887-1895.

Nock, A. D. "Erwin R. Goodenough, By Light, Light." Gnomon 13(1937), 156-65 (= book review).

Oldfather, W. A. Epictetus. 2 vols. Loeb Classical Library. Cambridge: Harvard University Press, 1925, 1928.

Philonenko, Marc. Joseph et Asénath: Introduction, Texte Critique, Traduction et Notes. Studia Post-Biblica. Leiden: Brill, 1968.

DuPlessis, P. J. ΤΕΛΕΙΟΣ, The Idea of Perfection in the New Testament. Uitgave J. H. Kok N. V. Kampen, 1959.

Pope, Marvin H. Job. The Anchor Bible. New York: Doubleday, 1965.

Quandt, W. Orphei Hymni. Berlin: Weidmannsche Verlagsbuch- handlung, 1955.

Rad, Gerhard von. Deuteronomy: A Commentary. Translated by Dorothea Barton. Old Testament Library. Philadelphia: Westminster Press, 1966.

_____. Genesis: A Commentary. Translated by John H. Marks. Old Testament Library. Philadelphia: Westminster Press, 1961.

Ringgren, Helmer. The Faith of Qumran. Translated by Emilie T. Sander. Philadelphia: Fortress Press, 1963.

Robinson, James M. and Köster, Helmut. Trajectories through Early Christianity. Philadelphia: Fortress Press, 1971.

Russell, D. S. The Method and Message of Jewish Apocalyptic. Old Testament Library. Philadelphia: Westminster Press, 1964.

Sowers, Sidney G. The Hermeneutics of Philo and Hebrews. Basel Studies of Theology, 1. Zürich: EVZ-Verlag and Richmond: John Knox Press, 1965.

Speiser, E. A. Genesis. The Anchor Bible. New York: Doubleday, 1964.

Spicq, C. L'Épitre aux Hébreaux. 2 vols. Études Bibliques. Paris: J. Gabalda, 1952-1953 (3rd. edition).

Strack, Hermann and Billerbeck, Paul. Kommentar zum Neuen Testa- ment aus Talmud und Midrash. Vol. 3. München: C. H. Beck, 1926 (2nd. edition).

Thiessen, Gerd. Untersuchungen zum Hebräerbrief. Studien zum Neuen Testament, 2. Gütersloh: Gütersloher Verlagshaus Gerd Mohn, 1969.

Thomas, P. Apuleius: De Platone et eius Dogmate. Bibliotheca Scriptorum Graecorum et Romanorum Teubneriana. Leipzig: Teubner, 1970.

Völker, Walther. Fortschritt und Vollendung bei Philo von Alexandrien. Texte und Untersuchungen zur Geschichte der altchristlichen Literatur, 49. 1. Leipzig: J. C. Hinrich, 1938.

Windisch, Hans. Der Hebräerbrief. Handbuch zum Neuen Testament, 14. Tübingen: J. C. B. Mohr (Paul Siebeck), 1931 (2nd. edition).

Witt, R. E. Albinus and the History of Middle Platonism. Cambridge: University Press, 1937.

Wolfson, Harry Austryn. Philo. 2 vols. Cambridge: Harvard University Press, 1968 (4th. edition).

Yadin, Yigael. "The Dead Sea Scrolls and the Epistle to the Hebrews." Scripta Hierosolymitana 4(1958), 36-55.

Zeller, Eduard. A History of Eclecticism in Greek Philosophy. Translated by S. F. Alleyne. London: Longmans, Green and Company, 1883.

Ziegler, Joseph. Sapientia Salomonis. Septuaginta: Vetus Testamentum Graecum. Göttingen: Vandenhoeck & Ruprecht, 1962.